Non dilexerunt animam suam usque ad mortem.
The Latin, *Non dilexerunt animam suam usque ad mortem,*
translates, "... they loved not their lives unto the death." Revelation 12:11

On The Cover: *Massacres at Salzburg* took place in 1528 when
Prince-Archbishop Cardinal Matthaus Lang of Salzburg issued
mandates sending police in search of Anabaptists. Many were
captured and killed. This engraving illustrates the sufferings and
sacrifices these Dissenters endured when their government, in
conjunction with established religion, attempted to coerce and
impose uniformity of religious belief. Hence, this picture is a
reminder of the cost of religious liberty and the ever-present need
to maintain the separation of church and state. We use this art to
represent our Dissent and Nonconformity Series.

THE

EARLY ENGLISH DISSENTERS

IN THE LIGHT OF RECENT RESEARCH

(1550-1641)

VOLUME II

April. 4. Anº. 1605.

Whereas allmost 3. quarters of a yeare since I published a booke intituled, Reasons taken out of Gods word &c. I do heere faithfully promise to disperse no more of them, nor to be a meanes that any other shall, but to hinder the dispersing of all that that shall com into my power,

Also I do promise that I will not speak against y Church-governmt & orders now amoung vs established by Law, for the time of my being vpon baile & till I shall see what Reasons against my opinion will com forth within this halfe yeare. wch if I shall perceave to be good & well grounded on Gods word, then I will speake for the said Church-governmt & orders now established.

Howsoever, I will allwayes heereafter behave my selfe quietly, & as one carefull of the Churches peace, god assisting me.

Henry Jacob.

The first promise I may easily keepe, seeing I have none of those bookes left.

The second limiteth a time viz. within this halfe yeare wherein I forbeare to speak against their orders. Yet in y meane while my booke speaketh my minde & judgmt most plainly every where.

Thirdly I will allwayes heereafter behave my selfe quietly wch also I have don allwayes heeretofore; I praise god.

FIRST PAGE OF HENRY JACOB'S COPY OF HIS SUBSCRIPTION, April 4, 1605. (*Facsimile.*) See Vol. I., page 285 and Vol. II., pages 151–3.

THE

EARLY ENGLISH DISSENTERS

IN THE LIGHT OF RECENT RESEARCH

(1550-1641)

BY

CHAMPLIN BURRAGE

HON. M.A. (BROWN UNIVERSITY), B. LITT. (OXON.)

IN TWO VOLUMES
Illustrated

VOLUME II
ILLUSTRATIVE DOCUMENTS

Cambridge:
at the University Press
1912

The Baptist Standard Bearer, Inc.

NUMBER ONE IRON OAKS DRIVE • PARIS, ARKANSAS 72855

Thou hast given a *standard* to them that fear thee;
that it may be displayed because of the truth.
-- Psalm 60:4

Reprinted
by

THE BAPTIST STANDARD BEARER, INC.
No. 1 Iron Oaks Drive
Paris, Arkansas 72855
(501) 963-3831

THE WALDENSIAN EMBLEM
lux lucet in tenebris
"The Light Shineth in the Darkness"

Copyright © 1912 by Cambridge University Press
Reprinted by permission

ISBN #1-57978-895-5

PREFACE TO VOLUME II

THE documents herein brought together illustrative of the history of early English Dissent cannot of course claim the dignity of forming a complete "Corpus" of the literature relating to the subject, but they have been carefully selected from the mass of material now available for investigation. My aim in publishing these particular texts has been to present to the reader a number of the more inaccessible or historically valuable writings, many of which have as yet been only imperfectly or partially reproduced. Others have remained entirely, or almost entirely, unnoticed. The contents of this volume are likewise intended to supplement the narrative of volume I., as well as to illustrate it.

Such a selected Corpus has long been needed, for students, it is to be feared, have generally been much more familiar with what has been said by writers and historians of different points of view concerning this literature than with the manuscripts themselves, with resultant misunderstanding, or only partial understanding. Such papers, too, as are herein reproduced are all, with one exception, carefully located, whereas often in earlier works the location was not stated, thus sometimes requiring long search before the originals could be found. Further, in some cases only an imperfect translation of a document has up to this time appeared in print, so that students have been dependent for information upon the skill or candor of a translator.

Special mention should be made of the texts of a number of papers procured in Holland which are now for the first time reproduced in England as nearly as possible in their original form. Some of these were most difficult to decipher accurately even with the occasional help of the ablest Dutch manuscript specialists in the University Library, Amsterdam. No doubt my copies contain minor mistakes and imperfections which keen-eyed critics will be quick to detect. Even so, however, in case any injury should ever befall the originals themselves, approximately accurate texts of these manuscripts ought now to be preserved.

A typographical error may here be corrected. On page 309 Boberti Baffam should read Roberti Baffam.

C. B.

Oxford,
   16 *December* 1911.

CONTENTS

VOLUME II

Contents

LIST OF ILLUSTRATIONS

(CHRONOLOGICALLY ARRANGED)

THE

EARLY ENGLISH DISSENTERS

IN THE LIGHT OF RECENT RESEARCH

(1550-1641)

VOLUME II

I

HISTORICAL DATA RELATIVE TO THE ENGLISH CONVENTICLERS AT BOCKING AND FAVERSHAM IN 1550 AND 1551

[Various Depositions made about 1550.]

Here Folowithe the deposytions
of Iohn Grey william Forshall Laurence
Ramsey and Edmonde Morres productid
apon the firste x[th] and xj[th] articles /
aforessaid. /[1]

Iohn Grey:

Item Examyned apon the firste article
Saythe that Cole of Fauersham apon /
Lammas daye laste paste saide and affirmed
that the doctryne of predestynation
was meter for divilles then for *christ*ian men /

Item Examyned apon the x[th.] and xj[th]
Articles saithe that henry harte aboute
bartholomewetide laste saide and affirmed
in the presence of divers that ther was
no man so chosen but that he mighte dampne
hime selfe Nether yet anye man soo /
reprobate but that he mighte kepe goddes
Comaundements.

He saide that Saincte paule mighte haue
dampnid hime selfe if he listed
And deposithe that harte saide that ∼/
Learned men were the cause of grete errors /

---

[1] Harl. MŚ. 421, fol. 133–34 verso, in the British Museum.

Laurentius Ramsaye

Item Examyned apon the xth article
saithe that henry harte saide and affirmed
as it is conteyned in tharticle that is
that ther is no man so chosen or predesty
nate. but that he maye condempne hime
selfe. Nether is ther anye so reprobate but
that he maye if he will kepe the commande
mentes and be salvid prout liquet in suis
depositionibus

Item Examyned apon the xth article
saythe that harte saide that lernyd men
were the cause of grete Errors /

Willelmus Forstall

Item Examyned apon the xth article he
dothe agree in his deposytion withe the
foresaide Laurence Ramseye

Item Examyned apon the xj[th] article
saythe that henry harte saide the same tyme
that his faithe was not growndid apon
Lernyd men for all errors were broughte
in by Lernyd men   ∝ ///.

> The depositions of m[r] Thomas
> Broke Roger Lynsey and Rycharde
> Dynestake Clarke productid apon the
> xiij and xiiij[th] articles of the Interrogatories
> aforesaid.

Item Examyned apon the xxj[?][th] article
he saithe that aboute xij monethes Sythen
George Brodebridge saide and affirmed
that goddes predestynation is not reteyne
but apon condytion &c

Item Examyned apon the xxxix[th] and
xl[th] articles he deposithe and saithe that the
contentes of those articles hathe byn affirmed
amonge them for a generall doctryne

Item Examyned apon the xljth and xlijth
articles he deposithe and provithe the congregation
and the fame And ther goyng into Essex

Item Examyned apon the xlvjth article
he deposithe that Cole of Maidestone
saide and affirmed that children were
not borne in originall Syne

Willelmus grenelande

Item in aunsweringe to the xlth article
he saithe that to playe at annye game for
money it is Synne and the worke of the
Flesshe

Item in aunsweringe to the xljth xlijth
and xliijth articles he confessithe
the congregation and their Meatinges at
diuers places and ther going into Essex
And also that he hathe contrybuted

Iohn plume de leneham

Item Examyned apon the iiij^{orth} and vth
articles apon his othe Saithe that he
beynge emonge the congregators he hathe
herde it diuers tymes affirmed as a
generall doctryne that they oughte not to
Salute a Synner or a man whome they
knowe not And that Luste after Ivill
was not Synne, if that were not committed

Item Examyned apon the xiijth and xiiijth
articles he saithe that vmfrey Middilton
beyng in Coles house at fauersham apon
Lammas daye he saide that Adam was
elected to be salved And that all men /
being then in Adams Loynes were
predestynate to be salvid and that ther
were no reprobates and in his defence
he alleaged the doctryne conteyned in
the xiiijth article

Item Examyned apon the ıxth article
he saithe that it is a generall
affirmation emonge them, that the
preachinge of predestynacyon is
a dampnable doctryne

Item Examyned apon the xvjth
article he deposithe and saithe that
Nicho*las* Yonge saide that they wolde
not comunycate w^t Synners /

[Extracts from the "Privy Council Register" of 1550–1553
relating to the year 1551.]

A Le*ttre* to the Lorde Chancello*ur* to sende hither [Vpcharde]
the man of Bocking that was examyned by him[1]. [Under the
date Jan. 26, 1550/1.]

　　　　　[2]Vpcharde of Bocking was brought before the
Counsaill tooching a certein assemble that had been made in his
howse in Christm*as* last who confessed that were [*sic*] certein
kenttishemen to the towne to ha[ve] Lodged w*i*th goode man
Cooke. And bicause Cookes wief was in Childebed, thei cam[?]
to this vpcharddes howse weare Cooke was th[en] at dinner and
by Cook*es* entreatie there thei were Lodged. And vpon the
morowe which was Soundaie[?] divers of the towne about xıj of
the clocke came in and there thei fell in argument of thing*es* of
the Scripture, spe*c*iallie wheather it were necessarie to stande
or kneele, barehedde, or covered at prayer. whiche at length was
concluded in ceremonie not to be materiall, but the hart*es*
before God was it that imported, and no thing els, And bicause
it seemed suche an assembley being of lx p*er*sons or moo, shulde
meane some great matter, therfore bothe the said vpcharde
and one Sympson of the same sorte was co*m*mitted to the

---

[1] "Privy Council Register 1550–1553", in the Public Record Office,
p. 205.
　　[2] *Ibid.*, p. 206.

Marshalsie, till further triall were had, and order taken that
lettres shulde be sent bothe into Essex and kent for thapprehen-
sion of these that arr accoumpted chief of that practise /.
[Under the date Jan. 27, 1550/1.]

A [1]Lettre of sir George Norton knight Shrief of Essex tapprehende certein persons wose [sic] names were sent enclosed in
a scedule and to sende them hither that none of them haue
conference with other.

The parsons sent for, were of those that were assembled for
Scripture maters in Bocking. viz

Iohn Barrett of Stamphorde Coweherde
Robert Cooke of Bocking Clothier
Iohn Eglise of the same clothier
Richard Bagge
Thomas pygrinde
Iohn kinge.
.   Myxsto
.   Boughtell
Robert Wolmere

A like lettre to sir Edwarde wootton and sir Thomas wyat
tapprehende and sende vp these persons folowing
William Sibley of lannams
Thomas yonge of the same
Nicholas Shetterton of Pluckley
Iohn Lydley of Asheforde
.   Chidderton of Asheforde
       Cole of Maydestone Sholemaster. /   [Under the date
Jan. 27, 1550/1.]

This daie [Feb. 3, 1550/1][2] william Sibley & Thomas yong
of lenham Nicholas Sheterenden and Thomas Sharpe of Pluckeley
       . Coole of Maydestone, appeared before the Counsaill,
being of those that assembled at Bokyng in Essex. /
like wise vij others of Essex appeared the same daie bothe
which being examyned confessed the cause of their assemble to
be for talke of Scriptures, Not denyeng but thei had refused

---

[1] " Privy Council Register 1550–1553", p. 207.   [2] *Ibid.*, p. 215.

the communyon aboue ij yeres, vpon verie superstitiouse and erronyose purposes: withe Divers other evill oppynyons worthie of great punyshement.   Wherevpon   Boughtell   Barrey   Coole william Sibley and Nicholas Shittrenden were commytted to

Iohannes Eglins, Thomas Myxer, Ricardus Blagge Thomas piggerell et Iohannes king de Bocking in Essex recognouerunt &c in xl^{libras} pro quolibet eorum.

The Condicon [*sic*] tappeare whan thei shalbe called vpon, and to resorte to their ordinarie for resolucion of their oppynyons in cace thei haue any doubte in religion

The like Recognisaunce taken of Thomas Sharpe of plukeley and Nicholas Yong of lenham. /

II

INFORMATION CONCERNING THE LIFE AND CHARACTER OF ROBERT COOCHE

[Part of a Letter of John Parkhurst, Bishop of Norwich, to Dr. Rodolphus Gualtherus, dated June 29, 1574.]

Magna nostra Comitia in 20 diem Octobris sunt dilata. Quo quidem tempore Thimelthorpus cogetur (vti spero) vnanimi omni consensu et Reginae et mihi satisfacere. Ante illud tempus nihil certi de illo possum pronunciare. De controuersijs nostris circà Ceremoniolas quasdam, de Roberto Coochaeo, et alijs rebus nonnullis, in superioribus meis litteris satis fusè scripsi[1].

[Part of another Letter of John Parkhurst, Bishop of Norwich, to Dr. Rodolphus Gualtherus of Zürich, dated, Feb. 6, 1574/5.]

Robertus Coochaeus est vir valdè humanus, et in arte musica bene doctus. Cum ego in Aula Reginae Catharinae concionator essem, fuit ille in Cellam vinariam promus. Contrà hunc scripsit libellum (dum in viuis esset Edouardus Rex) clarrissimus ille medicus et doctissimus Theologus D. Gulielmus Turnerus, in quo illius sententiam de peccato originali refutauit. Perperam item tamen de baptismo infantum sentiebat. Insolita de Caena domini somniauit. Saepissimè Couerdalo et mihi in hisce controuersiis[?] negotium facessebat, ità ut illius nos taederet. Erat verbocissimus. Cum Iuellus et alii docti viri mei inuisendi gratia in Aulam venissent, is statim de hisce rebus cum illis agere caepit, nec finem loquitandi facere potuit.

---

[1] MS. in the University Library, Cambridge, Press-mark Ee. 2. 34 (23).

Nunc etiam in Aula Reginae mansitat. Et Reginae in bella
est cantor ipse capella. Hec est illius conditio. Hanc quoque
conditionem ferè propter tales opiniones ante paucos annos
amisit. Sic enim dux Norfolciae cum viueret mihi narrabat.
Palinodiam quoque tamen temporis cecinit, ut ex eodem duce
audiui. Hactenus de Cochaeo. Non est respondendum stulto
secundum stulticiam suam. vt doleo...[1]

[1] MS. in the University Library, Cambridge, Press-mark, Ee. 2. 34 (20).

III

DOCUMENTS PERTAINING TO THE PURITAN PLUMBERS' HALL CONGREGATION AND TO THE SEPARATIST "PRIUYE CHURCHE" OF RICHARD FITZ, WHICH "SECEDED" FROM IT

[A List of the members of the Plumbers' Hall congregation taken prisoner on March 4, 1567/8.][1]

Parsons fownde to gether within the parishe of S^t martens in the felde in the howse of Iames Tynne gooldsmythe the forthe daye of marche 1567 as here after Followethe &c

1	Lawrence Ryppleye dwellinge at Allgate	.
2	Wylliam yonge dwellinge in Temesstrete	..
3	margarette Sawyer of temestrete	..
4	Elizabethe [?] Langtone at Algate	.
5	Androw [?] Waterhowse at Dowgate	...
6	Wylliam Tomlyne at Charterhowse Lane	::
7	Alis Appletaste in Sowthewarke	:·:
8	Markes Golddinge in Smythfylde	:::
9	Wylliam Collingham in Dysstafe Lane	7
10	Roger Nycolls of S^t martens in the fylde	8
11	Thomas Ludburte in Lyttell wodstrete	9
12	Myghell Bowyer in marke Lane	10
13	Bryane wylles in Charterhowse lane	::

[1] S. P., Dom., Eliz., Vol. 46 (No. 46). This valuable document was discovered several years ago by Dr F. J. Powicke, and the substance of its contents is given in his "Lists of the early Separatists", in the "Transactions" of the Congregational Historical Society, Vol. i., pp. 141–3. As the original document is much worn, a verbatim copy has now been made.

14 Annys Smythe at Crypplegate   11
15 Rowland Sclyforde at London stone   12
16 Ione Evanes in Holborne   13
17 Ione Edwardes at aldermaneburye   14
18 Randall partridge in olde fyshe strete   15
19 Thom[a]s Bowllande in temestrete   ..
20 will*i*am whighte at St Iones Strete [?]   16
21 Iohn Kynge at yslyngtone   17
22 Iohn Smythe at Dysstafe Lane   7
23 Robart Tod [?] in Dysstafe Lane   7
24 Thomas Hancoke in Aldersegate strete   18
25 Iames Irelande in Cheker allye in Sowthwark   :·:
26 Edwarde Burdbye and his wyfe at S^t gyles at ludgate   19
27 Elizabethe Langtone in Swethen Lane   20
28 Elizabethe Phennyxe at S^t marye overies   21
29 Rob[e]rte Bonde and his wyfe at S^t gyles at ludgate   19
30 Samuell Rodggers in Smythefelde [?]   :::
31 Symonde goldinge in Smythefelde [?]   :::
32 Wyll*i*am Nyxson at quenehive [*sic*]   22
33 margerye Vennye in Bred stretto   23
34 mawdelyne Vennye in Bred strete   23
35 Richard morecrofte and his wyfe in Aldersgat strete 18
36 Iohn Iohnsone in Bushopesgate strete   24.
37 Iohn Leonarde and his wyfe in holborne   13
38 Annys wrighte in Barmeseye strete   25
39 Alis Hassellwode in pater noster Rooe   26
40 Annys Lyttellcoate at Hoggesdone   27
41 Alis Vanes in the Tower   28
42 Ellyne Buggburte in hartestrete   29
43 Iohn Bovlte [Boulton ?] in S^t martens   30
44 Annys Rowles in Holborne   —13
45 Anne Phyllipes at St Thomas apostels   42
46 margarette Stockes in aldersgate [?] strete   18
47 George wayddye in flyt [?] stretto [?]   31
48 Thomas Harysone at [illegible words]   23
49 Iames Andertone in Dysstafe lane   7
50 Annys Staltone in Cornwell   32
51 Annys Lacye in aldersegate strete   18

52	Wyll*i*am grenne and his wyfe in holborne	13
53	Ione Strynger at St Androwes Vndershafte	33
54	Annys Ropper at S^t androwes Vndershafte	33
55	Elizabethe [?] Fawkener at St Andros Vndershafte	33
56	Avis [?] Carye at Bysshopes gate	24
57	margaret Iones at S^t myghells in Cornwell	32
58	margerye Browne in Burder Lane	34
59	Katheren Bawdwyne in aldersegate strete	18
60	Elizabethe Bamford in Bowe Lane	35
61	*chris*tofer poorke in olde fyshe strete	15
62	Annys Hawkes at St Antonyes	36
63	Katheren whighte at Ludburye	37
64	Cycillyc Holtore [?] in aldersgat strete	18
65	Elyne Esecoote in S^t bennet*es* p*a*rishe	38
66	Ione Knowles in St Bennet*es* p*a*rishe	38
67	Garrete Speker in St Clement*es* p*a*rishe	39
68	Edde Burris in more Lane	40
69	Elizabethe Turner in more Lane	40
70	Elizabethe gylte in Lyttell wodstret	9
71	Elizabethe Sclake at S^t gyles at ludgate	19
72	Katheren Hassellwode in berebynder lane /[1]	41.

["A promyse made by Will*i*am Bonam precher", 1569, together with the names of twenty-four members of the Plumbers' Hall Congregation who were discharged from Bridewell on April 22, 1569.][2]

A promyse made by William Bonam precher.

1569 Memorand*um* that I *William Bonam*, do Faiethfullie promise, that I will not at anie tyme hereafter vse anie publique prechinge or open readinge or expoundinge of the scriptures. nor cause, neither be *presente* at anie privat Assemblies of praier, or expoundinge of the scriptures or mi*ni*steringe the co*mmun*ion in anie howse, or other place, Contrarie to the state of religion nowe by publique authoritie established, or contrarie to the Lawes of this Realme of *England*, neither will I invaie ageinste any rites or ceremonies vsed or Receaved by com*m*on auctoritie *wi*thin this Realme. /

[1] Thus seventy-two persons from forty-two streets or localities.
[2] Lansdowne MS. xii., fol. 67–8, in the British Museum.

This promise was read and declared by the said *William Bonam*, before Mr Thomas Hinck Doctour of Lawe, and vicar generall to the right reverend Father in god *Edmond* Bisshop of *London*, at his howse in *pater noster Rowe* in *London*, the Firste daie of *Maie* i569 for the performaunce, whereof the said *William Bonam* hath faiethfullie promised for to obserue the same./ Beinge also *presente* at the readinge therof, Thomas Iones deputie to m^r *Bedell*, Clerk to the Quenes Ma*iestes* Commissione^rs for causes Ecclesiasticall //

1 *Iohn Smythe*
2 *Iohn Roper*
3 *Robert Hawkins*
4 *Iames Irelande*
5 *William Nyckson*
6 *Walter Hynckesman*
7 *Thomas Bowlande*
8 *George Waddye*
9 *William Turner*
10 *Iohn Nayshe*
11 *Iames Anderton*
12 *William Wight*
13 *Thomas Lydforde* [*Ludburte ?*]
14 *Richard Langton*
15 *Alexander Lacye*
16 *Iohn Leonarde*
17 *Robert Todd*
18 *Roger Hawkesworth*
19 *Robert Sparrow*
20 *Richard kinge*
21 *Christofer Colman*
22 *Iohn Benson*
23 *Iohn Bolton*
24. *Robert Gates* /

All theis persons before written wer dyschardged

out of *Brydewell*, besides seven women also prisoners there the xxij[th] day of Aprell 1569, by a warrant dyrectid from the right reuerende father in god Edmond Bishop of London to the Governours there.

The trewe markes of Christes churche, &c.[1]

The order of the priuye churche in London, whiche by the malice of Satan is falselie slaundred, and euell spoken of.

THe myndes of them, that by the strengthe and workinge of the almighty, our Lorde Iesus Christe, haue set their hands and hartes, to the pure vnmingled and sincere worshippinge of God, accordinge to his blessed and glorious worde in al things, onely abolishinge and abhorringe all tradicions and inuentions of man, what soeuer in the same Religion and Seruice of oure Lord God, knowinge this alwayes, that the trewe and afflicted churche of oure Lorde and sauyoure Iesus Christe, eyther hathé [*sic*], or else euer more continually vnder the crosse stryueth for to haue. Fyrste and formoste, the Glorious worde and Euangell preached, not in bondage and subiection, but freely, and purelye. Secondly to haue the Sacraments mynistred purely, onely and all together accordinge to the institution and good worde of the Lorde Iesus, without any tradicion or inuention of man. And laste of all to haue, not the fylthye Cannon lawe, but dissiplyne onelye, and all together agreable to the same heauenlye and allmighty worde of oure good Lorde, Iesus Chryste.

Richarde Fytz, Minister

[The Separatist Covenant of Richard Fitz's Congregation.][2]

BEyng throughly perswaded in my conscience, by the working and by the worde of the almightie, that these reliques of Antichriste be abominable before the Lorde our God.

---

[1] Printed in black letter on one side of a small leaf. S. P., Dom., Eliz., Addenda, Vol. xx (107. 1).

[2] Printed in black letter on one side of a small folio leaf. S. P., Dom.,

And also for that by the power and mercie, strength and goodnes of the Lorde my God onelie, I am escaped from yᵉ filthynes & pollution of these detestable traditions, through the knowledge of our Lorde and sauiour Iesus Christ:

And last of all, in asmuch as by the workyng also of the Lorde Iesus his holy spirite, I haue ioyned in prayer, and hearyng Gods worde, with those that haue not yelded to this idolatrouse trash, notwithstandyng the danger for not commyng to my parysh church. &c,

Therfore I come not backe agayne to the preachynges. &c, of them that haue receaued these markes of the Romysh beast.

1. ❡ Because of Gods commandement, to go forewarde to perfection. Hebrew. 6. verse .1. 2. Corinth. 7. verse .1. Psalm. 84. verse .7. Ephesi .4 verse .15
Also to avoyde them. Roma. 16. verse .17. Ephesi. 5. verse .11. 1. Thessal. 5. verse .22.

2. ❡ Because they are abominations before the Lorde our God. Deut. 7. verses .25. and .26 Deutero. 13. verse .17. Ezekiell. 14. verse .6.

3. ❡ I wyll not beautifie with my presence those filthy ragges, which bryng the heauenly worde of the eternall our Lorde God, in to bondage, subiection, and slauerie.

4. ❡ Because I would not communicate with other mennes sinnes. 2. Iohn. verses .9. 10. and .11. 2. Corinth. 6. verse .17. Touch no vncleane thyng. &c. Sirach. 13. verse .1.

5. ❡ They geue offences, both the preacher & the hearers. Rom. 16 ver. 17. Luke. 17. verse .1

6. They glad [*sic*] and strengthen the Papists in their errour, and

Eliz., Addenda, Vol. xx (107. ɪɪ). I think that Dr Waddington failed to see the significance of this paper. It evidently took the place of a church covenant, and was to be accepted by all the members of the congregation when they joined it. The document is not, therefore, a statement of the grounds whereby some one particular person justified his separation from the Church of England. It is rather a covenant (though the form of a covenant is more implied than manifest) with a statement of the grounds of separation added.

greue the godlie. Ezekiel. 13. verses .21. and .22. *Note this 21. verse. &c.

7. ⁌ They doo persecute our sauiour Iesus Christ in his members. Actes. 9. verses .4. and .5 2. Corinth. 1. verse .5.

Also they reiecte and despyse our Lorde and sauiour Iesus Christ. Luke. 10. verse .16.

Moreouer those labourers, whom at the prayer of the faithful, the Lorde hath sent furth in to his haruest: they refuse, and also reiect. Math. 9. verse .38.

8. ⁌ These Popish garments. &c, are now become very Idolles in deede, because they are exalted aboue the worde of the almightie.

9. ⁌ I come not to them because they shoulde be ashamed, and so leaue their Idolatrous garments. &c. 2. Thessal. 3 verse .14. Yf any man obey not our sayinges, note him. &c.

⁌ God geue vs strength styl to stryue in suffryng vndre the crosse, that the blessed worde of our God may onely rule, and haue the highest place, to cast downe strong holdes, to destroy or ouerthrow policies or imaginations, and euery high thyng that is eralted [exalted] against the knowledge of God, and to bryng in to captiuitie or subiection, euery thought to the obedience of Christ. &c. 2. Corinth. 10 verses .4. and .5. &c, that the name and worde of the eternall our Lorde God, may be exalted or magnified aboue all thynges. Psalm. 138. verse .2.

⁌ FINIS.

["B. of London. Puretans."][1]

O Englande, yf thou returne, returne vnto me, saythe the Lorde, Ierem[y ?] 4. [?] verse .1.

We the poore afflicted & your humble and obedient subiectes in the lorde most ernestly desyer, that the word of our god may be set to raygne, and haue the hiest place, to rule & reforme

---

[1] S. P., Dom., Eliz., Addenda, Vol. xx (107). This MS. was probably written by Harry Sparowe.

all estates and degrees [o]f men, to build and plante his holy
sygnes and true markes, to cut downe, to roote out, and vtterly
destroy by the axe of the same his holy word, all monumente*s*
of Idolatry, to wit, that wicked cannon law, which is the onely
roote, out of the whiche these abhominable braunshes do growe,
as forked cappes, & tipete*s*, surplices, copes, starche cakes,
[godfathers & godmothers]¹ popishe holy days, forbidding of
mariages and meate*s* which the holy gost our almighty calleth
doctrines of devills as in the .1. timothie .4. verses .3. 4. more
to destroy idol*es* [?] temples & chapels whiche the papistes or
infideles haue builded to the service of their god*es*. Our god
hath straytly commaunded & charged his people Israell chiefly

Dew. 31º.
23. Iosua.
1. verses.7.
8. 9. the governours as in dewteronomie .16. verse .20. with the note.
& so in them yᵉ maiestrates of our tyme, not to vse in his
service, the man*n*ers, fashions, or customes of the papiste*s*, but
contrary wyse vtterly to destroy them, to consume them, and
abhorr them dewte .7. verse .26. whiche holy commaundement
of the almighty our god yf it be not executed spedely, the
lord*es* wrathe will surely breake out vpon this whole reallme of
england as in numbers .25. verse .3. .9. & for such abhomi*n*ations
our god will cause this land to spew vs out as in leviticus .20.
verse .22. the allmightie our god will not allway suffer suche
dishonour to his blessed evangell, whiche for the sinnes and
tryall of his people he suffreth the papiste*s* and newters, faulse
brethren, and domesticall enemies to suppresse, to wrest, and
abvse to serve their purposes, (as they perswade them selves)
yet for all their policye and fyne pinnyng these abhominations
aboue named with many other, are no more able to stand in
presence before the word of our god having the power of
discipline, then dagon was able to stand before the lord his
holy arke the power wherof threwe downe dagon twyse to the
dust as in .1. samuell .5. verses .3 .4. Therefore according to
the saying of the almighty our god   mathew .18. verse .20. wher
ij or iij are gathered in my name ther am I. so we a poore
congregation whom god hath seperated from the churches of
englande [?] and from the mingled and faulse worshipping

¹ The words in square brackets appear to have been added in another
handwriting.

therin vsed, out of the which assemblies the lord our onely
saviour hath called vs, and still calleth, saying cume [?] out
from among them, and seperate your selves from them & touche
no vnclean thing, then will I receyue you, and I wilbe your
god and you shalbe my sonnes and doughters sayth the lord.
2. corinth .6. verses .17 . 18. so as god geveth strength at this
day we do serue the lord every saboth day in houses, and on
the fourth day in the weke we meet or cum together weekely
to vse prayer & exercyse diciplyne on them whiche do deserve
it, by the strength and sure warrant of the lord*es* good word as
in mathew. 18 verses 15 . 16 . 17 . 18 . / .1. corinth . 5 . / but wo
be vnto this cursed cannon Lawe the gayne [?] wherof hath
caused the byshop*es* and clargi of england to forsake the right
.2. peter .2. way and haue gone astray, folowyng the way of baalam sonn of
verse .15 bosor, which haue throughe their pompe and covetousnesse
broughte the gospell of our saviour Iesus christ into suche
sclaunder and contempte, that men do thinke for the most part
that the papist*es* do vse and hold a better religion then those
which call them selves christians, and ar not, but do lye
revela. 3 verse .9. the holy gost sayth.   I behold another beast
cummyng [?] vp out of the earthe which had ij hornes lyke the
lame, so this secrete and disguysed antechrist [?] to wit, this
cannon l[a]w w*ith* [?] the braunshes and [?] their [?] maintayners
thoughe not so openly, haue by lon[g]e inprisonment [?] pyned
mathew & kylled the lord*es* servant*es* (as our minister Rycherd fitz)
.23. verses thomas bowlande deacon / one partryge) & gyles fouler / &
.34. 35. besydes them a great multitude, which no man could number
of all nations and people and tounges as revela. 7. verse .9.
whose good cause and faythfull testimony though we should
cease to grone and crye vnto our god to redresse suche wrong*es*
& cruell handelyng*es* of his pore member*es*, the very walles of
the prisons about this citye, as the gatehouse, brydewell, the
counters, the kyng*es* benche, the marcialsey, the whyte lyon,
would testifye god*es* anger kyndlyde agynst [*sic*] this land for
suche iniustyce and subtyll persecucion.

O Lord god almyghty graunte, for thy mercyes sake, that as
Iehosaphat, in the iij[th] yeare of his raygne destroyed the hye

places and groves, out of Iudahe, and sent his prynces and
priestes, and gaue them the boke of the lawe with them to
reforme religion by, and so feare came vpon every citye that
they made not ware agaynst Iehosaphat So Lord we most
humbly beseche the to strengthen the quenes hi[g]hnesse [*sic*]
with his holy spirit that in the .13th yeare of her reygne
[1571], she may cast downe all hye places of Idolatrye with in
her land, withe the popyshe cannon Lawe and all the super-
sticion and commaundementes of men, and to plucke vp by the
rootes all filthi ceremonies perteynyng to the same, and that
her highnesse may send forth princes and ministers and geue
them the booke of the Lord, that they may bryng home the
people of god to the purity and truthe of the apostolycke
churche, Then shall the feare of the Lord cume vpon every
citye and cuntrye, that they shall not make warre agaynst her
highnesse, no the very enemies that be with out, shalbe
compelled to bring presentes to her grace, thus olord [*sic*]
graunt that her highnes may not onely haue a blessed, longe,
and prosperous reygne, with peace of conscience in this life, but
also in the lyfe to cum, her highnesse may enIoye [*sic*], by the
merites and death of christ Iesus our onely saviour, lyfe ever-
lastyng, to whome with the father and the holy gost be all
honour and glory for ever and ever amen.

Ioane Abraham [mark][1]	Ihon Thomas [mark]
Constance foxe [mark]	Annes. Evance [mark]
Eliz. slacke	Elizabeth Leanordes [mark]
Annes Hall [mark]	Ioane Ireland [mark]
Marg Race [mark]	by me Iasper weston
Helene stokes [mark]	Marten [?] tilmans [?]
Eliz. Balfurth [mark]	Ihon Davy [mark]
Sara Cole [mark]	edye Burre [?]
by me Harry sparowe.	Elizabeth Hill [mark]
By me Iohn King.	Ioane havericke [mark]
by me Iames awbynes	Mary wever
by me Ihon Leonarde.	Abraham foxe [mark]
by me George Hares. [mark]	Mary Mayer [mark]
	Eliz. Rumney [mark]

in white
Chappell
streate

---

[1] The signatures in the original are irregularly arranged in four
columns, but are here for convenience placed in two.

IV

MISCELLANEOUS DOCUMENTS RELATING TO THE EARLY BARROWISTS

[The names of certain Brownists (Barrowists) taken at a Conventicle in Henry Martin's House, October 8, 1587, and examined in the Episcopal Palace, London, on the same day.][1]

8° die mensis Octobris *1587*.
in palacio ep*iscopa*li London.

Brownest*es*.
1

Crane a mi*n*ister mad by 23 Grindall when he was Bushop of London, and before that he was a student in Lawe in the inner Chauncery— called for beinge at privat conventicles this daye in henry Martins howse in St Andrewes in the wardropp. /

he saieth that all the booke (meaninge the comon booke, is not gospell)

2   Henry M*a*rtin / of the same secte.

3   George Smells / of the same sect

for beinge at [p]rivat conventles

4   Edward Boyce / of the same sect

5   Anne Iackson / of the same sect

6   George Collier / of the same sect

7   Katherin Owin [Onyon].

8   Robe*r*te Lacy of St Andrewes in holborne of the
: : : ˙ ˙ · · · · }— same sect / he refuseth to take an othe. /

---

[1] S. P., Dom., Elizabeth, Vol. 204 (10), in the Public Record Office, London.

9   Thomas Freeman of the p*a*rishe of St Botulphe w*i*th owt aldersgate of the same sect and a Brownest.

i0   Edithe Burry of Stepney [?] /

ii   Mr Grenwood *pr*ea*cher* depr*iu*ed of his benefice [?] in norfolke about 2 yeres past takin at the said privat conventicles in m*a*rtins howse / he is comitted to the Clincke /

12   Margaret maynerd of Bredstreet she saieth ther is no church in England, she hath not bin at church theis x. yeres. / comitted to Bridwell

13   Alice Roe wydow. of St Andrewes in the wardrop

14   Agnes Wyman of Stepney.

15   Robe*r*te Griffith of the same sect

16   Iohn Chaundler of Stepney / of the same sect /

17   Edmond Thompson of Stepney / of the same sect

18   Henry Thompson eiusd*em* pr*aedic*te of the same sect

19   Robe*r*te Redborne &] servant*es* to m^r Boyce of the p*a*rishe of St Brigitt*es*

20.   Thomas Russell] in flet stret. /

2i   Peter Allen servant to m^r Allen a salter of the p*a*rishe of St Botulphe nere Billingsegat] of the same sect and at m*a*rtins howse a foresaid at the conventicle /

vacat ~~Clement Gamble~~ servante ~~to Anne Jackson~~

[Information concerning the Barrowists in 1590.]

A briefe of the positions holden by the nevve sectorie of recusants [i.e., the Barrowists][1].

. . . .

6.   That the Sacraments of Babtisme & the Lords supper, as they are administred now in the Church of England, be not true Sacraments.

[1] "A COLLECTION OF | CERTAINE SCLAVNDEROVS | Articles gyuen out by the Bisshops | ...", 1590 [p. 7].

7.   That infants ought not to be baptised, according to the forme of baptisme ministred now in the Church of England, but are rather to be kept vnbaptised.

[The experiences of the Barrowists at the hands of the Bishops were by no means pleasant.]

Now the course the BBs & their cleargie haue taken, to approoue themselues vnto all men to be no such deceitfull vvorkmen, theire building to be no such vvood, hay, stubble, hath not beene to bring their vvorkes to the light, & to submit yt & themselues, to be measured by the golden reed of Gods word, therby iustifying themselues, conuincing and perswading others : But in stead of this, they first imprison all such as make anie scruple or question of theire doings : yea all such as but speake against them, they shut vp in close pryson, there to continewe yvithout bayle or mainprice, all the daies of theire life, except they submit & recant : Some they cast into most noisome & vile dungeons, without ayre, foode, bedds, or so much as strawe to lye vppon, keeping them from theire vvyues, children, trades labours, to the vtter vndoing & affamishment of them, their wyues, & children ; Others they lade, with as manie yrons as they can beare ; some others they a while produced to the Sessions, there indicting them as recusants vppon the Statute made for the Papists ; publishing them by theire prynt with priuiledg Anabaptists, Hereticks, Schismaticks, Sectories, Donatists, Conuenticlers, seditious, turbulent ; sparsing abrode through all the land certeine Articles of theire owne deuising against them, to bring them into hatred vvith the vvhole land. vvhervnto also they haue not spared theire toungs, in theire pulpits, where euery one of their priests might forge what opinion he lyst against them, & confute it with the same mouth, in their name : and all this, vvithout once producing them, to anie christian triall vvhere they might haue place giuen them, to defend themselues, & produce theire reasons, or once endeuoring to perswade or confute them by anie one place of scripture ;......[1]

---

[1] "A COLLECTION OF | CERTAINE SCLAVNDEROVS | Articles gyuen out by the Bisshops | ...", 1590, sig. A$_{ij}$ recto and verso.

[The names of the persons belonging to the imprisoned "nevve sectorie of recusants" are the following:—][1]

Iames Forester⎫
Iohn Francys ⎬ prysoners in newgate

Robert Batkine — — in the Fleete

Thomas Freeman⎫
Thomas Settel ⎬ in the gatehowse
Iohn Debenham ⎭

George Collier⎫ in the Clynke
Iohn Sparowe ⎭

Edmond Nicolson⎫ in the Clynke
*Christ*ofer Raper ⎭

*Christ*ofer Browne⎫ in the Clynke
Quintan Smyth   ⎭

Androwe Smyth   ⎫ in the Clynke
William Blakborowe⎭

Thomas Lemar ⎫ in the Clynke
Thomas Michell⎭

Anthonye Clakston⎫ in newgate
William Forester ⎭

William Denford⎫ in newgate
Roger Waterer ⎭

Edeth Burrowghe⎫ in newgate
William Burt   ⎭

George Smels   ⎫ in the Counter wood-
*Christ*ofer Bowman⎭   street

Robert Iackson⎫ in Count: woodstr.
Nycolas Lee ⎭

Robert Andrewes⎫ in Count: woodstr.
William Hutton ⎭

Iohn Buser[2]⎫ in Count: woodstr.
Iohn Fissher⎭

---

[1] "A COLLECTION OF | CERTAINE SCLAVNDEROVS | Articles gyuen out by the Bisshops | ...", 1590, sigs. A_{iv} verso—B recto.

[2] Could Iohn Buser have been Leonard Busher's father?

William Clarke ⎫
Richard maltusse ⎭ in Count: vvoodstr.

William Fouller ⎫
Richard Skarlet ⎭ in Count: woodstr.

Roger Rippine ⎫
Iohn Clarke ⎭ in Count vvoodstr.

Rowland Skipworth ⎫ in the Counter
George Knifton ⎭ poultrye

Richard Hayward ⎫
Iohn Lankaster ⎭ in Count: poult.

Thomas Endford⎭ in Count: poult.

Henry Barrowe ⎫
Iohn Greenwood ⎭ in the Fleete

Daniell Studley ⎫
Walter Lane ⎭ in the Fleete

Edmond Tomson ⎫
Iohn Nicolas ⎭ in the gatehouse

William Dodson ⎫
Iohn Barrens ⎭ in the gatehowse

Iohn Cranford ⎫
Richard vvheeler ⎭ in the gatehowse

Thomas Canadine—in the gatehowse

[Part of a letter from Iohn Smith to Dr. [John] Reynolds, dated February 20, 1592/3.][1]

This daye it is reported the Baroists shalbe arraigned. yesterday m^r smith [*sic*] & I dealt with half a score of them at ye gatehowse concerning *our* church, & [?] ther errours in refusing to say the L. prayer, & to eate any thing vpon the Sabboth.   They denyed both at first, but at length yelded that thei held the former. The men be verye readye to ther poore [?] still, but as impudent, as obstinate, as proud & disdainfull as ever I talked with any; The L. geeve them humble & repentant hart*es* [?].... .
London the 20th of Febr.

---

[1] Corpus Christi College Library, Oxford.   MS. No. 318, present press-mark C. 3. 2 (fol. 143).

[The names of several Barrowists who were willing to conform and were evidently bailed some time after April 5, 1593.][1]

The names of suche Sectaries, as vpon
ther Conformitie the Commissioners have
bayled.

Iohn Hulkes [or Huckes] of Detford Shipwright. /
William Mason of wappinge Shipwright. /
william Curland of Detford Shipwright.
Edward Gilbert apprentice to Isack Frees Taylor,
of the parishe of St Gregories neere powles. /
Henry Brodewater of St Nicholas lane Scrivenor.
Thomas Mihilfield [*sic*] of St Saviours Ioyner. /
Thomas Farret servant to William Greene of
Aldersgate streete.
Henrye Withers of Detford Strand, Shipwright.

[Part of a Letter of Iohn Chamberlain to Mr Dudley Carleton at "Eaton", dated "From London", the "22th of October 1608".][2]

only there was a nest or assemblie of Brownists [probably Barrowists] discouered on Sonday about Finsburie, wherof Fiue or sixe and thirty were apprehended with theyre preacher one Trundle that vsed to exercise at christs-church.

[1] Harl. MS. 6848, fol. 210.
[2] S. P., Dom., James I, Vol. 37 (No. 25), in the Public Record Office, London.

V

EARLY MANUSCRIPT INFORMATION CONCERNING THE MARPRELATE PRESS AND THE ACTIVITIES OF SOME OF THE EARLY PURITANS

In[1] the yeare 1588 came fourth those hatefull libelle*s* of Martin Marreprelate, & much about the same tyme the *Epitome,* the *Demonstracion of discipline,* the *Supplicacion Diotrephes,* the *Mineralles, Have you any worke for a Co̅oper, Martin Iunior,* alias *Theses Martinianœ, Martin Senior, Moore worke for the Cooper,* all printed with a kinde of wandering presse wh*ich* was first sett vp at Monsey [Moulsey?] neare Kingston vppon Thames, & from thence conuaied to Fawsley in Northampton-shire, from thence to Norton, from Norton to Couentry, from Couentry to Wollston in Warwickshire, from thence the Setters were sent to an other presse in or neare Manchester where the presse was discouered in printing of More worke for a Coope*r,* wh*ich* shamelesse libell as like wise all the forenamed were fraught only with odious & scurrulous calumpniacio*n*s against the established gouerm*e*nt & such reuerend Prelate*s* as deserued honour with vprighter iudgem*ent*es, some of the Printers whiles they were busied about the last libell, were apprehended, who with the enterteiners & receauers of the presse were pr*o*ceaded against in the Starre Camber & their censured but vppon their submission, at the Archbi*shops* humble sute were both de-liuered out of Prison & eased of their synes. The Authors & publishers, were Iohn Penry and Iohn Vdall with others the cheefe disper*s*or was Humphrey Newman a Cobler (a fitt brooker for such souterly worke) of wh*ich* three hereafter we

---

[1] Cotton MS. Julius F. VI, fol. 76 verso and 77 recto, in the British Museum.

shall speake more in a fitter place   The factious Monsters of the pretended discipline hauing with these seditious libelles (as the forerunners & harbengers of their farther designes) made waie in the hartes of the vulgar who euer are apt to entertaine matter of Noueltie especiallie if it haue a shew of restraining the authoritie of their Superiours, they thought it the fittest time to prosecute their proiectes & while the one sorte of them, were maliciouslie busie in slaundering the state of the Church alredy setled, the other sor[t]e were as factiouslie eager in planting the discipline which they had newlie plotted Where vppon shortlie after Thomas Cartwright Edmond Snape, Andrew Kinge, Wilton Proudloue, Iohn Graine, Melanchton Iewell, Lord, Fennye, and Wright were called in question & proceeded withall in Starre chamber, for setting forth and putting in practise without warrant or authoritie a new forme of Commõn Praier & administracion of the sacramentes & presbiteriall discipline comprised in two bookes Intituled Disciplina Ecclesiæ sacra Dei verbo descripta and Disciplina Synodica ex Ecclesiarum vsu with other bookes and Pamphlettes of like nature, And so putt their reformacion & Hierarchie in practise they held their assemblyes & Classis in sundrie places of this Realme viz: at London, Oxford, & Cambridge, Warwicke, Northampton, Ketteringe, Daintry where they corrected & altered diuerse imperfections conteyned in the said booke, treating allsoe & concluding of sundry Articles & decrees in allowance of the bookes & of the Matters therin viz:

That the Queenes authoritie ought to be restrained in causes ecclesiasticall. /

VI

SOME OF THE EARLY BARROWIST DEPOSITIONS

["Certen wicked sect*es*
& opin*ions*.*ma*rche
1588 & 89 No 3i.Eliz."][1]

The Man*ner* of thassemblie of the secret Conventicklers to-gethe*r* *wi*th some Collections of there opynions /

Confessed by clement Gambell.

In the somer tyme they mett togethe*r* in the feilds a mile or more about london. there they sitt downe vppon A Banke & diu*er*s of them expound out of the bible so long as they are there assembled

Confessed by Clem*en*te Cambell

In y*e* wynte*r* tyme they assemble themselves by 5. of the clocke in y*e* morning to that howse where they make there Conventicle, for y*t* [?] Saboth daie men & woemen togethe*r* there they Con-tynewe in there kinde of praier & exposic*i*on of Scriptures all that daie They dyne togethe*r*, After dinn*er* make collection to paie for there diet [?] & what mony is left som*m*e [?] one of them carrieth it to the pr*i*sons where any of there sect be com*m*itted.

[1] Harl. MS. 6848, fol. 83 recto—84 recto, in the British Museum.

Confessed by Iohn
Dove[1]

> In there praier one speketh and the rest doe grone, or sob. or sigh, as if they wold wringe out teares, but...not after...that praieth, there praier is extemporall

Confessed by Clem*en*te
Gamble /

> In there co*n*venticles they vse not the lord*es* praier, nor of any forme of sett praier, for the lord*es* praier, one, who hath ben A dalie resorte[r] [to ?] there conventiclers [conventicles ?], hath [*sic*] this yeare & a half on the Saboth daies, co*n*fesseth y[t] he neu*er* hard it said emongest them, And this is the doctryne of the vse of it in there pamphlett*es*, To that w*h*ich is alledged, that we ought to saie the lord*es* praier, Bycause o*ur* savio*ur* Christ saieth when yo*u* praie doe yo[u] praie thus &c[?],...

. . . .

. . . .

. . . .

> for thuse of set or stynted praier (as they terme it,) this they teach that all stynted praiers & redd s*er*vice is but Babling in y[e] lord*es* sight,...

. . . .

. . . .

Confessed by Clem*en*t
Gambell

> In all there meting*es* they teach that there is noe heade or supreme gove[r ?]m*en*t of the Church of god, but Christe, That the *Queene* hath no aucthoritie to appoyn[t] mynisters in the Church nor to set downe any goverm*en*te for y[e] Church w*h*ich is not directlie com*m*anded in god*es* worde /

Taught in another of
there wryting[es] taken from

> To co*n*firme there p*r*ivat conventicles and expounding there

[1] John Dove, M.A., who published at least half a dozen books.

the for[e]said Smyth,
Confessed by Iohn dove /

they teach that A pryvatt man
being A Brother may preach to
begett faieth and nowe that
thoffice of thappostles is ceaseth
[*sic*] there nedeth not, publiq*ue*
mynistres but eu*er*y man in his
owne calling was to preache the
gospell.

confessed by Clem*ent*
Gambell,

They condemp*ne* [?] it as vtterlie
vnlawfull to co*mm*e to o*ur*
Churches in england to any
publicque praier or preching of
whome soeu*er*, for y^t they saie
as the Chirch [?] of england
standeth they be all fals teachers
& falce p*r*ophett*es* [?] that be in
it, there reason is for that o*ur*
preachers (as they saie) doe
teach vs that the state of the
realme of England is the true
Church (wh*i*ch they denye) and
therfore they saie that all
p*re*achers of england be fals
preachers sent in the lord*es* anger
to deceyve his people w*i*th lyes,
and not true preachers to bring
the glad tyding*es* of the gospell,

. . . .
. . . .

confessed by Io*hn* dove

and all that come to o*ur* Churches
to publicque praier or sermons
they accompt damnable soules

. . . .

. . . .
. . . .

. . . .
. . . .
Taught in the same
pamphlet taken from
R*oger* Iackson
Confessed in m^r Iohn
Doves examinac*i*on A
m^r of Arte who

. . . .
. . . .
. . . .
. . . .

Those who haue ben of there
secret Brotherhood and seing
there errours do fall from them

was at one of the
Conventyckles

and Submytt them selves to be
partakers of publique praiers
and hering of godes worde with
vs they condempne [?] as ap-
postates [?] and they saie it is A
greater synne to goe to our
Churches to publique praier then
for A man to lye with his fathers
wief /

Confessed by love
who is the partie
who[m] they so vsed
& by mʳ dove who
was present at this
Accion and was the
first man who
reveled this /

And when as one of late forsoke
there Conventickles they sent
for him, and when he gave them
many reasons whie he cold not
hold there opynions for good as
namelie that they reiected the
lordes praier, That they were
dissemblers in that two of them
had made A deede of gyfte of all
there landes to deceyve the
Queene and A nombre of other
reasons which he alledged to
them when they sawe they cold
not wynne hime they gaue hime
ouer to thandes of Satan till he
wold Submitt hime self to the
Church agayne and they all
kneling he that gave that sentence made A praier to desyre
god to ratiffie that censure
against hime

Wydowe Vnyon one
of there Chief
Conventickler[s] her
Child was Babtised
in Sᵗ Andrewes in
the wardrope

They held it vnlawfull to baptise
Children emongest vs but rather
Chewse to let them goe vnbaptized as in Somer 1588 A Childe
of one of theres [?] beinge xıj
yeres of Age was knowne [?] not
to haue ben baptized And when
the pore infant desyred the

mother often that it might be
baptized she and it was [*sic*]
borne of faiethfull parent*es* w*hi*ch
was enough for it w*hi*ch Child
was by the Chauncelo*r* of
london caused to be publiquely
Baptised, at a sermon made for
that purpose the last sommer [?]
and the mother ranne awaie for
feare of puishm*ente*

Confessed by
Clem*ent* Gamble

It cannot be learned where they
receyved the Sacram*entes* of the
lord*es* Supper and one who neu*er*
missed there meting*es* [?] of A
yere & A half confesseth that he
neu*er* sawe any min[i]strac*io*n of
the sacrem*ent* nor know*e*th where
it is donne

Confessed by
Clem*ent* Gamble [?]

for marradg*es* if any of there
Chirch Marry together some of
there owne Brotherhood must
marry them as of late A Cople
were married in the fleet

Thexa*minacio*n of Abraham Pulbery of London free
of the Cowpers of thage of xxv or thereaboutes.
taken vij° die martij 1592 as foloweth[1].

Item hee saieth that hee was in Cheapeside when the dead
Corps of Roger Rippon was caried thorowe the same, and
saieth further that hee heard there publikely redde the paper
w*hi*ch was sett vpon the Coffine but hee would not call the
same a libell, And the same libell being shewed vnto him hee
thinketh that it was in effecte the same hee heard redde in
Chepeside /
And beinge examined of what opynion hee was touchinge
the same libell he saieth that the mainteyninge of the Bishops
of Englande as namely the ArchBishop of Canterbury & the

[1] Harl. MS. 6848, fol. 43 recto, in the British Museum.

rest of the Bishops. whom hee termeth to bee Antichristian
Bishops as they are, that they are the mainteyners of Antichristian Authoritie sayeng further that the said Bishops haue
their authorities as they are Bishoppes from Antichriste & not
from her maiestie because there is noe suche authoritie in the
word of god for any Princes to make such Bishoppes to overrule
the Churches of god

And saieth further that when hee heard that paper redde in
Chepeside hee heard allso then reported that they mente to
carry the said Coffine to m^r Iustice youn*ges* house

And hee saieth further that hee was vpon Sonday laste in the
morninge at a wood neere yslington with others that were there
the nomber hee knoweth not and then & there had a sworde
aboute himselfe, and denieth to aunswere how often hee had
bene there before / and saieth allso that m^r Iohnson was their
expounder that daye. /

Item hee saieth that hee hath made a promise to the Lord in
the presence of his Congregacion when hee entred therevnto
that hee would walke with them as they would walke with the
Lorde /

Rychard young
Iohn Ellis

Thexaminacion of Iohn Nicholas of
Smithfeild Glover taken before vs
Henry Tounsend, Richard yonge and Iohn Ellis
Esquiers the viijth of Marche 1592[1]

Item beinge tendred his oath to aunswhere truly to such
matters as should be demaunded of him concerninge the
Quenes maiestie refuseth to take any oathe

Item beinge demaunded whether he were at newgate or in
Cheepesid when the Coffin was carried to Mr Yongs saith he
was not, nor was prevye of the makinge of the said Coffin onely
Rippons wyfe did tell him on Frydaye night (as he thinks that
hir husband was deade

Item he saith he did not knowe of the makinge of the Lybells
that were fixed on the Coffin nor did knowe whoe they were

---

[1] Harl. MS. 6848, fol. 61 recto, in the British Museum.

that made them beinge demaunded whether he knowes
Pendred [Penry] or not saith he hath heard of him but knowes
him not

Item he saith he knowes Abraham Pulbery /

Item he saith he knowes one   Iones but hath not bene
longe acquainted with him nor doeth he knowe where he
dwells

Item this Examinate saith that he with his company were at
the wood where they were nowe taken on sonday was a fortnight

Item he saith that the Lords prayer is noe praier for that (as
he saith) Christ did not saie it as a praier

> Thexaminacion of William Clerke, a worker
> of Capps, of the parishe of St Buttolphes, taken
> before vs Henry Townsend Richard yonge
> and Iohn Ellis esquiers the viij[th] of marche 1592[1]

Item he beinge tendred his oath to aunswhere truly to such
questions as should be demaunded of him on the behalfe of the
Quenes maiestie refuseth to take any oath:

Item he saith he did knowe Roger Ryppon but was not with
him duringe his imprisonment nor was at Newgate when the
Coffyn was carried from thens, nor was previe of yt nor of the
lybell fixed theron nor who wrote it /

Item he saith he *hath bene of the foresaid congregacion these
Fower or Fyve yeres*, and made *promise to stand with the said
Congregacion* soe longe as they did stand for the truthe and
glory of god, beinge then of that Congregacion at that tyme
present aboute twentie or there aboutes

Item beinge demaunded when he did see Pendred [Penry]
denies to aunswhere that Question /

And beinge demaunded whether he wold geve his consent to
repaier to his parishe Churche (as he is bound by the lawes of
the Land) saith he maye not soe suddenly yeld there vnto but
(soe that he maye be at libertye) he saith he will put in good
securytie to be of good behauioure towards the Quenes maiestie
and the state /

[1] Harl. MS. 6848, fol. 62 recto.

Thexamination of Richard Hawton shoomaker
taken before vs Henry Townsend Richard
yonge and Iohn Ellis esquiers the viij[th]
of marche 1592[1]

Item he denyes to take any oath to aunswhere to any question
but will aunswher truly soe nere as he can
Item he saith he hath bene of the foresaid congregacion a
fortenight or three weeks
Item he saith he hard noe notice of their meetinge at the wood
but meetinge with a shoomaker whome he knowes not went
with them /
Item he saith he knowes not Roger Rippon nor was at newgate
nor in Cheepesid when the Coffin was carried from newgate,
but he heard that a Coffin was carried throughe the streetes
and that Libells were fixed on yt but was not previe of them
nor knowes whoe wrote them
Item he saith he is nowe contented to repaier to his parishe
Churche as he ought and will hereafter refraine the Company
of that congregacion and will observe the Quenes maiesties [?]
lawes

Thexaminacion of Iohn Barns tayler
taken...the viij[th] of Marche i592[2]

......

Item he saith he did knowe Roger Ryppon and was at newgate
in the morninge before he was carried thens but was not prevye
of the carriynge[?] of the Coffyn to m[r] yongs, nor of the Lybells
fixed theron nor whoe wrote them

......

Item he saith that at his first entringe into that societie he
*made noe other vowe, but that he wold followe them soe farr
forth as the word of god did warraunt him......*

Thexaminacion of Daniell Bucke scrivoner of the
Burughe
of Southwarke taken the nyneth daye of marche
[1592/3]

---

[1] Harl. MS. 6848, fol. 61 verso.
[2] *Ibid.*, fol. 67 recto.   This MS. is an original.

before Henry Townsend Richard yonge and
Iohn Ellys Esquiers And beinge required to
be deposed vppon a booke refuseth to
take any other oath then to protest before god
that all his sayings were true[1]

Beinge examined whether he was with the Coffyn at newgate,
denyes that he was there and that he did not see the lybell
fixed on the said Coffin, but saith y^t afterwards a straunger
shewed vnto him the Coppie of the same at his owne shopp in
Southwarke and denyes that he knewe the name of the
straunger nor any thinge els of him, but that he was a
Wiltsheere man and came to see how he did /
And saith further that he was vppon sondaye last in thafter-
noone in the Cunstable his house in Islington where he did see
emongst others of their fraternitie Penrhyn [John Penry] /
And saith further that George Iohnson was Reader there in
the Cunstables house as aforesaid And saith alsoe that there
were there aboue fortye of them together and diuers others that
were not of their societie
And saith further that he was not in his parishe Churche thes
xij monethes, bycause it is against his conscience vnlesse there
were reformacion in the Churche accordinge as they be warraunted by the word of god
And as concerninge the Bushopps he thinkes that they haue
noe spirituall aucthoritie over the rest of the Clergie
Beinge asked what vowe or promise he had made when he
came first to their socyetye he aunswhereth and saith that he
made this protestacion, That he wold walke with the rest of
that congregacion soe longe as they did walke in the waye of
the lord and as ffarr as might be warraunted by the word of
god
Beinge demaunded whether there shold be any motion made
by some of their fraternitie that they should goe some where
in to the Cuntrye wherby they might be in more saftie denyes
that he herd any such matters / but saith that he herd that one
Myllers a preacher at St Andreas vnderashafte sayd that if

---

[1] Harl. MS. 6849, fol. 216 recto—217 recto, in the British Museum.

they did maynteyne the truth they should not keepe them
selves in Corners but should shewe them selves forth publiquely
to defend the same, and he thought that vnfitt lest it should be
a meane to stirr a Rebellion

And further beinge demaunded whoe was their pastor and by
whome he was Created saith that m^r Frauncis Iohnson was
chosen Pastor, and m^r Grenewood docto^r, and Bowman and
Lee deacons, and Studley and George Knifton potticary were
chosen elders, in the house of one Fox in St Nicholas Lane,
London / about halfe a yere sithence all in one day by their
congregacion, or at m^r Bylsons house in Crechurche he remembreth not whether / and that the Sacrament of Baptisme
was (as he called it) deliuered there to the number of vij
persons by Iohnson, but they had neither god fathers nor
godmothers, and he tooke water and washed the faces of them
that were baptised: the Children that were there baptised
were the Children of m^r Studley m^r Lee with others beinge of
seuerall yeres of age, sayinge onely in thadministracion of this
sacrament I doe Baptise thee in the name of the father of the
sonne and of the holy gost withoute vsinge any other cerimony
therin as is now vsually observed accordinge to the booke of
Common praier B[e]inge then there presente the said Daniel
Studley: william Sheppard, william marshall, Iohn
Beche, Roberte Bray Thoma[s] Lee. Arthur Byllet
Edmund Thompson Roberte Iackson william Mason,
George marten, Thomas michell, Robert Abraham,
henry wythers, Thomas digson[?], peter farland;
william weber, dauy Bristoe, Iohn Nicholas, Iohn
Barnes. George Smell[?], Christofer Raper, Christofer
Sympkins, Christofer diggins Roger Rippon Christofer
Boman, Thomas Settell Iohn Grenewood, aforesaid
Edward Graue, william Collins, Abraham pulbery,
Nicholas leye aforesaid George manners George Knyfton,
aforesaid m^{rs} Settell, katherine Onnyon[?], m^{rs}, Boyes,
margery daubin[?] Ellyn Rowe, Avis Allen, An homes,
Ione pulbery, nicholas lee his wyfe, frauncis Iohnes, An
Bodkyn, Elizabeth moore, Barbera Sampford, and others
whose names he doeth not remember.

Beinge further demaunded the manner of the lordes supper
administred emongst them, he saith that fyve whight loves or
more were sett vppon the table and that the Pastor did breake
the bread and then deliuered yt vnto some of them, and the
deacons deliuered to the rest some of the said congregacion
sittinge and some standinge aboute the table and that the
Pastor deliuered the Cupp vnto one and he to an other, and
soe from one to an other till they had all dronken vsinge the
words at the deliuerye therof accordinge as it is sett downe in
the eleventh of the Corinthes the xxiiijth verse

Beinge demaunded whether they vse to make any Collection
or gatheringe amongst them said that there is a gatheringe of
mony emongst them the which mony is deliuered to the deacons
to be distributed accordinge to their discretion to the vse of
the poore

And he herd saie that they did vse to marry in theire
congregacion

And further refuseth to comm to the Churche and obeye the
forme of service which is vsed in the booke [?] of Common
prayer sett oute by the Quenes maiesties [?] Iniunctions, bycause
there is not a reformacion accordinge to the word of god

Rychard Young

Thexaminacion of Iohn Penryn [Penry] taken

xxvj° martij 1593[1]

hee requireth that hee may haue a publike conference to bee
allowed or appointed by her maiestic & the Lordes of the
Counsell, if it so please their honours; or otherwise hee will not
confere for this present hee saith that there was a peticion
deliuered & allso there is a booke to bee deliuered into the
Parliament, conteyninge his Faithe and opinions & hee
expecteth to knowe their Censure thereof & allowance or dis-
allowance of the same /

......

Thexaminacion of sondry persons abidinge in
the prisons in & aboute London taken before

---

[1] Harl. MS. 6849, fol. 204. This is apparently the original MS. of this
deposition, signed by " Rychard young".

Doctor Goodman deane of westmi*nster* &
others iij°, iiij°, v*to*, et vj*to* April 1593[1]

Clinke   Henry Broadwater scrivene*r* in S*t* Nicholas Lane
aged xxix yeares was committed to prison by the
Bishop of London & others aboute vj weekes paste
......

Newgate.   Edward Grave Fishmonger of the pa*r*ishe of
S*t* Butulph in Thames streete aged xxv yeares was
committed to prison a weeke paste /
Item hee saieth that hee hath bene of this opinion
of the Sectaries this halfe yeare & was persuaded
by the Sermons of m*r* Gardener and m*r* Phillips;
who preached that men were bounde to heare & to
bee ruled by their pastor Elders & deacons Hee...
confesseth that hee had one of Barrowes his bookes
of conference wh*i*ch hee lent to Pedar the shoemaker,...
Christofer diggins weuer aged xxiiij yeares is
servaunte [?] to Nicholas haveren*n*[2] of the pa*r*ishe
of S*t* Olaves in Southwarke & was one of them
that carried the Coffine to m*r* younges dore /
......
Hee saieth that hee was in the Assemblies eu*e*ry
Lordes day by the space of two yeares now laste
paste
Item hee saieth that hee hath seene one of Barowes
his bookes in the handes of one Iohn wilkenson,
......
Iohn Clerke husbandman of the pa*r*ishe of wall-
soken in the Countye of Norffolke was committed
three yeares paste by the Sheriff*es* of London
beinge taken in an assembly w*i*th Barrowes......Hee
saieth that hee will not goe to any churche nor to
any Sermons /

---

[1] Harl. MS. 6848, fol. 32 recto—fol. 36 recto.
[2] This is apparently the name here written, but in these hastily penned
depositions mistakes were likely to be made.

yt was thoughte good by the Commissioners
that hee should bee sente to Bridewell. to
grinde in the mill

Roger waterer haberdasher servaunte [?] to Robert
Pavye [?] of the parishe of S^t. Martens at Ludgate
was committed to Newgate...three yeares and
a quarter paste / & was neuer examined / The cause
of his imprisonment (as hee saith) was for that hee
wente not to his parishe churche in three weekes
& was fetched out of his masters house /

hee saieth hee was once at an assembly in a
gardeyne house neere Bedlem where Iames Forester
did expounde the Scriptures.

......

William Marshall Shipwrighte dwellinge at wappinge aged xxxij yeares was taken in the wood...
hee saieth he hath bene of these assemblies halfe
a yeare & was with them three tymes in the woodes.
& yet was at churche vj weekes paste /

....

Thomas hewett borne in Swanton in the County of
Leicester pursemaker of the age of xxx yeares &
doth dwell at St Martens le Graunde with Iohn
Sutton & is his servaunte & was taken with the
Reste in the wood

....

George Knifton Apothecarye dwellinge in Newgate
markett of the age of yeares [*sic*] saieth that hee
hath mett at the assemblies at Barnes his house at
Billsons house & at Lees house & at the woodes &
at Rippons house & at deptford wood, & hee is an
Elder

Beinge demaunded whether hee will goe to Churche,
hee aunswereth that hee wilbee content to haue
conference & before that hee will not goe to the
churche, & refuseth to take an othe

hee is to bee sent to the deane of westminster
to conferre

willi*a*m Mason shipwrighte of thage of xxj yeares
was taken in the wood Hee saieth that hee hath
bene of these assemblies since a little before
Christmas laste & was p*er*suaded by Roger Rippon
& Edward Chaundler, & hath bene at there
assemblies xij tymes viz in Nicholas Lane, at
Daniell Buck*es* neere Allgate & at Nicholas Lee his
house, & hee gaue vj^d a weeke w*h*ich the deacons
receyued & hee saieth that Chaundler had Barrowes
bookes & did reade them

Beinge demaunded whether hee will goe to the
Churche, hee saieth he will & is bounde w*i*th
his brother Ri*c*h*a*rd Mason & Iames Tailor & so
discharged /

Henry withers shipwrighte dwellinge at deptford
Strande of the age of xxvij yeares was co*m*mitted
a moneth paste beinge taken at the assembly in
the woodes /

hee saieth hee hath bene of the said assemblies
this halfe yeare by meanes & p*er*suasion of the
Shipwrightes & they did assemble themselues
eu*er*y Sabboth daye at dyvers houses
......

Beinge demaunded whether hee will goe to Churche,
hee aunswereth that hee is willinge to goe to
Churche after that hee hath had conference /

*Christ*ofer Bowman goldsmithe of thage of xxxij
yeares & doeth dwell in weste Smithfield & was
Co*m*mitted by [i.e., for] the Coffine & libells /

Hee saieth hee is one of the Confused [?][1] Churche
& is a deacon amongest them beinge chosen in
September laste

hee saieth hee was imprisoned v yeares paste for
puttinge vp a petic*i*on to the Queenes ma*i*estie &
continued in prison iiij yeares for the same /

---

[1] The writing of "Confused" is plain, but some other word was
evidently intended.

hee saieth that the Forward preachers caused him
to fall into these assemblies & that m^r Chattertons.
printed Sermon was the cause that made him enter
into this Action

......

Hee [Christofer Bowman] saieth that hee hath beene
at their assemblies as often as hee could have time
& liberty viz at m^r Billsons house, at Penryns,
Lees; Rippons and Barnes there houses & in
St Nicholas Lane & in the woodes

......

Beinge demaunded where hee was maried, hee
saieth at Penryns house, and Settle did pray &
Grenewood was presente, & hee denieth to sweare
or subscribe

Thomas Micklefield Ioyner of thage of xxxiij yeares.
dwellinge in St Mary Overies parishe was taken in
the assembly in the woodes......

hee confesseth that hee hath bene of the Company
of these Sectaries this quarter of a yeare & was
persuaded thereto by m^r Phillips preachinge /

......

Dauid Bristowe tailor of thage of xxx yeares
dwellinge in St Martens le Graunde was taken in
the woodes......

......

hee hath bene in their company this halfe yeare &
saieth hee cannot goe to any Churche but to that
wherevnto hee hath Ioyned himselfe

Christofer Simkyn Coppersmith dwellinge in aldersgatestreete of thage of xxij yeares was taken in the
woodes...

hee...saieth that hee hath not bene at his parishe
churche these xviij moneths beinge thereto persuaded by hearinge m^r Sparkes m^r Cowper & others
their Sermons,

......

William Smithe of Bradford in the Comitatus [i.e.,

County] of willshire mynister of thage of xxx yeares
was made mynister by the Bishop of Couentrye &
Litchfield

hee saieth hee was imprisoned viij weekes since...
for the Carriage of the Coffine......

......

Arthur Billett borne in Flanteclex[1] in the Com*itatus*
[i.e., County] of Cornewall aged xxv yeares saieth
that hee hath bene a Scholler & a Souldiour & was
taken with Penryn and others at Ratcliffe aboute
a fortnighte paste /

hee saieth that hee hath bene in[?] drawen into this
Society these two yeares & hath bene three or foure
tymes at the woodes & in dyvers houses. and
receyued the Communion at Barnes house

hee was the man that putt Barrowes & Grenewood
their bookes to the printe at dorte & hee sawe one
of the bookes in a Countrey mans handes.

......

Iohn Parkes Clothworker of thage of L yeares was
taken in the woodes & committed...aboute a
moneth paste.

hee saieth hee serueth m^r Livesey his sonne & hath
meate & drinke of him & noe wages & hath no
habitacion

hee hath bene of this Secte a quarter of a yeare
& hath bene at these assemblies vj tymes in sondry
places,

......

Iohn Penryn mynister of the age of xxx yeares or
thereabou*tes*

......

The cause of his departure out of the Lande of
Scotlande was for that hee putt vp a petition to
the parliament & could not bee heard / & therefore
hee departed /

---

[1] "Flanteclex" is quite plainly written.

Leonard Pidder shoemaker of thage of xxx yeares dwellinge at blacke Friers was taken in the woodes......

......

William Curland Shipwrighte of thage of   [1] yeares was taken in the woodes neere yslington

......

William Giles Taylor aged xxij yeares servaunte to mr Cheryatt of walbroke was taken as hee was goinge to the assembly in the woodes

......

Thomas Emery is his felowe servaunte
Edward Gilbarte of thage of xxj yeares servaunte to Isaac Frize tronkemaker was taken in the woodes /

......

Frauncis Iohnson mynister was so made by the Sectaries & chosen their pastor is of thage of xxxj yeares & is of noe certeine abode

......

hee saieth that it is the power of their Churche that they may excommun[i]cate the Queene vntill shee acknowledge & confesse her selfe, and this is done to save her soule /

Hee [Francis Johnson] saieth that hee was committed the vth day of december 1592 by the Lord of Caunterbury & others, & hee hath bene examined two seuerall tymes by the Lord Chiefe Iustice at Sergeantes Inne

Item hee saieth that the Lordes prayer is a forme of prayer but not to bee vsed for the Apostles did not vse to saye it

Item hee saieth that hee was prisoner in Cambridge for a Sermon that hee made to this purpose for that hee would not take an othe foure yeares paste

Beinge demaunded by whom hee was persuaded to these assemblies hee saieth by the Scriptures & worde of god /......

......

Edward Boys haberdashed [haberdasher] aged xxxiij yeares dwellinge in Fleetestreete was committed xvj weekes paste by the Bishop of Caunterbury......

---

[1] There is a blank space at this point in the manuscript.

Beinge asked how longe hee hath bene drawen from his parish Churche, hee saieth that hee hath bene of this Societie these three yeares. & was moued thereto by m^r Egerton m^r Cowper & M^r wigginton their Sermons......

......

George Collier haberdashed [haberdasher] aged xxxviij yeares of the parishe of St Martens at Ludgate was committed by the Bishop of London & others v yeares paste

......

hee saieth that hee was taken with Grenewood & Crane & others & was neuer examined in all this time
Beinge required to goe to his parishe church & haue his liberty hee saieth hee will not /
William denford Scholemaster of the age of L yeares lodged at mayres house in Fosterlane & was taken in the wood & committed...aboute a moneth paste.
hee saieth that hee hath bene twise at the Assemblies in the wood & doeth vse to saye the Lordes prayer, but hee will not goe to Churche vntill the parishes bee reformed / hee saieth that the ministery is not duely called

......

Thomas Settell mynister of the age of xxxviij yeares hath bene in prison these xv weekes beinge committed by Sir Owen Hopton & doeth renounce his mynisterye / & was not examined since his committinge.
hee was taken in an Assembly at a Schoolehouse in St Nicholas Lane.
Beinge demaunded how longe hee hath absented himselfe from the church of England hee aunswereth, about a yeare paste & hath not receyued the Communion these three yeares & hath bene againste the discipline of the Churche of England these vij yeares; & refuseth to take an othe /

......

hee allso saieth that hee was at the excommunicacion of Robert Stokes & the wordes were pronounced by Frauncis Iohnson their pastor & confesseth that hee hath prophesied in their assemblies
hee saieth that hee did receyue the Communion in Barnes his

house in Smithfield in the Aforenoone, & hath persuaded
the people to their assemblies /

......

william wevar shoemaker of Grayes Inne Lane of thage of
XL yeares servaunt to George Smith...was taken in the
woodes...
Item hee saieth that hee hath frequented these assemblies
these xviij monethes...

....

hee saieth that hee hath made a Couenaunte to the Congregacion to bee of their Societie & refuseth to goe to the
churche /
Quintine Smith Feltmaker servaunte to his brother in Southwarke aged xxx yeares. was taken in the woodes...
hee saieth hee hath bene of these assemblies these two yeares

...

hee saieth that hee made a Couenaunte with the Assembly
that as longe as they did walke in the lawes of god hee would
forsake all other assemblies and onely folowe them /

......

Katherine Onyon spinster dwellinge at Allgate, is willinge to
goe to Churche, but shee is not able to putt in Suerties /

2. Aprilis. *1593*. Thexaminacion of William Clerke of St
Buttolphes without Bushopps gate. aged
xl. yeres, or ther aboutes,...[1]

First that he hath bene in prison in the Fleete this
moneth. /
Item, that he was committed by the Bushopp of London, and
other highe commissioners beinge taken in the woode, beyonde
Islington, wher he saieth they praied and exercised the word
of god, and ther George Iohnson vsed the exhortacion and
praier. /

...

Item, he saieth he hath refrained to come to churche but halfe
a yere, but hath held his opinions these fyve yeres, beinge

---

[1] Harl. MS. 6848, fol. 55 recto.

drawen therto first by Greenewood, then in prison, and since by one Crane who died in Newgate, /

...

Concordat cum Original

...

[April 2, 1593.]

> Thexaminacion of Iohn Nicholas of the parishe of St Pulchres London Glover aged xxxvj yeres or theraboutes...[1]

...

First that he hath bene in Prison a monthe.
Item that he was comitted...beinge taken in the wood beyond Islington amonge diuerse others ther assembled /

......

Item that he hath refrained from parishe churche assemblies thes fowre yeres, wherof he hath bene thre yeres and more in prison in the gate howse at westminster,...
Item beinge asked by whome he was drawen into his oppinions and when, sayeth by the word of god, and that he hath heard George Iohnson preache once or twice wherof once was in the wood, and hath heard Francis Iohnson preache once in S⁺ Nicholas Lane /
Item he sayeth that they vsed to meete in ther assemblyes in S⁺ Nicholas lane and in the woods beyond Islington wher he was taken /

......

Item he sayeth that one of his sonnes named nathaniell [?] beinge five yeres of age was baptized by Francis Iohnson in S⁺ Nicholas lane in the Scolehowse ther about Christmas last, and that he was never baptized before that tyme. /

......

Concordat cum Original

...

2. Aprilis 1593.   Thexaminacion of George Iohnson late Scholemaster in S⁺ Nicholas Lane. London

[1] Harl. MS. 6848, fol. 63 verso.

borne in Richmonshire in the Countie of yorke.
of the age of xxix. yeres,...[1]

First that he hath bene prisoner in the Fleete a monthe,
comitted...for beinge taken in an assemblye of people in
a wood beyond Islington /

...

Item beinge demaunded by whome he was drawen into his
oppinions, saieth he was drawne therto, by the worde of god,
and by hearinge of m[r] Egerton preacher, at his Sermons /

...

        .1.

3. Aprilis. i593.   Thexaminac*i*on of Iohn Dalamore of the
                    Cittye of Bathe brodeweaver of the
                    age of xxv yeres...[2]

First that he hath bene in prison in Newgate this monethe
being taken in the wood beyond Islington in thassembly ther...

....
Item being asked by whome he was drawen in to his opinions
sayeth by the word of god and that he hath hard one Smythe
& others preache at Kensham [Keynsham] and other places in
Sommersetshire. /

...

                    Concordat Cu*m* Orignall [?]

                            ...

        .2.

3. Aprilis i593.   Thexaminac*i*on of Robe*r*t Abraham se*r*vaunt
                   to Thomas Rookes dwelling in S[t] Olives
                   in Sowthewarke letherdresser of thage of
                   the [*sic*] xxvj yeres...[3]

First that he hath bene in prison in Newgate this monethe
being taken in the wood in the assembly...

....
Item he sayth he hath not bene at any Churche this twelve
monethes and hath bene of his opinions a yere & halfe

......
        [1] Harl. MS. 6848, fol. 63 recto.   [2] *Ibid.*, fol. 58 recto.
                [3] *Ibid.*, fol. 57 verso.

Item being asked how often they haue vsed to meete in their
assemblies saythe twyce a weeke commonly except they were
otherwise occupyed and saythe they mett somtymes at Smyth-
fielde in an house by the hospitall allwayes earlye in the
morninge And in the wynter about iiij⁰ʳ or v a clocke in the
morninge and somtyme by Algate besydes Christchurche and
they met by such direccion as they tooke alwayes at ther last
meetinges and somtymes about moregate[?]. they tooke their
direccion for meeting as they met ther And sayth they received
the Communyon[?] but once which was in a house about
Smythfyeld but he remembreth not the house and yt was at
the handes of Francis Iohnson ther pastor./

Item he confesseth that they met thre or fowre tymes at
Sᵗ Nicholas Lane and once at Rippons[?] house in Southworke
and in the field by Detforde somtymes and oftentymes in the
feilds & woods by Islington./

....

Item he sayth they vsed to geve ther pastor every man
accordinge to his abylitye./

Concordat cum original

......

3. Aprill. *1593*..Thexaminacion of Abraham Pulburye of the
                parishe of Crichurche pursmaker by trade, but
                free of the Coupers, of the age of xxiiijᵒʳ.
                yeares./ or their aboutes,......[1]

First, that he hath bin in prison this moneth...taken in the
Wood beyond Islington,...and saieth he had with him a Sworde
at the wood./

......

Item, he saieth he hathe byn at some of their assemblies at
diuerse places, viz. by Smythfeild, earlye in the mornynge, wher
they continewed most parte of the daye, and sometymes by
Crichurche, sometymes by Detford./

Item, he saieth that Francis Iohnson, was their Pastor, Greenewood their Doctor, Studley and knyveton their elders, Nicholas
Lee and Iohn [i.e., Christopher] Boweman their deacons./

[1] Harl. MS. 6848, fol. 47 verso and 48 recto.

Item, he saieth their hathe bene baptised in their assemblies in Nicholas Lane, at one tyme, iiij^{or}. or fyve children, wherof some wear of fyve yeres ould, some of sixe yeares, and some of vij. yeres ould. /

......

Item, he saieth he was about a twelmonth since, Commytted to prison in Sussex together with one william Collin, by the Bushopp of Chichester, and from him sent to Sir Henrye Goringe, and by him send [*sic*] to Arrundell, their to be kept, vntill the quarter Sessions /, beinge taken in Arrundell as suspected to be a Brownist, and then Continewed in prison vntill Thassises, whear he was Indicted, and Burned in the eare, for a vagabounde, and then prest for a souldier, which he saieth was done agaynst, all Lawe and Iustice. /

Concordat cum Original

...

3. Aprilis. *1593*. Thexaminacion of Roger Waterer late Servant to Robert Pavye of S^t martyns Ludgate, haberdasher, aged xxij. yeres...[1]

First, that he hath bin in prison in Newgate, these three yeres, and a quarter,...and the cause of his commitment, was (as he saieth) for not Comminge to Churche. /

......

Item, he Confesseth that before he was Committed to prison, he was in an assemblie in a garden howse by Bedlein, wher Iames Forrester expounded, before ther Churche was setled, and was perswaded to his opinions by one Coppye. /

......

....

The Reexaminacion of Robert Aburne [Abraham]; taken the thirde day of Aprell. 1593. before Doctor Goodman Deane of Westminster m^r Townshend m^r Dale, m^r Barne, and m^r yonge. /[2]

[1] Harl. MS. 6848, fol. 51 recto.
[2] *Ibid.*, fol. 41 recto and verso.

He saieth he is by trade a lether dresser and servaunt to one
m^r Rooks of Southwarke, he saieth he hath not bene at his
parishe Churche this yere and a halfe,

he saieth the first that euer brought him into this Congregacion
was one William Howton deceased, whoe perswaded him to
refraine his [sic] parishe Churche, and brought him acquainted [?] with the rest of the bretheren of that Congregacion,
beynge at bridewell, and thether he went to see ther orders,
beynge ther at at [sic] that tyme Studley, with others [sic]
prisoners ther, wher he harde at that tyme, one Stanhopp
preache, amongest them in the prison openlye, and then he this
examinant, beynge amongest them, was receaved and admytted
into ther societie and congregacion, without eyther examinacion,
or further enquirie of his conversation. /

he saieth that sithens he hath met with the said Congregacion
diuers tymes, as well privately in howses, as openlye in feilds
and woods, some tymes to the number of a hundreth, sometymes
lx. [60] at the least, once they mett about halfe a yeare sithence
at Roger Rippons in Southwarke, two other tymes at Algate
one [i.e., on] the left hand he knoweth not at whose howse, and
that m^r Iohnson was ther pastor when they wear in Southwarke,
and after at an other howse at Smythfeild almost halfe a yere
sithens but knowes not whose howse it was, and ther they
Receaved the Communion, Iohnson ministringe vnto them, and
mett once in St Nicholas Lane, the said Iohnson beinge Pastor,
& Greenewood ther teacher. /

They mett diuers tymes in the feild neere Detford, And about
the woodsides neere Islington, and ther have hard yonge
[George] Iohnson preache, sithence his brother the elder
Iohnson, was in troble. /

He saieth that at ther meetinge in St Nicholas Lane, when
m^r Yonge did take them ther, the[y] did then make Choyse of
their Doctor Teacher Deacons and elders, and that Iohnson
thelder then was chosen Pastor, Grenewood teacher, Studley
and knyfton Elders, Lee and Bowman Deacons. /

He saieth that their Doctor and Pastor weare mayntained by
Contribucion from amongest them euery one as his abilitie
was, by Weekelie colleccion, / and that he for his parte hath

yealded his contribucion this yere and this halfe, / and that the collection beynge gathered was deliuered to the Deacons to be distributed amongest those of that congregacion, which they [the] said Deacons did thinke good, and most to stand in neede. /

He saieth that they did vse to excommunicate amongst them, and that one Robert Stokes, and one George Collier, and one or twoe more whose names he Remembreth not, wear excommunicated, for that they discented from them in opinion but in what poynte he Remembreth not, and that the said Iohnson thelder did denounce thexcommunicacion against them, and concernynge ther manner of proceadinges to excommunicacion he saieth, that they the saide Stokes and the Rest beynge privatelye admonished of their pretended errors, and not conforminge them selves, and by Witnes produced to their congregacion, then the said Iohnson, with the Consent of the whole Congregacion, did denounce the excommunicacion, and that sithence they weare excomunicated which was a halfe yere and somewhat more sithence, they wear not admitted into their Churche /, And beynge demaunded whether he could be contented to forsake the said congregacion, and repaiere to his parishe Churche, or not, he saieth he knoweth not, nor can see any cause whye he should soe refraine the said congregation. /

Concordat cum Original

. . .

[April 4, 1593.]

George Kniveton [Knifton] of Newgate market potecary of the age of xxiiij^{or} yeres

......[1]

First that he hath bene in prison this fortnight...taken in the company of Penry and others in the howse of one Lewes in Stepney. /

Item he confesseth that he is one of the elders of their congregacion

......

Item he saythe he hath had conference with M^r [Robert ?]

[1] Harl. MS. 6848, fol. 76 verso.

Browne whoe perswaded him not to recive the Cómmunyon and synce hath had conference with Barrowe with Greenewood and with Penry and was made Elder about half a yere since and that he misliketh Cartwryghts plan[?] of Church goverment. /

Item he sayeth he hath bene at thassemblies most comonly vppon euery sonday and sometyme vppon the weeke dayes sometymes in St Nicholas Lane somtymes at Nicholas Lees and somtymes at m^r Bilsons by Chrichurch sometymes at the woodes by Islington and Detford and at Iohn Barnes his his [*sic*] howse by S^t barthelmewes. /

......

4. Aprilis. *1593*.   William Mason of Wappinge Shipwright
              of the age of xxiiij. yeres, or theiraboutes,...
              ......[1]

First, that he hath bene in prison in the Counter in the Poultrye,...beinge taken in the wood. /

......

Item, that he was never at Churche since Christmas last, and soe longe he hath held his opinions, perswaded therto by Edward Chandler a Shipwright, and went to the woodde, with Roger Rippon. / and hathe bene at ther assemblies about xij. tymes. viz. at Nicholas lane, at Roger Rippons howse, at Detford woodde, and at the woods by Islington, when he was taken, and at Daniell Buckes howse, a scrivenour by Algate. and hath seene diuerse children Baptised, and gave to the Deacons, vjd. a weeke when he had money.

....

Concordat cum Original

......

bayled

[April 4, 1593.]

              Henrye Withers of Detford Strande,
              Shipwright, aged xxvij. yeres, or theraboutes,
              ......[2]

---

[1] Harl. MS. 6848, fol. 69 recto.
[2] *Ibid.*, fol. 69 verso.

First that he hath bene in prison a month,...

Item, he saieth he hath held his opinions, but since Michaelmas last, and was drawen to his opinions, perswaded therto by the teachinge of Iohnson and Greenewood,

Item, he saieth he was most Comonlie, at ther assemblies, euerye Sondaye, sometymes at St Nicholas lane, at the woods by Islington, at Rippons howse, and in Smythfeild at Lees howse, and at the wood by Detford, and sawe diuers Children ther baptized. /

....

Concordat cum Original

......

bayled

[April 4, 1593.]

Thomas Hewet of St Martyns Le
grand pursemaker aged xxx yeares

.........^{1}

Fyrst he saythe he hath bene in prison a monthe...taken in the wood by Islington.

....

Item he hath not bene at Churche this half yere and soe longe he hath held his opinions and will not showe by whome he was perswaded to it but only by one Edward Hale a herteffordshire man. /

....

Concordat cum original

....

[April 4, 1593.]

*Christo*fer Bowman of Smythfeld Gowldsmyth
of the age of xxxij yeres,...

......^{2}

First, that he hath bene in prison in the Counter, in the Poultre, this v. weekes, comitted by m^r yonge, beinge suspected to have knowledge whoe made the Libell, and about the Coffyn brought to m^r yonges dore. /...

[1] Harl. MS. 6848, fol. 76 recto.
[2] *Ibid.*, fol. 70 recto and verso.

Item, he saieth he is a Deacon in the congregacion chosen in September last. /

Item, he saieth he hath not bene at Churche these fyve yeres last past, wherof he was iiij^{or}, yeres in prison, and soe longe hath held his opinions, and was one of them that deliuered the Supplicacion to the Queenes Maiestie the last parliament, before this. /

Item, he saieth he was drawen to his opinions, by the course that the forward preachers tooke, and by a booke, and by a booke [*sic*] of a sermon vpon the xij^{th}. of the Romans, made by master Chatterton, as he thinketh, and by the forward preachers, he saieth he meaneth one Snape, and kynge, with others, whose course made him enter into further searche of the matter of the reformacion. /

Item, he saieth he hath bene at ther metings as often as he Could, beynge at libertie, and in health, viz. at m^r Bilsons howse neere Chrichurche, at St Nicholas lane, in the woods by Detford, and Islington, at Penries howse, at Lees howse, and at Rippons howse, and at Barnes his howse in Smithfeld by St Bartholomewes. /

......

Item, he saieth if ther nomber should never soe moche have encreased, they ment noe Reformacion by stronge hande. /

......

Item, beinge asked wher he was maried to his last wief, saieth in Penries howse, wher m^r Settle vsed praier, and that his opinion is that mariage in a howse without a mynister by Consent of the parties and frends is sufficient. /

Concordat cum original

......

5. Aprilis. *1593* Thexaminacion of Iohn Penrie Clerke,
             of the age of xxx. yeres, or theraboutes,
         ....[1]

First, that he was in or about London, the xix^{th}. of marche, and that he and Edward Grave went that night to Hodsdon, wher they laie, at the Antelopp. /

[1] Harl. MS. 6848, fol. 86.

Item, beynge asked whether they went not from thence to
one Iohn millett*es* howse in hertfordshere, saieth he will not
saie... /
Item he saieth he came out of Scotland about September, last,
in the Company of Iohn Edwards /, and came to london, and
lighted at the Corke at longe lane end, and that night lodged
at Stretford bowe. /
Item, he saieth he made, and caused to be printed in Scotland,
a booke intituled a Reformac*i*on and noe enemye to her
Ma*i*estie and the State. / and a boke w*h*ich he translated called
Thesis genevenciu*m*. /
Item, beynge asked what other bookes he made and caused to
be printed ther he Refuseth to answear. /
Item, he saieth the cause of his dep*a*rtinge out of this lande,
was because he could not be in quiet here, for the ecclesiasticall
state of the land. /

Concordat cu*m* Original

......

[Apr. 5, 1593.]

> *Christ*ofer Simkins of Aldersgate strete
> Coppersmyth of the age of xxij yeres or ther
> aboute*s* examined before m*r* deane of Westm*inster*
> m*r* dale m*r* Barne and m*r* yonge, the
> daie and y*e*r*e* aforesaid, refuseth to be
> sworne but sayeth /[1]

First that he hath bene in prison this monthe, comitted by
m*r* yonge and others, taken in the wood by Islington examined
before m*r* Doctor Stanhop and others at his Comitment, and
not since, and never indicted to his knowlege
Item he saieth he hath not bene at his p*a*rishe Church this
yere and a half last past, and soe longe hath held his oppinions,
and drawen therto by the preachinge of m*r* Sparkes and
m*r* Cowp*er* and other forward preachers. /
Item he confesseth he hath bene often at the assemblies and
comonly every sabothe daye but refuseth to tell wher.

---

[1] Harl. MS. 6849, fol. 182

Item he refuseth to tell whether he hath had any of Barrowe or Penries bookes. /

Item he sayeth if ther nomber had increased they would not have don*n* [?] any other thinge but serve god /

Item he refuseth to come to his *pa*rishe Churche, and sayeth he is ioyned to their congregac*i*on from whence he will not depa*rt*e. /

Concordat cu*m* original

......

5. Aprilis *1593*

> Francis Iohnson minister, but by thassamblies
> chosen to be a Pastor of the congregac*i*on, beinge
> of the age of xxxj yeres or ther about*es*, examined
> before M**r** doctou*r* Cesar, m**r** doctou*r* Goodman deane
> of Westm*inster* m**r** Barne and m**r** yonge. whoe
> refuseth to be sworne, but saieth[1].

First that he was first comitted to the Counter in woodstrete by the Sherif of London and m**r** younge, beinge taken in an assemblie in S**t** Nicholas Lane, and lastlye comitted by the L. Archbyshop of Canterbury and others, beinge taken in m**r** Boyses howse in Fletestrete, and hath bene twice examined before the L. Chief Iustice of England, and the L: Anderson viz. once before the L. Chief Iustice of England, and once before them bothe.

Item he saieth he knoweth not that he is indicted for any offence.

Item beinge asked howe longe he hath held his oppinions saith he cannot definitely answer, but sayth he was comitted to prison iiij**or** [quatuor] yeres agoe, vppon the makinge of a Sermon in S**t** maries Churche [in Cambridge]. /

Item he confesseth he hath baptized diu*er*se children in their congregac*i*on, and saieth for mariage he doeth not accompt that an ecclesiasticall matter, nor laid vppon the minister of god as a dewetie of his ministerie, and also sayth they are not bound no**r** tied to the wordes of the Lordes praier, and touchinge the Com*m*union of the Lordes supp*er* he saieth it maye be

[1] Harl. MS. 6849, fol. 181 recto and verso.

received, at any tyme of the daie or night, when the congregacion is assembled and prepared thervnto. /

Item beinge required to shewe in what places they vsed to
meete in their conventicles and assemblies, refuseth to answer /

Item being asked whether he hath or had anye of Barrowe
Greenewood or Penries bookes, refuseth also to answer but
desireth he maye be accused. /

Item beinge asked whether he hath not labored and perswaded
others to the assemblies and Congregacion wherof he is a
Pastor, and howe manie he hath soe perswaded and drawen
saieth he hath and must doe that which god laieth vppon him
in dewtye accordinge to his worde, and otherwise refuseth to
answer /

Item beinge asked whether he wilbe contented to reforme him
self and come to Churche refuseth directly to answer but sayeth
he cannot Ioyne with this ecclesiasticall ministerie, in this estate
of Archbyshops Byshopps Parsons, Vicars, Curates &c. /

Concordat cum Original

......

[The deposition of Iohn Edwardes concerning John Penry
probably made on April 5, 1593.][1]

Iohn Edwardes came out of Scotlande with Penryn & laye by
the way euery nighte where hee laye, and saieth that Penryn
was not banished out of Scotland, but there was banishment
decreed againste him, and the mynisters euer staye the pro-
clayminge thereof.

Hee saieth that Penryn was of this assemblie and was taken by
the waye and broughte to the Conestables house and from thence
hee escaped away on sonday nighte and named himselfe Iohn
Harries, and there were two or three Countreymen comynge
towardes them wch were taken by the way and said they were
goinge to waltham & therefore the Iustice discharged them

Hee saieth that one Iones was taken & wente home to dynner
with Captein [?] Graye & was afterwardes broughte by him to
the Iustice

Hee saieth that on Satterday nighte hee this examinant walked

[1] Harl. MS. 6848, fol. 85 recto.

with Penryn alonge Cheapeside thoroughe Newgate & they
wente to Nicholas Lees house & there this ex*aminant* lefte
penryn & his wife aboute vııj of the clocke hee knoweth not
who should haue exercised that day, nor did not heare of any
purpose that they had to goe into the Countreye /

His comynge out of Scotland with Penryn was in Nouember
laste & they came firste to one m^r yretons house besides Darby
vj miles, and dyned there & came to Northampton to the house
of Henry Godley who is father in lawe to the said Penryn,
where the said Penryn lodged, & this ex*aminant* laye at the
signe of the Bull; & the next day they came from thence to
St Albans [?] & lodged at the signe of the *Christ*ofer & the
nexte day came to Stratford at bowe to the signe of the Crosse
keyes [?] where Penryns wife was & had a chamber, and this
ex*aminant* lefte them there & came to London & sawe him no
more vntill a little before Christmas that they mett at a garden
house at the dukes place neere Allgate, where Penryn did
preache & (as hee doeth remember) Grenewood did preache
there allso & this ex*aminant* wente downe into the Countrey &
came not vp vntill Satterday was Sevenighte & since hath laien
at his brother Rochford his house, And vpon wensdaye or
thursday morninge Penryn came to this ex*aminantes* chamber
before hee was vp & was booted

hee saieth that hee did heare that Penryn was lodged at
m^{rs} Settles house

Ry*chard* young

5. Aprilis. *1593.*   Will*iam* Smythe of Bradford in
wilts*hire* minister of the age of xxx. yeres or
theraboutes, made a minister by the Bushopp
of Litchefeld and Coventrie, and licenced
to preache by the Bushopp of Saru*m*...
......[1]

First, he saieth he hath bin in prison this vııj. weekes, or
ther aboutes, Comitted...for suspicion to be privie to the
matters concerninge the Coffin caried to m^r yonges Doore. /
......

<hr>

[1] Harl. MS. 6848, fol. 71 recto.

Item, he confesseth he hath bine at an assemblie, at Lees howse, by Smythfeld. /

Item, beynge asked whether he be of that Churche or Congregacion wherof Iohnson is Pastor, refuseth to answear. /

Item, he saieth he came of purpose to Lees howse to thassemblie there to heare and see ther orders in those matters. /

......

Item, he saieth he came vp to London to conferr with m^r Iohnson, Greenwood, and others. /

......

Concordat cum Original

....

[April 5, 1593.]

Arthur Billet of llanteglos by Fowhey in Cornwell Scoller, of the age of xxv. yeres, or theraboutes......[1]

First, that he hath bene in Prison this fortnight,...who was in the woode by Islington, and afterwards taken in the Companye of Penrye and others,...

Item, he hath bene drawen to his opinnions, these two yeres, / perswaded by certen conferences in the Fleete, betweene m^r Mullins, m^r Hutchinson, and Barrowe and Greenewood. /

....

Item, he denieth that he hath or had any of Barrowes, Greenewoods, or Penries bookes, but hath receivid some of the written Coppies, and caried them over into the Lowe Cuntries to be printed, and that he hathe seene one of Barrowes bookes, in Nicholas Lees howse......

....

Concordat cum Original

......

6. Aprilis. *1593.* Quintin Smyth of Southwarke Feltmaker of the age of xxx. yeres, or ther aboutes...

.........[2]

[1] Harl. MS. 6848, fol. 71 verso.
[2] *Ibid.*, fol. 79 recto.

First, that he hath bene in prison a moneth,...beynge taken in
a wood by Islington,...
Item, he saieth he hath held his opinnions about twoe yeres,...
....
Item, he sayeth he did covenaunt with the Congregacion to
walke with them in the lawes of god, soe longe as ther doinges,
should be approved by the word of god, and soe longe would
forsake all other assemblies /,

Concordat cum Original

....

["6. Aprilis. 1593."]

William Weaver of Grayes Inne lane
Shomaker, of the age of xl. yeres, or
theraboutes,...[1]

First, that he hath bene in prison a monthe,...beynge taken in
the wood neere Islington,...
Item, he hath bene of his opinions, about a yeare and a halfe
and somewhat more, / and hath bene often at assemblies, viz.
twice or thrice at the wood wher they weare taken and once in
Nicholas Lees howse in Cowe lane, and was drawen first to the
assemblies, by Robert Bodkin, in Grayes Inne lane, Taylor. /
....
Item, he saieth that if their Nomber had greatly encreased, yet
he thinketh thay ment nothinge against the peace or estate
[i.e., the State]. /
Item, he saieth that when he was ioyned to their congregacion,
they caused him to vse words to this effect, that he should
promise to walke with them, soe longe as the[y] followed the
ordinance of Christ. /
......

["6. Aprilis. 1593."]

Thomas Settle late of Cowelane,
minister, made by Bushopp Freke, but
nowe renownceth that ministrye, of the age
of xxxviij. yeares or their aboutes,...[2]

[1] Harl. MS. 6848, fol. 66.
[2] *Ibid.*, fol. 65 verso and 66 recto.

....

Item, he Confesseth that he was present in the Congregacion
in a howse nighe Algate, within the Wall, when Robert Stokes
was excommunicated, and that he was excomunicated by
Francis Iohnson the Pastor, the rest of the officers and the
Congregacion beinge present and consentinge, which was done
for his Apostacy./

......

Concordat cum Original

...

10 [?] Aprilis 1593 George Smelles of Fynchelane taylor of the
age of xl yeares or thereaboutes...[1]

Firste he sayeth he hath ben in prison ever since sondaye
laste...
Item he sayeth he hath his oppinions thes iiij$^{or[?]}$ yeares
perswaded thereto by an old man one father Grayves a Carpenter as he supposeth who is deceased

......

Concordat cum Original

...

[1] Harl. MS. 6848, fol. 59 recto.

VII

DOCUMENTS OTHER THAN DEPOSITIONS RELATING TO JOHN PENRY

[An undated Petition of Helen Penry's to Sir John Puckering in her Husband's Behalf, written in April, 1593.][1]

> To the right honorable S*ir* Iohn Puck-
> ering Knight Lord Keep*er* of her
> M*ai*esties greate seale of England. /

In all humblenes beseecheth y*our* honno*ur* y*our* poore suppli*cant* Hellen Penrie in the behalf of her poore husband Iohn Penrie, That whereas your suppli*cantes* poore husband is at this p*resent* kept close prisoner in the Counter in the Poultrie in London, none suffered to come to him to bring him such thinges as are necessary for the p*r*eservac*i*on of his life and sustanaunce, he of him selfe being a very weake and sicklie man not hable longe to endure so hard and miserable imprisonment w*i*thout hazard of his life, his allowaunce being nothing but bread & drinke, the keeper refusing to carry such necessaries as are sent vnto him for his sustenaunce, yf he were the veriest Traito*r* that ever was, if it is not her M*ai*esties pleasure that he shold be thus hardlie vsed, but how soeu*er* greate matters are laide to his charge, yet I hope he will prove him selfe an honest and good subiect to her M*ai*estie. Most humblie therefore she beseecheth y*our* honno*ur* for god*es* cause in considerac*i*on of her poore husbandes sicklie and weake estate, that it wold please yow to graunte her y*our* honno*urs* warrant that she maye have accesse vnto her poore husband, to administer such necessaryes vnto hi*m* as she may for the p*r*eservac*i*on of his life, And y*our*

---

[1] Harl. MS. 6849, fol. 207 recto.

poore Oratrice shall be bound daylie to praise god for so greate favour and Mercy shewed vnto her, wch the Lord wold not see vnrewarded in yow. /

[A Note by John Penry in defence of Mr. Gittens, Keeper of the "Cownter in the Poultrie in London", dated April, 1593.][1]

They doe m^r Gittens injury who say that I have wanted eyther meat or drink competent sync [?] I was committed vnto his custody. I am lyklyer to starve for could then for want of meate. my wife in deed cannot bee permitted to come vnto mee, shee knoweth not how I fare. And therfore she may bee in feere that I ame in regard of meat and drinke hardlyer [?] vsed then I ame or have been.

    the 4th moneth Aprill 1593.

                    Iohn Penry.

[A Subscription of John Penry's concerning the Authority of the Queen, of the Privy Council, and of Civil Magistrates, and three other articles which he declined to subscribe.][2]

That hir right exellent [?] ma*ie*stie, & the Lord*es* of hir honorable privy co[un]sell, yea the most inferiour civill magistrate [?] vnder hir highnes hath authority to call any church or churchman to give an account of the doctrine w*hi*ch they hould & not fynding [?] the same according vnto the word may p*u*nish [?] them for it.

                    Iohn Penry

I stande to proue it out of ther owne writing*es* [?] vpo*n* my life that they allowe not the magistrates of whatsoeuer [?] place they be ether supreme, or inferio*ur*, to haue any authoritie as they call it (authoritatem Iuris) in causes Ecclesiasticall, but only potestatem facti to execute that w*hi*ch their presbyterie or Synodes have decreed.

                    R. Vaughan.

---

[1] Harl. MS. 6849, fol. 206 recto.
[2] Harl. MS. 6848, fol. 93.

I hold.   That the inferiour ciuill magistrate hath no authoritie to call
the Church or any churchman to giue accounte of their
doctrine (without expresse commandement from the supreme
magistrate) by open & publike triall.

R. Vaughan.

I hold that the most inferiour magistrate hath nothing to doe
to examyne any Churchman concerning his doctrine but only
to presente him, ether to the Church governours, or to other
ciuill magistrates to take further order with him...

Rich. Vaughan /

He refused to subscribe
to any of these. or to
controuerte [?] them

["The offers & requestes of m^r Iohn Penryn"]¹

Vnlawfull

1   The offices
2   The maner of calling vnto ye offices
3   A great part of ye workes wherin the officers
    are employed
4   The living ore [or] maytenaunc wherby the
    officers are mayntayned.————

Thes thinges by the Lordes assistaunc wee wilbe
ready to make good by the word of god, & yff it
bee thought needfull by the writinges of ye holy
martyres of this land (wherof[?] some are privileged
by hir maiesties authority) and also by the
doctrine of ye reformed churches.————

A conferenc wee are most willing to yeald vnto.
Our humble request vnto hir maiestie & their
honours is that yf it may so stand with their
pleasure, wee may have but this æquity yealded
vnto vs in it.

1   That the questiones one [on] both sydes layed
downe in writing, the reasons briefly annexed
vnto them, the awnswers also may with ye lyke

¹ Harl. MS. 6849, fol. 209–210.

brevity bee returned in writing, & so every thing wilbe the more deliberatly sett downe & all bye speaches & matters shalbe avoyded.

2. That such of vs as are scollers one [on] the one syde, may conferr together (having also the vse of bookes) about the awnswers & replyes that wee shalbe to make [*sic*]— — —

3. That those of the ecclesiasticall state with whôme[?] wee are to deale may bee but partyes [?] in this conferenc & not judges. And that some of the civill state may bee appoynted by their honours (yf their Lordshipes will not tak y⁰ hearinge of y⁰ cause them selves w*h*ich wee had rather & ernestly crave) to see that both partyes[?]/ do contayn them selves w*i*thin boundes: least otherwise eyther the holy truth of god should not bee so delt in as it beseemeth the same: or so holy & necessary an action should bee vnprofitablie broken of, by the infirmytyes or other greater wantes of eyther partyes [?].

Iohn Penry.

[A Letter concerning John Penry's Confession of Faith and Apology dated, "Mon. 6. 12. 1593."][1]

Right hono*u*rable,...I am bolde allso to sende to yo*u*r Lord*ship* a shorte confession of faith, and an Apologie, drawe*n* by y*t* faithfull wittnes of Christe, o*u*r brother Penry, before his death, By w*h*ich plainely app*e*areth, what his fayth was towards god, & nowe is p*a*rtaker of y*t* crowne of life w*h*ich is promised by Christe to all them that are faithfull vnto deathe./. The poore remnau*n*te of poore christians(who are falsely called Brownistes) doe all of vs generally agree with y*t* o*u*r faithfull brother in y*t* confession of faith and allegiau*n*ce to god & her ma*i*estie as we have often declared to y⁰ worlde, in other lyke confessions,

---

[1] Harl. MS. 6849, fol. 143. Dr John Waddington in his "John Penry", 1854, pp. 279–80, indicates that the original of this letter was written by Francis Johnson to Lord Burleigh.

which now I have not by mee, to sende allso to your Lordship
as otherwise I woulde have donne,...

[John Penry's Answer to Fifteen Slanderous Articles, written
not long before his death.][1]

> A short and true answer to *the*
> partycular slanders conteyned in
> these—15—most false and maly-
> cyous Artycles which lately were
> cast abroad in reproch of the true
> Christians whom they vnChristianly
> call Brownistes.　And first to ther
> tytle as is in that Copy that came
> to our handes.

The tytle to the slanderous　An abstract of the opinions which
　　Artycles.—　　　　　　　*the* Brownists do mainteyn

That you call true Christians by *the* name of Brownistes we
meruaile not for we find that the Apostles were said to be of
the Sect of *the* Nazarites and therfore with them also we do
confesse that that way which you call a sect, and Brownisme,
we worshipp God the father of our Lord Ihesus Christ beleeuing
all thinges that are wrytten in the Law, the Prophettes and
Apostles and whatsoeuer according to this rule is published by
this State, or holden of any refourmed Churches abroad.　These
opynions therfore which are falsely [?] and malycyously fathered
upon vs, we vtterly renounce them as none of ours, because
they agree not with the word of God which is the rule of truth,
nor with the allegeance which in the Lord we owe, and are
carefully to perfourme to her Maiestie her Counsell, and this
State, and we returne them vpon the detractors themselues as
the true fathers of such blasphemous lyes and slanders, which
are the brood and ymaginations of their own corrupt hartes, as
shall more fully appeare by this short but true answer to the
partyculars—.

a. Acts. 24. 5.
b. [?] Acts. 24.
14.

---

[1] Add. MS. c. 303 (fol. 200–203 recto), in the Bodleian Library.

A PATERNE OF TRVE PRAYER.

A LEARNED AND COMFOR-
table Expofition or Commentarie vpon
the Lords Prayer: wherein the Doctrine of
the fubftance and circumftances of true
inuocation is euidently and fully
declared out of the holie
Scriptures.

By IOHN SMITH, *Minifter and Preacher of the*
Word of God.

AT LONDON

Imprinted by *Felix Kyngfton* for *Thomas Man*, and
are to be fold at his fhop in Pater-nofter row
at the figne of the Talbot. 1605.

TITLE-PAGE. (Size of original 6⅗ in. × 4⅞ in.) See Vol. I.,
pp. 227–9 and Preface, p. xi.

Article .1.—Inprimis they affirme that there is no true Catholik Church in all the world but theirs, and that all Churches elce whatsoeuer are the Synagogues of Sathan. /

We beleue and confesse that the Catholique Church consisteth of *the* faithfull and elect w*hi*ch haue bene or shalbe vpon the earth from the beginning to *the* end of the world, of all nations, people kindred and tongues, so far are we through the mercy of God from this palpable ignorance wherwith yt seemeth our aduersaryes are blynded, who as yet haue not learned to distinguish betwene a partycular Congregation and the Catholique that is the vnyversall Church [.] We hold a Christian and reuerend iudgment of the East Churches and of *the* refourmed Churches in this part of *the* world, and are so farr from affirming them to be the Synagogue of Antichrist, as we doubt not but they haue refused and cast of the Antichristian Prelacy Priesthood, Tyranny and superstitions, and endeuor to obey o*ur* Lord Ihesus Christ in his owne ordynances as by their owne publike confession and practyze yt appeareth. But let o*ur* aduersaryes looke vnto yt how they account of the refourmed Churches abroad seing they haue denyed such to be suffycyent and lawfull Ministers of the Ghospell of Christ, who haue bene of those Churches allowed & ordayned therevnto and on the other syde (as the Papis*tes* themselues report) haue allowed & receyued such as were of late made Pries*tes* at Roome or Rhemes vpon recantation of some of their Popish opynions to be ministers here of these assemblyes in England, without any other ordination then they there had receyued before—

Answer.—
Job. 10. 16.
Rom. 7. 9.

M*r* Whyting.
M*r* Trauers.
M*r* Wright.

Tyrrell &
Tythes.

Article .2.—Item. That they haue power to excommunicate all that will not be of their faction or (as they terme yt) of their Church, and *that* whosoeuer shalbe by them excommunycate, is damned vnlesse he shalbe by them absolued.—

No Church hath power to Excommunycate any but such as are members of the same Church, for can they excommunycate such as haue neuer bene in Com*m*unyon with them. and what haue they to doe to iudge them that are without. So as here

Answer.—.
1. Cor. 5. 11.
12..

againe [?] our adversaries while they belye vs, laye open their
owne grosse ignorance in the matters of God. If any member
of the Church deseruing to be excommunycate do refuse to
heare the Church, obstinatly persisting in his knowen and
greeuous Schysmes or synnes, and therevpon is by the Church

Mat. 18. 17. 18. cast out in the name and power of the Lord Ihesus according
to his word then Christ hath said let him be to thee as
a heathen, verely I say vnto you whatsoeuer ye bind &c.—
And doth not also the Apostle wryght vnto the Churches of
Corinth, that they should forgyue and Comfort him vpon his
repentance of whom before he had wrytten to them, that in

2. Cor. 2. 7. regard of this synne, he hauing bene a brother, they should
Compare with being gathered together by the power of Christ delyuer him
1. Cor. 5. 4. 5. vnto Sathan for the destruction of the flesh that &c. That in
the Pryde of theyr hartes they call the Church of Christ
a faction we leaue vnto God who iudgeth.—

> Article .3.—Item that they haue excommunicat [*sic*] the
> Churches of England & Ireland aswell the
> Queen as the Counsell and all others, and
> therfore she and all the rest of her subiects are
> damned vnlesse they wilbe absolued by them
> and so admytted into the Church.—

Answer.— Such is our Innocency herein (blessed be God) as we do appeale
to God to whose eyes all thinges are naked and open after
thexample of Dauyd when he was likewyse falsely accused and
slaundred by Cush, saying. O Lord our God, yf we haue done
this thing if this wickednes be in our handes, nay yf yt entred
into our thoughtes, let thenemy persecute our soule and take
yt, yea let him tread our lyfe downe vpon the earth, and lay
our honor &c. Aryse O Lord and lift vp thy selfe against the
rage of our enemyes, and awake for vs according to the iudgment
which thou hast appoynted. Iudge thou vs O Lord according
to our righteousnes, and according to our ynnocency. O let
the malyce of the wicked come to an end, but guyde thou the
iust, for the righteous God tryeth the very hartes and reynes.
Our defence is in God, who preserueth the vpright in hart.
Furthermore we acknowledge, that yt were greeuous synne for

vs to Condemne any, and therfore (as we ought) we leaue all others and *our* selues to the iudgm*en*t of God in that day, when all flesh shall appeare before him to receyue according to that they haue done in their bodyes whether yt be good or euyll [.] And in the meane tyme (as yt becometh vs to iudge) we are perswaded *that* her Ma*ie*stie and many thowsandes of her Subiect*es*, (who as yet differ in iudgm*en*t amongst themselues and from vs in many thing*es*) are the deare Children of God, and heyres of saluation through faith in Christ Ihesus, and according to *our* duty (God being wyttnes to *our* soules) we do dayly acknowledge, and do dayly prayse God for the great and wonderfull thing*es* w*hich* God by the most gracyous gouernm*en*t of her most excellent Ma*ie*stie and her honorable Counsell hath brought to passe both for the matters of God in relygyon, and for the matters of the land in the Peace and safetie thereof. And we pray God to encrease the same every day more and more to the prayse of his most gloryous name and to *the* honor of *our* Prince to whom we wish the dayes of Methuselah yf yt be the will of God, that she may be an ancyent mother in Israell. to the comfort of her Subiect*es* in *pro*tecting them that do well, and taking vengeance on them that do euyll.—

1. Cor. 4. 5 *with* .2 Cor. 5. 20.
Phil. 1. 6. 7.

Gen. 5. 27.
Iudg. 5. 7.

Article .4.—It*em*. that the ministers of the Church of England are not true and lawfull ministers, but they are the hirelings of Antichrist and that the B. B. [Bishops] are the forerunners.—

The ministers of these assemblies haue bene often and earnestly intreated to shew out of the scriptures their ministery in their offyce, and execution of their offyce, according to the rules of the Testament of Christ, which hetherto they haue not done, neither are able to do, Moreouer euen themselues haue taught and published that *our* Lord Ihesus Christ hath in his word for the administrac*ion* of holy thing*es*, appoynted *the* offyces of Pastor, Doctor Elders, and Deacons to contynue to the end of the world together with their lawfull entrance and execution of their duties, that his Church may be instructed, and gouerned, and holpen according to his owne ordynance, to w*hich* only he hath promysed his presence and blessing. Also that they haue

Answer.—

Admon*ition*.
2 treat./ sect.
20.

not this ministery, but that they haue (w*h*ich are their owne wordes) an Antichristian Hierarchy, and a Popish ordering of Ministers, strange from the word of God, and the vse of all the refourmed Churches in *th*e world [.] If that which is here spoken of B B, be meant of the Bishopps w*h*ich were in the Primitiue Church, then we hold no such thing of them as is here ymagined, For those Bishopps were eyther Pastors, Doctors, or ruling Elders, whom the holy Ghost by the immediate calling of the Church, made ouerseers not of whole

Act. 20. 17. 28.
cum. 14. 23.
Tit. 1. 5. 7.
1. Tim. 5. 17.
Phil. 1. 1. 2.
Rom. 12. 7. 8.

Prouynces and Shires but of their partycular flock and Church as is evident by the scriptures noted in the margin and by these expresse wordes κατ᾽ εκκλησιαν. κατα in euery Church and euery Cyttie and such like. If they meane of *th*e Prelates of this age let themselues be their owne Iudges.—

Article .5.—That for stealing a man ought not to be put to death, because his body is the temple of the holy ghost distinguishing sophistically betwen [*sic*] fur & latro [.]

Answer.—

We do acknowledge that by the word of God in some cases of stealing a man may be put to death, as If one sett vpon a man in the hye way, If a thief be found breaking into a howse in the night or such like, but that euery stealing should be punished with death, the lawes of the land do not requyre, as appeareth by the oth*er* punishment*es* sett downe, of whipping, boring through the eare, marking the hand*es* and such like, as when a man stealeth a little to satisfie his soule because he is hungry. Sophisticate distinctions are their owne, we do not vse nor acknowledge them for o*ur*s—

Article .6.—Item. That all we that are baptized, are not baptized rightly & therfore must be baptized againe.—

Answer.—
a. harmo. of
conf. sect.
10.—

We confesse with the French Church who haue published yt, that they which are baptized in Papisticall assemblies need not to be baptized the second tyme, no more then the Circumcysion w*h*ich was had in the defection of Israell and false ecclesiasticall constitution with them, and euen as those sinned greeuously

which abode and had their children Cyrcumcysed in that
defection of Israell, So in that case they hauing indeed plaid
the harlott and forsaken God (whatsoeuer they pretend) and
God having cast them away and geuen them a bill of diuorcement,   Ier. 3. 8.
the Sacrament*es* and seales of God his couenant do not belong
vnto them, neyther do those where they vse [*sic*], seale vnto
them in that estate the Couenant of grace. And further how
they administer or receyue baptisme aright without a true and
lawfull ministery, yea sometymes by a woman and in pryvate
houses with a devised Litargie, Idolatrous crossing, and pro-
pounding questions to the Infant which vnderstandeth not
wherto the Godfathers and Godmothers must make answer,
and such like, we leaue to theyr [?] owne examynations by the
scriptures, and their owne publike wryting*es*.—

Article .7.—Item. we receyue the Sacrament of the Lordes
        Supper not rightly as Christ did constitute the
        same & therfore we receyue to condemnation.—

It doth not follow that yf any receyue the Supper of the Lord   Answer.—
not rightly that he shalbe condemned, for yt is a synne which
God pardoneth as other the synnes of his Children. The
Church of Corinth synned greeuously in not receyuing this   1. Cor. 11. 20.
Sacrament aright according to the institution of Christ, and   21. 23. 29. 30.
were therfore indeed chastyzed of God, some by sicknes, some   1. Cor. 11. 32.
by weaknes, and some by death. and yet the Apostle saith
expressly they were thus corrected of God, that they might not
be condemned with the world. No Lutheran which holdeth
consubstantiation can in that error receyue this Sacrament
aright according to Christ his institution, yet we doubt not but
many of them which erre herein, are the elect of God and saued
by his grace. What is yt then ? surely when they eate of that
bread and drinck of that Cupp vnworthylie and not aright they
eate and drinke iudgment vnto themselues. But as we said,
such is *the* mercy of God to his Children, as washeth away this
with their other infinite synnes, in the blood of that immaculate
Lamb the Lord Ihesus Christ, which yet should not encourage
any in the same, but seing there is such infinite mercy with   Psal. 130. 4.
God, the more to feare him, and to stryue by all meanes to eate

of that bread and to drinke of that Cupp worthely. But how these assemblies in this State can receyue yt aright according to Christ his institution, let them selues iudge, when as by their owne Confession and practise all their ministers are Arch-Bishopps, Lord Bishopps, and Priestes or Deacons made and ordeyned by these Prelates, so as they haue not that true and Lawfull ministery, which Christ in his last Testament hath appointed for the administracion of his holy thinges there bequeathed vnto his Church, when as also themselues being wyttnesses they vse not the wordes of Christ his institucion. Take, eate, this is the body &c. Not to speake here of their pryvate Communyon stinted Litargie, Epistles. Ghospells and such like, all which in that vse, Christ neuer instytuted

Admon. to the Parl. treat. 1.

Article .8.—Item. They hold a communyty of goodes.—

We hold no Anabaptisticall Communytie of goodes at all, only such communyty as the Apostles and Primitiue Church held and vsed. We confesse yt to be our duties and the dutie of all Christians to hold and vse the like (that is) that euery one according to his ability as God hath prospered him be ready to minister succor vnto the Brotherhood, and to distribute to their necessyties as is wrytten Iho. 3. 17. Whosoeuer hath this worldes good and seeth his brother haue need and shutteth vp his compassion from him, how dwelleth the loue of god in him?. Other communytie hold we none, but as the Apostle said to Ananius. Whilst yt remayned appertayned yt not to thee? and after yt was sold was yt not in thy power? So we also hold, that the right and propertie of whatsoeuer any possesseth, appertayneth vnto him who is the owner and possessor thereof only he is carefully to looke vnto yt that he be a good and faithfull Steward of that which God hath commytted vnto him, doing good to all, but chiefly to them which are of the houshold of faith.

Answer.—

Act. 11. 29.
1. Cor. 16. 12.
Rom. 12. 13.

Gal. 6. 10.

Article .9.—Item. He that wilbe a brother, must geue for his admission into their fellowship the tenth penny of his goodes, to which he must be sworne.—

We do no such thing, but *our* aduersaries haue framed this as Answer.— the rest, of their owne Corrupt hart*es* : we are p*er*swaded yt is the free and gracyous worke of God to add to the Church from day to day such as shalbe saued. Tything became *the* Iewes priesthode better then the ministery of the Ghospell, yf we marke the manner of mayntenance that was in *the* Apostles tymes : And indeed we thinke that her Ma*ie*stie might greatlie gloryfy God, and bring much peace to her Subiect*es*, in taking the Lordly revenewes of the Prelat*es* and Priest*es* into her owne handes, to employ them otherwyse as her Ma*ie*stie shall thinke good to her highnes owne vse, and the benefyte of the land. Only for this error and for endevoring to serue Christ and obey him in his own ordynance ecclesiasticall, do the Prelates *our* great aduersaryes persecute vs, although they do yt vnder another colour.—

Article .10—Item. Baptisme must be administred with rayne water.—

We hold no such thing, but this also hath the father of lyes by Answer.— these his ministers forged as the rest. Indeed the scryptures say that vpon the wicked god will rayne snares fire and Psal. 11. 6. brimstone and stormy tempest, the portion of their cupp. Let *our* aduersaries fear (yf they repent not) that they shalbe babtized with this baptisme of rayne, because the Lord of hostes hath determyned yt and who shall disanull yt ?

Article .11.—Item That all set prayer is blasphemous, and therfore *the* Lords prayer printed [.]

We thanke God we are so farr from thinking blasphemously Answer.— any manner of way of that most absolute fourme of prayer called the Lordes prayer, as we doubt not to affyrme, that whosoeuer holde yt to be blasphemous they are horrible wicked men, worthie to be cutt of from the face of the earth. As for *our* selues we hold yt Canonycall scripture, that yt is a most abolute fourme and rule of all trew [?] prayer, that no Angell or man whatsoeuer are able to sett downe the like, that yf they should sett downe anie other, yet all Christians ought to pray Mat. 6. 9. only by this rule w*hi*ch Christ *our* Sauyor the wisdome of the Luk. 11. 2.

father hath prescribed. That herein he hath taught vs .1. to whom to pray, that is, to God only, and not to any Angell or Saint whatsoeuer .2. with what affeccion, that is, with faith and confidence of his willingnes to heare and help vs as being our father and of his abilitie thereunto as being in heauen, that is (as the Scrypture expoundeth yt) able to do whatsoeuer he will. 3. To what end. That God in and ouer all may be gloryfyed. 4. For what thinges to pray. According to the seuerall occasyons and necessyties which God ministreth and layeth vpon vs, here being in few wordes comprised* but indeed fully comprehended all the occasyons and necessyties that euer haue bene or shalbe offered of prayer vnto God by the Church or anie member thereof, in any age place or State whatsoeuer, as may appeare by this, that all the prayers sett downe in the scriptures, which the men of God vpon so manie seuerall occasyons offered vp vnto God, are all comprised in this most absolute patterne, who yet did not vse these very wordes, so as it is plaine that our Sauyor Christ himselfe did not tye his disciples or thers to the vse of these wordes, which yet men now a dayes in their ignorance & superstition are not ashamed to do. If yt be obiected that Christ said. λεγετε. say Our father &c. We answer first that the scrypture yt selfe sheweth his meaning herein to be, not that the disciples or others should be tyed to vse these very wordes, but that in prayer and geuing of thankes they should followe his direction and patterne which he had geuen them, that they might know to whom, with what affeccion and to what end to pray as yt is expresslie sett downe in these wordes. After this manner therfore pray ye, and not as men will now haue vs. Say ouer these very wordes. Secondly we doubt not but we may vse anie of these wordes as others applying them to our seuerall necessyties as we see Christ himselfe did when he prayed. O my father yf this cupp cannot passe from me but that I must drinke yt, thy will be done where yt is plaine that Christ himselfe who gaue the rule doth shew vs how to vse yt, to weet, not in a superstitious saying ouer those very wordes but in praying according to that rule as our specyall necessyties shalbe, whether we vse any of these wordes

* This is the opinion of Mr Caluyn. Mr Beza. Mr Vrsinus &c./

Luk. 11. 2.

Mat: 26. 42.

or other, or pray with sighes & groanes that cannot be expressed. And here thirdly we would gladly know of *our* aduersaries yf Christ hath tyed vs to say these wordes when we praye and that such saying of these wordes be true prayer, how they will reconcyle vnto [*sic*] the assertion of the Apostle, *which* sayth. We know not what to pray as we ought, but the spyryt yt selfe maketh request for vs with grones that cannot be expressed. For we might haue answered the Apostle yes we know what to pray, to weet the Lordes prayer: neyther needed the spyryt to make request with sighes *that* cannot be expressed, for the saying of these wordes is enough, conteyning whatsoeuer we need to aske [.] And againe, it would be knowen how that same Apostles question in another Epistle will stand where he sayth. When thou prayest or geuest thankes in a strange tongue (for of that he speaketh) how shall he that occupieth the room of the vnlearned say Amen at thy geuing of thankes? seing he knoweth not what thou sayest. For yf they had bene tyed to the very fourme of the wordes of the Lordes prayer, or to any sett stinted wordes, yt might haue bene answered. Yes I know what he sayth when he prayeth or geueth thankes, he sayth the Lordes prayer, or some stinted or prescribed fourme of prayer *which* I know before hand, and therfore to yt, though yt be said in a strange tongue I can say Amen. Fourthly the Apostles. and disciples to whom first this rule was geuen were carefull no doubt to keep yt according to the meaning of *our* Sauyor Christ. But they did not tye themselues to these wordes, but prayed as they had seuerall occasyons according to this rule, as appeareth by their prayers expressly mencyoned in the scripture quoted in the margin, and when they wryte vnto others exhorting them vnto this heauenly duty of prayer they neuer in all their Epistles chardge them when they pray to say ouer the Lordes prayer, *which* doubtlesse they would haue done yf so yt had bene the will of Christ to haue yt vsed, but they teach and exhort them according to their seuerall necessyties and occasyons in all thing*es* to shew their request*es* vnto God in all maner of prayer and supplycac*io*n in *the* spyryt *with* geuing of thankes

Rom. 8. 26.

1 Cor. 14. 16.

Act. 1. 24. &. 4. 24.
Mat. 14. 30. And by necessary consequence.—
Phil. 4. 6.
Eph. 6. 18.
Iam. 5. 13.
1. Thes. 5 [?].
17. 18.
Ioh. 5. 14 15. 16.

and herevnto to watch with all perseuerance, for this is *the* will of God in Christ Ihesus. Fiftly, Christ hath geuen an expresse Commaundm*ent.* When you pray say. &c. But to breake the Commaundm*ent* of Christ is synne, therfore yf Christes meaning were to tye them or vs to this fourme of wordes, yf they or we pray at anie tyme and not vse these wordes yt is synne: But before yt appeareth that th'apostles [?] prayed and vsed not these wordes and yet synned not, and so we doubt not do all Christians dayly according to their dyvers occasyons and Conditions. Fynally. If Christes meaning were to haue vs vse these very wordes yt were great and intollerable presumption to offer vnto God any other, seing all thing*es* whatsoeuer we need aske for *our* selues or for others are here comprehended, & seing Christ hath enioyned when you pray say. Our father &c.

Article .12.—Item. They affirme that our Communyon booke is blasphemy against the maiesty of God.—

Answer.—

The primitive Churches, w*h*ich by th'apostles were taught and setled in all *the* ordynances of *our* Lord Ihesus, were neuer tyed to any sett prayers or devised wayes of ministracion, but were taught to worshipp God and to administer his holy thing*es* according as he had prescrybed in his Testament, w*h*ich he sealed with his blood, and this only we hold yt *our* dutyes to follow as the Lord enableth vs, as for their booke of Common prayer wherein is prescribed the whole worshipp and rules of administration, let them first consyder what the best preachers haue wrytten of yt aboue 20 yeares sythence to *the* Parliament viz: That yt is an vnperfyt booke culled and picked out of *that* Popish dunghill the masse booke, full of abhomynations, that they prophane the holy scriptures, that in all this order of seruyce there is no edification according to the rule of the apostle but confusion, and againe, that that fourme ys not commaunded of God. That in *the* Primitiue Churches the ministers were not so tyed to any fourme of prayers inuented by man, but as the spirit moued them, so they poured forth

1. Cor. 4. 17. &. 11. 23.

Mat. 28. 20. Rom. 16. 17.

Admon. to *the* Parl. treat. 2. Admon to *the* Parl. treat. 1.

harty supplications to *the* Lord, but that now they are bound
of necessytie to a prescript order of servyce and booke of
Common prayer, in which a great number of thing*es* contrary
to God his word are conteyned: patched yf not alltogether, yet
the greatest peece out of the popish portise [portasse]: When
these thing*es* stand thus, euen in the Confession of the godlyest
preachers and professors of these assemblies, let them selues
next consider how meet this is for the Ma*ies*tie of God, and
how acceptable vnto him to whom notwithstanding they dayly
offer yt in the mediation of Ihesus Christ, who hath geuen Eph.4 . 8.
gift*es* vnto men for the worke of his ministery, and maketh his
Church an holy priesthood to offer vp spyrytuall sacryfyces 1 Peter. 2. 5.
acceptable to god through him, neyther doth he or the father
accept anie other sacryfyce, worshipp or worshippers, whatsoeuer
men do deeme or ymagine.

Article .13.—It*em*. to reade any but the Canonycall scripture
is Sacrilegious

We ground *our* faith only vpon the Canonycall scriptures, being Answer.—
assured *that* they were geuen by inspirac*ion* of God, and that Pro. 30. 5. 6.
they conteyne the whole reuealed will of God, vnto w*hich* none
may add, and from which none may take away, and therfore
also we reade them only when the Church meeteth together
for the seruyce of God, and to edifie in *our* most holy fayth: Act. 13. 15.
Yet notw*i*thstanding in our pryvate howses and studyes, we
reade and vse any other bookes and helpes w*hich* through the
blessing of God may further vs vnto the better vnderstanding
of this word of God. But yt seemeth *our* aduersaries would
insynuate [?] that [yt] is Lawfull in the Church for the edification
thereof to reade the Apocrypha bookes aswell as the Canonycall
scryptures. We are not ignorant that this indeed is their
practise, yea that they haue published that they leaue some of Book of Com-
the Canonycall scriptures vnread as lesse edyfying, and w*hich* mon praier in
might better be spared meaning the booke of the revelation *the* rubrick of
partycularly, whereof yet the spyryt of God wyttnesseth saying. reading *the*
Blessed is he that readeth and they that heare *the* word Scripture.
of this prophecy, and kepe those things which are
written therin.—Let themselues therfore consider how

a. Iudi. 9. 2
with Gen.
42. 5.
Machab. 14.
37. 4i, 42..
with Exod.
20. 13.
Esther

directly they go against the spiryt and word of God herein. Moreouer let them know that in the Apocrypha book*es* there is a Contradiction with the Canonicall scriptures, blasphemy, Magick, errors and lyes, and therfore not lawfull to reade them in *the* publike assemblies of the Church.

Apocr. 12. 5. with Ester Canon. 6. 3.   b[?].   Tob. 12. 15. with Reuel. 8. 2. 3. 4.   Hebr. 3. 9. 24. C[?].   Tob. 6. 7. 8.   d.   Ecclesiast. 26. 20.   Comp. with Esay. 57. 2. & Reuel. 14. 13.   Also in Toby 12. 15[?]. with Toby. 5. 12.   Iudith. 10. 12. & 9. 13.——

> Article. 14—Item. they deny the Queen to be supreme head of the Churches of England and Ireland.

Answer.—
Hebr. 2. 8./
1 Cor. 15. 27.
Eph. 1 22. &
4. 15. & 5. 23.
Coloss. 1. 18./

The word of God teacheth that God hath made all thing*es* subiect vnder Christes feet and hath appoynted him ouer all thing*es* to be the head to the Church w*hi*ch is his body, euen the fullnes of him that filleth all in all thing*es*.

> Article .15.—Item they make a question of her Ma*ie*sties legitimacy, and therfore they are enemyes to God and Traytors to the Queen.   God eyther conuert them or cutt them of Amen.—

Answer.—
Ioh. 8. 44.

We pray the readers not to be offended, yf in grief of o*u*r soules we be co*n*streined to say to o*u*r aduersaries as yt is wrytten.   Ye are of *y*our father *the* deuyll who was a lyar and murtherer from the beginning.   God is wittnes, that we gladly acknowledge her Ma*ie*stie to be o*u*r Lawfull and Soueraigne Prince by right descent from the vndoubted right king*es* of theis realmes her royall Progenitors, w*hi*ch the king of king*es* from heauen hath also sealed and assured by his most wonderfull and mightie delyuerances of her Ma*ie*stie from so many trayterous conspyracyes and wicked purposes entended against her both by forreine and home enemies, so as we may iustly

Psal. 21. 1. 8.
9.

say.   The Q*ue*ene shall reioyce in thy saluation thy hand shall find out all thine and her enemyes.   Thou shalt make them as a fyery oven in tyme of thine anger, the Lord shall destroy them in his wrath and *the* fire shall deuoure them.—

And for o*u*r Enemies who drew and spread these false & slanderous artycles against vs, we must needes say, that they could neuer come from a hart and mind loyall to her Maiestie. We pray God that her Maiestie and Counsell may more and more discerne betwene such false dissembling hypocrytes and her true and faithfull Subiectes, And we pray God be mercyfull to our Aduersaries, forgeving their synnes in Ihesus Christ to whom be praise for euer. Amen.—

[John Penry's Confession of Faith and Apology prepared not long before his death in 1593.][1]

> I Iohn Penry do here (as I shall answer before the Lord my God in that great day of iudgment) sett downe summaryly, *th*e whole truth and nothing but the truth of all that I hold and professe at this hower eyther in regard of my fayth towardes the Lord my God, or touching my allegiance to her right Excellent Maiestie my most gracyous and deare Soueraigne Queene Elizabeth, vnto whom only of all the Potentates in the world I owe all duty, reuerence and submyssion in the Lord

First, because my allegeance vnto her Maiestie is chiefly called in question, I protest I am not at this day, nor yet euer was in all my life eyther guilty or privy vnto any purpose, consultacion, or intent of any sedition against, or disturbance of her Maiesties royall State and peaceable gouernment and yf I were privy to any such godlesse, wicked, and vndutyfull accions or purposes, as might any way impayre or disquyet the peaceable State of my natiue Prince and Cuntry, I would reueale, disclose and withstand the same to the vttermost of my power in all persons forraigne and domesticall of what profession or Religion so euer they were.

Her supreme authorytie within her Realmes and Dominions I acknowledge to be such ouer all persons in all causes, as no person eyther Civile or ecclesiasticall may exempt himselfe or his cause, from the power & censure of her lawes and word.

I do also acknowledg, That her Maiestie hath full authorytie from the Lord by her royall power to establish and enact all

---

[1] Add. MS. c. 303 (fol. 204–207 verso) in the Bodleian Library.

Lawes both ecclesiasticall and Civile amongst her Subiect*es*, In the enacting whereof the Lord requireth, that her ecclesiasticall be warranted by her wrytten word, which expressly conteyneth fully whatsoeuer belongeth to the true worshipp of his Ma*i*estie: Her Civile be grounded vpon the rules of Common equyty and Iustyce, the w*hi*ch bondes are so farr from weakening the authorytie of king*es* and Princes, as they are the only inexpugnable walles thereof.

This Soueraigne authorytie and prerogatiue of her highnes, I am most most [*sic*] willingly readie to defend against all the States, persons & cretures vnder heauen to *the* losse of my life. 1000 tymes yf yt be needfull.

And I take the Lord to record, that that daye hath not passed ouer my head (doth not I am sure) synce the first tyme that the Lord vnder her gracyous raigne brought me vnto the knowledge of his Ghospell, wherin I haue not and do not pray for the blessing of my God both inwardly and outwardly to be powred with a full horne vpon her right excellent Ma*i*estie, her throne, regiment and dominions euen for ever, and that he would eyther conuert or speedyly ouerthrow in his wrath all his & her enemyes with their enterpryses whether they be home or forrayne. Hereof I call the searcher of the hartes as a wyttnes of truth against myne owne soule, yf eyther I dissemble or feigne in the premisses.

Secondly touching my faith, I do beleue with my hart and confesse with my mouth, that there is no God but that true God only, w*hi*ch *the* holy wrytten word doth shew to be one in substance and three in person, the Father, the sonne, and the holy Ghost, three distinct persons of one and the selfe same Deitie. This most hye God, who also is my God in Ihesus Christ, I beleue to be *the* Creator, preseruer, maynteyner, Soueraigne Lord and supreme commaunder of all creatures in heauen and earth, of men and Angell*es*, good and bad [.] I do beleue that nothing doth or can come to passe eyther in heauen or earth but by the forebounded and determinate will, purpose, Counsell and directio*n* yea without the most wyse and most vpright commaundm*ent* of this euerlasting and true God who worketh all thing*es* after the Counsell of his owne will.

All men by nature I beleue to be the Children of wrath and saued only by grace through the sufferinges and righteousnes of Christ Ihesus apprehended by a true and lyvely faith.

Christ Ihesus in regard of his natures I beleue to be God and man, euen God aboue all blessed for euermore, and in respect of his offyce, to be the only king, Priest and Prophet of his Church, the which his offyces he so fully accomplished in the daies of his flesh, by the manifesting the whole will of his father through his preaching and teaching the full redemption of his Church by his death & resurrection and the receyuing of full and absolute power in heauen and earth from his father in such sort, as he is not to receyue a successor in any of these his offyces, but is consecrated alone to them all for euermore

True Fayth I beleue to be that persuasion of the hart, wherby the soule is truly assured of remission of synnes, and imputation of righteousnes through Christ [.] This true Fayth, belongeth only to Gods elect, and hath perseuerance vnto the end ioyned with yt: with this true Faith also is vnseparably ioyned (as the fruytes thereof) a dying vnto synne, and a lyuing vnto righteousnes in such sort as the members of Christ haue a contynuall battaile within them against synne, the which by the power of Christes death is so wounded, as the same in some measure decayeth more and more in them vntill at the length yt be vtterlie consumed, when the bodies and soules are separated and not before.

By the quyckening power of Christ, I do beleue, that his members here vpon earth are drawen more and more to like of his blessed will, and to practize the same yea to giue their lyves rather then to dishonor their God in the voluntarie and willing denyall of his truth, and the breach of his law and will reuealed to them[.] His reuealed will, I beleue to be perfectly conteyned in the wrytten word of the old and new Testament geuen by the holy Ghost for the instruccion and comfort of his poor Church, so long as the same is a Pilgrim here vppon earth.

This Church, I beleue to be the Companie of those whom the word calleth Saintes which do not onlie professe in word that they know God, but also are subiect vnto him, vnto his lawes and ordinances indeed: With this Church, I do beleue that the

Lord God of his meer fauor hath entred into Couenant that he
wilbe their God and that they shalbe his people.   The seales of
this Couenant are two only—Baptisme and the Supper of the
Lord.

This Church here vpon earth I do beleue not to be perfect,
(although in regard of *the* order *which* the Lord hath appointed
for the same yt be most absolute) but to haue many blemishes
and want*es* in yt, yet assuredly that all *the* true members
thereof shall at *the* day of iudgment receyue their perfect
consum*ma*tion by Ihesus Christ, and be crowned in him
with eternall glory, of his meer grace and not of any meryt of
theirs.

Of w*hi*ch blessed, free, and vndeserued reward, I professe my
selfe to rest in most vndoubted and gloryous hope through the
mercyes of my God, and therfore I am most willingly content
to vndergoe any trobles in this life for his names sake, who be
gloryfyed of me both in soule and body, and of all his Saint*es*
for euermore Amen

I detest all heresies, sect*es* and schysmes and errors whether
new or old, by whomsoeuer they haue bene inuented. as
Puritanisme, Donatisme, Anabaptisme, Libertinisme
Brownisme, all the dreames and dotages of the famylie of
loue, but especyally all Popery, that most dreadfull Religion of
Antichrist, *the* great enemye of the Lord Ihesus, and the most
pestilent aduersary of the thrones of king*es* & Princes[.] So
that I abhorre from my sowle, that whole body and euery part
of *that* Romish religion, called the sonne of perdition by the
spiryt of God, because *the* Lord hath determyned to consume
yt by his appearing in the brightnes of his Ghospell before his
second coming.

I detest that prowd superiorytie of that man of synne, wherby
(as the Apostle forespake) he either exalteth himselfe in his
members and their power to beare rule and raigne ouer the
truth and members of Christ, euen ouer all that is called holy,
or opposeth himselfe as a most bloody aduersary against all
those truthes and seruant*es* of the Lord, w*hi*ch will not suffer
him with his said infernall power to raigne ouer them in stead
of Ihesus Christ in his blessed ordynanc*es*

I detest in regard of their offyces (I speake not of the mens persons touching *the* Lordes election) the head of that body the Pope, his cursed triple Crowne, his vsurped iurisdiction of eyther of both swordes [*sic*]

I detest the rest of *the* Lymmes of that body and their spyrytuall power, as Cardinall*es* ArchBishopps Lord Bishopps, Suffraganes, Abbott*es*, Pryors Deanes, Archdeacons, Com*m*ysaryes, Chancellors, Offyciall*es*, Monkes, Fryars, Chanons, Prebbendes, Priestes, Deacons, I detest the invented maner of calling wherby they are placed in their cursed offyces, their devysed workes wherein they are employed by reason of their offyces, as the false doctrine and false worshipp of that kingdome, with the lyving and mayntenance wherby they are mainteyned in their offyces.

And forasmuch as the members of Christ must haue no Com*m*union of or with any of these cursed inventions, insomuch as they can haue no lawfull vse or spirytuall communyon of or with any of these offyces, calling*es*, workes, and maintenance, because they cannot lawfully be subiect vnto any part of the ecclesiasticall power of these offyces, Therfore yt is, that I dare not participate in those assemblies or with anie of these offycers bere rule ecclesiastically, and intermeddle with the holie thinges of God wherein any of these devised calling*es* (and none els) workes and maintenance are to be found: For I am forbidden to haue any Communyon with those vnfruytfull workes of darkenes, though yt be vpon pretence of enioying the truth and Sacrament*es* of Christ, vpon paine of everlasting torment*es* daye and night for euermore.

And yf I may not be subiect to the Ceremonies of Moses, as Circu*m*cysion &c w*h*ich were sometymes the Lords owne sacred ordinances, how dare I or any other creature be in bondage to those inuentions of Antichrist the great enemy of o*ur* Lord Ihesus whereof *the* Saint*es* of God neither can neither yet euer could haue any sanctified vse.

The truth of the doctrine touching the holy Trinitie, touching the natures and offyces of o*ur* Sauyor, Iustyfying fayth, Sacrament*es*, eternall life &c. established by her Ma*iesties* Lawes, and professed by her selfe, their Honors, and such as haue knowledge

in the assemblies of this Land, I acknowledge from my hart to
be such, as yf I mainteyned not the vnitie and held not the
Communyon of *the* same doctrine with them in these point*es*,
I could not possibly be saued.   For out of the vnion of
the true profession w*hic*h her Ma*ie*stie hath established in
these and in the like truthes there is no hope of saluation
left : But to ioyne notwithstanding with the publike worshipp
in these assemblies of this Land I dare not for the former
reasons.

I do moreouer willinglie confesse, that many both of *the* teachers
and also of the professors in these Parish assemblies, haue so
embraced the truth of doctrine established and professed in this
land, as the Lord of his infinite goodnes hath graunted them
the fauor to shew outwardly many tokens, wherby in regard of
the Lordes election, I professe before men and Angell*es* that I
doe iudge them to be members of that bodie, whereof the sonne
of God Christ Ihesus is the head, only herein the lord be mercyfull to them as vnto my selfe in regard of my synnes, that they
are not vnder that outward order w*hic*h Christ Ihesus left in
his Church, but instead thereof are first subiect vnto many of
the forenamed offyces, Secondlie, haue Com*m*union with their
false manner of calling vnto their offyces, Thirdly partycipate
with a great part of their devysed workes where offycers are
employed, Fourthly with the false maintenance and lyving*es*
sometyme, consecrated to Idolatrie for the most part, wherby
these offycers are mainteined, Fiftly, are mingled with the
knowen prophane, ignorant, and disordered persons, w*hic*h are
ioynt members with them of these assemblies.

This is the Som*m*e of my faith and allegeance vnto my God and
Prince.   Here is the Som*m*e of that whole difference that is
betwene me and the Clergy of this Land, and the som*m*e of
that whole cause for the w*hic*h I and dyvers other of my poore
brethren are iudged to be Schysmatik*es*, Felons, Heretick*es* &c.
If this may come vnto the royall handes of my Soueraigne and
to the view of their honors, I doubt not by the mercyes of my
God, but her Ma*ie*sties hart and their Lord*shi*ps wilbe soone
induced, that neither I, nor any that hold not the same
profession with the aforenamed offycers of assemblies in this

land, do deserue the shortening of our dayes by her Maiesties sword for these thinges.

And there is all that euer we hold: For as touching that error concerning the not repeating of the Lordes prayer wherwith we are charged, Far be yt, euen farr be yt that we should deny the same or any the like scriptures, to be an holy fourme of prayer, conteyning not only an exquisyte patterne of doctrine, according to which all our prayers are to be squared, but also a fourme of petition request and wordes, which a Christian soule may vtter not only lawfully, but also with great comfort: The vse for which yt was geuen, we hold indeed to be rather for doctrine then for praier, the abuse in the often repetition thereof we condemne, and this I am sure was the iudgment in this point of those holy seruantes of Christ [i.e., Henry Barrowe and John Greenwood], who now rest from their labors.

The good which this land getteth outwardly, by these false offyces aforenamed and the lyuinges belonging to them, is, That the trayterous Iesuytes and semynary Priestes are drawen by the hope they haue of possessing this this [*sic*] Babylonish gold, to become the vnnaturall betrayers of their Naturall Prince and Cuntrie into the handes of strangers, whereas yf these offyces and livinges were by publike authorytie once remoued and conuerted to her Maiesties Civile vses, the Pope would haue no occasyon to send ouer these Locustes, there would be no baytes to allure them hether, and the home Papistes would be vtterlie voyd of hope to see their expected daye. So that the mainteyning of those offyces and lyvinges, and their devised workes and callinges which would fall with them, is ioyned with that contynuall danger of her Maiesties Royall person and the whole State of the land. I do but point at the inconuenyence which in Conscyence towardes her Maiestie and my Cuntry, I am bound to showe, they that are wise will thinke of the cause with seryousnes, and will not (I hope) thinke me worthie to be smytten for shewing the danger.

Whatsoeuer I hold of these pointes controuerted, I hold the same of meer conscyence towardes my God, and of that meer detestation which in Conscyence I am bound to haue of all the inventions of man and Angell in Religion, and of that care in conscience I ought to haue of *the* saluation and safegard of her Ma*ies*tie (whom the Lord preserue for euermore) and of my Cuntrye.

I haue for my warrant in all these thinges not only the wrytten word, which is suffycyent, but also in these causes of greatest moment, the doctrine of the Church of England, established by her Ma*iesties* authorytie, and confirmed by the Wrytin*ges* Testimonies and blood of these famous seruant*es* and Martyrs of Christ. viz m^r. Wickliff Mr Brute, m^r Aston, m^r. Purvey, m^r. Whyte, m^r Thorp &c. with many other the holy wittnesses of the Lord in former tymes as m^r Tyndall, m^r Lambert m^r Barnes, m^r Latymer, m^r Ball, and the famous seruantes of God in this latter age together with the vnitie and consent of the refourmed Churches at this day in the point*es* (I saye) of specyall weight.

My soule is so resolued by the power of God in all of them as I am readie to yield my lyfe by the aide of my God for the truth of this my testymonie and *the* testimony of the forenamed servantes of God, and holy martyrs and Churches of Christ. Yet yf any man can shew by the wrytten word of God that I erre in any thing, I will most willingly refourme my iudg-m*ent*, craue pardon earnestly for my oversight yea and be most willingly content to suffer due punishm*ent* for my temerytie.

But yf on the other syde I testifie nothing but verytie in these poynt*es* as I am vndoubtedly persuaded, I humbly craue that the piercing edge of that sword may not in heate be turned against me and my brethren, w*hich* was neuer pr*o*ffessedly violent against the open and sworne enemyes of *our* natiue Prince and Cuntrye.

Death (I thanke God) I feare not in this cause especyally, for I know *that the* sting of death is taken away, and *that* they are blessed that dye in the Lord for wyttnessing against anie of the former corruptions. Reuel. 14. 9. 13. Life I desire not, yf I be giltie of sedition, of defaming and disturbing the quiet state of her Ma*iesties* peaceable gouernm*ent*

Lastly, I humbly and earnestly beseech their honors and wors*hi*pps into whose handes this wryting of myne may come,

to Consider, that it is to no purpose *that* her Ma*i*esties subiectes
should bestowe their tyme in learning, in *the* study and medy-
tation of *the* word, in reading the wryting*es* and doing*es* of
learned men and of the holy Martyrs *that* haue bene in former
ages, especyally the wryting*es* published by her Ma*i*esties
authorytie, yf they may not without danger professe & hold
those truthes w*h*ich they learne out of them, and that in such
sort, as they are able to convince all the world that will stand
against them, by no other weapons then by the word of God.
I beseech them also to consider, what a lamentable case yt is,
that we may hold fellowshipp with the Romish Church in
th'inventions thereof without all danger, and cannot but with
extreme perill be permytted in Iudgm*ent* and practize to dissent
from the same where yt swarueth from the trew way : And as
they find these consideracions to be of specyall moment, so I
beseech them in the bowell*es* of Ihesus Christ to be a meanes
vnto her Ma*i*estie and their honors that my cause may be weyed
in euen balance. Imprysonm*ent*, yndytem*entes* arraignm*entes*
yea death yt selfe, are no meet weapons to convince the conscyence grounded vpon the word of the Lord, accompanied with
so many testimonies of his famous seruantes and Churches.
The Lord blesse her right excellent Ma*i*estie my most gracyous
Soueraigne blesse theyr honors, this whole land, and all his
Saint*es* euen for his names sake. Amen. Amen.
Subscribed with heart and hand by me I. P. now in streight
& hard bondes for the afore recyted testimony of Christes
truth.

Iohn. Penry.

Apology eiusdem.

Although yt were altogether most reasonable, that these my
poore, publike, deliberate and digested wrytinges should bind
vp and heale that wound w*h*ich my most secrete vnbalanced
and confused observations are iudged to make, yet I craue not
so much that equytie in this case, wherein my allegeance and
dutyfullnes towardes my most gracyous Prince is called in
question, as chiefly this I desyre, that what in the Conscyence
of her right excellent Ma*i*estie, and of all those both honorable

and worshipfull into whose handes I entreat that these my
wrytinges may come shalbe thought most likely to agree with
truth may be determined touching my case, and that accordingly
I may be acquyted or condemned of the guylt layd to my chardge,
as for the penalty thereof, I will not refuse to susteine the same
yf yt shall seem good to her highnes to inflict yt vpon me
whether yt be the vndeserued mulct of myne ynnocency, or the
iust demeryt of my guiltynes, that I referre vnto *the* Lordes
determynacion and her gracyous Maiestie whom he hath placed
over me: Myne ynnocency only heerby I desyre to be many-
fested without any further regard, that whether I lyue or dye
my vprightnes towardes my Prince and her State may survyue.
Whatsoeuer then in those my pryvate intercepted wrytinges,
(being the secret & confused obseruations of myne owne study)
touching her Maiestie is mencyned [*sic*], the same I protest was
sett downe by me, eyther as obiected indeed by others, whereof
I thought to haue Considered further, yf at all, yt should be
done for her Maiesties cleering where occasyon should be offered,
or as being groundes of a brief treatize, w*h*ich w*i*th myne owne
handes (yf euer the Lord should graunt meanes and oppor-
tunytie therevnto) I purposed to haue delyuered vnto her
highnes for the manyfesting of my fayth and allegeance towardes the Lord and her Maiestie wherein (as in a pryvate
advertisement) euen for the dischardge of my Conscyence, I
meant to haue offered to her Consideracion. viz. Whether
many thing*es* besides her knowledge were not done vnder
gouernm*ent* to the hindrance of the free course of the Ghospell
for the w*h*ich she standeth blamed amongst forrayn nations and
yt may be wold be further charged amongst their posterytie
These my wrytinges also are not only most vnperfect, but euen
so pryvate as no creature vnder heauen was privy vnto them
(my selfe excepted) vntill now they were seised vpon, and therefore yt wilbe the great fault of those into whose handes they are
come, and not any vndutyfullnes of myne yf they be made more
publike then they are.   Myne I dare not acknowledge them to
be for a thousand worldes, because I should therby most
fearfully synne against *the* Lord and myne owne Conscyence,
in bearing false wyttnes against my selfe.   I neuer conceyued

that anie man would haue made any thing of them, especyally against my selfe, by whomsoeuer they had bene interpreted, otherwise yt might be well thought that I would neuer haue reserued them being to my so small vse, as all men will iudge them to be. Now for the cleering of my selfe towardes her Maiestie, and of the purpose I had to referr my selfe into her Maiesties handes, yt shalbe found in those my intercepted writinges, how earnestly I haue entreated the Lord, and often (especyally toward the tyme of my coming out of Scotland) to graunt me fauor in her sight, and to enclyne her hart vnto my petition, which was only *that* yt would please her so to conceyve of me as I was in hart towardes her, and to permytt me to employ my small talent amongst my poore Cuntrymen in Wales, for their calling to the knowledge of Christ [.] Their ignorance I know (alas) to be ouer-lamentable. It will also appeer in my said wrytinges, that report coming into Scotland of her Maiesties departure out of this life, I humbled my selfe when I heard yt in fasting and prayer before the Lord, entreating him euen with many teares, that the same report might proue vntrue, as I thanke his Maiestie yt did, shewing what a great stroke (in my Conscyence) the taking her out of this life would be vnto the Church of God, at this day especyally, and vnto her kingdome, my deare and natiue Cuntrye. How heavy the newes were vnto me in partycular, those my wrytinges do partly testify, my Conscyence knoweth, and the Lord God I am sure will reveale vnto my clearing in that great daye. This was long synce I had occasyon to sett downe all the thinges wherwith I am like to be so heavyly chardged. No Creature was privy to this accion of myne vntill my wrytinges were now intercepted, neyther did I purpose to haue revealed the same. Now that my secret, confused and vnadvysed obseruations are brought against me euen to the spilling of my blood, I humbly beseech that these my papers also may be looked vppon and brought to light aswell as the other, wherby myne adversaryes thinke to ympeach my allegeance which (I thanke God) neither man nor Angell shall euer be able to effect. This was done in Ianuary or Febr was Twellvemoneth— 1592—. It wilbe easily found out in those papers of myne, which conteyne a diarie or daily obseruacion of myne owne synnes and corruptions, and of the specyall requestes which I made to the Lord, being thinges of *that* secrecye as I know well all the world would thinke yt shamefull that they should be laid to my charge: yet I thanke the Lord I refuse not to be tryed by them. Touching the partycular thinges that concerne her Maiesty in those my papers, I had great occasyon in the tyme of my contynuance and being in Scotland to take notyce of them, for the purpose before mencyoned, and surely most of them are expressed in the very same or the like wordes wherein they were obiected to me, euen by those whom I iudge to wish well to her Maiestie and gouernment. For the gentlemen, ministers and people of Scotland, that are not acquainted with the State of this Land thinke by reason of the Prelacy here mainteyned, (the yoake whereof they fell within these few yeares), by reason of the multytude of dumbe ministers that were tolerated and dayly made in this land, and because they heare that preachers are suspended, sylenced, ymprysoned and depryued thinke (I say) and haue spoken yt vnto me, that lyttle or no truth is permytted to be taught in England, that which is taught, ys measured by the length of her Maiesties Scepter, and that the Common wealth indeed is much but the Ghospell lyttle beholuding vnto her. Whereunto I answered that the Ghospell (in my Conscyence) was asmuch behoulding to her Maiestie as to all the Princes in Europe besides. They haue replyed then that Princes dissemble then, for none of them that appeare to defend *the* Ghospell do suffer the ministers and professors thereof to be sylenced and ymprysoned for their Conscyence sake and for mainteyning the truth which reformed Churches do generally embrace, wherevnto as I haue allwayes suffycyentlie answered (I thank the Lord) in her Maiesties behalfe, so haue I sett downe confusedly the tenor of my speeches in those my wrytinges, that so I might vpon better leysure consyder of them, and make some vse for the discharge of my Conscyence as before I haue sett downe. Hereof also I haue had specyall occasyon vpon pryvate conferences had with the ministers of the Cuntrye wherein I haue otherwyse informed them of the state of thinges here then they were generally certyfyed by the

marchantes or such other as travayled thether, in such sort,
as I being invited with some of them by a godly gent*leman*
of that Cuntry, then told him, that yt was not without
great reason (seing he had so often speech with me) that he
being in such a noble mans Chamber, where her Ma*iesties*
picture was sett belowe the pictures of divers other kinges
and Princes, he tooke the same and placed yt aboue them all,
for he thought her to be no less worthy, yf the speeches w*hich*
I gaue of her highnes were trew. The gentleman answered
that he was glad to learne that of me who as he iudged would
not report otherwyse then truth, w*hich* he allwayes conceyved
of her. viz. That the Euangely of Christ was mickle deale bound
(for those were his wordes) vnto the Qu*een*e of England, as vnto
all *the* Princes on this syde of the Alpes the w*hich* he durst the
more boldly avouch vppon the credyt of my report [.] These
and such like (I say) haue bene the occasyon of whatsoeuer in
my pryvate wrytinges seemcth to make most against me : and I
could name Englishmen who (yf they would speake yndifferently)
must testyfy, that they haue heard no lesse obiected of others,
and no less answered by me then I haue here sett downe, as
convenyence of tyme and place hath bene ministred : yea when
myne owne case, or the case of any oth*er* (who professing the
Ghospell are iudged to be hardly dealt with vnder her Ma*iesties*
gouernm*ent*) hath bene alleadged, I haue answered. Vt
parentum sic patriæ & principis seueritatem patiendo
& ferendo seminda*m* esse. The which saying, as also some
other of Marc*us* Tulli*us* vnto Lentulus as I remember shalbe
found noted in those my wrytinges to this very purpose.
Whereby yt may appeare that what now I wryte hath some
credence in yt though those my obseruations be most confused,
such as out of which no man (my selfe excepted) can possibly
gather my purpose. I haue not looked vpon most of those my
wrytinges these—14—or—15—moneths, whereby consydering
how they are sett downe, I might also well forgett *the* purpose
for the w*hich* they were wrytten : yet I will not desyre to be
accounted (as I thanke God I am) a Loyall subiect to my
Prince, yf I shew not any speech conteyned in them touching
her Ma*ies*ty to haue reason vppon the former occasyons, and to

haue bene noted for the purposes I spake of, namely, eyther
the advertysing or further cleering of her Maiestie as the Lord
would offer occasyon, the w*hi*ch latter purpose of myne, is also
cleered, in a treatyse w*hi*ch I published now toward 2 yeares
synce wherein, wryting vnto the Parliam*ent*, I shewed that the
Papist*es*, either Brystow or Saunders yf my memory faile not,
had geuen out *that* her Maiestie regarded not the Ghospell any
further then yt may be for her standing, and therfore desyred
the Parliam*ent* that they would withstand that slaunder, by
provyding that the people of Wales may be better taught,
saying that whatsoeuer the Parliam*ent* should do, I did gain-
saye the same, as being a speech vndutifull and slanderous
against my Prince, as lowd as ynke and paper could do yt.
These are my wordes, and as I shall answer before the Lord
my God, I had no other then this dutyfull meaning in setting
downe whatsoeuer is now so heynously interpreted in those my
wrytinges. Briefly the most reuerend and dutyfull regard w*hi*ch
I haue caryed towardes her Maiestie in my publike wrytinges
whensoeuer I haue mecyoned her or her gouernm*ent*, the tenor
of my life that way, together with the testimonie of all those
w*hi*ch haue knowen me and my wrytinges especyally of such of
my cuntrymen as know me in Scotland, will clear me of whatsoeuer may touch me in loyaltie towardes my Soueraigne. And
I do here, (in this last wryting w*hi*ch is like to proceed from me
for ought I know) protest before all the world, that although I
regarded neither the feare of God nor man, nor the testimony
of a good conscyence, yet the respect w*hi*ch I haue and allwayes
had that my native Cuntry Wales should not cary the blemish,
that euer it brought forth (for my part) any *that* would defame
or deale vndutyfully with so gracyous a Prince as her Maiestie
is, and hath bene allwayes vnto vs, should and would kepe me
from all vndutyfull attempt*es* against her highnes. Nay (I
thanke God) I haue all reasons that do and allwayes haue
stirred me vp to all dutyfullnes towardes my Prince but neuer
any that moued me so much as in a secret wandring thought
vnto any such disloyall cogitation of her Maiestie. Lastly those
my intercepted wryting*es* w*hi*ch are now brought against me,
conteyning in them not only a peculiar record of my dayly

Corruptions, for and against w*h*ich I craued mercy and strength
at the Lordes hand, but also of all the specyall synnes whereof
my conscyence could accuse me in all my lyfe, euen to the last
daie of my coming out of Scottland yt will easyly appeare,
whether my soule was euer privy to any offence com*m*ytted
by me against her Ma*i*estie, saue only this whereof I there
complayne namely that I was not so carefull in prayer for her
perseuerance and wellfare, as I desyred and laboured to haue
bene[.] And yet (I thanke the Lord) I remember not that day
hath passed ouer my head, synce vnder her gouernm*e*nt I
first came to *th*e knowledge of *th*e truth, wherein I haue not
recom*m*ended her estate vnto his Ma*i*estie[.] I deale in those
my most secreat wryting*es* w*i*thout guile, as in his sight whom
I know to be the revealer of secrett*es*, at whose hand I craued
the healing of my brused Conscyence, wherfore yt concerned
me not to collude w*i*th him though I would do the same w*i*th
man, such dealing might well augment the intollerable burthen
of my woryed soule, but cure my wound yt could not, and therfore I may truly say If euer I had bene gilty of any such cryme
there yt should haue bene sett downe, euen when I powred the
secret*es* of my hart before *th*e mercy seat of the euerlyving, and
the rather in such a case of confession vnto the Lord of my
secret synnes neuer expressed in action, wherof also I was most
sory *that* any such should be brought against me. But in this
point of my Loyaltie towardes my Prince, I feare not (I thanke
the Lord) the aduerse testimony of myne owne Conscyence
much lesse[1]

[A Letter of John Penry's to Lord Burghley, written
May 28, 1593.][2]

Although Right honorable my thoughtes athis present are
wholy employed as it is meet, rather vpon y*e* meditation of that
heavenly lyf whervnto of the Lord*es* infinite favor, I ame now
to passe, then vpon any earthly consideration whatsoever; yet

---

[1] Here with the last two words as catch-words the manuscript
at present abruptly ends.

[2] Egerton MS. 2603, fol. 49, in the British Museum.

to the end your Lordship may see, that I have in in [sic] no
wise slightly regarded your last speach vsed vnto mee; I do
heer most humblie crave entreat the vse of penn and inke, yᵗ I
may writ vnto hir majestie my most gracious soveraing, to see
yf the Lord will thcrby encline hir roiall heart to hould forth
vnto mee, the compassionate hand of hir wonted clemency
towardes hir distressed Subjectes in my case.

For your Lordship [?] I beseech you, to beare patiently these
few lines following which in the discharge of my conscienc, I
write vnto you; & for no other respect. I do confess then &
your [?] Lord[ship] lay it not vnto my charge, that I betrayed
myne owne innocency at yᵉ barr, because I did not lay open,
the clearnes of my case, as in lawe it is well knowen [?] to bee.
Lett mee speak without prejudice vnto any. I will not say much
vnto your Lordship this way. Only this, I should have beene
indighted of those thinges within one yeer after I writ them. I
should have been convinced [?] to have written them with a
maliciouse intent, to diffame hir majestie, or to stirr insurrection
[among hir subjectes]¹ from which purposes, how farr I [?] have
been allwayes, I refer it vnto yᵉ voyc of yᵉ whole world, even vnto
the consciences of adverseryes them selves yf I haue any.   Yf
I weare a papist [fallen away & to err from yᵉ true Christ] as
farrbeit I might writ in the defenc, of yᵉ sixt article, & labor to
draw hir majesties subjects to bee of my wicked [?] mynd, & yet
shal be in no wise thogh[t] nor adjudged [?] a felone by yᵗ statute
of.23. Eliz. I may publish & vtter Bellarmyns readinges Sanders
Demonstration. &c which directly mak hir majestie & yᵉ whole
state to be & yet bee in no wise within yᵉ daunger of yᵉ sayd
statute. These bookes & such lyk any [?] other [?] are comonly
sold by all stationers. And therfor my Lord, I beseech your
wysdome in the mercyes [?] bowelles of Iesus Christ, whose
truth you profess, to consider what a lamentable case it is, yᵗ
the playn [?] error in the missvnderstanding of yᵉ law should
bee written with my blood.

Touching these my confused, & most secrete indeavors [?]
writtinges [I] refer you vnto yᵗ which els where I hav written
to this..., as your Lordship knoweth [?] I am sure. And how

¹ Words within dark brackets are in the margin of the MS.

farr I ame from any such thoughtes of hir ma*jes*tie, I shall
declare, yf you will grant [?] mee the vse of ink & paper.

That I spak not at y⁰ barr what in law might have cleared my
case, it was partly in that y⁰ Iury wear sent away. befoʳ I cold
have tyme so to doe, but especially in that I was content in
this case, rather to comitt myne innocency vnto him, yᵗ judgeth   1. Pet. 2. 23.
righteously, & to referr my self vnto hir ma*jes*ties handes, then
any wyse to contend with your Lordshipes their present, whome
I saw to bee playnly overseen in the mysvndersta[n]ding of that
statute.

But my Lord, I beseech you lett mee appeale vnto your second
considiration as this way, & have y⁰ favor thereof, for the
defenc of my lyf: And I dare assure your Lordship, yᵗ it shall
not repent you, eyther in this, or the lyf to come, you have
beene the mcanes of my preservation frome vntymly [?] death.
wherwith, as I thank god I ame well content because I know
whether to goe after this lyf; of this erthly breath becaus
becaus [*sic*] it is y⁰ Lord [who gave it.] not you, where [?] now
have yoᵘ use therof it beseemeth mee in no wise to bee over
profuse.   And therfor agayn, I beseech your Lord*ship*, yᵗ I may
not only reaceave the same at Queen Elyzabeth my soverainges
hand*es*, but also be indebted vnto Sir Iohn Popame hir highnes
Supreme Iustice for the reposs thereof.   And my Lord you
shall fynd, that the continuance of my lyf (wh*i*ch I thank god
for my self I respect not becaus I ame assured, yᵗ a better is
prepared for me) wilbee farr more beheefull [?] for the apeasing
& quiet taking vp, of the differences in relligion between mee
& y⁰ Ecclesiasticall estate of this land then. my death in the
said tymes possiblie can bee.

What my purposes are, yf I shold live yᵗ way, what maner of
disposition I am off even in heart, I canot hide it yf I wold, for
my...privat writing*es*, wh*i*ch wholy shew, the very lineaments of
my soule, & y⁰ very vnreveled [?] secrett intent*es* of my heart
are in ther hand*es*, with whose judgment*es* &...in this lyf I
canot wholly accord.

You ar not to bee putt in mynd, yᵗ as y⁰ cry of y⁰ widow & y⁰   Exodus 22. 22
fatherless, peerceth deeply into y⁰ eares of y⁰ just judge, so y⁰   23. 24.
blessing [?], of y⁰ distressed & y⁰ orphan especially of him that is   Deut 24. 13.

ready to perish, is much avaylable befor god & man, vnto them,
y[t] deserve the same therefor good my Lord cloth y*our* self
therew*i*th as w*i*th a robe, the garment, wherw*i*th yo[u] are

Iob. 29.12 .13. adorned, That w*i*th y[t] great [?]...wholy man [?] Iob yo[u] may
say. I deliu*e*red y[e] poor, y[t] cryed, & y[e] fatherless & him, y[t] hade
none to helpe him.   The blessing of him y[t] was ready to perish
came vpon mee & I caused y[e] widowes heart to rejoyc. I was
a father vnto y[e] poor & when I knew not y[e] cause (or had
mistaken it), I sought it out y[e] more dilligently

And[1] shall fynd in the mercyes of god y[t] veryfyed of you, wh*i*ch

verse 18. followeth in the same place of holy story openly [?] y[t] you shall
.19. dy in y*our* nest & multiply y*our* dayes as the sand [y[t] y[*our* ?]
root] shalbe spread out by y[e] waters & y[e] dew vpon y*our*

20 branch, y[t] y*our* honor shalbe renued [?] towardes yo[u] & y*our*
21 bow continue [?] firme in y*our* hand, y[t] vnto you men shall
22. still [?] give eare & hold their tong at y*our* counsell, & y[t] yo[u]
25. shall appoynt al their way & continue [?] still to sitt as cheife,
& be truly accounted lyk him, y[t] comforteth y[e] mourners.
Thus preparing my self vnto y[e] tribunall of y[e] Supream judg,
I humblie referr my...estate vnto y*our* Lords*h*ipes due consideration, & y*our* self w*i*th all yours into his hand*es*, whoe
tryeth y[e] hear*t*es & y[e] reines, y[t] hee may give vnto every man
according as his workes shalbee From...& close prison, the 28 of
y[e] 4 month Maij [?] 1593

Your Lords*h*ip[es] most

Suppliant

Iohn Penry[2].

---

[1] At this point about ten words have been crossed out.

[2] The text of this letter took the present writer some hours to decipher,
even with the aid of the magnifying-glass and with the help of two of the
officials in the British Museum. The handwriting is in places very fine
and indistinct, and the ink is much faded. Penry's corrections, also, are
by no means as clea*r* as they might be. The present text, therefore, is
not perfect, but it is perhaps as good as under the circumstances might be
expected.

VIII

DOCUMENTS RELATING TO HENRY BARROWE

[An undated Letter of Henry Barrowe's asking for a "christian and peaceable conference" for the settlement of "theis Ecclesiasticall controuersies".][1]

My humble desier is to any that feare god even to my gratest aduersaries in theis Ecclesiasticall controuersies (or I hope) but brotherly differences yf we may come to christian and peaceable conference with some Learned and moderate persons, where the reasons of each syde may be with deliberacion set downe and exponded by the worde of God and so his treuth therin appearinge may be imbraced and we brought to vnitei [sic] in the treuth. And theis woundes (woh now ar made and Lykely to shedd eeven streames of christian bloode may be healed Those faythfull of oure mynde woh yet remayne and such as god no doubt will rayse vp in this cavse of christes may be revnited yea rather all of vs vnited to Christe oure Head with ioye. And what so euer it shall please god and her excellent maiestei to dispose of oure Lyves, yet we therby beinge brought to the sight of such faultes as we ar chardged to have committed (but yet see not) may then humbly acknowledge the same and suffer such punishment as ar [sic] inflicted to the good example of others to the honor of her maiestei and this State. And this as in sight of Christe I vowe by his grace, and dare assure in the behalf of my christian bretheren. Lyke mynded that you or any

1 Harl. MS. 6849, fol. 211 recto.

of yo" takinge this christian and brotherly paynes shall
recou*er* and Lead vs by every word of God to agree w*i*th
yo" and be obedient vnto his whole will /

Henry Barrow

[Another undated Letter of Henry Barrowe's, requesting a
"peceable disputaci*o*n" for the settlement of "sondrie Ecclesiasticall differenc*es*".][1]

M y moste humble and submissiue [?] desire vnto yo*u*r
wor*ship* was and is, That for so much as, there remaine
sondrie Ecclesiasticall differenc*es* of no smale weight
betw*i*xt me w*i*th sondrie others hir h*i*gh*nes* faithfull
subiect*es* now impr*i*soned for the same, on the one side
and this pr*e*sent ministerie now by aucthoritie established
in this land on the other vndecided, or as yett indis-
cussed [?], yo*u*r wor*ship* would vouchaffe [*sic*] to be a
meanes to hir moost excellent ma*ie*stie, That a Christian
and peceable disputaci*o*n by the scriptures might be
vouchaffed vnto some fewe of vs, w*i*th whom or how
manie, of o*u*r adu*er*saries herein shall in wisedom be
thought meete, for the readie & happie deciding or
composing the same. Protesting to yo*u*r wor*ship* in the
sight of god, at whose finall Iudgem*ent*, I looke howrelie
to stand, that I hould not anie thing in thes differences
of anie singularitie or pride of spirit, but as I am hetherto
certainlie p*er*swaded, by the vndoubted ground*es* of god*es*
worde, the profession and practise of other reformed
Churches, and learned of other Countreis, wherof if wee
hir ma*ie*st*ies* said few impr*i*soned subiect*es*, shall faile to
make evident and assured prooffe, and that those learned,
shall shew anie other thing by the word of god in the
said Christian conferrence desired, That then, I for my
parte, vow vnto yo*u*r wor*ship* through god*es* grace, as
also [I] am p*er*swaded, my said impr*i*soned brethren
permitted this conference will doe [?] the like, that I will
vtterlie forsake anie erro*u*r I shall be so proved to holde,

<hr>

[1] Harl. MS. 6849, fol. 214.

and in all humble and glad consent to submitt to o*ur*
now discenting adue*r*saries in all those matters wherin
now wee differ, if theie shall approve them vnto vs by the
word of god.   By w*h*ich charitable [?] Acte your wor*ship*
maie put end to theise pr*e*sent controue*r*sies reduce [?] as
wherin wee erre and a peace [*sic*] manie a Christian
soule. /

your wor*ships* humble suppliant

henry Barrowe

["Reasons against Publike disputac*i*on w*i*th (Henry) barow."]

It is not equall, safe nor fitte
to graunt a disput*acion* to Sectaries[1]

.1.   It hath ever been denied by the state to papistes, a secte
that had possession of the Church for some hundred
yeares before.

.2.   To call the ministerie, and co*n*fession of the Church of
England into question were to call all other Churches
likewise into question against whom also ther exceptions
extend.

.3.   The Church of England hath submitted her selfe to
disputation thrise .1. in K*i*ng Ed*ward*s tyme, in Q*ueene*
marie in Q*ueene* Elizabethes.

4.   The erroneous opinions of these men have been already
co*n*demned by iust treatises of the most famous learned
men that have lyved since restitut*i*on of [*sic*] relligion.

.5.   It is no reason that relligion, and the controversies therof
the same beinge alreadie established by parlament [*sic*]
should be examyned now by an inferio*ur* authoritie by
way of disputation

.6.   It is no reason (that all the Reformed Churches in Europe
acknowledginge o*ur* Church of England for a sister) the
same should be now brought into question at the will &
request of a fewe sectaries.

[1] Harl. MS. 6849, fol. 212.

7—2

.7. Their principall errours have been already discussed by disputations and writinges in the dayes of S[t] Augustine, and that by himselfe, &c.

.8. To call the ministerie of England into question is to strengthen y[e] papistes, and to dishable all the exercises of the mysteries of relligion ever synce the establishment thereof.

9. It hath ever been the manner of Heretiques to require [?] the same by great importunities, and continuall exclamations [?], as Novatus, Arrius,...

.10. It hath already been discussed by bookes written, out of which the truth may better appear, then by a tumultuarie disputation.

.11. They that require disputation of the Ciuill magistrate will not stande to the Iudgement of the Ciuill magistrate

.12. If the Church should satisfie everie sect that riseth [?] there were no ende of disputations.

Mr Barrowes letter written a little before his death.

To the right honorable, &c.[1]

THough it be no new or strange doctrine vnto you, right honorable and excellent Ladie, who have ben so educated & exercised in the faith and fear of God, that the crosse should be joyned to the gospel, tribulation & persecution to the faith & profession of Christ: yet may this seem strange vnto you, & almost incredible, that in a land professing Christ, such crueltie should be offred vnto the servants of Christ for the truth & Gospels sake, & that by the chief Ministers of the church, as they pretend. This no doubt doth make sundrie, otherwise wel affected, to think hardly of vs & of our cause; & specially, fynding vs by their instigation, indicted, arraigned, condemned, & readie to be executed by the secular powers, for moving sedition and disobedience, for diffaming the renowmed [*sic*]

[1] From "AN APOLOGIE | OR DEFENCE | OF SUCH TRUE CHRISTIANS | As are commonly (but vniustly) called | Brownists: | ...", 1604, pp. 89–95.

person & government of our most gracious Soveraigne Qu.
Elisabeth & this state. But, right honorable, if our adversaries
proceedings, & our suffrings with the true causes therof, might
be duly expended by the scriptures; I doubt not but their
malice and our innocencie should easily appear to al men:
howsoever now they think to cover the one and the other, by
adding slander vnto violence.

Your Ladyship readeth, that the holie Prophets who spake
in the Name of God, yea our blessed Saviour himself and his
Apostles, have suffred like vsage vnder the same pretence of
sedition, innovation, rebellion against Cæsar & the state, at the
hands & by the means of the chief Ministers of that church,
the *Pricsts*, Scribes, and *P*harisees; men of no lesse account
for holines learning and authoritie, then these our adversaries.
The faithfull of all ages since, that have witnessed against the
malignant synagogue of Antichrist, and stood for the Gospel of
Christ; have suffred like vsage, at the hands of the same
Prelacie and Clergie that now is in the land, though possessed
of other persons: The quarrel stil remayneth betwixt the two
opposite kingdomes of *C*hrist and Antichrist; and so long shal
endure, as any part of the apostasie and vsurped tyrannie of
the man of sin, shal remayne. The apostasie and tyrannie of ² Thes. *2. 8*
Antichrist, as it sprung not at once or in a day, but by degrees
wrought from his mysterie to his manifestation & exaltation in
his throne: so was he not at once wholly discovered or abolished:
but as Christ fro*m* time to time by the beams of his appearing, Reu. 16.
discovered the iniquitie, so by the power of his word, which can
not be made of none effect, doth he abolish the same, & shal
not cease this warr, vntil Antichrist with his army, power, &
ministerie, be wholly cast out of the church. Assurance & Rev. *19.*
manifest revelation hereof, we have both in general & particular,
in that historical prophesie given of Christ vnto his church by
Iohn the divine in the book of the Revelation, from the 10. to
the 20. chapter: proof & accomplishment hereof, we have
hitherto found in the abolishing of al the errors, idolatries,
trumperies & forgeries discovered and witnessed against, by
the faithfull servants of Christ in former ages. Neither is
there cause why we should doubt of the like sequel & event in

the present & future times; seing the enormities remayning, are no lesse hateful to God, & contrarie to the kingdome of Christ: and God that condemneth them is a strong Lord to execute his will, which no opposition or tyrannie of his adversaries, shalbe able to hinder or resist.

Rev. 18. 8

Whiles then we be in the mercies of God, holding the most holy & glorious cause of Christ against them, that hee might reigne in his Church by such Officers and lawes as he hath prescribed in his testament; we fear not our adversaries in any thing, knowing that their malice & opposition herein, is made to them a token of perdition, and to vs of salvation, and that of God. For this cause we are bold, both to stand for the holy Ministerie government & ordinances of Christ prescribed in his word; and also to withstand and witnesse against this antichristian hierarchie of the Prelacie and Clergie of this land, in their Ministerie, ministration, government, Courts, Officers, Canons, &c. which I by writing, have shewed to have no ground or warrant in Gods word; not to be given, or to belong vnto the church of Christ, but to be invented by man; the very same that the Pope stil vseth, and erewhile vsed & left in this land. The like, others of vs more learned, have offred and do stil offer vpon the dispence of our lives to prove by the expresse word of God, in any Christian & peaceable conference, against any whosoever, that wil there stand for the defence of the same.

Philip. 1. 28.
29.
2 Thes. 1.

The Prelats, seing the axe thus layd to the roots of the tree of their pomp, not able to approve their Ministerie, ministration, government, which they vsurp & exercise in the church, by the Scriptures; sought to turne away this question, & to get rid of their adversaries by other subtil & hostile practises: as at the first by shutting vp the chief of vs in their close prisons; by diffaming vs in their pulpits, printed books and sparsed libels in the land; by seeking to invegle vs with certaine subtil questions to bring our lives into danger; by suborned conferences with certaine their select instruments: Not to speak of the manifold molestations, and cruel usage at their commaundment shewed vs in the prisons. To their reprochful & slaunderous books, being set of God, though most vnworthie,

& suffering for the defence of the faith, & being thus provoked by them, I held it my dutie, according to the small measure of grace received, to make answer. Which I also did more then three yeres since. Likewise to deliver our selves from the false report and witnes that might be made against vs in those Conferences, we thought good to publish them to the land. For these books written more then three yeres since, after well neer six yeres imprisonment susteined at their hands, have these Prelates by their vehement suggestions and accusations, caused vs to be now indicted, arrayned, condemned, for writing & publishing sedicious books, vpon the same statute made the 23. yere of her Maiesties reigne. Their accusations were drawen into these heads:

> *First, That I should write and publish the Queenes*
> *Maiesty to be vnbaptized.*
> *Secondly, the state to be wholly corrupted from*
> *the crowne of the head to the sole of the foot, in*
> *the lawes, iudgments, iudges, customes, &c.*
> *so that none that feared God, could live in peace*
> *therin.*
> *Thirdly that all the people in the land are infidels.*

To these indictments I answered, generally, that eyther they were mistaken, or els misconstrued; that neyther in my meaning, matter, or words, any such crime could justly be found: My meaning, being just & without evil towards any man, much more towards my Soveraigne & the state, whom I from the hart honored: The matters, being meerly ecclesiastical, controverted betwixt this Clergie and vs: My words, being eyther in answer of their slanders, or in assertion of such things as I hold: That if I had offended in any of my words, it was rather casual through hast, then of any evil intent.

More particularly to the first, concerning the Queenes baptisme; I answered, that it was vtterly mistaken, both contrary to my meaning and to my expreesse words in that place of my book, as manifestly there appeareth to any indifferent reader: That I there purposely defended her Maiesties baptisme received, against such as hold the baptisme given in Poperie to be no baptisme at all; where I proved, that it needed not to be repeated: yet there I also shewed such baptisme given in Poperie, not to seal Gods covenant to the church in that estate; & therefore that the abuse ought by all that had there received it, to be repented.

To the second indictment, I shewed the words by me vsed to be drawn from Isaiah, 1. & Revel. *13*. That I had no evil mynd towards the state, lawes or Iudges; but onely shewed, that wher the Ministerie, the salt, the light is corrupted, the body and all the parts must needs be vnsound: which I immediatly in the same place of that book, shewed by the general breach of the lawes of both Tables, by all esstates, degrees, persons, &c. setting down the particulars.

To the third indictment I answered, that I gladly embraced & beleeved the common faith received & professed in this land, as most holy & sound: That I had reverend estimation of sundrie, & good hope of many hundred thousands in the land: though I vtterly disliked the present constitution of this church, in the present communion, ministery, ministration, worship, government & ordinances ecclesiastical of these cathedral & parishional assemblies.

Some other few things, such as they thought might most make against me, were culled out of my writings, & vrged: as, That I should hold her Maiesty to be antichristian, & her government antichristian. To which I answered, that it was with great and manifest injurie so collected: seing in sundry places of that book, and every where in all my writings & sayings, I have protested my exceeding good opinion & reverend estimation of her Maiesties royal person and government, above al other Princes in the world, for her most rare & singular vertues & indowments. I have every where in my writings acknowledged, all dutie and obedience to her Maiesties government, as to the sacred ordinance of God, the supreme power he hath set over all causes & persons, whether ecclesiastical or civil, within her dominions: Alwayes desiring to be intended of this false ecclesiastical government, forrayn power canons and courts brought in and vsurped by the Prelates and their accomplices.

But these answers, or whatsoever else I could say or allege, prevayled nothing; all thinges being so hardly construed and vrged against me; no doubt through the Prelates former instigations, & malicious accusations. So that I, with my fower other brethren, were the 23. of the third moneth, 1593. condemned, & adiudged to suffer death as fellons, vpon these indictments aforesaid. Vpon the 24. early in the morning, was preparation made for our execution: we brought out of the Limbo, our yrons smitten of, & we ready to be bound to the cart; when her Maiesties most gracious pardon came for our reprive.

After that, the Bishops sent vnto vs certaine Doctors & Deanes, to exhort and confer with vs. We shewed, how they had neglected the time; we had ben well nigh six yeres in their prisons, never refused but alwayes humbly desired of them Christian conference, for the peaceable discussing & deciding our differences, but could never obteyne it at their hands: neyther did these men all this time come vnto vs, or offer any such matter: That our time now was short in this world, neyther were we to bestow it vnto controversies, so much as vnto more profitable and comfortable considerations: Yet if they desired to have conference with vs they were to get our lives respited therevnto. Then, if they would ioyne vnto vs, two other of our brethren in their prisons, whom we named vnto them, we then gladly would condiscend to any Christian & orderly conference by the Scriptures, with such or so many of them as should be thought meet.

Vpon the last day of the third moneth, my brother Grenewood & I were very early & secretly conveyed to the place of execution: Where being tyed by the necks to the tree, we were permitted to speak a few words. We there, in the sight of that judge that knoweth and sercheth the hart, before whom we were thence immediatly to appear, protested our loyaltie & innocencie towards her Maiestie, our nobles, governors, magistrates, and this whol state: That in our writings we had no malicious or evil intent, so much as in thought, towards any of these, or toward any person in the world: That wherin we had through zele, or vnadvisedly, let fall any word or sentence that moved offence, or caried any shew of irreverence, we were hartily sorie, and humbly besought pardon of them so offended for the same. Furder, we exhorted the people to obedience & hartie love of their Prince & Magistrates, to lay down their lives in their defence against all enemies: yea at their hands meekly and paciently to receive death, or any punishment they shall inflict, whether justly or vnjustly. We exhorted them also vnto orderly quiet & peaceable walking, within the limits of their own calling, to the holy fear & true worship of God. For the books written by vs, we exhorted all men, no further to receive anything therin conteyned, then they should find sound proof of the same in the holy Scriptures. Thus craving pardon of al men whome we had any way offended, and freely forgiving the whole world, we vsed prayer for her Maiesty, the Magistrates, people, and even for our adversaries. And having both of vs almost finished our last words; behold one was even at that instant come with a reprive for our lives from her Maiesty: Which was not onely thankfully received of vs, but with exceeding reioysing & applause of all the people, both at the place of execution, & in the wayes, streets, & houses, as we returned.

Thus pleased it God to dispose the vttermost violence of our adversaries, to the manifestation of our innocencie, concerning the crimes whereof we were accused & condemned: and not onely so, but also to the further shewing forth of her Maiesties princely clemencie, rare vertue, & Christian care over her faithful subjects, to the yet further manifesting of her renowned fame & love amongst all her people. And sure we have no doubt, but the same our gracious God, that hath wrought this marvelous work in her Maiesties princely hart, to cause her of her owne accord & singular wisdome, even before she knew our innocencie, twice to stay the execution of that rigorous sentence; wil now much more after so assured & wonderful demonstration of our innocencie, move her gracious Maiesty freely and fully to pardon the execution therof, as she that never desired, & alwayes lothly shed the blood of her greatest enemies; much lesse wil she now of her loyal Christian and innocent subiects: especially if her Maiesty might be truly informed, both of the things that are passed, & of our lamentable estate & great miserie wherin we now continue in a miserable place & case, in the lothsome gayle of Newgate, vnder this heavie iudgement, every day expecting execution.

Herevnto if God shall move your noble hart, right vertuous Ladie, not for any worldly cause, (which for my present reproch & basenes, I dare not mention to your honour,) so much as for the love and cause of Christ, which we though [through] the grace of God professe ; to informe her Maiesty of our intire faith vnto God, vnsteyned loyaltie to her Highnes, innocencie and good conscience towards all men; in pardoning our offence and judgement, or els in removing onr [our] poore worne bodies out of this miserable gayle, (the horror wherof is not to be spoken vnto your honour,) to some more honest & meet place, if she vouchsafe vs longer to live : Your Ladyship doubtlesse shall herein doe a right Christian and gracious act, acceptable to God, behoovefull to your soveraigne prince, comfortable to vs the poor condemned prisoners of Christ; yea to his whol afflicted church, and most of all to your own prayse and comfort in this life, and in the life to come. Herevnto further to exhort your honor, by the examples of the godly of like condition, in such times of publick distresses and danger, I hope I need not so much, as to stirre vp that good gift and grace of God which is in you, not to neglect or put from you this notable occasion sent vnto you from God, to shew forth the naturalnes of your faith vnto him, of your fidelity to your Prince, of your love to the members of Christ in distresse, whom as you succour or neglect herein, so assure your self wil Christ in his glorie esteme it as done or denyed to be done by you to his own sacred person.

Let not therfore, right dear and elect Ladie, any worldly or politick impediments or vnlikelyhoods, no fleshly feares diffidence or delayes, stop or hinder you from speaking to her Maiesty on our behalf, before she go out of this citie; least we by your default herein perish in her absence, having no assured stay or respite of our lives; and our malignant adversaries readie to watch any occasion for the shedding of our blood, as we by those two neer and miraculous escapes have found. Onely, good Madame, do your diligent indevour herein, and commit the successe as we also with you shall, vnto God in our prayers: which howsoever it fall out, magnified be the blessed name of God in these our mortall bodies, whether by life or by death. His mighty hand, that hath hitherto vpholden vs, assist vs to the finishing vp this last part of our warfare, to the vanquishing of our last enemie death with all his terrors, and to the atteyning of that crowne of glorie which is purchased for vs in the bloud of Christ, layd vp and surely kept for vs in the hand of God: and not onely for vs, but for all that keep the faith and commaundements of Iesus. Of which number, noble Ladie, I hear and hope you are, and shal not cease (God willing) whiles I heer live, to further the same vnto you by my prayers & vtmost indevours. His grace and blessing, the prayers of the saincts, and myne vnworthy service be with you. This 4. or 5. of the 4. moneth [i.e., 4 or 5 April]. 1593.

Your Honors humbly at commaundement during life,
condemned of men but received of God:

Henry Barrowe.

IX

THREE EARLY BARROWIST PETITIONS.

The humble, most earnest, & Lamentable Complaint
& Supplication, of the persecuted & proscribed
Church & Servant*es* of CHRIST, falsely called
Brownists: Vnto the high Court of Parlament./[1]

The most high God, possessor of Heaven & Earth bringeth
at this present before Y*our* L*ordshi*ps & Wisdomes
(right Honor*a*ble) his owne cause, his owne people, his
owne sworne & most trecherous Enimies, together w*i*th
the most shamefull vsage of his truth & servant*es* that
ever hath been heard of in the dayes of Sions professed
peace & tranquilitie.

His Cause & People he offreth vnto y*our* consideration &
defence in *our* profession & persons: his Enimies &
theyr outrage against his truth & servant*es*, in the
persons & bloody procedin*ges* of y*e* Prelat*es* of this
Land & theyr Complices.

Wee professe y*e* same Faith & Truth of y*e* Gospel w*hi*ch
her Ma*ie*stie, w*hi*ch y*our* L*ord*ships, this Whole Land,
& all y*e* reformed Churches vnder Heaven this day doo
hold & mainteine. Wee goe beyond them (beeing *our*
only falt, even in y*e* iudgm*ent* of *our* most tyrannicall &
savadge enimies) in y*e* detestation of all Popery, y*t*
most fearefull Antichristian Religion; & drawe neerer
in some poinct*es* by *our* practise vnto Christs holy

---

[1] Harl. MS. 6848, fol. 150, in the British Museum. This petition was
written between March 4 and 11, 1592/3.

order & Institucion.   This is our faith, this is our
cause (right Honorable) yea the Lordes Cause in our
sinfull handes.

For the profession & maintenance of Which Faith, the
forenamed Enimies of GoD deteine in theyr handes
Within the Prisons about London (not to speake of
other Gaoles throughout the Land) about threescore &
twelue persons, men & Woemen young & old, lying in
cold, hunger, dungeons & Yrons: Of which number they
haue taken the Lordes day last, beeing the 4th of this
.3. Moneth March *1592* about some .56. persons hearing
ye Word of GoD truly taught, praying & praysing GoD
for his favors shewed vnto vs, vnto her Maiestie, Your
Lordships, & this whole Land; and desiring our GoD
to be mercifull vnto vs, vnto our gracious Prince, & to
our Contrey.   Beeing employed in these holy actions &
no other (as the parties who disturbed them can testifie)
they were taken in the very place where ye persecuted
Church & Martyres were enforced to vse the like exercises in Queene Maryes dayes.

The former nomber are now vnbayleably committed by the
Prelate or Bishop of London &c vnto close (for ye most
part) severall Prisons: As Brydewell, the Lymboe or
dungeon in Newgate; the Fleet, the Marshalsea, the
Counters, the Gatehouse, the Clynke, the White
Lyon: Wherein wee willingly acknowledge the Lott &
inheritance in this life of our Fore-fathers & Brethren
the holy Martires of ye former age, and ye entayled
Aceldema or bloody possession of the Sea of London
& y^t whole linadge.   Well, heere our Brethren lye (how
long Lord holy & true thow knowest) in dungeons, in
hunger, in cold, in nakednes & all outward distresse:
For those bloody men will allowe them neyther meate,
drinke, fyre, lodging, nor suffer anie whose heartes the
Lord would stirr vp for their releif to haue accesse vnto
them, purposinge belike to emprison them vnto death,
as they haue doon 17 or 18 others in the same noysome
Gaoles within these .6. yeeres.

The Wife & Husband beeing now taken by them, they permit not to be in yᵉ same, but haue sent them to be closely kept in diverse Prisons : What theyr poore familie doth at home in yᵉ meane tyme your *Lordsh*ips may consider & iustly pittie. Some of this companie had not anie penie about them When they were sent vnto close Prison; nor anie thing beeing abrode (w*h*ich is the case of the most of them, if not of all) to procure themselves & theyr poore families anie maintenance, saue only their handy labors & trades. Whereby it is come to passe, yᵗ these enimies of GoD doo not only starue & vndooe a number of men in Prison, but even a lamentable companie of poore Orphanes & servant*es* abrode. Their vnbrydled sclanders; Their lawlesse privie serches; Their violent breaking open & rifling of o*ur* houses; Their lamentable & barbarous vsage of woemen & young Children in these hostile assaul*tes*; Theyr vncontrolled theeverye, robbing & taking of whatsoever they thinke meete fro*m* vs in this case; Their vnappeased and mercilesse pursuite of vs from our houses, trades, wives, Children; But specially from yᵉ holy societie of yᵉ Sainct*es* & Church of GoD wee are enforced to omitt, lest wee should bee over tedious vnto Y*our Lordsh*ips. But theyr dealing this way toward vs is so woefull (right Honor*able*) as wee may truly demaund wᵗ greife of heart, whether the forreigne Enimie or our naturall Contrymen doo possesse & beare rule over vs in our deare & natiue Contrey./

Their whole dealing heerein is most barbarous, most inhumane, but especially most vnchristian, & such as exceedeth the crueltie, of the heathen & popish professed Tyrant*es* & persecuto*ʳˢ*. The Record*es* of the heathen persecution vnder Nero, Traian, Decius, Galienus, Maximinian, &c. can scant affoord vs anie examples of the like crueltie & havock: For the heathen Romans would murther openly & professedly; These godlesse men haue put the blood of warre about them in the day of that peace & truce w*h*ich this Land

professeth to hold w^t Iesus Christ & his servant*es*.
Bishop Boner, Storye, Weston, delt not after this
sort: For those whome they com*m*itted close, they
Would also eyther feed, or permit to be fedd by others;
And they brought them in short space openly into
Smythfeild to end their miserie, & to begin theyr
never ending ioye. whereas Bishop Elmar, D. Stanope,
& Mr Iustice Young w^t the rest of that persecuting &
bloodthirstie facultie doo neyther of these.   No Fellons,
no Murtherers, No Traytors in this Land are thus delt
with.

There are manie of vs by the mercy of GoD still out of theyr
hand*es*.   The former holy exercises & profession Wee
purpose not to leaue by the assistance of *our* GoD.
Wee haue as good warrant to reiect ye Ordinanc*es* of
AntiChrist, & to labor for ye recoverie of CHRISTS
holy Institut*i*ons, as *our* Fathers & Brethren in Queene
Maryes dayes had to doo ye like.   And wee doubt not
if *our* Cause were truly knowne vnto her Ma*i*estie &
Your wisdomes, but wee should finde greater favor then
they did, whereas *our* estate now is far more lamentable./

And therfore wee humbly & earnestly craue of her Ma*i*estie
& *Your Lordshi*ps both for our selves abrode, & for our
Brethren now in miserable captivitie but iust & equall
tryall accord*i*ng to her Ma*i*estis [*sic*] Lawes.   If
wee prooue not our Adversaries to bee in a most
pestilent & godlesse course, both in regard of
theyr Offices & theyr proceedings in them, and
our selves to bee in ye right way, wee desire not
to have the benefit of her Ma*i*estis true & faithfull Subiects, w*h*ich of all earthly favors wee
accompt to bee one of the greatest.   Are wee
malefactors?   Are wee anie wise vndutifull vnto our
Prince?   Maineteine wee anie errors?   Let vs then
bee iudicially convicted thereof, & delyvered to the
Civill authoritie; But let not these bloody men both
accuse, condemne & closely murther after this sort,
contrarie to lawe, æquitie & Conscience, Where they

alone are the plaintiff*es*, the accusers, the Iudges, and
the Executioners of theyr most fearefull & barbarous
tyrannie.

They should not by the Lawes of this Land goe anie further
in Cases of Religion then theyr owne Ecclesiasticall
censures, and then referre vs vnto y⁰ Civill power.
Their Fore-fathers Gardyner, Boner, Story, delt
thus equally And wee Craue but this æquitie.
Oh Let her excellent Ma*i*estie our Sovereigne & Yo*ur*
Hon*ours* consider & accord vnto this our iust petition.
For streames of innocent blood are likely to bee spilt in
secret by these bloodthirstie men, except her Ma*i*estie
& Yo*ur* Hon*ours* doo take order with theyr most cruell
& inhumane procedinge*s*

Wee craue for all of vs but the Libertie eyther to dye
openly or to lyve openly in y⁰ Land of our
nativit[i]e. If wee deserue death, it beseemeth the
Maiestie of Iustice not to see v[s] closely murthered, yea
starved to death with hunger & colde, & stifled in lothsome dongeons. If wee be guyltlesse, wee crave but y⁰
benefit of our innocencie Viz. That wee may haue
peace to serve our GoD & our Prince in the place
of the sepulchres of our Fathers./

Thus protesting o*ur* innocencie, complayning of violence &
Wrong, & crying for Iustice on the behalfe & in the
name of y*ᵗ* righteous Iudge the GoD of æquitie &
iustice, Wee contynue our prayers vnto him for her
Ma*i*estie & your Hon*ours*, whose heart*es* wee beseech
him to encline toward this our most æquall & iust
suite, Through CHRIST IESVS our Lord./

[The humble
Petition of
[the imprisoned Barrowists]

["To the...Magistrates of our Most mercifull
sou*e*raigne Lady Queene Elizabeth in their
seu*e*rall plac*es*".]

For Goddes sake
For Queene Elizabeths sake
For Englandes sake &
For *you*r owne sake
     pervse yt W*i*th favoure
       Yt tendethe to
        mercy & vnitie]¹

[Written just after the death of Barrowe and Greenwood in 1593.]

       The firste parte of
     A tretise conteyning Motions touching
         Mercie & vnitie

Sent by a few of those whoe are falslie & Maliciouslie called
     Browni*stes*.
     For Christ*es* sake, For Queene Elizabeths, For
     Englandes sake, and for *you*r owne sakes²

       *pe*ruse it, &
       Neglect it not

If the confession of offence against her Ma*i*estie, in some
falt*es* escaped in those book*es* and the suffering death for yt by
the Two principall doers, may be found sufficient punishment in
conscience, for the qualletie of those faltes: The Lord graunte
that None maye diswade her highnes from her Wonted Mercy,
but that some may have Will and power to *pe*rswade her grace
to *pa*rdon all former offences in theis poinct*es*,: And it shalbe a
Warning to vs all to looke better vnto that wch our penns lay
downe (quia litera scripta manet), And We shall also be the
more bounde, to praise our God, and to pray Vnto him for her
Ma*i*est*ie*s most longe & prosperous raigne, and the *pr*esent &
ever lasting comfort of her soule and boddie./

---

¹ Harl. MS. 6848, fol. 2–7, in the British Museum. Throughout the
text here given words enclosed by dark brackets are such as have been
inserted by the corrector of the Petition.

² The person who wrote this petition forms many of his small "m"s
and "w"s, and even some other letters, with a long preliminary curved
stroke of the pen, so that they much resemble capital, or if one may so
express it, semi-capital, letters. When thus formed they are here given as
capitals.

To the most honorable & Worshipfull Magistrates of our Most mercifull soueraigne Lady Queene Elizabeth in their seuerall places (specially her highnes moste honorable privie counsell, in their digneties, her reverend Iudges in their seates, the right honorable the Lord Maior of London, and the Worshipfull Iustices there in theire roomes) To all & euerie of them, aboundaunce of heavenly Wisdome be Multeplied./

In Most humble and lamentable manner beseech your honnours and worshipps, a fewe of the poore people, falslie and Maliciouslie called Brownistes, in behalfe of our selves at libertie, and more then Threskore [three score] poore prisoners now shut vp in the seuerall Gaoles and prisons of this most noble Cittie. That whereas all the bookes, letters, wrytinges, examinacions speeches and accions of anie particuler person, or of the whole congregacion, are vndoubtedlie knowen to be quite contrarie to Infidells, Papistes, and Atheistes. And whereas none can prove that we hold anie heresie, or Mainteyne anie filthines amongest vs, (the thought whereof we thanke our God we abhorre) And lastlie, Whereas we doe here protest before his heavenly Maiestie (whoe knoweth all secrettes) that we hartelie desyer the glorie of our God to shine more and more in this nacion by increase of true holines and Godliness in all the people thereof even with intire and fervent love to him, our Queene and one an other, togeather with the abundant peace plenty and prosperretie of our Countrie, and all this vnder the longe and most blessed government of our dread and soueraigne Ladie and Queene Elizabeth to Melchisedeches age, yf such be his good pleasure (whose princelie spirites and boddie we praye that he will refreshe or renew as he doth the Eagles Bill) Yt may therefore please your honnours and worshipps for Godes sake to increase all charitable thoughtes of vs, and to be Mercifull vnto vs as our heavenlie Father is mercifull, and as our noble Queene doth plentifully and daylie ymitate * * him therein: Hereof we have late experience by her highnes pro-longing * * our deare Mr Barrowes and Mr Greenewoods life, when the instrumentes, and Man and sheetes and flowers and grave,

" * * [From margin.] sequens pagina expungatur [?] (in fine)" of death Were all prepared, and they both reddie (as they had lived togeather like Two Turtles) to yeld vp their sperit*es* togeather (like Two lambs) in all meekenes and obedience: Now blessed be our God for such a ruler of his people; Let them deepelie repent or p*er*ishe foreu*er* that once seeke one drop of her bloud, or peece of her land, or blemishe to her renowme. What is our cheife request in this Introduc-tion? Having Twoe or Three Motions concer*n*ing Mercy, and more touching vnetie, whereby we verelie hope that this con-troversie shalbe the sooner taken vp, Wee most humblie beseech You to harken vnto them w*i*th patience and then to favo*ur* them so farre as they shalbe found Godlie, lawfull & convenient. Y e reu*er*end Magistrates, ye God*es* (so called in the scriptures, because yow are in his stede to doe righteous Iudgment vppon the earth) Hath not the almightie given yow vnderstanding to trye the depth of all attempt*es* w*i*thin this land? Wee trust he hath, Oh search vs deeper then, try our wayes, And if none can alleadge anie thinge against vs save onelie this one error (yf it be so) touching the law of our God. deale tenderlie w*i*th tender conscienc*es*: Wee are Yet p*er*swaded that we shold shew our selves disobedient and vnthankfull to our maker, except we hold fast this ca*u*se: Yow know not how rich his mercie hath ben vnto vs, for we verelie suppose that yow never offended his divine Ma*i*estie so much or so often as most of vs have donne (like the prodigall childe, yea like Mary Magdelin) But he hath wasshed vs & clensed vs, and given vs vnspeakable Ioye and peace of conscience sence we came to this companie: Mervell not then at our zeale, but pittie vs and helpe vs wherein yow know it to be a Misse. Behold a people wholly bent & vowed to s*e*rve the God of heaven in that course w*ch* they may p*er*ceive to be most tending to holines & righteousnes. Yf yo*ur* honno*ur*s & Worshipps can bring anie to shew vs that We shall doe more true s*e*rvice to our God, our Queene and Countrie by comyng to the p*ar*ish assemblies, verelie we will harken vnto them w*i*thout obstinacy (& o that some of yow wold be the Witnesses and Iudges). Alas it is not our worldlie ease to be thus tossed as we are, yt is onely this matter of conscience that causeth all our suffering*es*, and yo*ur* troubles w*i*th vs./

like poore
Daniels
case. Chap.
6. 5. u*er*se

Wherefore for Christe Iesus sake (whose true servauntes we strive to be) for Queene Elizabeths sake, (whose true subiectes we are,) For Englandes sake (whose loving Countrymen we remaine) and for the honnour of your owne names and helth of your owne soules, let no man cause yow to fixe your eies and your thoughtes whollie vppon that our supposed falte (or falt indeede) but rather vppon some holie and Mercifull meane [whereby] this our too much heate may be cooled and tempered (yf it be adust [*sic*]) in all meekenes & love:[?] Howe? As becommeth them, that wold spend their blood against the Pope and Spanishe Kinge to deale with those that are most willing to doe the like: As it becometh Englishmen to deale with Englishmen, Protestantes with Protestantes, Fathers with their children, and breifely Christians with Christians: Men & Fathers yf yow cannot helpe vs presentlie, yet suffer vs to ease our hartes a litle by expressing our Woundes sorrowes and suites at large (even as a childe mourneth to the nurse) vnder God, we have no helpe but our Queene and Yow. And whoe knoweth Whether he will (even this Mournefull Moneth) by increasing our affliccions, cause yow to behold our loyaltie and innocency More then ever yow did, And thereby release vs the sooner, The Mercy of God, and the Mercifull inclinacion of our most gracious Queene, doth feede vs with vndoubted hope, that so manie of [the rest of] vs as cannot be found Traito\[^rs\] or Herretickes, shall [yet] fynde favour & pardon. The God of Daniel, our Most mercifull Father, graunte all true Wisdome & prosperetie to our most gratious Queene Elizabeth, and to as manie of yow and yours as desyer to increase in true feare and love & service of that mighty God of Izraell. Amen.

Motions tending to mercy

First That it may please your honnours and worships (the promysses christianlie pondered) never to hearken vnto them, Whoe shall goe aboute to perswade Yow that this people deserve the like terror and punishment, as treacherous and Idolatrous Papistes doe./ **1**

Secondlie, That yt may please yow to take order for releasing **2** theis pore distressed protestantes, freelie from those contagious Gaoles, yf that may stand with lawe and conscience./

3 Orels, To baile them vppon sufficient securetie, to answer at a reasonable Warning vnto whatsoever shall be obiected against them./

4 Lastlie, yf it be not thought convenient that Wee her Maiesties naturall and loving subiectes shold have the same libertie graunted vs in the Worship of God, Wᶜʰ her highnes giveth to strangers, French, Dutche, and Italian (sithe our practise is no othe[r] in every cheife poinct, then that of theirs, and Geneua, and all other reformed Churches.) Yet that we maye have Summam misericordiam, Not summum ius: Sed quorsum hec de Gallis. &c:? Inuidus alterius? Non equidem inuidemus (honoratissimi et nobillissimi viri) miramur magis vndique totis vsque a deo &c. En nos &c: (sed tempus non datur).

The other motions tending to vnitie (wᶜʰ wee trust wilbe acceptable to your honnours and Worshipps) shalbe now [alsoe] delivered to yow [and more partes] God willing very shortlie, yf theis firste, and the Women that bring them doe fynde such favour in your eies, as not to be turned back or Misliked: Otherwise wee know not what course to take (so greate is our Misery and want of men and Meanes to expresse it) Wee are like enough to offend in not Wryting with such discression as we ought, and they in not delivering with such modestie as they shold: But wee are simple men, and they are silly Women. Therefore howsoever either Wee now or others of late have failed in Manner or matter, Wee most humblie beseech your honnours and worshipps to be perswaded, that it was not for lack of care and conscience, but onelie for Want of Iudgment and experience, and therefore to pardon vs the sooner: If he that hath but his foote out of ioynct can scarce doe anie thing currantly, What can they doe whoe have [all] their cheife members troubled and almoste quite cut of? No Marvell yf their accons [*sic*, for "*accions*"] be distempered (some too violent, some too cold) In such a case have we ben theise manie Weekes The knee (as it were) is faine to ronne for the foote and a few litle fingers (wch cold never helpe them selves) to labour for the Whole bodie: Howbeit we truste that in such tymes and cases, your *Lordships* & *Worshipps* will ymmitate all Godly men of trades (si liceat magna paruis) when Children or servauntes are sent vnto them, they Will give better Ware and Measure, and dispatch them sooner then yf the parentes them selves shold come to buye: Necessety compelleth vs to make mone & signes vnto yow: Ah barre vs not of that comfort for then shall our greate distresse be made vnspeakable. Heu, quanta miseria est, in tormento, nec vocem, nec pennam, nec signum habere: O vos qui Dij appellamini, nolite istiusmodi silentiam iniungere: ferme omnes perimus (dolore et paupertate oppressi) Iuniores carent gubernatione, et aliqui seniores sepulti sunt: si non remedium statim, saltem lachrymas suspiria, Declarationes, supplicationes, et verba concedite (presertim matri pro filio, sorori pro fratre vxori pro marito) Aliter, regia (quasi) petendi via obstructa erit, quod adhuc non factum esse vidimus (Deo gratias) Ecce feminas petentes pro charissimis suis in causa lamentabili, cum motionibus honestis, legitimis et pijs: Estote misericordes, qui sub Deo et Elizabetha ([ipsius] Ancilla Regina nostra) judicatis et gubernatis Angliam.

In all humble and pittifull manner Wee intreate Yow not to make question whoe shold begynne to releive vs: But as we have ioyned Yow all in one humble peticion: soe all of yow to ioyne togeather in one Christian compassion and euerie one in his place according to his lawfull aucthoritie to helpe vs: The cause whie We made our direction thus generall, was, to the ende that one or a few coppies might passe from manie handes to manie hartes: Wee beseech Yow then, send our papers from one to an other, & lett our lamentable case remaine in Your bosome till there be some godlie & Mercifull order taken for vs./

** Whereas We spake of her maiesties imitacion of God in
** mercy, lest some might misconster [*sic*] vs as liers or flatterers, thus We say. We are persuaded that their reprive as from her highnes, was in mercy, and that their execution (sone

after) Was rather importuned & hastened by others then easily
consented vnto by her grace For hath she not ben alwaies very
mercifull to her veriest enemies ?   Therefore howsoeu*er* yt fell
out, we still retaine a good hope of her ma*ie*sties favour towar*des*
vs when God shall fynd meanes to revele *our* inocencie vnto her,
and still we pray that nothing may w*i*thdrawe *our* loiall [?] hart*es*
from her[1]

[The second
    parte]

Motions tending to Vnitie

1 That yf we maie not heare publique conference for anie
  inconvenience (in regard Whereof it were better We shold
  suffer Mischeif) Yet that our Teachers may (in our hearing yf
  it be thought Meete,) have such as Was graunted Campion and
  his fellowes

2 Orels, That there may be some conference betwene ij or iij of
  either side, before a good nomber of *you*r honno*ur*s and worshipps
  in some private Chamber, the Manie questions agreed vppon
  before hand (w*i*th preparac*i*on by fasting and prayer) and when
  the tyme com*m*es [?] omytting all taunt*es* and by Matters, onely
  searching the truth in love.   To the touchstone, To the
  lawe and the Testament.

3 Orels such a conference as was graunted H art, the Papist.
  Yf it be obiected that none of our side are Worthie to be thus
  disputed or Wrytten W*i*th (publiquelie nor privately) Wee
  thinke that this will prove the contrary viz, because there are
  3. or 4 in this Cittie and More els Where, Whoe have ben
  zealous preachers in the p*a*rish assemblies, Not ignorant in the
  Lattin Greeke & Hebrew tongues (nor otherwayes vnlerned)
  and gen*er*ally confessed to be of honest conversac*i*on.   To be
  breife, as gentle and lerned M[r] Reynoldes of Oxford and others
  like him are yet alive, so are there right honorable and godlie
  disposed p*er*sonages of s*i*r Frauncis Walsinghams mynde (and

---

[1] The corrector of the petition evidently wished this paragraph omitted
from the text, as he has expressed in Latin in the margin of fol. 2 verso.

alyance and mynde), Whoe have power Wee know, and good
Will we hope to furder such lawfull Mocions tending to so good
purposes./

If theis mocions take effect wee are verely perswaded that the
controvercy Will soone ende (with all or moste of vs) For by
theis Meanes shall Wee poore Wretches whoe onelie Make this
sepperacion (as knoweth the Lord) for love we have to kepe his
commaundimentes and for feare to disobey him, perceive more
plainely Whether (as men & simple soules) we be deceived by
a false light, orells (as his deare children (for soe we. hope)
honored and trusted with the first view of and faithfull standing
in a cause of holines and righteousnes. Wherefore in most
humble and earnest manner, and even as yow feare God and
love righteousnes (and as yow strive to resemble him in liking
better of them that are hott, then of those that are luke Warme)
We intreate your honnours and Worshipps to labour in obteyn-
ing theis or some better Mocions for procuring vnitie and
Mercye, that the blessinges promysed to Mercifull Men and
peacemakers, maye light vpon Yow and yours, and the curses
threatened for the contrary maye be farre from Yow. Ye
reuerend Magistrates and noble guides of this most florrishing
common Welth, We beseech Yow againe and againe in the Lord
Iesus, searche your selves narrowlie when Yow seeke him
whome your soule loueth.and thinke how yow wold desyer
to be dealt with yf yow were in our case, and so deale with vs
and our Teachers; If yow suppose them and vs to be in a
grevious error, for common humanities sake (were there no
further cause) let vs not perishe either secretly in prisons or
openlie by execucion for want of that vtermost helpe wch lyeth
in your power to afford them that are not obstinate./

If anie adversary shall obiect that we are Worthie of close
ymprisonmentes in Most contageous ayre, withoute bayle, and
vnworthie of having or hearing anie greate prepared conference
or of anie favour because some of vs have ben conferred with
alreadie, and yet remaine in greate error as lerned men Iudge,
We make this answer, and praye eache one of tender harte to
ponder it deepelie./

God forbid that all they whoe [erre] greately in some opinions

shold have no other Meanes to convert them but sodden
vnequall conference*s* by [startes] [?] (with snatching & [?] and
Catching) without good order and indifferent hearing and
Iudges, (such have all or the moste of our conference*s* ben)
and then yf they Will not by and by yeild, be thought Worthie
of as bad prisons as theeves and Roges: The holy ghoste
seemeth to be of another Mynde. 2 Tim. 2. 24, 25, 26. even
towardes those Whoe are in the snare of the Devill taken
prisoners by him to doe his Will (can We be worse then such)
And also Galla. 6. 1, 2, 3, O that the Bisshope*s* and all the
zealous preachers of this land, wold aske their owne harte*s*
whether we [have] ben soundlie and lovinglie delt with according to theise rules. If they be true Pasto*rs* to vs, then
though we goe a straye and be intangled in errors (as sillye
sheepe with thornes) yet ought they to follow vs seeke vs vp,
and vnlose vs with all tendernes (not so much for feare of
loosing of our fleece as of our soules,) The love of a naturall
brother is greate, and Will not easely cease, but more of a
naturall Mother but much More of a supernaturall father (such
are Pasto*rs* and therefore they Will not easely give over the
leaste and leanest of their flocke, though he have a greate
disease, a greate error): O why then doe theise or anie of them
so revile vs in their bookes & common speeches, Whie doe they
Wishe and perswade the Civil Magistrate to deale With vs
by the sword and not by the Word, by prisons and Not by
perswations, Whie doe they vse vs thus whiles we praye for
them and wish them no more harme then we desyer to our
owne soules and bodies, naye whilest we grone and longe to
heare some of them, so wee might doe it with a saife conscyence? Is there no other remedy but yf wee erre We must
be thus dealt With? Alas our first parente*s* Adam and Eve
did fall: The Patriarke*s* had their faltes, the holiest Prophete*s*
Were not free from them, the Appostles erred and dissented,
The Auncient Fathers of the Prymative Church retracted divers
opinions, greate *par*liament*es* & gene*r*all counsells have fouly
erred The lerned of this age, Yea of this land, (, Naye of one
profession and Church) differ very Much in Iudgment aboute
moste of the same poinct*es* w*ch* we doe, And whoe is cleere from

synne error & ignoraunce But so longe as men are not in
herresy nor in trechery, Nor in filthie conceiptes nor in
obstinacy but erring (yf they doe faile) on the right hand
in poinctes uncondempned, still hating all falce wayes and
loving the pathes of righteousnes, thus long there is apparant
Mercy in the Moste high, and so is there in those Pasto[rs], those
Magistrates those people Whoe have feeling compassion (when
God bringes meanes Whereby they vnderstand the truth of
accions.)   As for dungeons, Irons, close ymprisonment, honger,
cold, want of meanes to mainteyne their famulies [?], theise
may cause some to make shipwrack of a good conscyence or to
lose their life, but they are not fitt Wayes to perswade [honest
men] to anie truth or diswade them from errors./
Her Maiestie hath shewed greate Mercy to [her] vndoubted
enemies, the trecherous Papistes.   What then Wold her
Maiestie shew to vs yf she knew that w[ch] some of yow doe
now see.   O that her grace and Yow did vnderstand of all our
accions, and did see [the] seuerall declaracions of our faith and
loyalty (longe sence penned) Wee shold not then be longe in
such hazard of vtter spoyle to our bodyes and Myndes (of evel
ayre and dyet) and of the poore remnant of our goodes, and of
our famulies [?] distruccion through lack of guiding.   Doubtles
right honorable & Worshipfull) vnles there be some speedie &
Mercifull order taken With vs, both Wee our selves are like to
perishe in the gaoles (as divers of our bretheren & sisters have
donne) and our famulies [?] & housholdes fall to vttur ruen
and decaye through Want of government and teaching./ [Alas
(reverend Fathers) What is Youth Without governement? and
What governement can there be in those howses whose shop
Windowes are alwaies shut, Whose masters are continuall
prisoners, Whose dames [?] are dayly cold sutors, and whose
teachers & overseers are so enclosed as they cannot performe
any dutie vnto them vpon the Lordes day, or wekely from
howse to howse] Mercifull Magistrates yf anie of yow fynde
the bowells of your Christian compassion stirred by theise
lamentable yet true reportes, let not your eyes rest untill your
heartes have made a promise to cause your tonges to speake,
and Your bodies to labour for Mercy & vnetie.   And the God

of righteousnes graunte that Yow maye fynde peace & favour
with him in the dayes of trouble, sicknes, and death (whereto all
flesh is subiect). Amen. /

To the right honorable Syr   . Roe[1] nowe Lord major of
        London abundance of all blessing*es* be multiplied
                to Godd*es* glorie

Right honorable seinge God disposeth of everie action
(accordinge to his surpassinge Wisedome) and sith he and his
Angell*es* behold all the doing*es* of men, We humblie beseche
yo^u to consider with your self that yt is not without some
providence of his (to your good if you deale mercifullie) that
these thing*es* touchinge Mercy and Vnitie are first brought
to your Lord*ship*s hand*es*: Many of our bretheren are in the
prisons belonginge to your Libertie, Nowe as your Citie is
accounted the most noble (even as the Princ*es* chamber) and
as You are the honorable and chefe officer therein, so we
beseche our God that your Lord*ship* may be made a noble
honorable & Worthy instrum*ent* in bringinge these twoe most
blessed and acceptable thing*es* (in the sight of God & man) to
good passe: If we sent you vile thing*es* (dishorable [dishonor-
able] to God our Queene & Contrey) ought you not to make
the superior magistrates acquainted with them? surely you
ought: But howe if we acquaint your Lord*ship* with honest
motions (tendinge to the glorie of God, the ho*nour* of her
ma*iest*ie and the benefit of our Contrey) should you not doe
the like? dowtles you should: If you hide yt or neglect yt, yet
the almighty may fynd waies to bring yt to the sight of her
highnes right ho*norable* Counsell and her grac*es* reverend
Iudges: But if you vouch-safe to be a charitable and godlie
meane for effectinge such lawfull & conscionable [?] Suites,
You shall dischardge the dutie of a most honorable officer of
a most famous & populous Citie, and we and all ours shalbe

---

[1] Evidently Sir William Rowe, but Joseph Hayden in his "Book of
Dignities", London, 1890, appears to give Sir William's year of office as
9 November, 1591, to 9 November, 1592. It is not unlikely that during
this time of trouble and imprisonment the separatist leaders had forgotten
that a new Lord Mayor had already assumed the dignities of that position.

the more bound to pray vnto our God that he will blesse your Mayraltie with all manner blessinges of trewe peace (both inward & outward) and of healthe, with all other prosperities soe as may tend most to his owne glory and your and our comfort in hym: And that he will continnewe those blessinges to your successors and to all England in such sorte as moche happines may redound to you & vs and all her maiesties dominions for many Yeares (if yt be his will) vnder the blessed governement of our most gratious Zoueraigne Ladie & Queene Elizabeth

Amen

The humble Petition of her
highnes faithfull Subiects falsly
called Brownistes [of 1597][1].

......

To the Right Honorable the Lords of her
Maiesties most honorable priuie Councell:

𝖂𝖍𝖊𝖗𝖊𝖆𝖘 wee her Maiesties naturall borne Subiectes true and Loyall now lyving many of vs in other Countries as Men exiled her highnes Domynions, and the rest which remaine within her Graces land greatlie distressed thorough imprisonment and other great troubles sustained onlie for some matters of conscience in which our most lamentable estate, wee cannot in that measure performe the dutie of Subiectes, as wee desier. And also Wheareas meanes is now offered for our beeing in a forraigne and farre Countrie which lieth to the West from hence in the Province of Canada where by the providence of the Almightie, and her Maiesties most gratious fauour, wee may not onlie worshippe god as wee are in conscience perswaded by his Word, but also doe vnto her Maiestie and our Country great good service, and in tyme also greatlie annoy that bloodie and persecuting Spaniard about the Baye of Mexico. Our most humble suite is that it may please Your Honors to bee a meanes vnto her excellent Maiestie that with her most gracious

---

[1] S. P., Dom., Elizabeth, 1593, Vol. 246 (No. 56), in the Public Record Office, London.

fauour and protection wee may peaceablie Depart thither, and there remayning to bee accounted her M*aiesties* faithfull and loving Subiect*es*, to whom wee owe all dutie and obedience in the Lord. Promising heerebie, and takeing god to record who searcheth the hartes of all people. That wheresoeuer wee become wee will by the grace of god liue and die faithfull to her highnes and this Land of our Natiuitie:/

X

HITHERTO UNNOTICED TESTIMONY CONFIRMING ROBERT
BROWNE'S OPINION OF THE REFORMATION IN SCOT-
LAND AS PUBLISHED IN RICHARD BANCROFT'S SERMON
PREACHED AT PAUL'S CROSS: TOGETHER WITH SOME
OF THE GROUNDS ON WHICH ARCHBISHOP WHITGIFT
RECOMMENDED BANCROFT'S APPOINTMENT AS BISHOP
OF LONDON

[A Letter of Sir Robert Naunton to Dr. J. Copcoat, Master of
Corpus Christi College in Cambridge, relating to the publica-
tion of Richard Bancroft's famous "Sermon preached at Pavles
Crosse", and dated November 12, 1589.][1]

Sir My Humble dutie to your Worship precommended &c. [?]
The ould inveterate [?] grudg conceived by this Clergie against
m^r Doctour Bancrofte for meer medling with their anarchie [?]
here established; how soeuer it seemed for a time to have bene
divested or at least voyded [?] together with such cholericke
humours & termes of splene as they disgorged their stomaches
of at ye first receipt: yet is it at length descried [?] to haue
impostuned [?] & rankled inward [?] all this while, by ye late
fostering & drawing to a heade which we [?] here perceive
allready [?], and is like er longe to breake out to some further
anoyance there, if discrete remedie be not foreseene in time.
A man wold hardly beleeve that such professours of Charitie,
should be such reteiners of enmitie Et tamen istos si quis forte
vel verbo commoverit, manet alta mente repostum. etiam
plumbeas iras gerunt [?]. He that shall heare their protested
sinceritie & see their practised extremitie he may iustly
exclame with that Poeticall admiracion—tantaé ne animis

---

[1] Add. MS. 32,092. fol. 106–7, in the British Museum.

coelestib*us* irae ?   At y*ᵉ* first publishing of M*ʳ* Bancrofts
sermon, there was nothing but breathing out threatninges of
I know not what Canonicall confutac*i*on to be set forth by y*ᵉ*
generall consent of their p*r*ovinciall Synode, anathematizing as
well y*ᵉ* read*e*rs [?] as y*ᵉ* autho*ur* of that schismaticall libell for
so it pleased some of their brotherhoods to intitulate [?] that
booke).   Since when, eith*e*r vpon their kings earnest intreatie
(his H*igh*n*e*s standing so intirely well affected to y*ᵉ* inter-
teignem*e*nt & p*r*eservac*i*on of all good amitie betwene the two
Crownes) or rather bethinking them selves that there was
nothing in that sermon wh*i*ch might gall them any way, but
was literally derived out of the acts of their owne p*a*rleam*e*nt
declared by publicke autoritie, they have vpon mature de-
liberac*i*on (vt su*n*t istor*um* hom*in*um secundae cog*i*tat*i*o*n*es
aliquanto saniores) revoked that p*u*rpose of controverting y*ᵉ*
matt*e*r by pen for feare of ripping vp their old sores &
vncou*e*ring y*ᵉ* shame of their reformac*i*on [?] alla Scotcese (y*ᵉ*
searching wher*o*f they haue no list to heare of) but haue
reserved notw*i*thstanding [?] y*ᵉ* ranco*ur* of their brotherly
μνησικακία still boyling in their brests, till the first oppor-
tunitie shold serve [?]. when to belche it forth.   To wh*i*ch
intent waiting all pacience still [?] swelling [?] on w*i*thout
vent, might at length indanger them to brast [burst] for
envie like Asops tode, they haue taken their advantage of the
time p*r*es*e*nt p*e*rsuading them selves that now in absence of
their kinge (of whose sailing into Norwey to fetch home his
Queene I doubt not but yo*u* have heard long since) bearing so
highe a saile in y*ᵉ* state as they do, & being earnestly moved
from her Ma*i*estie to p*e*rforme all good offic*e*s [?] they may to
keepe this people on good terms till their Soue*r*aines returne
(wherein I denye not but their endevo*ur*s haue bene well
imployed) & therupon presuming that this is their time wherein to make their market in England.   Her Ma*i*estie having
p*r*omised them all good Correspondence in recom*p*ence of their
paines taken for y*ᵉ* peaceable qualificac*i*on of her vnruly neigh-
bo*ur*s in so dangerous a time [?]; they made resort to my
L. Amb*ass*ador here, acquainting him w*i*th their [?] greife [?],
craving his assistance for their redresse, & offringe their l*e*tt*re*s

of Complainte vnto her Maiesty of such & such abuses against yᵉ puritie of their reformacion [?] not only committed by one of her Highnes subiects, but permitted & allowed by her Highnes publicke autoritie to their [?] greate slander, scandale & I know not what. My L. having received late instructions from yᵉ Councel to put in execution all good meanes he mought to winne & reteine [?] their kindnes in a time so necessarye (& therefore [?] being to temporise & second them in all their motives [?] in convenient sorte) had much adoe [?] to [?] withstand their vrgent importunitie with all the earnest intreatie he could make for the delaie of their Complainte herein, alleging that how fitt soeuer the present might seeme to serve their turne for exhibiting of their supplicacion, yet that it was on yᵉ other side as vnseasonable a time for her Maiestie to intende their redresse, being so encombred as she now is with diuerse other her greate affaires both domesticall & forein [?], promising that if they woulde referre yᵉ matter to him, he would of him selfe worke privatelie for their satisfaction as he could, or at least to watche them a fiter time to present their complaints with better hope of taking place &c. And so after much debating to & fro they were intreated [?] thoughe halfe malecontente to suppresse their supplicacion till some better opportunity, not dessembling [?] yᵉⁱʳ purpose to selicite her Highnes further herein by some other extraordinarie meanes, vnles some speedy satisfaction were procured by my Lᵈ dealing to that effecte. Wherupon being glad of so fitte an opportunity [?] to declare my due regard of my humble dutie & service aswell to my Lords grace as to your worship hereof, I vndertoke to my L. Ambassador that he would aduertise your worship thereof in such time, as my Lᵈˢ grace might take knowledge of their designements before hand, the better to prevent any such inconvenience as might insue hereupon, specially in such a time wherein her Maiestie having so necessarie occasion to vse their service here, may happilie be drawen the rather to respecte yᵉ [?] importunitie of their Clamorous complaints whatsoeuer. I may please your worship to acquainte my Lords grace herewith if so you shall thinke good & to recommend my L. Ambassadors most affectionate

devocion to his Hono*ur*, who (if[?] he might p*r*esume so farre)
wold gladlye knowe his graces direction how to deale therein,
or othe*r*wise to impa*r*te it to m^r Bancrofte that he may the
better bethinke him selfe[?] postqua*m* irritavit hos cra-
brones quib*us* armis aut consilijs hor*um* aculeis eat*ur*
obviam. Sunt enim & Stoicis sua πάθη, & his etiam
Sanctis sua bilis. Nimirum q*uod* in alijs scelus, id in
his zelus quid nj habeat*ur*? And so most humbly p*r*e-
senting my humble· dutie & service, craving yo*ur* best
acceptance of my perfite[?] good meaning herein how soeu*er*
imperfectly vttered, I cease further to be tedious to yo*ur*
wo*r*ship.

At Edenb*urgh* this xijth of November 1589.

Yo*ur* worships most intirely devoted

R. Naunton

[A Letter of Richard Bancroft's, dated December 23, 1589,
also relating to his Sermon at Paul's Cross.][1]

> To my good frend M^r
> Nanton attendinde
> vpo*n* ye L: Embassador
> in Scotland.

Good Mr Nanton. Althoughe we have no acquaintaunce together, yet by the letter yow writt not longe since to Dr Copcot
I find my selfe exceedingly beholden vnto yow. Towchinge the
effect of which letter there hath been consideration taken by
my good Frend*es*. I had written a letter to the chief of the
great Rabbies: but bicawse I am certaynly enformed that there
is a booke written agaynst my sermon which shall w*i*thowt
doubt be printed I have thought good w*i*th some advice to
stay the same. It appeareth likewise by your letter how
greatly I am bownd to my L: Embassador: I doubt not but
that both my L: of Canterbury and my L: Chauncelor who are
acquainted therw*i*thall will give him thank*es* on my behalfe.
The truth is I had no intent to have offended any of the

---

[1] Egerton MS. 2598 (fol. 242–3) in the British Museum.

ministers there [in Scotland]. Yow know we are pressed with
examples of other Churches to the imbracinge of that most
counterfeyt and falsly patched vp government which is tearmed
the presbitery, a meere humane device devised by shiftinge and
sleight, attayned by tiranny and bloud, and mainteyned with
vntollerable pride and with most straunge boldnes in expoundinge the scriptures and falsifyinge of all antiquitye. In which
respect I thought it agreable with my duty and the since
beinge called to that place to give warninge by the miserable
estate of the Church of Scotland least we should fall into the
like desolation. But howsoever it is taken I shall be redy for
them : especially if I may crave your favor by satisfyinge the
particular poyntes conteyned in the sheet of paper here inclosed. For other matters towchinge the course which hath
been held for the erectinge of that government ever since
Iames the fifte I am well acquainted with yt. I have read of
the last stratageme and exployt at Strivelinge when the kinge
was taken. But peradventure yow may learne more therof
then is mentioned in our English late Chronicle of Scotland.
For of that poynt I have litle more then there is conteyned.
Furthermore I doe perceave vpon diverse occasions that the
chiefest of the ministers of Scotland (especially Mr Melvin
[probably Andrew Melville]) have procured sondry lettres from
Mr Beza and other learned men beyond the seas concerninge
theyr ratefyinge of the Church government there established.
Which lettres or the copyes of them if by the strength of your
device yow be able to compasse they will greatly pleasure me.
For thereby it will appere what very false reportes have been
made by them both of the kinge and of the Bishopes there.
Vpon which vntrue suggestions the sayd learned men did write
otherwise then they wold have done if they had knowen the
truth, I can not see how yow can accomplish this poynt except
yow insinuate your selfe into them as one desirous to embrace
theyr devices if yow might see the same confirmed by the
iudgmentes of Beza and other learned men of Fraunce &c:
Thervpon peradventure they will show yow the sayd lettres,
If also yow could procure the Copyes of theyr owne lettres
sent to Beza &c that were notable what paynes yow shall be

pleased to take herein, and to certifye me thereof from time to time whilest yow stay there yow may signify vnto me with all securitye if yow direct your lettres to Mr Ashly one of the Clark*es* of her Ma*iesties* privy counsell. But I wold have yow to seale such lettres as yow write vnto me and to inclose them in a letter to him of my direction to yow and then I am sure he will be very carefull to deliver them vnto me. Mr Dr Copcott my very frend I thinke will ioyne with me for your good favor in the premises: Yow may thereby as I suppose furnishe your selfe with good experience: and if hereafter yow shall have any occasion wherin I may doe yow any pleasure assure your selfe yow shall commaund me. And so with my harty commenda-tions I committ yow to god: from Lambeth ye 23 of December, 1589.

Yo*ur* Lovinge frend

Rich: Bancrofte[1].

[Some of the " Reasons alledged by the Arch B*isho*p of Canterbury, for D^r (Richard) Bancroft's being promoted to the B*isho*prick of London."][2]

" He was by his diligent search the first Detector of Martin Mar-Prelats Press & Books, where & by whom they were printed[3].

" He was an especiall Man, that gave the Instructions, to her Maj*es*ties learned Council, when Martin's Agents, were brought into the Star Chamber.

" By his advice, that Course was taken, w*hich* did principally stop Martin & his Fellow's [sic] mouths viz: to have them answered after their own vein in writing.

" By his diligence to find out certain Letters & writings,

---

[1] Only the signature and the words beginning with " from Lambeth " are in Bancroft's own handwriting.

[2] Baker MS. 36, pp. 333–5, in the University Library, Cambridge. It is possible that the original manuscript of which this is a copy, is to be found in Harleian MSS. 6848 or 6849 in the British Museum. I think that I have somewhere seen the original.

[3] P. 333.

Heare, o King, and dispise not ye counsell of ye poore, and let their complaints come before thee.

The King is a mortall man, & not God therefore hath no power over ye immortall soules of his subiects, to make lawes & ordinances for them, and to set spirituall Lords over them.

If the king have authority to make spirituall Lords & lawes, then he is an immortall God, and not a mortall man.

O King, be not seduced by deceivers to sin so against God whome thou oughtest to obey, nor against thy poore subiects who ought and will obey thee in all things with body life and goods, or else let their lives be taken from ye earth.

God save ye Kinge.

Spittlefeild neare London.   Tho: Helwys.

THOMAS HELWYS' AUTOGRAPH INSCRIPTION TO KING JAMES I, 1612. See Vol. I., page 252.

M^r: Cartwright & his complices, their setting up their Discipline secretly in most shires of the Realm, their Classes, their Decrees, & Book of Discipline were first detected." [1]

" By his only diligence, Penry's seditious writings were intercepted as they came out of Scotland, & delivered to the now *Lord* Keeper.

" His earnest desire, to have the slanderous Libels, against her Majestie answered, & some pains of his taken therein, wold not be omitted because they show his true Affection, & & [*sic*] dutifull heart unto her Highness." [2]

"Though he hath been carefull & zealous to suppress some sort of Sectaries, yet hath he therein shewed, no tyrannous Disposition, but with mildness & kind dealing, when it was expedient, hath reclaimed diverse." [3]

[1] P. 334.　　　　[2] P. 334.　　　　[3] P. 335.

XI

THE NAMES OF VARIOUS PERSONS WHO HAD BEEN
MEMBERS OF FRANCIS JOHNSON'S CONGREGATION
BEFORE 1613, INCLUDING THE NAMES OF SOME WHO
HAD WITHDRAWN FROM IT OR BEEN EXCOMMUNI-
CATED, AND OF OTHERS WHO HAD BECOME WAN-
DERERS

GATHERED FROM GEORGE JOHNSON'S "A discourse of some
troubles/", 1603 ; from "The Prophane Schisme of the Brownists
or Separatists", 1612 ; and from Christopher Lawne's "Brovvnisme
Tvrned The In-side out-ward", 1613

W. Adams
Henry [Henrie] Ainsworth
R. Appleby
William Asplin (?)
William Barbor [? Barbones[1]]
Elizabeth Bates
Robert Bayly [Baylie]
Mr. Bellot [Arthur (?) Billet]
Edward Benet
Mr. & Mrs. Thomas Bishop [Bishopp]
Francis Blackwell
Christopher Bowman, deacon, later an elder.
—— Braithwait, deacon.
Robert Bulward, excommunicated.
Thomas Canadine
Mr. Castel
Alexander Carpenter
Richard Clarke

[1] See E. Pagitt's "Heresiography", fourth edition, London, 1647, 4o,
p. 65.

George Cleaton
Iohn Clifton
Iohn [Jean] de Cluse [de l'Ecluse]
Thomas Cocky
Anne Colyer
G.[eorge] Colyer
Mr. Crud
Christopher Dickons
G. Dickons
William Eiles
Iohn Fovvler
R. Frank
William Gilgate, Ainsworthian, formerly a minister in England.
Mr. Greene
Mr. Hales [? Halies]
Mother Heas
Mistresse Hinton
Iudith Holder
William Holder
Henrie Homline
I. Huntley
Cvth.[bert] Hvtten (?)
Mr. Isaac
Robert Iackson
Lewis Jenkins
Francis Iohnson & his wife Mrs.
Tomison Iohnson
George Iohnson
Iacob Iohnson, who had returned to England before 1603.
Iohn Iohnson, Francis Johnson's father.
Mr. Knifton, an Elder.
Christopher Lavvne
Charles Leigh, Captain of the " Hopewell " in which Francis
    Johnson and Daniel Studley sailed for Canada.
Mr. [Nicholas ?] Ley [? Lee]
Richard Mansfield, Ainsworthian.
G. Marshal

George Martin
Henry May
Marie May [Maie], "the victualler".
Stanshal Mercer
Philipp Merriman, in 1603 a man of sixty years of age, who
    had been excommunicated "about 20. Years".
Thomas Michel [Mitchell]
Iohn Nicholas
Thomas Odal
Mr. Onyon
[Mrs (?) Catherine Onyon (?)]
Richard Ore
—— Pecksall, "the Prophet".
Father Perriman
Iohn Phelps
T. Pring
Abraham Pulbery [Pulburie]
Widdow Roules
Clement Sanders
Mat.[thew] Savnders [?]
Mr. [Thomas] Settel, a preacher, and about 1595 prisoner in
    the "Gate-House", London. [By 1609 he was in
    Norfolk.]
W. Simson, an Ainsworthian (?).
Mr. [Matthew ?] Slade, once an Elder.
Daniel Studley
Mr. & Mrs. Sutheby
Ioseph Tattam
Anthony Thatcher
Martin Thatcher
Edward Tolwine
Iohn Trappes
Ellen Vpton
B. W.
Roger Waterer
I. Whatley
I. Wheler

Geffrey Whittakers
" vvandering brethre*n*, (vvandering starres)", who go "hither
    and thither / to and from England abiding in no certaine
    place."
Iohn Beacham
William Shepheard
Iohn Nicholas
Richard Paris
David Bristoe
William Houlder.

XII

TWO DOCUMENTS RELATING TO THE CONTROVERSY BETWEEN THE BARROWISTS AND THOMAS DRAKES

[The "Seven Demands" of Francis Johnson and his Followers, 1595.][1]

SEVEN QVESTIONS which have ben propounded to divers of the Ministers of these assemblyes, with request that they would aunswer them directly and syncerely from the Scriptures. Which also still is desired at theyr hands.

1 WHether the Lord Iesus Christ have by his last Testament given vnto and set in his Church, sufficient ordinary offices, with theyr calling, vvorks, and maintenance, for the administration of his holy things, and

---

[1] First published on page 141 of [Francis Johnson's] "A TREATISE | [Device] Of the Ministerp of the Church | of England. | Wherein is handled this question, | Whether it be to be separated from, | or joyned vnto. | ... | Also in the end of the treatise, | Some notes touching the Lordes prayer. | SEVEN QVESTIONS. | ..." The work is a quarto, chiefly printed in Gothic Letter. No date or place of printing is given, but on p. 137 at the close of the main text is the date 1595. In the above citation I do not distinguish between the Gothic and the Roman type.

Wil.[liam] Euring in his "Ansvver to the Ten Covnter Demands Propovnded by T. Drakes", 1619, fortunately gives on Sigs. A₂ verso, and A₃ recto and verso, a copy of the Barrowists' "7 Demands", and remarks that they had been "propounded" "some good space since". Euring modifies the text a good deal in section 2, and slightly in some of the other sections. Without Euring's copy the original publication of the "7 Demands" might never have been identified as Francis Johnson's "Seven Questions" printed almost twenty-five years before Drakes' "Ten Counter Demands". At this period the word "demand" evidently could be used as a synonym for the word "question".

for the sufficient ordinary instruction guydance and service of his Church, to the end of the world, or no ?

2. Whether the offices of Pastors, Teachers, Elders, Deacons and Helpers, be those offices appoynted by Christ in his Testament, as aforesaid ? Or whether the present ecclesiasticall offices of Archbishops, Lordbishops, Suffraganes, Deanes, Subdeanes, Prebendaryes, Chauncelors, Priests, Deacons or half Priests, Archdeacons, Subdeacons, Commissaryes, Officials, Doctors, Proctors, Registers, Scribes, Apparitors, Parsons, Vicars, Curates, Stipendaryes, Vagrant peachers, Chapleynes or howse priests, Canons, Petticanons, Gospellers, Epistlers, Chaunters, Virgerers, Queristers, Organ-players, Churchwardens, Sidemen, Collectors, Clerks, Sextans, and the rest now had in these Cathedrall and parishionall assemblyes, be those offices appoynted by Christ in his Testament, as is aforesayd, or no ?

3. Whether the calling and entrance into these ecclesiasticall offices last aforesayd, theyr administration, and maintenance, now had and reteyned in England, be the maner of calling, administration, and maintenance, which Christ hath appoynted for the offices of his Church aboue named, or no ?

4. Whether every true visible Church be not a company of people called and separated out from the world and the false worship and wayes thereof by the word of God, and ioyned together in fellowship of the Gospell, by voluntary profession of the faith and obedience of Christ ? And whether the ecclesiasticall assemblyes of this land be such, or no ?

5. Whether the Sacraments [being seales of righteousnes which is by faith] may be administred to any other then the faithfull and theyr seed, or in any other Ministery and maner thẽ is prescribed by Iesus Christ the Apostle and high Priest of our profession ? And whether they be not otherwise administred in the Cathedrall and parishionall assemblyes of England at this day ?

6. Whether the book of common prayer with the feasts, fasts, holy dayes stinted prayers and leiturgy, prescribed therein and vsed in these assemblyes, be the true worship of God commaunded in his word, or the devise and invention of Man, for Gods worship and service.

7. Whether all Churches and people (without exception) be not bound in religion onely to receyv ãd submit vnto that Ministery, vvorship, and order which Christ as Lord and King hath given ãd appoynted to his Church: Or whether any man receyv and joyne vnto another, devised by man, for the service of God? And consequently, whether they which ioyne to the present ecclesiasticall Ministery, vvorship, and order of these Cathedrall and parishionall assemblyes, can be assured by the word of God they ioyne to the former ordeyned by Christ and not to the latter invented by Man, for the worship and service of God?

¶ Let him that readeth, consider.

[Woodcut border at the bottom of the page]

[Sig. A recto]   [Device]

Αντερώτήματα *Thomæ Draks.*[1]

T E N   C O V N T E R-
D E M A V N D S   P R O-
pounded to those of the Separati-
on, (or *English* Donatists) to be directly, and
distinctly answered.[2]

1. Hether, that their rent, Schisme, and Separation from the Church and Con-gregations of *England*, can (in any probabilitie) bee pleasing vnto God, seeing, it hath such vnhappy beginnings, the *a* first founder of it, comming to

Maister Bolton. *Iudas* his shamefull and fearfull ende, hanging himselfe: and
Maister Browne. the *b* second totally recanting it, and reioyning himselfe to our

---

[1] The "*s*" in "*Draks*" is very indistinctly printed and might easily be taken for an *i*, but I think that the reading here given is preferable.

[2] This work appears to have been composed of only four leaves and to have had no separate title-page. The last page is blank. No date and no place of printing are given, but the date is probably 1618 or 1619. It is uncertain whether the pages were numbered. There are a number of marginal corrections in the copy I have seen.

Church, as diuers of their proselites doe daily: seeing also it
hath had so small encreases, and so many dismall and fatall
euents, and diuisions: one side excommunicating the other,
some of them turning Anabaptists, and *c* others dying and
distracted, by reason of irresolution.

*Maister Nowell
of Sheldon in
Warwicke-shire,
&c.*

2. Whether, that the quintessenced profession, Religion
and discipline of these *Nouations* and *In-*

A   *nouators,*

[Sig. A verso]   [*Ten Counterdemaunds.*]

nouators, as it standeth in opposition to the Church of *England,*
and the rest of the reformed Churches) can bee of God, or, haue
any approbation from God, seeing that it hath no vertue, power
and efficacy in it (as the Gospell preached in our English
assemblies by Gods blessing abundantly hath) to winne, conuert,
and drawe vnto their partie and profession, *Atheists, Papists,
Heretikes, rude, profane* and *ignorant people*: The Apostles,
Euangelists, and ther [marginal correction: their] holy successors, conuerted all sorts vnto God, but these refined reformers,
onely seduce the sound, and peruert and estrange from vs, those,
that are otherwise well affected, and of some vnderstanding and
make them twofold more refractary then themselues.

3. Whether that (in the very separatists conscience) our
reformed assemblies, (wherein the Gospell of Christ is sincerely
preached and professed, and the Sacraments duly and rightly
administred) are worse then the Iewes *Synagogues,* in which
notwithstanding Christ his *Apostles* preached; & our *Ministers,*
worse then the *Scribes* and *Pharisees,* that sat in *Moses* Chaire,
when [marginal correction: whom] *Christ* commandeth the
people to heare, and obserue and doe, whatsoeuer (according to
Moses Lawe) they did bid them obserue. Wherefore (to reason
à minore ad maius) if our Lord Iesus, his Disciples, and the
people did not separate from their Synagogues and assemblies,
that were in faith and maners farre more defectiue then ours
are, much lesse ought they to separate from our Church and
assemblies, wherein, all the grounds of Christian Religion are
soundly held, and professed.   4. Whe-

Mat. 23. v. 2. 3.

[Sig. A 2 recto]   *Ten Counterdemaunds.*

4.   Whether that those great multitudes of people (though
hitherto wanting the pretended Church-constitution of the
Separatists) that euen fasting heard our Lord Iesus preach, and
professed themselues his Disciples, (albeit many of them were
drawen, not by doctrine but by miracles, report, & with a desire
to be fed) can with any reason bee denied to bee members of
the visible Church, and whither those three thousands [marginal
correction: thousand] which blessed *Peter* at one Sermon
conuerted (for they were baptized, continued in the Apostles
doctrine, fellowship, breaking of bread and praiers.) were not,
before that Presbyters and Deacons were chosen, true members
of a visible Church, and this cannot bee refuted, and why are
not our Church assemblies in *England*, (much more grounded
in the truth) &c. a true visible Church? and then with what
conscience, doe, or can these Separatists sequester and rent
themselues from them?

5.   Whether, (to ascend no higher, and neerer the Apostles
to me [marginal correction: time] as I might) that in *Con-
stantines* [marginal correction: *Constantine*] the first Christian
Emperours time, and euer since vnto M^r. *Iohn Caluins* dayes,
for the space of some thirteene hundred yeares, there was no
Christian Churches in *Asia, Africke, Europe,* because they had
the same outward constitution, formal State, *Bishops, Archbishops, Metropolitans,* & Church-gouernment (for substance and
substance of doctrine) that our English Church hath, and
retaineth.   And if those were true visible Churches, why are
not ours (also?)

6.   Whether, that the reformed Churches in the
                         A 2   lower

Mat. 14. 13.
14. 15. 16. 17.

Ioh. 6. 5. 10.
11.

Ioh. 6. 27.

Act. 2. 37. 38.
41.

[Sig. A 2 verso]   *Ten Counterdemaunds.*

lower, and higher *Germany*, in *France*, the Church of *Geneua*
&c. (that come neerer to their constitution and discipline, then
ours doe in England,) bee true visible Churches, or no? if they
be such, why then doe they not adioyne themselues to some of
them, but distast them as much as they doe ours?   And why

doe they not in iudgment assent vnto any or all of those reformed Churches, that with a ioynt consent (as may appeare by the harmonie of Confession [marginal correction: Confessions]) acknowledge the Church of England to be a true visible Church, and giue vnto it the right-hand of fellowship? how dare they refuse such a cloude of witnesses? will these μονόσοφοι put out all their eyes? is there no Church in the world but their Platonicall Idea?

7. How can the Church, or, Church-assemblies of England, bee false, Antichristian, bastardized, wherein the Gospell, is so soundly and solemnly and substantially taught and professed, and the Sacraments, so rightly administred and receiued, whose Bible translations, (specially the last English translation done by his Maiesty [marginal correction: Maiesties] command) are so pure, that the very Separatists rest in them : wherein are so many thousands, yea hundred thousands of true Converts and orthodoxe Christians, that hath bred and brought forth so many excellent and renowned *Martyrs*, who haue sealed the trueth of our religion with their bloud, and died members of the protestant Churches; wherein so many Christian *exiles* are comfortably harboured, wherein so many sound, religious and learned *Pastors, Doctors, Preachers,* as (for proportion) no Country in the world
can

[Sig. A 3 recto]   *Ten Counterdemaunds.*

can afford the like; and by whose doctrine, writings, disputes, (not to speake of the Magistrates sword) the *Romish Ierico* hath bin more shaken, and the second beast the Antichrist, more fatally wounded, then by any nationall Church whatsoeuer: and which Church, and the members thereof, haue beene so wonderfully blessed and protected, and so strangly deliuered from the rage, tumults, designes, treasons, conspiracies of the Romish Antichrist and all his adherents: and in which Churches (as one of the princiall [principall] Separatists I. R. [? Iohn Robinson] in his admonition *ad lectorem,* in his owne name and in the name of his faction, lately prefixed before the third booke of M. Robert Parker, de politia ecclesi. [title underlined by the

corrector] pag. 368. confesseth, that the grace of God by the
Gospell, in respect of the cheife heads of true Christian faith,
by diuers of the faithfull preached, doth so abound, that there
are very many godly and holy men in these assemblies, both of
Reformitants and Conformitants, which they acknowledge for
brethren in Christ &c. We haue (by their owne confession)
sound faith, and holinesse, why then doe they or how dare they
sunder and rent themselues from such a Church, and why will
they for accidents and circumstances, denie and renounce the
substance of a Church? And if they (vpon bettercōsideration
[*sic*]) esteẽe [marginal correction: esteeme] vs brethren, with
what warrant cã they seperate from holy brethren in Christ, *is
it not good and pleasant for to see brethren to dwell together in
vnitie?* Did not the conuerts in S. Peters dayes continue dayly
with one accord in the Temple &c. And why doe not our
Separatists[,] who would
be

[Sig. A 3 verso] *Ten Counterdemanunds.* [sic]

accounted? [*sic*, and the interrogation point has been crossed out
by the corrector] conuerted Saints[,] imitate them. must wee
leaue and forsake a goodly Cittie, for the weaknesse of *the walls?*

Act.
2. 46.

8. How can the formall state (as they call it) of the
Prouinciall, Diocesan, Cathedrall & Parishionall Churches of
England, and the regiment thereof, be vnlawfull, papall, Antichristian? And how doe, or, can the Lawes of the land, and
Ecclesiasticall Cannons confirme it? seeing that the name,
calling & office of BB: [Bishop] whether we respect ordination
of ministers or power of iurisdiction, is (as hath ben, & will be
proued) for substance expressed in diuers places of the new
Testament; seeing, it hath had a continuall succession from
the Apostles time to this day, as all auncient Fathers and
Counsells acknowledge: and seeing that (at least) this formall
estate of *Diocesan, Parishionall* and *Cathedrall* Churches, hath
bin in vse, long before Antichrist was hatched, for the Pope
was not Antichrist before he had gotten the Title of vniuersall
Bishop, nor complete vntill he had gotten into his hands both
swords, that is, both Ciuill and Ecclesiasticall *Dominion*: Doth

Anno.
1607.

not euery Bishop amongst vs, euery Pastor and ecclesiasticall officer, abiure the *Prpes* [marginal correction: *Popes*] vsurped supremacie? Doe not our statutes, and Cannons directly make againg [marginal correction: against] papistry and Idolafry [marginal correction: Idolatry]? What will Sathan expell Sathan, and will the members of Antichrist fight against Antichrist? And admitt all bee, as you pretend, doe we not (at least) kill Antichrist with his owne sword and weapons?

9. Whether, any new lawes can, or ought to be enacted, or any further reformation made without

the

[Sig. A 4 recto]   *Ten Counterdemaunds.*

the Christian Princes or Magistrates consent, or euer in a well ordered Church hath bene enacted, or made [marginal correction: ":"] and whether, they haue done well, to seperate with, [*sic*, with the comma crossed out by the corrector] out the Kings Maiesties leaue and licence, and consent of the state?

10. Whether, it were not the separatists best course, toreturne [*sic*] to Gods true Church and people, from which (vpon some concealed hard dealing) they haue made an vnlawfull rent, and therein to confer with the best learned, and if still their consciences be somewhat tender, to supplicate for some fauour and liberty, or if they will not take this course, whether it were not good for them, for the avoiding
of scandall, and in expectance of some prosperous successe, by the permission of our
noble King, and honourable Counsell:[1] to remoue into *Virginia*, and
make a plantation there, in
hope to conuert in-
fidels to Christi-
anitie?

FINIS.

[1] *Sic*, but the colon has been crossed out by the corrector.

XIII

PAPERS OF HENRY JACOB'S WRITTEN DURING THE YEARS 1603—1605

[A Copy of the Text of Henry Jacob's Letter to the Puritan Preachers, sent from Woodstreet, London, on June 30, 1603, with the accompanying form to be signed for use in connection with the presentation of the Millenary Petition to King James I.][1]

Moreover I ame to let you vnderstand, y^t many learned and godly ministers *are about to exhibite* to ye Kings maiestie à Petition, for the reformation of thing*es* amisse to o*ur* Church. Whervnto à consent of as many, as conveniently we can gett, is very behooefull [?]. my opinion and truste is concerninge you, that you wilbe, not only à p*ar*taker, but also à furtherer of this Christian dewty ; I haue sent you heere inclosed, ye forme to be subscribed by all such as haue good-will [?] to this purpose./ I praye you, let me haue an awnsweare [?] heerof from you, asone [as soon] as you may ; with so many of your well affected frends hands therevnto as shalbe thought good./ It is not intended, that your names shalbe rashly shewed to any mans preiudice, but reserved to a fitt opportunity, if we shall p*er*ceaue that they altogether beinge brought forth, will further o*ur* desires and sute ; of ye good succese wherof, we conceaue good hope, thank*es* be to god./ Thus beseechinge god to keepe and sainctify vs for his service and to geue vs Wisedome in all

[1] Harl. MS. 6849, fol. 254.

thing*es*. I bid you hartely farewell. Woodstreet in London.
30. of Iune 1603.

Yours to his powre,

Henry Iacoob

I could Wishe you to conferre with
D^r. Airey about this matter.

———————————

The copie of Henry Iacoob his letters,
Written to procter Dale ; and by him
shewed to m^r Searchfeeld.—5. Iulij.
and by him shewed, to .R. H.—6°. Iulij.
1603.

The copie of the subscription

We whose names are vnder Written, doe agree *to make our
humble* petition to ye Kings ma*ie*stie that y^e *present state of* our
Church may be further *reformed in all things* needfull accordinge
to the rule of god*es* holy woord, and agreeable to example of
other reformed Churches, which haue restored both the doctryne
and disciplyne, as it was *deliuered by* our *Sauior Christ*, and his
holy Apostells.

[The Text of a later, undated, general Letter, also sent from
Woodstreet by Henry Jacob with an abbreviated text of the
earlier form of subscription and a list of abuses which the
Puritans wished removed.]

[" Mr Iacobs | papers."][1]

Reverend, & wellbeloved, notwithstanding I suppose you have
ben already written vnto, or at at [*sic*] the least have ben

---

[1] MS. 113, fol. 242–253, in Lambeth Palace Library, London, first
published by me in " The Review and Expositor" (Louisville, Kentucky)
for October, 1907, pp. 489–513, under the title, " Lost Prison Papers of
Henry Jacob." This letter, as well as all the following documents here
included relating to Jacob, are to be found in the above-mentioned pages
of this one manuscript. One paper entitled, "Kneeling in ye very act of
Eating and Drinking | at the L. Table is simply evill", as well as some
minor jottings by Jacob, I have not attemped to present here.

communicated with by those who have ben written vnto by som from hence to procure a consent of the faithfull Ministers of your Country [?] according to yᵉ tenure [?] of yᵉ inclosed, yet I thought good againe & that by advice of others heere with vs by a word or two to stirre vp your godly minds to this necessary duty, & the rather because they to whom the blemishes of our Church are profitable & in their conceipt honorable leve no stone vnremoved to hinder a further reformation. Besides the tyme draweth neere wherein the declaration of your consent in yⁱˢ busynes will be of great vse, & therefore yᵉ matter requireth the more expedition. It is not intended yᵗ your names, which we desyre to be sent vp hither, shall be rashly shewed to your prejudice, but reserved to a fit opportunity if vpon the exhibiting of our peticion the same shall be found expedient for yᵉ further-ance of our cause, of yᵉ good successe whereof we conceave good hope thanks be to God. Thus beseeching God to keepe & sanctify vs for his service & to Give vs wisdom in all things I bid you hastily farewell. Woodstreet in London.

We whose names are vnderwritten do agree to make &c holy word. ——. And agreeably &c Apostles. —— In particular we desyre the removing of the Ecclesiasticall Courts, yᵉ dumb & idle ministers, Nonresidencyes, offensive & superstitious Cere-monies, Subscription beyond Law, the Oth ex Officio, Excom-munication for trifles, by Lay men, &c.

If any think not good to go so far as the example of other Churches &c let them stay at the first line. If any thinke good to descend into particulars let yᵉᵐ go beyond yᵉ 2 line, & reckon vp as many & as few as they please.

[An undated Petition written by Henry Jacob to the Bishop of London, requesting that he may be released from imprison-ment in the Clink.][1]

I humbly beseech your Lordship [the Lord Bishop of London] to consider Christianly of my estate. I am committed by your

---

[1] This petition appears to have been written not long before April 3, 1605.

selfe & others in authority with you for publishing my Treatise,
which is written only in way of Reasoning & not inveyghing
against our Church Traditions. I vse not therein any detracta-
tion or reproch any way: I do but argu[e ?] & reason the matter,
being no new but an ancient controversy amon[g] vs. I beseech
you waigh with your selfe, what evill is there in th[is ?] wherin
nothing is said but only against Ecclesiasticall Vnwritten Traditions.   Specially considering the Evidence which is...against
them, the consent of many Christian Churches & Writers, my
faithfull care to give heerein to Cesar whatsoever is Cesars & to
God that which is Gods, the necessit[y ?] of mine owne defense
& purgation as also this present time of yᵉ Kings first entrance,
& other circumstances[1].   I hope it is not vnlawfull nor new for
Christian Subjects lowly to desyre reformation of such things at
the Princes hands. Besids it would have ben thought yᵗ The[re ?]
had ben small feare of God in vs or respect to yᵉ Scriptures
honour against vnwritten Traditions (for so still [?] I say we do
conceave of this whole matter) if no[ne ?] of vs had now spoken
in this cause. We are condemned by many, & verily we
oug[ht] so to be as Schismatikes & contentious persons if
we should differ from you & yet gi[ve] forth vnto yᵉ world
no Reasons of our difference.   While we were silent & sai[d]
nothing we were insulted vpon for a long time togeather. Now
when one of vs doth...some Reasons with all due respect, is it
an offense to do it? We have consciences desyrous to serve
God by yᵉ...of his word which move vs to do this thing. Gods
word only stayeth yᵉ conscience: & these Reasons included [?]
are built only...vpon. Let yᵉ Reasons therefore [?] be...
answered [as ?] you sayed vnto me yᵗ they shalbe; & then
let obstinacie & perversnes where it is found be censured.
The Kin[gs ?] first entrance & setling among vs (whom God
long preserve) requireth also of vs that we should shew causes
if we will dissent from others: chiefly sith he hath often
signifyed he will reforme whatsoever can be shewed contrary
to Gods word. Yea he hath specially willed vs to...by patience
& well grounded Reasons to perswade all yᵉ rest to like of
our ju[dg ?]ments. How can we perswade all yᵉ rest to like

[1] I give in this place what seems to have been the original text.

of our judgments, but by publishing Reasons to al[l?] And
now [?] seeing I have don no more I beseech you let not y^s seame
so great a fault. Further ye pr[o]vokings of many & their vrging
vs to shew som reasons, yea their plaine affirming y^t we have
nothing to say for our selves, which not only in speach they
expresse very often in most frequent & honorable Assemblies,
also in a nomber of printed bookes, togeather with ye generall
expectation of all men at y^s season wi[ll?] excuse (I hope) y^is y^t
I have don humbly & dutifully. But more y^en y^is the Answer
from Oxford to ye Ministers [?pe]tition hath vanely traduced
me as a schismatike in y^is respect. Doth not all equitie &
religion per[mit?] me correspondently to publish Reasons for
my necessary cleering? I beseech your Lordship waigh with
your self these things indifferently. moreover my booke is
dedicated to ye King to whose godly co[nsi]deration &
clemency I do alltogeather submit my selfe. His Majestie
I hear hath a good while sinc[e] taken knowledge of it.
I doubt not his grace is minded y^t my Reasons (whatsoever
they be) should by better grounds of Divinity [be?] reproved
before I should be thus punished. In my Treatise whatsoever
words I have besides Arguments, they all tend to y^is y^t we should
all dutifully seeke to his Majestie fo[r] reliefe to our consciences
in this behalfe, who only hath authority vnder God to give
generall redr[esse?] in these things. Where[fore?] I beseech
your L. to remember y^t I freely & from my heart do give y^e
King his just & full supremacie over all persons causes ecclesiasticall whatsoever, reserving no jot of power heer but what is
proper to Christ alone. viz. to be our absolut Prophet & sole
Teacher in all matters of ye Church[.] If Humane discretion
will...alone to warrant vs any thing of y^is sort, we feare him
who saithe [he?] will not give any glory to an other. And who
can think that Christs Testament is no perfecter in tea[ching?]
vs Church matters, then it is in shewing vs Civill? In a word
therefore, whatsoever I have wri[tten, (?)] or do hold, cometh to
y^is one point (which is ye old profession of Protestants) to refuse
Vnwritten Ecclesiasticall Traditions or inventions of men. I do
in this treatise no more, neither intend I any more, ye Lord is
witnes. I say of all but as Cyprian said long ago of one Ec-

clesiasticall Tradition: Vnde est ista traditio? Vtrumnè de
Dominicâ et Evangelicâ authoritate descendens, aut de Aposto-
licis preceptis et Epistolis veniens? Implying y^t otherwise it is
to be refused whatsoever it be. And touching ye true state of
Christs Visible Church, as Chrysostom (if it be his) in y^e
Vnperfect worke saith; Ecclesia cognoscite tantum odò per
Scripturas. And as Augustin, Nec ego, nec tu, sed Chris*t*us
interroge*tur* vt indicet Ecclesiam suam. Lege Evangeliu*m*, et
respondet tibi &c. w*hi*ch I hope is no evill now for me to affirme
likewise. And more y^{en} y^{is}, or y^t w*hi*ch necessarily cometh from
y^{is} I do not affirme. Last of all as I came to yo*ur* Lordship
freely w*i*thout comma*n*deme*nt* when only my servant told me
from yo*ur* messingèr y^t yo*ur* L. would speake w*i*th me, so I
beseech you deale kindly w*i*th me. I beseech you restore me
to my poore wife & 4 small children, who w*i*thout my inlarge-
me*nt* are in much distresse.

Your Lorships humble suppliant
Henry Iacob prisoner in y^e
Clink.

To the right reverend the Lord
Bishop of London.

[Henry Jacob's Copy of his Subscription.]

April. 4. An°. 1605.

Whereas allmost 3. quarters of a yeare since I published a
booke intituled, Reasons taken out of Gods word &c. I do
heere faithfully promise to disperse no more of them, nor to be
a meanes that any other shall, but to hinder the dispersing of
all that shall com into my power.

Also I do promise that I will not speak against ye Church-
governme*nt* & orders now among vs established by Law, for
the time of my being vpon baile & till I shall see what
Reasons against my opinion will com forth w*i*thin this halfe
yeare. W*hi*ch if I shall perceave to be good & well grounded
on Gods word, then I will speake for the said Church-governme*nt*
& orders now established.

Howsoever, I will allwayes heereafter behave my selfe quietly, & as one carefull of the Churches peace, God assisting me.

Henry Iacob.

The first promise I may easily keepe, seeing I have none of those bookes left.

The second limiteth a time viz. within this halfe yeare, wherein I forbeare to speak against their orders. Yet in yᵉ meane while my booke speaketh my minde & judgment most plainly every where.

Thirdly I will allwayes heereafter behave myselfe quietly, which also I have don allwayes heeretofore, I praise God.

Let all men vnderstand that touching yᵉ first promise I may easily performe it, considering I have never a one of these bookes in my power nor am like to have: except only one which I have & will keepe for mine owne vse.

Touching the second I do promise within halfe a yeare not to speak against yᵉ publike orders in question. Neither yet in this while am I altogeather silent in the cause, for my booke speaketh sufficiently, & sheweth my judgment therein; which I still do hold, though for a time I cease to talke against yᵉ matters in question.

Touching the third I promise to behave my selfe quietly allwayes heereafter; which yet also I have don heeretofore, as my conscience beareth me witnes.

　　Whosoever do make any other sense of my words they do me wrong. Henry Iacob.

For the time of my baile shall be no longer if it like my selfe. I can appeare before Authoritie & so withdraw my baile at that time, if I think good, & if my baile cease not before. Besides the true construction of yᵉ very words do shew yᵗ halfe a yeare is the appointed & vttermost terme of this my promise. The 2. clauses are conjoyned & referred togeather to these words in yᵉ end of the sentence ["within this halfe yeare"]. Neither can there be any other perfect & proper sense of this whole speach. The Archbishop expresly said to me yᵉ day before [i.e., April 3,

1605.], y^t ye maner of bailes is to be but for a time, & mine should be but for a time, & for no long time. Vnto y^{is} I have relation heere where I speake of the time of my being vpon baile.

[The earliest completely developed Independent, or Congregational, Puritan (non-separatist) Catechism in existence: written by Henry Jacob.][1]

Principles & Foundations
of Christian Religion.

---

1.   Concerning God.

Question.

What doest thou believe concerning God?

1.
God.

Answer.

I believe that There is [1.] one God [2.] Creator & [3.] Governor of all things; who is distinguished into the [4.] Father, the Sonne, & the Holy Ghost.

2.   Concerning Man.

Question.

What doest thou believe concerning Man?

2.
Man.

Answer.

All men by Nature are [1.] wholly corrupted with sinne through [2.] Adams fall; & so are become [3.] bond-slaves to Sathan, & subject to eternall damnation.

3.   The Author & Principall Meanes
of Salvation.

Question.

What meanes is there to escape this damnable estate?

3.
The Authour
of salvation.

Answer.

The holy & heavenly meanes of salvation given vs of God are of 2. sorts. Principall, & Instrumentall.

[1] This Catechism, though undated, was evidently written in 1604 or 1605.

Question.

What is the Principall meanes?

Answer.

Hebr. 12. 2.
I. Tim. 2. 5.
I. Cor. 3. 10.
Act. 4. 12.
Ioh. 14. 6.
Isa. 42. 8.
I Tim. 3. 16.

The Principall meanes is Iesus Christ, (yea indeed he is the [1.]whole Authour being the eternall Sonne of God & also true Man . who perfitly alone by himselfe accomplisheth all things that are needfull for the salvation of mankind.

4.   The Instrumentall Inward meanes.

4.
Our Instru-
mentall In-
ward mea-
nes.

Question.

What are the Instrumentall meanes of Salvation?

Answer.

They are of 2. sortes: Inward, & Outward.

Question.

By what Inward meanes is a man made partaker of Christ & his benefits?

Answer.

A man of a [1.]contrite & humble spirit by Faith alone appre-hending & applying to himselfe [2.][*sic*] Christ in his 3. maine Offices (that is, as he is *our* Prophet, King, & Priest) with all his Merits in them, is justifyed before God & sanctifyed? [*sic*]

Question.

What is Christs Propheticall Office: or what did Christ for vs as he is *our* Prophet & Teacher. [*sic*]

Answer.

[1] Ioh. 4. 25
and 16. 13.

[1.]He himselfe (in his owne word & Testament only) teacheth vs all things Religious as properly belonging to the Church, both Outward & Inward.   Wherein standeth his whole true Worship, & the meanes of *our* salvation.

Question.

What is Christs Kingly Office. [*sic*]

Answer.

He himselfe alone [1.]ruleth & guideth vs Spiritually.   And this is called Christs [2.]Kingdom of grace./

Question.

How may we further know this his Kingdom of Grace?

Answer.

Christs Kingdom of Grace heere in this life is of 2. sorts: Inward & Outward.   And this later is the meanes & ordinary cause of the former.

Question.

Wherein standeth Christs Inward spirituall Kingdom?

Answer.

In that he ruleth & guideth *our* [1.] hearts by his Spirit to the obedience of his Law, w*hi*ch is his word.

Question.

Wherein is his Outward Spirituall Kingdom?

Answer.

In that by himselfe or by his Spirit in his Apostles w*hi*ch is all one, (& by none other) he constituteth & injoyneth the forme of all his Visible Churches w*i*th their Ministeries, & admitteth (wheresoever) none other.   Also in that he ordinarily ruleth, guideth, & blesseth vs in them only by his owne Ministeries & ordinances, & by none other.

Question.

What is Christs Priestly Office?

Answer.

To offer vnto God a Sacrifice allsufficient for all *our* sinnes, w*hi*ch he did by his infinit Sufferings [?] in this life, & to make Intercession for vs in Heaven by vertue thereof for ever.   And all this in his owne only person w*i*thout any other w*i*th him whomsoever.

[Question.]

Doth not Christ save vs only by his death & sufferings?

Answ.

No; He redeemeth vs in deed only by his death & Sufferings: but he is *our* Saviour & mediator by his Doctrine teaching vs, by his kingdom ruling vs, & by his death once vpon y*e* Gibbet.

That is not by any one, but by all 3. his...& proper Offices apprehended & applyed to vs by a true faith.

Question.

What vse hath *our* Sanctification in this life?

Answer.

Our Sanctification, *our* Obedience to the Word, or our Good works have 2. vses./ 1. They are the fruits & sure witnesses of true faith justifying vs. 2. They are the high way necessary for all men to walke in vnto salvation.

5. The Instrumentall Outward Meanes.

Question.

5.
Our Outward meanes.

What are the ordinary Outward meanes given by Christ for his outward true worship & for *our* obtayning of faith & salvation?

Answer.

The ordinary Outward meanes (wh*i*ch Christ as *our* Prophet & King gave vs & sanctifyed for vs) are of 2. sortes: Generall, & Speciall.

Question.

What is the ordinary Generall meanes?

Answer.

The ordinary Generall meanes is, to be joyned a Member in som true Visible or Ministeriall Church of Christ.

Question.

Are there many in the world, or is there only one Vniversall Visible Church?

Answer.

In the time of the Law there was only one Visible Church vnder one High priest of the Iewes. But since the Gospell went out of Ierusalem into all the world, by ye Divine ordinance there allwayes have ben & are many in nomber, & not only One Visible or Ministeriall Church of Christ, as the Catholiks do falsly believe.

Question.

How then do we say in the Creed; I believe the Catholik, y^t is, the Vniversall Church?

Answer.

There we signify the Invisible Church Catholik, either Militant,
or els the whole nomber of Gods Elect in Heaven & in Earth.
It can not be contrary to yᵉ Acts & Writings of yᵉ Apostles,
where a multitude of proper & distinct Ministeriall Churches
are shewed vs: one at Corinth, an other at Antioch, an other at
Ephesus & many in Asia, many in Iudea, many in Galatia,
Macedonia, &c. &c.

Question.

What is a true Visible or Ministeriall Church of Christ?

Answer.

A true Visible or Ministeriall Church of Christ is a particular
Congregation being a spirituall perfect Corporation of Believers,
& having power in it selfe immediatly from Christ to administer
all Religious meanes of faith to the members thereof.

Question.

How is a Visible Church constituted & gathered?

Answer.

By a free mutuall" consent of Believers joyning & covenanting
to live as Members of a holy Society togeather in all religious
& vertuous duties as Christ & his Apostles did institute &
practise in the Gospell. By such a free mutuall consent also
all Civill perfect Corporations did first beginne.

Math. 18. 19, 20.

Question.

If every particular Church be an intire Church & independent
of any other, how shall Vnitie be preserved & obedience to
Magistrats?

Answer.

Vnitie in conscience standeth not vpon one Church or Pastor
over the rest, but vpon yᵉ one Word & Testament of Christ
taught ordinarily by that Church vnto vs whereof we are; as
Gods Ordinance is. Also thus ²most easily ¹may yᵉ meanest
next dwelling Magistrat ³rule any Church in outward peace;
yea in peace & concord of Religion far more easily & more
readily then otherwise.

Question.

What are the ordinary speciall meanes of faith ?

Answer.

In speciall sort faith cometh only by yᵉ preaching of the word, & increaseth dayly by it, as also by the administration of the Sacraments, Discipline, & Prayer.   And heerein consisteth the whole true outward Worshipping of God.

Question.

What is the Word that is preached vnto vs. [*sic*]

Answer.

It is the Word of God.   That is, his Will & Testament revealed & confirmed vnto vs in yᵉ holy Scriptures only.

Question.

What is the effect & scope of the Scriptures ?

Answer.

Their scope is to specify & shew most perfectly all the wayes of worshipping God a right, & so also yᵉ whole meanes of *our* salvation.

Question.

W*hi*ch are the holy Scriptures. [*sic*]

Answer.

The Bookes of yᵉ Prophets & the Apostles, called the Old & New Testament.

Question.

From what authority com they ?

Answer.

Those holy men of God (the Prophets & Apostles) writ them as they were inspired by yᵉ Holy Ghost.

Question.

How know we that they have Divine authoritie, & were written by inspiration of the Holy Ghost ?

Answer.

First the tradition of all times telleth vs so much. Secondly & chiefly the Heavenly matter contained in them vnder such simplicity of words doth now assure vs of it; with many other like reasons taken out of the Scriptures themselves.

Question.

What short Summe have we of all the holy Scriptures, as concerning any duty which we ought to do?

Answer.

The 2. Tables divided into 10. Commandements are a short & perfect Summe of all the Scriptures.

....
....[1]

Question.

Is there not then any outward thing Indifferent.

Answer.

Yea, there are many indifferent Civill matters. But of y⁰ parts of Divine Service & Church vse, there is nothing at all Indifferent. All such things are heere simply commanded or forbidden.

....

Question.

How many Sacraments are there; or holy Signes?

Answer.

Two; Baptisme, & the Lords Table. One other also may be reckoned as a holy Signe of lesse dignity & inferior nature; yᵗ is, Laying on of hands. But beside these Christs Testament knoweth none.

Question.

Wherein standeth the Churches holy Government [?]

Answer.

In their Election of Ministers, & Their Spiritual Correction of offenders.

---

[1] The portions here omitted are questions and answers concerning the Commandments.

Question.

Is it Christs ordinance y^t ye whole Church should Elect their Ministers, & Correct their Offenders?

Answer.

They are to do no more of necessity, & in their ordinary carriage, but freely to consen[t] to their Guides preparing & directing every matter.

Question.

What Ministers ought the Church to chose for her ordinary guidance & government.

Answer.

A Pastor or Bishop, with Elders, & Deacons.

Question.

What is ye Pastors Office?

Answer.

In Gods & in ye Churches Name to administer the Wo[rd, (?)] the holy Signes, the holy Government, & publik Prayer. Not any one, or so[me?] of these, but all.

Question.

What are the Elders?

Answer.

The Pastors assistants & coadjutors in ye holy government.

Question.

What are the Deacons?

Answer.

They are faithfull men trusted to gather & distribut ye Church[es?] publik treasure for Ecclesiasticall vses.

Question.

Wherein standeth ye Churches spirituall Correction of Offenders which is properly called the holy Discipline.

Answer.

In their Admonishing (twise or thrise at least) & Exhorting to repentance, & y^en in cutting of & Excommunicating ye vnrepentan[t.]

Question

What is Prayer ?

Answer.

A Calling vpon God in *our* wants & necessities. Whereof ye Lords Prayer is a perfect rule & direction for vs.

6.   The End of all.

Question

What is the estate of all men after death ?

Answer.

All men shall rise againe with their owne bodyes to the last judgment. W*h*ich being ended, the godly shall possesse the Kingdom of heaven: but the Vnbelievers & wicked shalbe in Hell tormented with the Divell & his Angells for ever.

[A detached Definition by Henry Jacob of a "true Visible or Ministeriall Church of Christ".]

A true Visible or Ministeriall Church of Christ is a constant & comple[te ?] societie of Christians or spirituall Body politike ordayned by Christ in his word, w*h*ich any one member the[re] of (having neede) may (& must on occasion) go vnto, consult with, heare & obey intirely & wholly togeather & yet with keeping due order & distinction of degrees the[y] all of them being vnited vnder one Ecclesiasticall govern*m*ent with themselves & proper vnto y^{em}.

A third humble Supplication of many faithfull
Subjects in England, falsly called Puritans directed
to ye Kings Ma*i*estie. 1605[1].

In most humble wise doe beseeche y*o*ur Ma*i*estie, a great nomber through out y*o*ur realme of y*o*ur Ma*i*est*ies* sworne

---

[1] Only the title of this "Supplication" was originally written by Henry Jacob, but he evidently corrected it throughout. The document as at first drawn up contained six numbered sections, but Jacob does not seem finally to have approved of this arrangement. I give here therefore the corrected text. The title as originally written was "The second humble Supplication...."

loyall subiect*es* and most dutifull people. Forasmuch as wee are in conscience throughly p*e*rswaded, that Gods most holy word in the New Testament is absolutely p*e*rfect, for delivering the whole maner of Gods worship, the holy government & forme of all his Churches, p*a*rticularly specifying vnto vs all things whatsoeu*er*, both inward and outward, great and small therein as y° Old Testament did vnto the Iewes, Except only meere circumstances of Tyme, Place, Person &c w*hi*ch have ben, are, and must be variable by necessity of nature; So that wee cannot p*e*rceiue anie humane Ecclesiasticall tradition whatsoever, as being simply w*i*thout Gods word, to be lawfull. And yet we yo*ur* Ma*ie*sties said loyall Subjects are forced against o*ur* consciences to submit o*ur* selves to such vnlawfull Traditions & Inventions of men in y° Churches governm*ent*, ministery, & Divine Service, to the high displeasure of Allmightie God against vs, and the ruine of y° soules of many. Considering also that this is a point singularly making to the honor of Christ Iesus. and to the magnifying of his loving care for his Churches, namely to believe that he left vs his word so p*e*rfect (as hath ben said) in all things Ecclesiasticall and touching the Soule: & contrariwise greatly derogating to Christs personall most perfect Propheticall Office, & also to his Kingly Office to say y*t* he hath not in his word so perfectly p*r*ovided for vs, but hath left sundry of these things to y° discretion of men. And because thus indeed to honor Christ and his word as by this meanes wee shall and ought to doe, no way harmeth the State nor the Princes authority, peace, & [Marginal note: "See o*ur* Protestation of y° Kings Supremacie."] security; but doth truly advaunce & blesse all estates, when they shew them selves helpfull & favorable herein. And Considering that it maketh singularly to vnity and agreement in Religion, when our wholl forme of Ecclesiasticall orders & exercise of religion shall be held by vs to be specifyed exactly in Scripture. W*hi*ch happy fruit appeareth comfortably in all those Christian Churches of this day y*t* do want those Traditions & Humane Hierarchie w*hi*ch are among vs. As namely in the in the [*sic*] well ordered and peaceable Churches of the French and Dutch, w*hi*ch by yo*ur* Ma*ie*sties gracious protection and allowaunce doe liue within

your Realme, and also in all the Churches of the Countryes
of Fraunce Scotland, Low Countryes, and your Ma*iesties* owne
Ilands of Iersey and Garnsey.   In these it is much to be regarded (to Gods great praise be it spoken) that there are no open
dissentions in matters of religion among them selves but most
rare concord; w*hi*ch wee think cannot be, nor ever wilbe found
elswhere, where humane Tradic*i*ons are professedly observed
besides Gods word.   As wee see by experience here in England,
where grevious distraction of myndes among o*u*r selves in
point*es* of religion appeareth, only because wee are not resolved (as it doth seeme) simplie and absolutely to rest on the
written word.

All w*hi*ch things considered, as also that wee y*ou*r Ma*iesties*
sworne loyall subiect*es* aforesaid haue ben now a great manie
Yeres grevously afflicted and molested, defamed, impoverished,
yea and otherwise extraordinarily punished, for no other cause
in the world, but only for our conscience in the matter before
rehersed, w*hi*ch yet wee cannot discerne, but that it is a most
Christian, holy, and right opinion.   Therfore it may please
y*ou*r gracious Ma*iesty* of your Princly regard towards the glory
of God and vs y*ou*r ever faithfull subiect*es*, to tolerate and to
graunt vnto so manie of vs as shall declare that o*u*r consciences
are in this respect constreyned and bound before God, to
Assemble togeather somwhere publikly to y*e* Service & Worship
of God, to vse & enioye peaceably among o*u*r selves alone the
wholl exercyse of Gods worship and of Church Government viz.
by a Pastor, Elder, & Deacons in o*u*r [?] severall Assemblie[s]
w*i*thout any tradic*i*on of men whatsoeu*er*, according only to
the specification of Gods written word and no otherwise, w*hi*ch
hitherto as yet in this o*u*r present State we could never enjoye.

Provided alwayes, that whosoeu*er* will enter into this way,
1 shall before a Iustice of peace first take the oath of your
Ma*iesties* supremacy & royall authority as the Lawes of y*e*
2 Land at this present do set forth the same; And shall also
afterwards keepe brotherly com*m*union w*i*th the rest of our
English Churches as they are now established, according as
3 the French and Dutch Churches do; And shall truly pay all
payment*es* and dutyes both ecclesiasticall and civill, as at this

present they stand bound to pay in anie respect whatsoever;
4 And if anie trespas be committed by anie of them whether
Ecclesiastically or Civilly against good order and Christian
obedience; That then the same person shalbe dealt withall
therein by anie of your Maiesties Ciuill Magistrates, and by the
same Ecclesiasticall government only wherevnto he ordinarily
ioyneth him self, according as to Iustice apperteyneth, and not
to be molested by anie other whomsoever.

Most humbly beseeching your Maiestie with all, to forbid
others to revile vs, & to accuse vs of comitting schisme in this
doing. which iustly wee know they cannot accuse vs of. Considering that wee doe not pretend herein to haue anie thing
but that which the Scripture deliuereth even by the opinion of
the learnedest that mislike our desyer, Considering also that
this is the wholl somme of that which wee professe in our
differing from our bretheren, namely that the Scriptures are
absolutely perfect for vs forever in matters Ecclesiasticall: And
this wee are well assured is no Schismaticall assertion. Neither
shall it seeme strange wee hope that wee crave here of your
Maiestie, & of your most honorable Counsell this benefit in
Religion only for some, namely for those whose consciences are
perswaded herein; doing by this practise otherwise then heeretofore we have don. For seeing wee see, that numbers of
Christians of all degrees in England are not yet perswaded of
this Article of religion (as wee are, and as, wee in the presence
of God cannot otherwise choose but be) of whome notwithstanding wee hold our selves bound to think brotherly &
charitably: & because we are vndoubtedly sealed in our
consciences that for vs there is no way of religion to save
our soules by ordinarily but only to walke in this way…in-
stituted by Christ in his word. Therefore wee haue thought
it best humbly & instantly to seek & crave the same for our
selves in maner and forme as is before shewed. Which being
graunted by your gracious Maiesty and by your said most
honorable Counsaill it shall doubtles giue much comfort and
peace of conscience to manie most loyall subiectes, and shall
preiudice no other Protestant whose iudgment is not herein
yet informed, & shall procure to yᵉ most Excellent Governours

of our State everlasting praise both with God & all good men.

[Part of a Paper apparently written by Henry Jacob nearly a year after his Release from the Clink, and defending his book published in 1604 against the five principal criticisms which had been brought against it.]

A yeare now allmost past being in trouble for publishing my little Treatise, intituled *Reasons taken out of Gods word & y* best Humane Testimonies proving a Necessitie of Reforming our Churches in England*, I had this answer given me by men in great authoritie, that all the grounds of those my *Reasons* should be shaken & overthrowen by a man of knowen learning who (as I vnderstood otherwise also) had taken in hand the same, & would quickly do it. In ye meane while my Treatise was sharply censured by sundry of all sorts in divers points. But specially in these following: 1. Because I resolve vpon this conclusion, y^t Only a particular ordinary Congregation of Christians, & every such Congregation in ye New Testament is appointed & reckoned to be a visible Church...2. Because I affirme y^t our Ceremonies in controversie in England are parts of Gods Outward worship & Service, albeit invented by men.... 3. Because I expound those words of Christ Tell ye Church math. 18. 17. of a whole Church intirely & properly taken, as it containeth not only ye Guides but ye people also....4. Because I affirme that No Synod vnder ye Gospell hath power by Gods ordinance to prescribe & rule Ecclesiastically sundry whole Churches if they severally consent not...5. Because in my Epistle to ye Pastors of ye Churches in England pag. 81. I vse these words; *Looke to your charge, fullfill your Ministerie wch yo^u have receaved of ye Lord.* Wherein som gathered y^t I exhort ye Pastors of ye Severall Churches in England who do hold themselves ²to be *rightly & truly Pastors of their severall flocks,* & ¹not *ye Diocesan Bishops Curats & Substitutes,* but ³themselves to *have properly ye charge of their peoples Soules;* that they should *fullfill their Ministerie,* y^t is, set vp & exercise ye Ecclesiasticall Discipline among yem whether ye King will or no. To this last point I will first answer. My meaning & intent in this place is nothing so. But only to do as in yᵉ next page I do plainly expresse; *to seeke vnto God by prayer & to our most wise & noble King by humble & earnest Suit, both for their owne, for their peoples, yea & for Christs due right.* Which indeed if they obtaine not, then to *consider how they can be in such an Office & not to do yᵉ Office, nor intend to do it.* For so they do not, whosoever remaineth & continueth therein still not medling with yᵉ holy Discipline & government meerely Ecclesiasticall touching his more particular flocke. And yis albeit I answered by mine owne hand writing heeretofore to yᵉ Archbishop of Canterbury privatly, yet I thought it needfull also even in publik to deliver the same. As concerning yᵉ other severall matters before going I answered then in yᵉ time of my trouble, yᵗ if I should perceave from any man Reasons given contrary to my present resolution such as should be *good & well grounded on Gods word,* then I would by Gods grace change my judgment therein. And I promised also, (yᵗ it might appeare how ready I was to all Christian reason,) yᵗ for a time I would stay my selfe & see what would be brought against my opinion by any man within halfe a yeare, notwithstanding it was given out yᵗ out of hand [?] my small treatise should be shaken to pieces. Nothing whereof is performed, nor so much as likely to be performed for ought I heare....[1]

[1] Later in this MS. Henry Jacob begins an answer to the first four criticisms of his book mentioned above, but this part of his papers only covers two pages, and the presence of these MSS. in Lambeth Palace may indicate that they had been suddenly seized. This document suggests to me that Jacob may have gone to Holland in 1606, instead of in 1605, as I state in Vol. i., p. 290.

XIV

AN UNNOTICED LETTER OF THOMAS HELWYS'S

XXVIth of September 1608
A note sent by [Thomas] Ellwes [Helwys] one
of thelders of the Brownest
Churche, sent to his bretherne[1]

I desire to certefie yo[n] some thinge howe matters goe here [in
Amsterdam] wth vs, and that concerninge the differences betwixt
o[r] bretherne and vs, And therefore we Differ in parte in the
mÿnistrie, worshipp, Goverment, & Treasurÿ [?] Theire ministrie
consisteth of Pastors & Teachers, o[rs] of Pastors only, & we approve of no other officers in the ministrÿ but of Pastors. They
as partes or meanes of worship read Chapters Text*es* to preache
on, & Psalmes out of the translatioñ, we alreddÿ as in prayinge,
so in prophesiinge [?] & singinge Psalmes laye aside the trans-
lac*i*on, & we suppose yt will prove the truth, that All book*es* even
the originall*es* them selves must be laÿed aside in the tyme of
spirituall worshipp, yet still retaÿninge the readinge, & inter-
pretinge of the Scripturs in the Churche for the preparinge to
worshipp, Iudginge of doctrine, decidinge of Controversies as
the grounde of o[r] faithe & of o[r] whole profession And thus
we refuse not to vse the translatioñ, holdinge them notwith-
standinge muche inferÿor to the originall*es*. And this we
professe & thereof I desire yo[u] to take notice, and to give
notice to as manÿe as possiblÿ yo[u] can, This I assure yo[u] is
the truth of o[r] causes nowe in controu*er*sie, whatsoeu*er* yo[u]

---

[1] MS. 709, fol. 117, recto and verso, in Lambeth Palace Library. This
introductory description of the letter is written on the back of it in
another hand.

heare to the contrary, And hereof assure yor self as farrforth
as yo^u thinke there is any truth in me./Nowe concerninge
the Goverment, they holde that the presbetory Consisteth of
pastors, Teachers, & Rulinge elders Wee holde it Consisteth
of pastors only/For the Threasury they suffer them that are
without to Comunycate together with them, and doe not
sanctefie theire Almes with prayer, wee make a seperacion of
our Almes from the gift*es* of Strangers, whiche wee thankfully
receave And wee sanctefie the whole Actioñ by prayer, before
& after, as all the ordena*n*ces [?] of God ought to be./of theis
thing*es* [?] if God p*er*mitte [?] Yo^u shall here more at lardge.

[monogram or marks meaning] T H [?]

XV

PAPERS RELATING TO WILLIAM SAYER

The opinions defended & published by William Sayer[1]
imprisoned in the gaole for the Countie of Norff[olk], be
hereticall, scismaticall, & disloyall, & so scuerally may
be distinguished.

[Evidently written by "Io: Redmayne", " this xxv[th] of
Nouember 1612."]

1. The Baptisme of Infants is meerely vnlawfull, by the word of
   God, for that they have no actuall faithe.
2. A Christian man maye weare weapons and serve in warres at
   the Commaundement of the magestrate, against such as be
   enemies to the Church of God, which is only y[e] Church of the
   separation from the Church of England; and to beare armes
   or serve in warres against any which are of his opinion is
   vnlawfull by y[e] word of God /
3. That it is vnlawfull to take an oath before any ecclesiasticall
   officer, though it be to the detecting of a Iesuite, or an heretick,
   or making knowne his brothers offence being a delinquent
4. That it is vnlawfull to sue in any Criminall cause, before an
   ecclesiasticall magestrate; neither ought any heretique to be
   accused or sued for that offence of heresie before any Bishop,
   but before the Church, which he sayth are y[e] elders.
5. The Kinges maiesties aucthoritie graunted to Bishops for y[e]
   punishment of offenders, is meerely vnlawfull by y[e] word of
   God; neither can they have any cognizaunce of Criminall
   causes, or of any offender therein, though the Cause be of
   ecclesiasticall Cognizaunce (as they pretend. /.

[1] Add. MS. Mm. 6. 58 (fol. 180), in the University Library, Cambridge.

6. His maiestie hath no power by the word of God, to graunte any Iurisdiccion for the Cognizaunce of Causes to any prelates or priestes: And that his aucthoritie therein is vnlawfull & not warranted by the worde of God.

8. [7.] The Calling of the ministers in the Church of England, is vnlawfull & not according to the word of God /.

> He refuseth to recant & abiure publiquely his first defence, & publishing of his deniall of the Godhead of Iesus Christe & of the holie ghost; & obstinately persisteth in the defence of the former opinions; & saieth that he will never retreate, recant, & abiure his deniall of the Godhead of the twoe former persones in Trinitie before any ecclesiasticall Iudge or magestrate /

The Iudiciall processe vsed against him, have bene often in all mildenesse & lenitie. Greate care had for his better instruccion by often conference privately, & publiquely by learned & dis-creete divines but still he continueth obstinate, & will not submitt him self, or be reformed; but proudly peruerteth & interpreteth all scriptures, for the mainteyning & defence of his opinions, according to his owne vnderstanding & sense. And though in some pointes, as touching the lawfull bearing of armes, taking of an oath, and sueng [sueing] in any Con-trouersye; he seeme to approve the power & authoritie of the Civill magestrate yet when he is interrogated whom he meaneth or taketh for such a magestrate; he restrayneth that word, to the elders of the Church of the separation /

[Part of a letter of G:(eorge Abbot, Archbishop of) Cant:(erbury) to John Jegon, Bishop of Norwich, dated "Lambithe [?] Decemb: j. *1612*", concerning William Sayer.][1]

My very good lo:[rd] I haue receaved your lettre making mention of one William Sayer a desperate Hereticque, who out of malice rather then out of vnderstanding mainteineth manie prophane & scismaticall opinions. Those .8. positions conteined in the inclosed paper, are the doctrines of the

---

[1] Add. MS. Mm. 6. 58 (fol. 181, recto), in the University Library, Cambridge.

Baroists & Sep*a*ratists of this Age, but ioyned with some points of the Anabaptists;......But it will neu*er* be assented to, that hee should burne as an Hereticque, vnlesse hee denie something expressly conteyned in the three Creeds or in the foure first Generall-Counsells. I doe finde an obscure mention in the later p*a*rte of y*o*ur paper, as if this Sayer had denyed the Godhead of Christe, and of the Holie ghoste. If hee p*er*sist obstinately therein, the Lawe will holde of him, as it did this last yeare vpon Legate, and Wightman, to frie him at a Stake. But it is not clearly deliu*e*red what hee affirmeth in those points, and therefore I can giue no certein answer vnto it.

XVI

DOCUMENTS RELATING TO THE HISTORY OF THE EARLIEST ENGLISH ANABAPTIST CONGREGATIONS

[An undated Letter sent by "Hughe and Anne Brom-head" to their cousin, (Sir) William Hammerton, at London, probably written some time in 1609.][1]

This Brownists letter idle vile and vayne
I doe protest Ile nere read or'e againe. /[2]

Grace with Increase of grace, peace even from the father and god of peace, with all true comforte and consolation In Iesus Christe be wth you beloved Cosen and all yours, and that forever [?]. Beloved Cosen we receyved A letter from you dated the xiij of Iulie wherin you write that you expect an answer from vs of the said letter. The first part of your letter is, that leaving oure Countrie we removed to Amsterdam, wch removing was, you hope, but to make tryall of the Countrie. Cosen we gyve you to vnderstande that though Natura hominis est novitatis avida,......A seconde part of your letter is that you wold perswade vs to returne home into England, which you make no Question wold be much pleasing [?] to god, but we make great Question therof yea we [?] hold it w^thow^t all Question, the same [?] should be much and highly displeasing

---

[1] Harl. MS. 360 (fol. 70-1), in the British Museum. Portions of this MS. are now so faded as to be almost illegible. An attempt is here made to reproduce only certain parts. In Vol. I., p. 236, I assigned this letter to the autumn of 1608, but that date now appears to be too early. (See Mr Burgess's "John Smith", London, 1911, pp. 169-70.)

[2] This couplet is in a different, but contemporary, hand-writing. Mr Burgess misreads "alle" for "idle" ("John Smith", p. 169).

vnto vnto [*sic*] oure good god and father, that hath in his mercifull providence brought vs ow[t] of Babilon the Mother of all abhominations the habitation of devils [?] and the holde, of all foule spirites [?] and A cage of every vncleane and hatefull birde :...

..........................In oure Cosen [?] Nicholas, we can but be sory and lament his fall wishing him to remember...and good vse of the wordes of the apostle paul vnto the gala. .3 .3. *verse* and also of the wordes of the apostle peter in his .2. epistle .2. 10 [?]. 20 21 [?] & 22 [?] verses, yet we hope better thing*es* of him and such as accompany Salvation. Concerning the 4 p*arte* of yo*ur* letter wherin you seeme to desire to know wherin your churche might be reformed although I know not herin, where to begynne or where to ende, the corruptions therof be so many and Infinitt [?], yet in some measure to satisfie yo*ur* request I will geve you a vewe and taste of them but before I will geve you A brief Som*me* of the causes of oure Seperation and of our purpose in practise[1]. fyrst we seeke above all thing*es* the peace and protection [?] of the most high and the kingdome of oure lorde Iesus Christ .2.[lie] we seeke and fully purpose to worshippe god Aright according as he hath com*maunded* in his most holy worde .3.[lie] we seeke the felowshippe of his faithfull and obedient servantes and together wth th*em* to enter Covenant wth the lorde, and by the direction of his holy Spirit to proceed to A godly free and right choice of Ministers and other officers by him ordeyned to the Service of his church .4.[lie] we seeke to establish and obey the ordina*nces* and lawes of oure Saviour Christ left by his last will and testament to the governing and guiding of his church w[th]ow[t] altering, changing, innovating, wresting, or leaving ow[t] any of them that the lorde shall gyve vs sight of .5.[lie] we purpose [(]by the assistance of the holy ghost) in this faith and order to lead oure lyves, and for this faith and order to leave [?] oure lyves if such be the good will of oure heaven*ly* father. And 6.[lie] now that oure forsaking and vtter

---

[1] This part of the letter is evidently a citation taken from Barrowe and Greenwood's "A Plaine Refvtation", 1591 [ed. 1606], pp. 1–2. Mr Burgess has done well in calling attention to this point ("John Smith", pp. 172–73).

abandoning of these disordered assemblies as they generally
stand [?] in England, may not seeme strange or offensyve [?] to
any that will Iudge or be iudged by the word of god, we alledge
and affirme that heinoush guiltie in these .4. principall trans-
gressions. .i. they worshippe the true god after A false Maner
the worshippe being made of the Invention of Man, even of
that Man of Sinne, erroneus [?] and Imposed vpon them. .2.
for that the prophane, vngodly…w^{th}ow^{[t ?]} exception of any one
person, ar wth them receyved [?] into, and reteyned in the
Bosome of the church[.] .3. for that they have A false & Antichristian ministerie imposed vpon them reteyned wth them and
maynteyned by them .4. for that these churches ar ruled by and
remayne in subiection vnd[er] an Antichristian, and vngodly
goverment, contrarie to the institution of oure Saviour
Christe [. (?)] for the better confirmation of these .4. we have
thought good to add certayne argumentes .1. no Apocrypha
must be brought into the publick assemblies, for there [?] only
godes word and the lyvely voice of his owne graces must be
heard in the publique assemblies.   But mens writinges and the
reading them over for prayer ar apocrypha, therfore may not
be brought into the publique assemblies[.] .2. argument. we
must do nothing in the worshippe of god w^{th}ow^{t} warrant of his
worde. but re^{a}dd prayers have no warrant in his worde.   Therfore re^{a}dd prayers ar not to be vsed in the worshippe of god.
.3. argument we may not in the worshippe of god receyve any
tradition wch bringeth oure libertie into bondage :   Therfore
readd prayer &c. .4. argument because true prayer must be of
faith vtterred wth hearte and lyvely voyce, It is presumptuous
Ignorance to bring A booke to speake for vs vnto god &c.
5. Argument to worshippe the true god after an other maner
then he hath taught, is Idolatrie. but god commaundeth vs to
come vnto him heavy loaden [?] wth contrite hartes to cry vnto
him for oure wantes &c Therfore we may not stand reading A
dead letter in steade of powring foorth [?] oure petitions.
6. argument we must stryve in prayer wth continuance &c but
we cannot stryve in prayer and be importunate wth continuance
reading vpon A booke, Therfore we must not reade when we
should praye. 7. argument we must pray as necessi[tie ?] re-

quireth but stinted prayers cannot be as necessitie requireth,
Therfore stinted prayer is vnlawfull. 8. Argument read prayers
were devised by Antichrist and Maynteyne superstition and an
Idoll Ministerie. therfore read prayers and such stinted service
ar intollerable &c. 9. argument the prayers of such C[hristian ?]s
and people as stand vnder a false goverment are not acceptable,
not only because they aske [? ami]sse, but because they kepe
not his commaundements. The prayers of such ministers and
people as be [s]u[bie?]ct to antichrist ar abhominable. Th[o?]s[e?]
ministers and people w^ch[?] stand subiect[?] to the [? Bisho]ppes
and the Courtes[?] ar subiect to antichrist &c therfore the
prayers &c / [?] Touching the last[?] part of your letter w^ch
concerneth the differences of these dayes, [?] the apostle paul
saith he heareth that there be heresies among them that they
wch ar approved amongest them may be knowen, therby
teaching vs that it is no new thing that differences in Religion
ar in the church, for the end therof god often turneth to greater
manifestation of his truthe & the furthering of the same, as
also to the procuring much glorie to his owne Name and to the
good of his church and children so tryed and approved. we
reade in the prophecy of the prophet Isaiah these wordes, My
beloved had a vyneyeard in A very fruitfull hill and he hedged
it and gathered the stones ow^t of it and he planted it wth the
best plantes, and he built a tower in the mydest therof and
made a wynepresse therin...he [?] looked that it should bring
forth grapes but it brought forth wilde grapes, and in the
same prophecy in an other place, he calleth them trees
righteousnes the planting of the lorde [*sic*] that he might be
glorified. now to make vse and application of these testimonies,
if the vyneyearde and church of Israell wch was of the lord*es*
owne planting and constitution brought foorth wilde grapes,
what Marvell though your [?] church [?] Englande wch is not of
the lord*es* owne planting and constitution [?], but of Antichristes
planting and of the constitution of the Man of Synne bring
foorthe wilde [?] grapes...of Christe [?], do men gather grapes of
Thornes or figg*es* [?] of thistles [?], every good tree bringeth [?]
foorth good fruite, And A corrupt tree bringeth forth evill
fruite...fruite neither can A corrupt tree bring foo[rth] good

fruite, therfore by their[?] fruites ye shall knowe them...As the
said prophet Isaiah spake of the people of the Iewes[?] so may
we speake of the churche of Englande, from the Sole of the
foote vnto the head, there is nothing hole therin but wounds,
and swelling and sores, full of Corruptions, the whole heade is
heavy. And we confidently deny that ever the English nation
or any one of oure predecessors were of the king[dome?] of
Christe, or at any tyme beleved visibly in A true constituted
church, but were come of the race of the pagans, till Rome the
mother came and putt vpon vs her false baptisme worshippe
and ministerie, and so oure[?]...is...paganish and the holy
ghost in the scriptures compareth vs to the worst kynde of
pagans calling[?] persons aapostating from the true constitution
of the church, Babilonians, Egiptians Sodomites[..?] teaching
vs the church of England that he estemeth no otherwise of the
church or baptisme then of the Sinagoges of Babilon, then of
the washinges of Egipt, then of the worshippe of Sodome, your
church of England therfore being of Antichristes constitution
is A false church. And can there be any thing[?] true in A
false church but only the Scriptures and the truthes therin
conteyned but your church hath a false constitution, or false
ministerie, a false worshippe, A false goverment and A false
Baptisme, the dore and entrye into the church, and so all is
false in your church. wherfore beloved Cosen we wish you in
the lorde diligently and seriously to consider and weigh your
vniuersall state and standing, that it is most sorofull[?] and
lamentable, and now at the last to harken to the lordes voice
that sounded from heaven, saing goe ow^t of Babilon my people
that ye be not partakers[?] wth her in her Synnes & that ye
receyve not of her plages.

Beloved Cosen concerning your request of A booke of oure
present setled goverment, there is none [?] extant though ther
be dyvers bookes[?]...the matters of [?] controversie betwene
the church of England and vs, and touching the differences
betwene vs and the other churches here.

The order of the worshippe and goverment of oure church
is .1. we begynne wth A prayer, after reade some one or
tow chapters of the bible gyve the sence therof, and conferr

vpon the same, that done we lay aside oure bookes, and after a solemne prayer made by the .1. speaker, he propoundeth some text ow^t of the Scripture, and prophecieth ow^t of the same, by the space of one hower, or thre Quarters of an hower. After him standeth vp A .2. speaker and prophecieth ow^t of the said text the like tyme and space. some tyme more some tyme lesse. After him the .3. the .4. the .5. &c as the tyme will geve leave, Then the .1. speaker concludeth wth prayer as he began wth prayer, wth an exhortatation to contribution to the poore, wch collection being made is also concluded wth prayer. This Morning exercise begynes at eight of the clock[e?] and continueth vnto twelve of the clocke the like course of exercise is observed in the aft[er]n[o]wne from .2. of the clock vnto .5. or .6. of the Clocke. last of all the execution of the g[over]ment of the church is handled /

...I have by this Bearer[?] sent vnto yow[?] A booke of...of Mr Smithe[1] oure[?] pasto^r. I wish[?] you diligently to pervse[?] and seriously[?] wth Iudgment to examyn the same[?]. And[?] if you...any moe of this or any other argument[?] written by him, either for your self or for your friendes to signify the same vnto vs[?] by your letters, and we will (the lorde willing) procure the same so that you send[?] A faithfull messenger[?] to whom we may safely committ the Cariage therof / for we have heretofore[?] sent divers Bookes Into England and they have...of the...and...vnto whom they were sente[?] /

Yours[?] In the lorde at all tymes to vse.
Hughe[2] and Anne Bromheade. /

[A List of the names of those English people who formed the Remnant of John Smyth's Congregation, and who, probably about February, 1609/10, petitioned that they might be received as quickly as possible into the " true church of Christ ", i.e., the church of the Waterlanders.][3]

[1] This book was evidently "The Character of the Beast", 1609.

[2] Hughe Bromhead had once been "curate of North Wheatley", Nottinghamshire, and was probably about sixty years old in 1608 (W. H. Burgess's "John Smith", 1911, p. 173).

[3] MS. B. 1347 in the Mennonite Archives, Amsterdam. The names and text are written in the clear handwriting of John Smyth. The names

Nomina Angloru*m* qui hunc errore*m* suu*m* agnoscunt
ejusqu*e* penitentia*m* agunt, viz : quòd [?] inc*œ*perint
seìpsos
baptisare, co*n*tra ordine*m* a Christo constitutu*m* :
quiqu*e*
jam cupiunt hinc ver*œ* Christi ecclesi*œ* vniri, eâ
quâ fieri possit expeditione.

Nomina[1] viroru*m*.	feminaru*m*.
Hugh Bromhead.	Anne Bromhead.
Iervase Nevill.	Iane Southworth.
Iohn Smyth.	Mary Smyth.
Thomas Canadyne.	Ioane Halton.
Edward Hankin.	Ales Arnefield.
Iohn Hardy.	Isabell Thomson.
Thomas Pygott.	Margaret Stavely.
Francis Pygott.	Mary Grindall.
Robert Stavely.	Mother Pygott.
Alexander Fleming.	Ales Pygott.
Alexander Hodgkin.	Margaret Pygott.
Iohn Grindall.	Betteris Dickenson.
Salomon Thomson.	Mary Dickenson.
Samuell Halton.	Ellyn Paynter.
Thomas Dolphin.	(Ales Parsons.)
	(Ioane Briggs.)
	Iane Organ.

Cupimus vnanimiter votu*m* hoc nostrum ecclesiæ significari.

[A Short Latin Confession of Faith, probably written early
in 1609/10 by John Smyth.][2]

I have placed within round brackets were originally signed by marks.
An imperfect text of this document is given in Dr B. Evans' "The Early
English Baptists", London, 1862, Vol. I., pp. 244–5, and a translation on
p. 209.

[1] Some of these names as printed by Mr Burgess ("John Smyth",
London, 1911, p. 185) are slightly incorrect.

[2] MS. B. 1348 in the Mennonite Archives, Amsterdam. Professor
Dr Müller's translation of this document is printed in Dr B. Evans'
"The Early English Baptists", London, Vol. I., 1862, pp. 253–4.

Corde credimus, & ore confitemur:

1. Vnum esse Deum, optimum, maximum, gloriosissimum, Creatorem et conservatorem omnium: qui est Pater, Filius, et spiritus sanctus.
2. Deum creasse & redemisse genus humanum ad jmaginem suam, omnesque homines (nemine reprobato) ad vitam predestinasse
3. Deum, nullam peccandi necessitatem cuiquam imponere, sed hominem liberè impulsu sathanæ a deo deficere.
4. Regulam vitæ a deo primitùs in observatione Legis positam; exinde ob infirmitatem carnis dei beneplacito, per Christi redemptionem in justitiam fidei translatam esse: quam ob caussam, neminem deum justè incusare, verum potius ex intimis visceribus ipsius misericordiam revereri, admirari, & celebrare debere; eum possibile homini reddiderit Deus per gratiam, quod prius homine lapso impossibile fuerat per naturam.
5. Nullum esse peccatum originis verum omne peccatum esse actuale & voluntarium viz: dictum factum aut concupitum contra legem dei: ideoque infantes esse sine peccato.
6. Iesum Christum esse verum Deum & verum hominem: viz: Filio dei assumente et sibi vniente hominis veram et puram naturam ex vera anima rationali, et vero corpore humano consistentem.
7. Iesum Christum, quod ad carnem attinet, per spiritum sanctum in vtero Virginis Mariæ conceptum fuisse, postea-natum, circumcisum, baptisatum, tentatum fuisse,: etiam ipsum esurivisse, sitivisse, comedisse, bibisse, crevisse, tum statura tum cognitione: defatigatum fuisse, dormivisse, denique crucifixum, mortuum, sepultum fuisse, resurrexisse, in cælum ascendisse: ipsique, vtpote soli Regi, Pontifici, et Prophetæ Ecclesiæ, omnem tum in cælo tum in terra potestatem commissam esse.
8. Gratiam dei per Christi redemptionem impetratam omnibus sine discrimine paratam et oblatam fore, idque non fictè sed bona fidé: partim per creaturas quæ invisibilia dei declarant, partim per evangelij predicationem.
9. Homines ex dei gratia per Christi redemptionem posse (spiritu sancto per gratiam ipsos preveniente) resipiscere, Credere, ad

12—2

deum convertere, et vitam eternam adipisci: sicut e contrâ, posse ipsos spiritui sancto resistere, á deo deficere, et in eternum perire.

10. Justificationem hominis coram dei tribunali (qui est et justitiæ et misericordiæ thronus) subsistere, partim ex imputatione justitiæ Christi per fidem apprehensa partim ex justitia inherente in ipsis sanctis per operationem spiritus sancti quae Regeneratio sive sanctificatio dicitur; si quidem justus est qui facit justitiam.

11. Fidem, bonis operibus vacuam, mortuam esse,: veram autem et vivam fidem per bona opera dignosci:

12. Ecclesiam Christi, esse coetum fidelium post fidei et peccatorum confessionem baptizatorum, potestate Christi præditum.

13. Ecclesiam Christi habere potestatem sibi delegatam, verbum[?] anuntiandi, sacramenta administrandi, ministros constituendi & abdicendi, denique excommunicandi,: vltimam autem provocationem esse ad fratres, sive corpus ecclesiæ.

14. Baptismum esse externum symbolum remissionis peccatorum mortificationis et vivificationis, ideoque ad infantes non pertinere.

15. Cœnam Domini esse symbolum externum communionis Christi et fidelium ad invicem per fidem et charitatem.

16. Ministros ecclesiæ esse, tum Episcopos quibus facultas dispensandi tum verbum tum sacramenta commissa est: tum Diaconos viros et viduas, qui res pauperum et fratrum infirmorum curant.

17. Fratres post tertium gradum admonitionis in peccatis sibi cognitis perseverantes excludendos esse é communione sanctorum per excommunicationem.

18. Excommunicatos quod ad civile commercium attinet non esse devitandos.

19. Mortuos (vivis momentó mutatis) resurrecturos ijsdem corporibus, non substantià, sed qualitatibus mutatis

20. Post resurrectionem omnes sistendos fore ad Tribunal Christi judicis, secundum opera judicandos: Pios post sententiam absolutionis, vita eterna cum Christo in cœlis fruituros: Impios verò damnatos, in Gehenna cum diabolo angelis ejus eternis supplicijs cruciandos.

Iohn Smyth.

[An undated Latin Letter from Thomas Helwys's Congregation to the Waterlanders at Amsterdam, probably written early in 1609/10, urging them not to admit John Smyth and his followers into their church membership.][1]

Ecclesia Anglicana, Ecclesiæ Belg[icæ]
Amsterdamiæ. / Gratia vobis et pax, a
deo patre nostro, et domino Iesu Christo. /

Charissimi fratres fidei vinculo, (in eo, ad quod pervenimus) oportet nos, vt eadem simul incedamus regula: et hoc profitemur in omnibus erga vos prestare, secundum eam scientiæ et gratiæ mensuram, quam deus nobis dedit aut daturus est: idem a vobis expectantes, quum tale indicium de vobis ferendum est. / Idcirco nostra interesse iudicavimus [?] (cum auditur idque a semetipsis: quod, quidam, qui era[nt] ex nobis: sed nunc temporis, propter eorum in peccato impenitentiam, quum nos esse Christi ecclesiam, et potestatem recipiendi, eijciendi membra habere negent: sancta Christi censura nobis, eius ecclesia[e] concessa: e comunione enim sanctorum iuste excluduntur, et nunc conantur seipsos vobis adiungere:) vos certiores facere, vt caveatis, ne tales recipiatis, quibus polluamini, cum optime sciatis paulolo fermenti, totam massam fermentari. / Et vos in timore dei obsecramus, vt nobis ipsis attendatis, ne in inconsulto improbos iustificetis, innocentesque condemnetis, a quo scelere, vt vos deus avertat, summis precibus oramus: / Sed perswasimus nobis de vobis, istis meliora, assidue expectantes, vos operam vestram potius in reformandis contumacibus, quam in ipsis corroborandis in peccatis suis daturos: et adhuc vestrum auxilium in nobis superstruendis, non diruendis collaturos: Et sic sperantes, vos in omnibus rebus vestris, verbum dei regulam vestræ directionis secundum vestræ fidei professionem, sequuturos, commendamus vos deo et Sermoni gratiæ ipsius, qui potest superstruere, et dare vobis, quod hæreditatis iure possideatis cum sanctificatis omnibus:

Valete. /

---

[1] MS. B. 1349 in the Mennonite Archives, Amsterdam. Apparently not cited in Dr B. Evans' "'The Early English Baptists".

[A Latin "Synopsis" of the Faith of the "true English Christian Church" at Amsterdam under the Leadership of Thomas Helwys, delivered (probably between Feb. and Mar. 12, 1609/10) to the Waterlanders there, with thanks for the teaching they had given them.][1]

Synopsis fidei, veræ Christianæ
Ecclesiæ Anglicanæ, Amsterodamiæ. /

i. Quod tres sunt qui testificantur in Cælo, Pater, Sermo, et Spiritus sanctus, et hi tres sunt vnus Deus, per quem omnia in Cælo, et terra creantur et preseruantur. /

2. Quod hic Deus creavit hominem secundum Imaginem [?] suam, qui peccavit et per cuius inobedientiam, omnes peccatores constituti sunt: sed per obedientiam Iesu Christi, iusti constituimur omnes. /

3. Quod deus necessitatem peccandi nemini imponit. /

4. Quod nullum sit peccatum per generationem a parentibus nostris. /

5. Quod deus vult omnes homines seruari, et ad agnitionem veritatis venire, et non vult mortem morientis. /

6. Quod Iesus Christus in plenitudine temporis, manifestans erat, in carne, factus ex muliere, conceptus et natus ex ea, spiritus sanctus inumbrans eam, fructus vteri eius, semen Abrahami Isaaci, Iacobi, et davidis secundum carnem, Et sic verus homo, circumcisus erat, baptizatus, precatus est, tentatus erat, metuebat, ignarus diei iudicii [?], esuriebat, sitiebat, defatigatus erat, edebat, bibebat, somnum oculis capiebat, statura et cognitione crescebat, crucifixus erat, moriebatur, sepultus, resurrexit, in Cælum ascendebat, omni potestate in Cælo et terra ei tradita, existens solus Rex, Sacerdos, et Propheta eius ecclesiæ. Et vna persona, verus Deus et verus homo. /

---

[1] MS. B. 1350 in the Mennonite Archives, Amsterdam. Apparently not given in Dr B. Evans' "The Early English Baptists".

7. Quod hominis iustificatio coram deo solummodo consistit in Christi obedientia et iusticia, per fidem apprehensa [?]: fides tamen absque operibus mortua est. /

8. Quod homo dei gratia per Christi redemptionem, facultatem habet (spiritu sancto in eo operante per predicationem evangelij) resipiscendi, credendi, ad deum revertendi, et ad finem perseuerandi, atque et iam est in homine facultas spiritui sancto resistendi, et a domino avertendi. /

9. Quod Eccliesia [sic] sit Cœtus populi fidelis, baptizatus in nomen patris, filij, et spiritus, tempore, quo confitentur fidem et peccata eorum: potestatem Christi habens, verbum predicandi baptismum et Cænam dominicam administrandi: ministros suos Eligendi, et abdicandi: et membra sua recipiendi et eijciendi secundum Christi Canones. /

10. Quod baptismus sit signum externum remissionis peccatorum mortificationis, et vitæ renouationis: et Idcirco ad Infantes non pertinet. /

11. Quod Cæna dominica sit signum externum spiritualis comunionis Christi et fidelium mutuo in fide et charitate. /

12. Quod vnumquodque membrum corporis oportet se mutuo cognoscere, vt sic prestent omnia charitatis fraternæ munera, tam animæ, quam temporis, mutuo sibi invicem: et presertim Presbiteros oportet totum gregem cognoscere, in quo eos spiritus sanctus constituit Episcopos. /

13. Quod Ecclesiæ ministri sint, aut Episcopi, quibus ab ecclesia commissa [?] est potestas, verbum predicandi, baptismum, et Cænam dominicam administrandi: aut Diaconi, viri, et viduæ, qui pro ecclesia, fratrum pauperum et infirmorum necessitates sublevant. /

14. Quod oportet ecclesiam (iuxta Christi discipulorum, et primitauarum ecclesiarum exemplum[)] vnoquoque primo die hebdomadis conveniendi: ad precandum, prophetandum [?], deum celebrandrum [sic], panem

fragendum, et prestandum cetera omnia munera spiritualis comunionis, quæ pertinent ad divinum cultum, membrorum mutuam ædificationem, et preseruationem veræ religionis et pietatis in Ecclesia : Et Idcirco seponendi sunt ordinarij nostrarum vocationum labores, qui in eo nos impedire possent. /

15. Quod fratres in peccato impenitentes, post tertium admonitionis gradum per ecclesiam actum; per excomunicationem eijciendi sint ex ecclesiæ comunione. /

16. Quod Excomunicati respectu civilis societatis non sint fugiendi. /

17. Quod adiaphora non fuit ecclesiæ, aut alicui membro ecclesiæ imponenda : sed Christiana libertas...restituenda est. /

18. Quod mortui resurgent (et vivis momento mutatis) eadem corpora quoad substantiam, etsi quoad qualitates diversa habentes. /

19. Quod omnes homines post resurrectionem, comparere oportet coram tribunali Christi, ad [?] iudicandos secundum opera eorum, vt pij iustificati æterna vita fruantur, et impij condemnati in gehenna cruciatus æternos ferant. /

Et Sic per dei misericordiam, Christum, secundum eius verbum didicimus: agnoscentes tamen nosipsos simplices et ignaros; et semper paratos cum omni reverentia et humilitate a deo instrui per huiusmodi instrumenta, quæ dominus noster excitaverit pro nostra, in veritate, ampliore informatione : et deo benedicentes pro huiusmodi optimis medijs quae a vobis nobis suppeditata sunt: dominum nostrum Iesum Christum suppliciter invocantes, vt vos et nos per spiritum suum in omnem dirigat veritatem. /

Gratia sit vobis, et pax, a deo patre nostro, et a domino nostro Iesu christo. /

[A Letter from Thomas Helwys, William Pigott, Thomas Seamer, and John Murton at Amsterdam to the Waterland

Church there, dated March 12, 1609/10, dealing chiefly with the cause of their so-termed ejection of John Smyth and his followers.][1]

Beloued in the lord. Your approued care, diligence, and faithfulnes in the aduancement of Gods holie truth, being by good experience (to God be giuen the glorie) well knowne vnto vs: makes vs that wee can do no lesse then with our best hopes, hope, that through the grace of God (his word, and spiritt directing you) wee shall find you so still; and therefore wee are with much gladnes and willingnes stirred vp to write vnto you, praieing you as you loue the lord and his truth, that you will take wise councell and that from Gods word, how you deale in this cause betwixt vs and those that are iustlie for their sinnes cast out from vs. / And the whole cause in question being Succession, (for so it is indeed and in truth) consider wee beseech you, how it is Antichrists cheife hold, and that it is Iewish and Ceremoniall, an ordinance of the old testament but not of ye new. / Furthermore let it be well considered, that the Succession *which* is stand [*sic*] vpon, neither the time, Person, nor place, can be proued to anie mans conscience, and so herein wee should ground our faith, wee cannot tell vpon whome, nor when, nor where, . / Wee beseech you consider how can wee of faith forsake ye euident leight of Gods truth to walke in such darknes. / And this is our warrant by ye word of truth. First for our baptisme. / Iohn Baptist being vnbaptized preached the baptisme of repentance and they that beleeued and confessed their sinnes, he baptized, . And whosoeuer shall now be stirred vp by the same spiritt, to preach the same word, and men thereby being converted, may according to Iohn his example, wash them with water and who can forbid. / And wee pray that wee may speake freelie herein, how dare anie man or men chalenge to themselues a preheminence herein, as though ye spiritt of God were onelie in their harts, and the word of God were onelie to be fetched at

[1] MS. B. 1351 in the Mennonite Archives, Amsterdam. A modernized text is given in Dr B. Evans' "The Early English Baptists", London, Vol. I., pp. 209–210.

their mouethes, and the ordinances of God onelie to be had
from their hands, except they were Appostles, hath y⁰ lord thus
restrained his spirit, his word, and ordinances as to make
particuler men lords over them, or y⁰ keepers of them, God
forbid. / This is contrarie to the libertie of the gospell, which is
free for all men, at all times, and in all places, yea as our
Sauiour Christ doth testifie, wheresoeuer, whosoeuer, and
whensoeuer two or three are gathered to gether in his name,
there is he in the middest of them. / And thus much in all
christian loue wee do aduertise you, that this ground of truth
is, and wilbe mainteyned against all the world, and that by the
great aduersaries of our faith in diuers other maine pointes, who
wilbe glade to haue such an aduantage against you, if you shall
publish or practice anie thinge against this ground in y⁰ 18. of
Matth: and the profession of Christ shall sustaine much
reproach by it; and therefore wee earnestly intreat you euen
by the loue of Christ that is in you, that you wilbe well aduised
what you do in these thinges. / And now for the other question,
that Elders must ordeyne Elders, if this be a true perpetuall
rule, then from whence is your Eldership come, and if one
Church might once ordeyne, then whie not all churches alwaies.
Oh that wee might be though[t] worthie to be aunswered in
these thinges, or that the poore aduise of so few,, so simple,
and so weake might preuaile with you to cause you to looke
circumspectlie to ycur waies in these thinges. The lord that
knoweth all harts knoweth ours towards you herein, that wee
do desire that there may be found no way of error in you, but
that you and wee might walke vprightlie in the waies of God:
casting vtterlie away all the traditions of men, and this wee are
perswaded is your vnfained desire also; now fulfill our perswasion herein, and trie your standing in these pointes, and
respect not how manie hold these thinges with you, but respect
from what ground of truth you hold them. /

Thus beseeching the lord to perswade your hart, that your hand
may not be against his truth and against vs y⁰ lords vnworthie
witnesses, wee take leaue, commending you to y⁰ gracious
protection of y⁰ almightie, and to the blessed direction of his
word and spirit, beseeching y⁰ lord to do by you according to

the great loue and kindnes that you haue shewed vnto vs. /
Grace and peace be with you. Amen.

Your brethren in the faith

Amsterdam. this

Thomas Helwys

12th of March. 1609

William Pigott

· /

Thomas Seamer

Iohn Murton. /

Wee haue written in our owne tonge, because wee are not able
to expresse our mynds in anie other, and seeing you haue an
interpreter. / And wee haue bene much greeued since our last
conference with you because wee dishonored the truth of God
much for want of speach, in that wee were not able to vtter
that poore measure of knowledg which God of his grace hath
giuen vs. /

A short confession of fayth[1]
[evidently prepared and partially signed by the Remnant of
John Smyth's Congregation early in 1610.]

[1] MS. B. 1352 in the Mennonite Archives, Amsterdam. A modernized
text of this document is given in Dr B. Evans' "The Early English Baptists",
London, 1862, Vol. I., pp. 245–52. This MS. consists of twelve unnumbered
pages, the last two blank. The paper is somewhat worn and yellow with
age, but the hand-writing is generally clear. The text of this MS. is an
English translation of the Confession of Faith of Lubbert Gerrits and
Hans de Ries (omitting articles 19 and 22), and is not, therefore, an
original expression of the views of the English Anabaptists who have
here signed it. The text of this Confession on the contrary was used
as a means of testing the general orthodoxy of their faith. Dr Evans
incorrectly printed a number of the signatures, and Professor W. J.
McGlothlin in his "Baptist Confessions of Faith", London [1911], p. 65,
has painstakingly reprinted them. Mr Burgess ("John Smith", London,
1911, pp. 188–9) dates the *signing* of this Confession "between July 14
and the end of August", 1612, and he may be right, but I think that other
evidence in the Mennonite Archives points to the date given above. Some
of the later signatures, however, were certainly not written until after
July 14, 1612, and Mr Burgess has done well in calling attention to this
fact.

The first article

Wee beleeve through the powre & instruction of the holy scripture y^t ther is one only god, who is a spiritt, eternall, incomprehensible, infinite, almighty, mercifull, righteous, perfectly wise, only good, and the founteyne of life, & all goodnes: the creato^r of heaven & earth, thing*es* visible & invisible.

2.

This only god in the holy scripture is manifested & revealed, in father, sonne, & holy ghost,: being three, and neverthelesse but one god.

3.

The father is the originall and beginning of all thing*es*: who hath begotten his sonne fro*m* everlasting before all creatures: The sonne is the everlasting word of the father, and his wisdome: The H. Ghost is his virtue, powre, & might, proceeding fro*m* ye father & ye sonne: These three are not divided nor seperated, in Essence, Nature, property, Eternity, powre, glory or excellency.

4.

This only god hath created ma*n* good, accordinge to his jmage & likenesse, to a good & happy estate, & in him all men to ye same blessed end. The first man was fallen into synne & wrath: And was againe by god, through a sure comfortable pr*o*mise, restored, & assumed to everlasting life, wi*t*h all those y^t were guilty through him: so y^t none of his posterity, (by reaso*n* of this resolutio*n*) is guilty synfull, or borne in originall synne.

5.

Man being created good & continuing in goodnes, had hability, the spiritt of wickednes tempting him, freely to obey, assume or reject ye propounded[?] evill: man being fallen & consisting in evill, had hability, the Lord[1] himselfe moving him, freely to obey, assume, or reject ye propounded[?] good: for as he through free powre to the choise of evill, obeyed & assumed y^e

[1] Dr B. Evans in "The Early English Baptists", Vol. I., p. 245, has "the T——" for "the Lord", and Prof. McGlothlin faithfully reproduces this incorrect reading.

evill: so did he through free powre to the choise of good, obey
and reassume y⁰ propounded good. This last powre or hability
remayneth in all his posterity.

6.

God hath before all tymes forseen & foreknowne all thing*es*
both good & evill, whither past, present, or to come: Now, as
he is y⁰ only p*er*fect goodnes, and y⁰ very founteyne of life it
self; So is he y⁰ only author, originall & worker of such things
as are good, holy, pure, cleane, & of nature like vnto him; but
not of synne, or of damnable vncleanenes: He forbiddeth y⁰
evill, he forwarneth to avoyd evill, and threatneth the evill
doer: he is y⁰ Permitter, & Punisher: But Evill men through
free choise of all synne & wickednes together w*i*th the spiritt
of wickednes w*hi*ch ruleth in them, are the Authors[?], originall,
& workers of all synne, and so worthy y⁰ punishm*en*t.

7.

The cause & ground therfor of mans destructi*on* and damnati*on*
is th[e] mans free choise of darkenes or synne & living therein:
Destruction therfor commeth out of him self, but not from y⁰
good creator. Fo[r] being p*er*fect goodnes & love itself (following
the nature of love and p*er*fect goodnes) he willed the health,
good, & happinesse of his creatures: therfor hath he pre-
destinated none of the*m* y*t* they should be condemned, nor
ordeyned or willed the synnes or meanes[?] wherby they should
be brought to damnation: Yea much more (seing he hath no
delight in any mans destructi*on*, nor willeth y*t* any ma*n* perish,
but y*t* all men should be saved & blessed) hath he create[d]
them all to a happy end, and being fallen & restored in Christ,
hath forseen & ordeyned in him a medicine of life for all their
synn[es?] and hath willed y*t* all people or creatures through
the preaching of y⁰ gospell, should have this tiding*es* published
& declared vnto them: No[w] all they y*t* w*i*th penitent &
faythfull hart*es* receave & embrace, this gracious benefitt of
gods, manifested in Christ for y⁰ reconciliati*on* of y⁰ world,
are & continue the Elect w*hi*ch god hath ordeyned before y⁰
foundati*on* of y⁰ world, to make p*ar*takers of his kingdo*m* &

glory. But they wh*i*ch despise & contemne this profered grace of god, wh*i*ch love the darknes more the*n* the light, per*s*evere in impenitency & vnbelief, the[y] make themselves vnworthy of blessednes, & are rejected & excluded fro*m* the end wherto they were created & ordeyned in Christ; & shall not for ever tast of y*e* supper of y*e* Lord, wherto they were invited.

8.

The purpose, wh*i*ch god before y*e* foundatio*n* of y*e* world had for y*e* reconciliation of y*e* world, (wh*i*ch he saw would fall into wrath & want of grace) h[e] hath in the fulnes of tyme accomplished; and for this purpose hath se[nt ?] out of heaven his everlasting word or sonne for y*e* fulfilling of the pr*o*mises made vnto the fathers, and hath caused him to become flesh o[r] man, in the womb of a holy virgin (called Mary) by his wonde[rful ?] powre & working of y*e* holy ghost. Not, y*t* y*e* Essence of god, y*e* eternall word, or any p*a*rt thereof[?] is chandged into a visible, morta[l] flesh or man, ceasing to be spiritt, God, or gods essence: but y*t* th[e] everlasting sonne of god continuing [?] y*t* he was before, namely God and spiritt, became y*t* he was not, y*t* is, flesh or man: and s[o] is in one p*e*rson true god, & man, borne of Mary, being visibly & invisibly, inwardly & outwardly, y*e* true sonne of y*e* living god.

9.

This p*e*rson god & man, the sonne of the living god, is come into the world to save synners, or to reconcile the sinfull world to god the father: Therfor wee acknowledg him to be the only mediator, king, Preist, & prophett, Lawgever & Teacher, wh*i*ch god had. promised to send into the world, whom wee must heere, beleeve & follow.

10.

In him is fulfilled, & by him ther is taken away an intollerable burthe*n* of the law of Moses, even all the shadowes & figures: as namely the Preisthood, Temple, Altar, sacrifice: also the kingly office, kingdom, sword, Revendg appointed by y*e* law, battell, and whatsoever was a figure of his p*e*rson or offices, & so thereof a shadow or representatio*n*.

11.

And as the true promised prophett he hath manifested &
revealed vnto vs whatsoever god asketh or requireth of the
people of the new testament. for as God by Moses & the other
prophettes hath spoken & declared his will to the people of the
old testament: so hath he in these last dayes by this prophett
spoken vnto vs, & revealed vnto vs the mystery (concealed from
 yᵉ beginning of the world): & hath now manifested to vs what-
sover yᵗ remayned to be manifested. He hath preached the
promised glad tidinges, appointed & ordeyned the sacramentes,
Offices, & ministeries by god therto destinated[?]: & hath
shewed by doctryne & life yᵉ law of Christians, a rule of their
life, the path & way to everlasting life.

12

Moreover as a high Preist and mediator of the new testament,
after yᵗ he had accomplished the will of his father in the
foresaid workes, he hath finally given himself obediently (for
the reconciliation of yᵉ synnes of yᵉ world) to all outward
sufferinges, and hath offered vp himself in death vppon the
crosse vnto the father for a sweet savour & a common oblation.

13.

Wee acknowledge yᵗ the obedience of the sonne of god, his
sufferinges, dying, bloodshed[?], bitter passion, death, & only
sacrifice vppon the crosse, is a perfect reconciliation & satisfaction for our synnes, & the synnes of yᵉ world; so yᵗ wee
therby are reconciled to god, are brought into peace, & have
a sure hope, & certaynty to the entranc[e] into everlasting life.

14.

Iesus Christ our prophett & Preist, being also, the promised,
only spirituall, heavenly king of the new testament, hath
erected or built a spirituall kingdom & vnited a company of
faythfull spirituall men: These persons hath he indued with
spirituall kingly lawes, after yᵉ nature of his heavenly kingdom,
& hath established therin justice, righteousnes, & the ministers
therof.

15.

Having accomplished & performed, heer vppon the earth, by dying the death, his office of yᵉ Crosse; he was afterward buryed, therby declaring yᵗ he was truly dead, the third day he rose againe, & stood vp from the dead, overcomming death & testifying yᵗ he was Lord over death, & yᵗ he could not possiblie be deteyned by yᵉ bands of death, hereby comfortably assuring all the faythfull of their resurrection & standing vp from death

16.

Afterwards 40 dayes space he conversed among his disciples, and oft tymes showed himself vnto them, that [?] ther [?] might no doubt be had concerning his resurrection: after yᵗ, being compassed by a cloud, he was caryed vp into heaven, & entred into his glory, leading captivity captive, & making a show [?] of his enemies, hath gloriously triumphed over them, & is sett at yᵉ right hand of yᵉ majesty of God, & is become a Lord, & Christ, Glorifyed in body, advanced, lifted vp & crowned with praise & glory, & remayneth over mount syon a Preist & king for everlasting.

17.

The holy office of this glorifyed Preist, king, Lord, & Christ, in this heavenly glorious being, is, to help, governe, & preserve by his holy spiritt, his holy Church & people in the world, through the storme, wind & troubles of the sea: for according to his Preistly office, as an overseer or steward of yᵉ true tabernacle, is he our intercessor, Advocate & mediatoʳ by yᵉ father: He teacheth, comforteth, strengthneth & baptizeth vs with yᵉ holy ghost, his heavenly giftes, & fiery vertue: & keepeth his spirituall supper with yᵉ faythfull soule, making it partake of yᵉ Life-giving food and drinck of yᵉ soule, yᵉ fruit vertue and worth of his meritts obteyned vppon the crosse, the only true necessary good signified in yᵉ sacraments.

18

And according to his kingly office in his heavenly being, he gouerneth the hartes of yᵉ faythfull by his holy spiritt & word: he takes them into his protection, he covereth them vnder

the shadow of his wings,: he armeth them with spirituall
weopens[?] for y⁰ spirituall warfare, against all their enemyes
namely y⁰ spiritts of wickednes vnder heaven, and whatsoever
dependeth vppon them in this earth. He their most glorious
almighty, heavenly king, standeth by them, delivereth & freeth
them from the hands of their enemyes, giveth them victory &
y⁰ winning of y⁰ field: & hath prepared for them a crowne of
righteousnes in heaven. And they being the redeemed of the
Lord, who dwell in the howse of y⁰ Lord, vppon the holy mount
syon, do chandg their fleshly weopens[?], namely their swords
into shares, & their speares into sithes, do lift vp no sword,
neyther teach nor consent to fleshly battell./

19.

All these spirituall good thinges and benefittes with Iesus
Christ by his merites hath obteyned for y⁰ saving of synners,
wee do graciously enjoy through a true living working fayth.
Which fayth, is an assured vnderstanding & knowledg in the
hart, obteyned out of y⁰ word of god, concerning God, Christ,
& other heavenly things, which are necessary for vs to know &
to beleeve to salvation; together with a harty confidence in y⁰
only god, that he as a gracious heavenly father will give &
bestow vppon vs through Chri[st] & for his meritts, whatsoever
is helpfull & profittable for body & soule to salvation.

20.

Through such a fayth wee obteyne true righteousnes, forgivenes
or absolution from synne through y⁰ bloodshed of Christ Iesus,
and true righteousnes, which through Christ Iesus by y⁰ cooperation of y⁰ holy ghost is plentifully shed & powred into
vs, so y' wee truly are made of evill men, good: ·of fleshly,
spirituall: of covetous liberall,: of Proud, humble: & through
regeneration are made pure in hart, and the children of God.

21.

Man being thus justified by fayth liveth & worketh by love
(which the holy Ghost sheddeth into their hartes) in all
goods [good] workes, in the lawes, preceptes & ordinances given

them by god through Christ, he prayseth & blesseth god by
a holy life, for every benefitt, especially of yᵉ soule: And so are
all such Plants of yᵉ Lord, Trees of righteousnes, who honour
god through good works, and expect a blessed reward.

22.

Such faythfull righteous people, scattered in severall parts of
yᵉ world being yᵉ true congregation of god, or yᵉ church of
Iesus Christ, whome he loved & for whome he gave himself
yᵗ he might sanctify them, yea whom he hath clensed by yᵉ
washing of water in the word of life: of all such is Iesus
yᵉ head, yᶜ shepheard, yᵉ Leader, yᵉ Lord, yᵉ king, & maister.
Now although among these ther may be mingled a company
of seeming-holy-ones & hypocrites; yet neverthelesse they are
& remayne only yᵉ righteous true members of yᵉ body of Christ
according to yᵉ spiritt, & in truth, yᵉ heyres of yᵉ Promises:
truly severed from yᵉ hipocrites & dissemblers:/

23.

In this holy church hath god ordeyned yᵉ ministery of yᵉ
Gospell, yᵉ Doctryne, of yᵉ holy word, the vse of yᵉ holy sacraments, yᵉ oversight of yᵉ poore, & yᵉ ministery of yᵉ same
offices, furthermore yᵉ exercise of brotherly admonition &
correction, & finally yᵉ separating of the impenitent: which
holy ordinances conteyned in the word of god are to be
administred only according to the contentes thereof.

24.

And like as a body consisteth of divers parts, & every part
hath his owne proper work, seing every part is not a hand,
eye, or foot: so is it also in yᵉ church of god: for although
every beleever is a member of yᵉ body of Christ, yet is not
every one therfor a teacher, Elder, or deacon: but only such
which are orderly appointed to such offices. Therfor also the
administration of yᵉ said offices or dutyes perteyneth only to
them yᵗ are ordeyned therto, & not to every particular common
person. /

25.

The vocation or Election to yᵉ forsaid offices is performed by yᵉ church with fasting & prayer to god. for god knoweth yᵉ harts; hee is amongst yᵉ faythfull which are gathered together in his name: and by his holy spiritt doth so gouerne yᵉ myndes & harts of his, that he by them bringeth to light & propoundeth whom he knoweth to be profitable to his churches.

26.

And although yᵉ Election and vocation be performed by yᵉ foresaid meanes yet neverthelesse yᵉ investing into yᵉ said service is accomplished by yᵉ Elders of yᵉ church, through laying on of hands.

27.

The doctryne which by the foresaid ministers must be propounded to the people is even the same which Iesus Christ hath brought out of heaven, which he by word & work, yᵗ is by doctryne & life hath taught the people: which was preached by the Apostles of Christ by the commaundement of Christ & yᵉ spiritt: which wee find written (so much as is needful for vs to salvation) in the scriptures of yᵉ new testament, wherto wee apply whatsoever wee find in the Canonicall Bookes of yᵉ old testament, which hath affinity & vnity with the doctryne of Christ & his Apostles, & consent & agrecment with the government of his spirituall kingdom.

28.

Ther are two sacraments appointed by Christ in his holy church, yᵉ administration whereof he hath assigned to yᵉ ministery of Teaching, namely yᵉ Holy Baptisme, & yᵉ Holy supper: These are outward visible handlings & tookens setting before our eyes, on gods side, yᵉ inward spirituall handling, which god through Christ by yᵉ cooperation of yᵉ Holy Ghost reacheth forth in yᵉ justification of yᵉ penitent faithfull soule: & which on our behalf, witnesse our Religion, repentance, fayth, & obedience through yᵉ obliging of a good conscience to yᵉ service of god.

29.

The holy baptisme is given vnto them, in yᵉ name of yᵉ father, yᵉ sonne, & yᵉ holy ghost, which heere, beleeve, & with penitent hartes receave yᵉ doctryne of yᵉ holy gospell: for such hath yᵉ Lord Iesus commaunded to be baptized, and no vn-speaking children.

30.

The whole dealing in the outward visible baptisme of water setteth before the eyes, witnesseth, & signifieth, yᵗ Iesus Christ doth inwardly baptise the repentant faythfull, man in the lavoʳ of regeneration & renewing of the holy ghost, washing yᵉ soule from all pollution & synne, by yᵉ vertue & meritt of his blood-shed, & by yᵉ powre & working of the holy ghost the true hevenly spirituall living water clenseth the inward evill of yᵉ soule, & maketh it heavenly, spirituall & living in true righteousnes or goodnes. Therfor the baptisme of water leadeth vs to Christ, to his holy office in glory & majesty: & admonisheth vs not to hang only vppon yᵉ outward, but with holy prayers to mount vpwards, & to begg of Christ yᵉ good thing signified.

31.

The holy supper according to the institution of Christ is to be administred to the baptised, as the Lord Iesus hath com-maunded yᵗ whatsoever he hath appointed should be taught to be observed.

32.

The whole dealing in the outward visible supper, setteth before yᵉ eye witnesseth & signifieth, yᵗ Christes holy body was broken vppon yᵉ crosse & his holy blood spilt for yᵉ remission of our synnes: That he being glorifyed in his heavenly being, is the alive-making bread meate & drinck of our soules,: it setteth before our eyes Christes office & ministery in glory & majesty by houlding his spirituall supper with yᵉ beleeving soule, feeding & meating yᵉ soule with spirituall food: it teacheth vs by yᵗ outward handling to mount vpwardes with yᵉ hart in holy prayer to begg at Christes hands yᵉ true signified good: and it admonisheth vs of thankfullnes to god, & of vnity & love one with another.

33.

The church discipline or externall censures is also an outward handeling among ye beleevers, wherby the impenitent synner after Christian admonition & reproof is severed by reason of his synne from ye communion of ye saynts for his future good: and the wrath of god is denounced against him vntill the tyme of his conversion and reformation: and ther is also, by this outward seperation of the church, manifested, what god before had judged & fore-handled, concerning this seperate synner, by reason of his synne: Therfor first before ye Lord, the prejudging & predetermining of the matter must passe in respect of the synner impenitent, and the after-judging & handling by ye church Therfor the church must carefully regard, that none in the church be condemned which is not condemned in the word of god./

34.

The person seperated from the church may not at all be admitted (so long as he proceedeth in synne) to the vse of ye holy supper or any other ecclesiasticall handling, but he must be avoyded therin, as also in all other thinges betokening ye communion of ye saynts or brotherhood. And as the rebellious life, conversation, or dayly company of ye godlesse and perverse; or mingling with them is daungerous & hurtfull, & oft tymes procureth scandall & slaunder to the godly, so must they withdraw themselves from the same rebells, avoyding them in all workes & endes wherby their pure soules might be polluted & defiled: yet so y^t alwayes the word of god take place & y^t nothing take place or be preferred y^t is contrary to love mercy, Christian discretion, necessity, Promise, or any other like matter.

35.

Worldly Authority or magistracy is a necessary ordinance of god, appointed & established for ye preservation of ye common estate, & of a good naturall, politique life, for ye reward of ye good, & ye punishing of the evill: wee acknowledg ourselves obnoxious, & bound by ye word of god to feare, honour, & shew obedience to the magistrate in all causes not contrary to the

word of the Lord. wee are obliged to pray god almighty for
them, & to thank the Lord, for good reasonable magistrates.
& to yeeld vnto them without murmuring beseeming Tribute,
Toll, & Tax.   This office of the worldly Authority the Lord
Iesus hath not ordeyned in his spirituall kingdom the church
of the new testament: nor adjoyned to the offices of his church:
Neyther hath he called his disciples or followers to be worldly
kinges, Princes, Potentates, or magistrates: neyther hath he
burthened or chardged them to assume such office, or to
governe the world in such a worldly manner: much lesse hath
he given a law, to the members of his church, which is agreeable to such office or government.   Yea rather they are called
of him (whome wee are commaunded to obey by a voyce heard
from heaven) to yᵉ following of his vnarmed or vnweopened life,
& of his crosse-bearing footsteps.   In whom appeared nothing
lesse then a worldly gouerment, powre, & sword.   This then
considered: (as also further, yᵗ vppon the office of yᵉ worldly
authority many other thinges depend, as warrs, [*blank space*] to
hurt his enemies in body or goodes etc [?], which evilly or not
at all will fitt or consort with Christ, & yᵉ crucified life of
Christians): so hould wee yᵗ it beseemeth beseemeth [*sic*] not
Christians to administer this office: Therfor wee avoyd such
offices & administrations, notwithstanding by no meanes therby
willing to despise or condemne the reasonable discreet magistrate nor to place him in lesse estimation, then he is described,
by the holy ghost, of Paull.

36.

Iesus Christ the king & lawgiver of the new testament hath
prohibited Christian [*sic*] yᵉ swering of oaths: Therfor it is not
permitted yᵗ the faythfull of yᵉ new testament should swere
an oth.

37.

The marryed estate or matrimony hould wee for an ordinance
of god, which according to yᵉ first institution shalbe observed:
Every man shall have his one only wife, & every woman shall
have her one only husband: these may not be seperated but
for adultery.   Wee permitt none of our communion, to marry

THE
PATRIMONY
OF CHRISTIAN
CHILDREN:
Or,
A DEFENCE OF INFANTS
Babtiſme prooued to be conſonant to
the Scriptures and will of GOD (againſt
the erroneous poſitions of the
ANABAPTISTS.

By ROBERT CLEAVER, with the
ioynt conſent of Mr IOHN DOD.

MAT. 21. 16.
Haue yee neuer read, Out of the mouth of Babes and
Sucklings, thou haſt perfeᶜted praiſe?

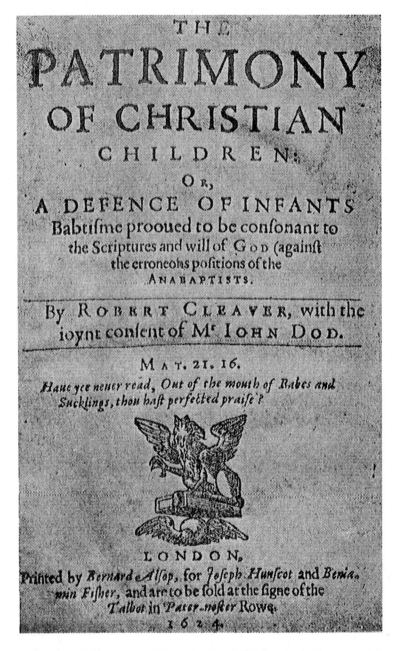

LONDON,
Printed by *Bernard Alſop,* for *Joſeph Hunſcot* and *Benia-*
min Fiſher, and are to be ſold at the ſigne of the
Talbot in *Pater-noſter* Rowe.
1 6 2 4.

TITLE-PAGE. (Size of original $7\frac{1}{10}$ in. × $5\frac{5}{8}$ in.)
See Vol. I., pages 268–9.

godles, vnbeleeving, fleshly persons out of yᵉ church; but wee
censure such (as other synnes) according to the disposition
& desert of yᵉ cause.

38.

Lastly: wee beleeve & teach the Resurrection of yᵉ Dead: both
of yᵉ just & vnjust, as Paul: 1. Cor. 15. soundly teacheth and
witnesseth: The soule shalbe vnited to the body, every one
shalbe presented before yᵉ judgment seat of Christ Iesus, to
receave in his owne body wages according to his workes: And
the righteou[s] which heer have lived holyly, & through fayth
have brought forth the workes of love & mercy, shall enter into
everlasting life with Christ Iesus yᵉ Brydegrom of yᵉ Christian
host: But the vnsanctified, which have not knowne god, & have
not obeyed yᵉ gospell of Iesus Christ, shall goe into everlasting
fier.

The Almighty, Gracious, mercifull God, preserve vs from the
punishment of the vngodly, & grant vs grace & gifts helpfull
to a holy life, saving death, & joyfull resurrection with all the
Righteous.   Amen.

Wee subscribe to yᵉ truth of these
articles, desiring further instruction

Iohn Smyth.[1]	**Garuase Neuile.** /
Hugo [?] **Bromhead**	
his wife X Iohn Grindall	
	Elizabeth Tomson
Thomas Cannadine [?]	**Mother Pigott.**
	Mary Smyth
Samuel Halton	Iane southworth
Thomas Pigott	Margarett Stavely.
Iohn Hardie	**Isabell** [?] **Thomson.**
Edward hankin [?]	Iane Organ.
	Mary Dickens.
Thomas Iesopp	
	Betteris Dickens.
Robert Staveley	Dorottie Hamand.

[1] The names in this list printed in dark type have been crossed out
in the original.

Allexander fleeminge[?]
Iohn Arnfeld

Fraunces Pigott
Thomas Dolphin
Salomon Thomson.

Alexander Hodgkin
Vrsulay Bywater
dorethie Oakland
Iohn......

....

Ellin[?] **Paynter**

Anne Broomhead
Ales Parsons.
Ioane Houghton.
Ioane Brigges
Ales Pigott.
Margarett Pigott
Ales Arnefield.
Elizabeth White
Dorethie Tomson
Margaret Maurice

[A Copy of a Letter sent in April, 1610, by the Waterland Church at Amsterdam to the Waterland Congregations outside the city, concerning the admission of the Remnant of John Smyth's congregation into their church membership.][1]

Iesŭs de ewighe wijsheyt des vaders zij met v, behertichde broeder en mededienaer inden heere,

Dus voornemen is welbeminde in Christo v by desen bekent te maken de gelegentheyt der saken alhier met ons en die engelse personen, (daer v voor desen wat van bekent is geworden) die de vereeninge met onse Gemeenten van oŭer lange gedŭijrichlijck versocht hebben. Vnde eerstelyck wetet, dat wij deur het vijerich aenhoŭden vande personen voorgenoemt, als oock het aendringen van sommige onser broederen, by de welcke haer doen en godtsalige wandelinge best bekent was, soe verre gebracht zyn, dat wij de oore voor haer niet langer slŭijten en conden met goeder conscientien, maer haere sake onse gansche broederschap hebben voorgestelt, om met onse Gemeijnte te sien, wat wtcomste ons de genadige Godt verlenen wilde, also ons hier de sake principalyck aenginck: en hebben eerst wy

<hr>

[1] MS. B. 1357 in the Mennonite Archives, Amsterdam. The date when this letter was written is not given, but only the date when it was sent. Professor Dr Müller's translation of this document is given in Dr B. Evans' "The Early English Anabaptists", Vol. i., London, 1862, pp. 211–13.

dienaren, wt last der broederen, dese engelsen voor ons
ontboden noch eens perfectelyck ondersocht inde leere ter
salicheyt, ende regeringe der Gemeynte, als oock bevraecht
t'fondament en de forme van haer doop, en hebben niet
bevonden datter enich verschil soe in t'een als int'ander
tüsschen haer ende ons was, oock aengaende haer doop voor
antwoort gecregen, datse in haer dopen ogemerck genomen
hebben op[1.] [i.e., 1.en] Act: 2, 38, doet boete ende een yegelyck
late hem dopen inden name Iesŭ etc om nade wijse Petri
alhier de boete voor te hoŭden, en t'sterŭen der sonden,
(oock door den doop beteeckent) grondich te verclaren:
2.en op Act: 8, 37. glooffdy van ganscher herten soe macht
wel geschieden etc. om t'gcloŭe aen Iesum Christŭm, dat
hy de Sone godts is, daer by te voegen, en van ganscher
herten te eysschen van die boetveerdigen, en daerop hebben
sy gedoopt met belofte vanden dopelinck hem te willen
bŭijgen onder het gansche eŭangeliŭm met syne leere, sy
verstondense dan ofte sy verstondense noch niet. Hebben
dan, mercken wij, geen onsŭyŭere verstanden geleert, en
den dopelinck voorgehoŭden, om haer doop op enige mis-
verstanden te fonderen, gelyck by de andere doopsgesinden
wel geschiet, maer alleen het schriftŭerlyck fondament daer
inne gevolcht, ende also eenvŭldelyck gehandelt.

Dit alle is daernae op een gesette tijt den broederen ver-
claert ende onse oordel van haer doop, wt begeerte der
broederen, also wy de voorstanders der gemeynte geacht
waren, voorgestelt, en den broederen daer op haer bedencken gegeŭen, (gelyckse oock begeerden,) en vermaent
haer met godt te beraden inden gebede. en nae enige
weecken wederom te samen gecomen zynde hebben wij
geeyscht by stemmen van persoon tot persoon wat haer
Godt soŭde mogen int herte gegeŭen hebben, en gevonden
dat meest de broederen, alleen sommige wtgenomen, ons
gevoelen, haer voorgestelt, toestendich waren, ende be-
stemden.

Soe is nŭ, hoewel wij hier een redelycke wtcomste inde
sake hebben onder onse broederen, dat wy nochtans, om
beters wille, geaccordeert syn niet voort te varen, voor en

all eer wij de sake onse naest gelegene mededienaren
hebben aengegeűen, om soe wy dolen, ons met onse gemeente van haer te laten onderwysen metten woorde des
Heeren.

Is dan onse gevoelen en*de* naeste insien dat dese engelsen
sonder wederom te dopen, soűden aengenomen worden,
en*de* wij vinden ons te blode, en*de* en soűden niet dorűen
haren doop ver*nieűwen*, gelyck dit met ons van verre
t'meesten-deel der gemeente bestemt is, als geseyt is,
en dat om dese reden; namelyck, dat wy weten en selffs
gesien en bevaren hebben datmen al eer die gene, die
vande műnstersche, naeckt lopers van Amsterdam, vande
Hazersoűsche[?][1], en die van oűde Clooster gedoopt
waeren, niet heeft dorűen weerdopen, maer sonder te
weerdopen heeft aengenomen,: en wat voor dopen noch
heden ten dagen voor goedt gekent worden: en op wat
wijse en met wat gront dese lieden haer doop geschiet is,
te weten een veele betere, en Christelijckere, nae onse
oordel, die wij vande sake hebben als wyse teugen malcanderen hoűden, dan de vorige die by ons geleden zyn,
en*de* noch geleden worden. Ist nű lieűe b*roede*r dat v
dűnckt dat wij hier inne dolen, soe doet wel, is onse en
der ganscher gemeente vrűndelyck en broederlyck bidden
en begeren, en coomt hier en onderwijst ons en de
Gemeynte metten woorde Godts, wij willen ons geerne
van een ygelycken laten onderwijsen, soe wy dolen en
hier inne de waerh*eyt* missen, onderwijst oock de engelsen wtten woorde godts, datse weer behoren gedoopt
te worden; want sy presenteren haer wel te willen laten
weer dopen, somen haer wtten woorde godts met reden
bewysen can, dat haer doop min een doop mach strecken
dan de doöp der Flamingen, Friesen en andere doopsgesinden, (ve*r*staet wel met onderscheyt de doop der gener
die van haer predicker gedoopt is; want van syn doop,
daer mede hy hem selűen gedoopt heeft, hebben wy selue
een ander onderscheijt, dat is een stűck op hem selűe,

---

[1] Evidently pertaining to Hazerswoude, a village south-east of Leyden

van de andere is nŭ de vrage, dit wilt ondescheyden) wij
hebben daer geenen moet toe, also het verstandige lŭijden
zijn, die niet sonder reden te paijen zyn. Wy bidden v
noch eenmael aenmerckt wat wy begeren lettet[?] op
t'propoost, en bedenckt v wel, hebdy dat gevoelen by v.
dat wy dolen, coomt tot ons en verlost ons vande dolinge,
en helpt ons te rechte : soe niet condy voldoen met stille
sŭijgen, en de sake godt en onse conscientie beuelen, [*sic*]

[A Letter from the Waterland Congregation at Leeuwarden
to the Waterlanders at Amsterdam, dated May 5, 1610 (Old
Style), urging that a union with the Remnant of John Smyth's
Congregation be not too quickly consummated.][1]

> Genade ende vrede van godt onsen vader ende
> den heere Iesŭ christo sij seer lieŭe beminde br*oederen*
> met ons allen die daar lieffhebben onsen heere
> Iesŭm christŭm onuergancklyck Amen

Seer lieŭe ende In godt beminde broeder mede dienaer Inden
heere Lŭbbert gerritsz met v lieŭe mede dienaren wij wenschen
v l te samen van haerten alles goets vanden heere met christe-
lijcke groetenisse[.] v l brieff aen ons gesonden hebben wij
ontfangen den inhoŭt vandien ten deile verstaen dat ghij
l. br*oederen* aen ons versoecket begeerende sydt seer ootmoede-
lycken om by v l tot Amsterdam te komen op den 23 Maij
stilo noŭo die oorsaeke Soe wij verstaen van dien is om met
den engelschen aldaer by v sijende vrede te maeken, waer op
wij onse l broederen op desen tijt voor antwoort schrieŭen dat
het komen voor ons Lŭijden nŭ ter tijt seer ongelegen is, Oock
laet ons mede het ongeŭall op het woort mercken want wij sien
op verscheijden tijt doer verschrieŭen ende begeerten In hollant
geweest om verscheijden saeken hebbende doenmaels onsen
besten raet dien wij hadde gegeŭen, maer heeft seer wenich
moegen helpen dat het tott vrede hadde moegen dienen, Iae

---

[1] MS. B. 1358 in the Mennonite Archives, Amsterdam. Professor
Dr Müller's translation of this letter is given in Dr B. Evans' "The Early
English Baptists", Vol. I., pp. 214–15.

maer tot ondanck ende onlŭst, dat ons Immers van haerten
leijt is weet die heere, daerom beminde broederen ofte het al
gelegen waer geweest voor ons om te komen doer v l ernstige
begeerten, Soe sijn wij doch oŭer dese saeke om met den engelschen vrede te maeken, sonder meerder kennisse te hebben
van haerder saeken niet vrijmoedich tis oock seer bedencke-
lycken ende wel te oŭerleggen, watter all aen onser sijden die
noch in vreden sien daer wt soŭden moegen ontstaen want die
erŭarenheijt leert het ons seer wel etc

Hierom dan lieŭe broederen soŭde onse meeninge weesen in
deser saeken dat wij met onser gemeenten die wij onweerdich
bedienen met open doeren onbedeckelycken soŭden begeeren te
handelen, want het haere lŭijden soe wel aengaet als ons, Ende
ofte wij luijden all by v l waeren saegen ende hoorden Soe en
soŭden doch niet gesinnet syn voor onse persoonen in eenighe
saeken te consenteren ofte ten waere dat wij ten eersten van
v l schrieftelycken hadden, die cortte bekentenisse der voor-
naemster stŭcken onser leere ende gebrŭijcken der gemeenten
die ghij haer luijden in schrieft gestelt hebt waerop dat sy
lŭijden den vrede soŭden willen aennemen, op dat wij dat selfde
by onser gemeenten oŭer all moechten proŭen, diewile dat die
saeke l broederen naer v eijgen schrieŭen wijt ende sijdt loopen
sall sonder dien soŭde het veele verantwoordens behoouen,
Daerom soŭden wij gesint sijen ons voor onse gemeenten om
te qŭijteren alles wat wij in deser saeken soŭden doen ende
ingaen dat sij dat selfde mede wijsten ende oock in vreden
ingingen op dat wij ons naemaels in geen moeten nochte
onrŭste en braechten, diewile wij doch sonder de gemeenten
niet en syen nochte sy mede niet sonder ons als een lichaem,
Soe en behooren dan ofte wij alschoen onwerdïge dienaers
sijen, Immers sonder haeren voorweten in sŭlcke saeken niet
te handelen want wij kennen lieŭe broederen den stant onser
gemeenten alhier seer wel, dit is op het naeste onse eenvoedich
insien van deser saeken [?] hoŭt het ons ten goeden, Soŭdet
anders gaen dan wel dat soŭde ons van haerten leijt syen voor
dijtmael niet meer dan blyft den heere in genaden te samen
beŭolen met vrientlycke groetenisse in den heere des vredens
bidt godt voor ons wij blyŭen seer gerne ŭwe schŭldenaers

desen 5 maij oŭden stijll anno 1610 In Leeuwarden by ons
ondergeschreŭene

by mij Hans mathijs zoon

Ane Anesz   Dijrck Doedesz

Ian Ians. zoen   1610

Schellinckwoŭ   5
            _____
                    6

Yeme de Rijnck

[A Letter of Yeme de Ringh at Harlingen to Lubbert
Gerritsz., Hans de Ries, and Reynier Wybrantsz., dated
May 15 [?], 1610, and expressing the wish that the Confession of Faith of the Remnant of John Smyth's congregation (in 38 articles) might be sent to Friesland for the
perusal of the Waterlanders there.][1]

Den
Eersamen Vromen Man
Renier Wybrants glaes⸍
maker in sint Lucas op de
Sijngel inde Menniste
Kercke.
            Tot
Amsterdam
            Loont den boode[2]

Laus deo XV [?] Mayo 1610 in Harlynghen
Van herten 1 beminde broederen ende mede Dienaers in
christo Lubbert ger:[ritsz.] Hans der rys Renier Wibrants
vl [v.l.] brieff van t' versoeck om aldaer by v te comen
om d'engelsen handel te spreecken, is ons geworden de
reste zyn terstont bij mij wort gesonden onse Leraren
behalŭen Iacob tiewes hebben bij een geweest ende haer
menijnge hier Ingaende gesonden an vl / het welcke [?]
vl mocht visiteren / t schijnt dat zij liefst d'articulen die

---

[1] MS. B. 1359 in the Mennonite Archives, Amsterdam. Apparently
not given in Dr B. Evans' "The Early English Baptists".

[2] This address is not a part of the text of the letter.

bij vl dEngelsen syn ouergegeuen : Eerst hadden / om met
den broederen die zelŭe te oŭersien op datter naderhant
gheen moeyte wt en quame soo zij zorghen. Dus de
vrienden connen doen wat haer Inne geraden Denckt„
k'en dencke nijet soo wij der schoon al quamen „dat wij
misschien eendrachtig int verstant souden zijn ende dat
mochte dan wel wat moyten maken sorgh ich„doch dat
vl hier an de leraren uwe ouergegeue[ne ?] articulen sont
en sije [zie] ick nijet voor quaed in. Want mij is zeer lieff
dat syt nijet opt stŭck des doops (soot schynt) nemen
waerom ick hoope soo se met onse geloue ende huys-
houdijnge te vreeden connen syn, dattet wel door ouer-
schriuen ten goeden einde conde comen soot godt belieft.
Dus bedenct v ten besten / want ick voor myn persoon
hadde wel geern de zahe wat op een ander manijer gesien
als dese / naemtlijch dat syselue getrocken hadden om alle
dynghen te hooren en zien / ofte soo se nijet getrocken
hadden dat syt ŭl [v.l.] hadden gantslijch in handen gestelt.
Dan dit soot schijnt en heeft soo wel nijet conne[n?] gaen /
ende dat soo ick merke wt sorgvuldigheijt vande gemeenten hier. Daerom bidde Ick vl doet soo wel ende
schrijft na hare begeeren d'articulen soo ghij se haer hebt
ouergegeŭen ende al waert dattet de dienaer der engelsen
mede ondertekende / ten soude nijet schaden mijns bedencken, doch doet soot v geraden denckt„ick hebbe dit
mede ondertekent oftet wel soo gants na mijn menijnge
nyet is / soo en can ick t toch soo quaet nijet schouwen,
want als wy wat sonder onse gemeenten doen / soo crighen
wij gemeynlich moeijte / want wij hebben vele stijŭe
hoofden daer wy wat moeten na omsien / en ten is niet
moglyck altyts in twist te leuen want onse gemeenten
bloeyen nŭ redelijck god loff soo dat wy nu [?] in twee
mael yn een maent oft 5 weken tyts / 40 personen onder t
Doopsel gecregen hebben / en t ware ommers [immers] nyet
goet onrŭst daer onder te brenghen. Voorder gaet hier by
eenen brieff die ick ter s[ton]t [?] van Rippert ontffangen
hebbe ende by mij onwetend opgebrooken..en [?] [? ni]et al
gelesen / alsoo ick noch op t bedde lach / doen den brieff

quam / dit met al mijn [?] ten besten afnemen t is onwetend
geschiet. nyet meer dan syt hartlyck gegroet met al die v
lieff zijn.

V. L. D[ienaer] yeme de Rijnck

[A Letter of Willem Janszoon, Teacher at Rynsburg, to
Reynier Wybrantsz. at Amsterdam, dated May 18, (1610),
concerning the proposed meeting on May 23 for discussion of
a union with the Smyth Remnant.][1]

Den
Eersaemen ende vroemen reijner
Wybrant soen wonende tot amsterdam[2]

Weest hertelick gegrüet

Nae wenscinge alles güets vanden here sao laet ick mijn
lieüe ende ingodbeminde brüeder ende medehelper inden
evangelio reijner wijbrant soen weten dat ick v scriüen
ontfangen hebbe ende hebbe daer wt verstaen als dat
daer sommige iverige herten wt engelant gecaemen syn
die daer met v l soecken te verenigen ende dat gy met
haer daer meermaelen van onse hüishoüdinge gesproecken
hebt ende wterlick in belidinge met malcanderen enich syt
soe ick verstae ende scrijft aen ons onwaerdich om daer op
den 23 mey met sommige van onse mede dijeners daer te
coemen om met malcanderen te oüer leggen om op het
beqüaemste met haer te spreecken ende dat ick sommige
soüde mede brengen die latijn verstaen ende spreecken
connen soe laet ick mijn l b [lieve broeder] ende mede-
diener weten dat het mijn op dien dach niet gelegen en
comt want mijn woort staet om die dach op een ander
plaetse te comen dat welcke ick niet mach verleggen om
redens wille mer hebbe meester Iacob ende Cornelis van
beest daer tüe beweecht om dan daer by v l te wesen die
wijle sy latijn verstaen ende spreecken connen ende dat gy
meer helps van haer sült hebben dan van ons die wijle wy

[1] MS. B. 1360 in the Mennonite Archives, Amsterdam. Apparently
not given in Dr B. Evans' "The Early English Baptists".
[2] This address is not a part of the text of the letter.

die spraeck niet en verstae*n* die heer wil v altesaemen
wijsheit ende verstant geŭen dat het mach gescieden tot
eere des euangeliŭms tot stichtinge van veele godtvrŭch-
tigen en*de* tot lof en*de* dancbaerheit van gods heylige naem
en*de* tot salichkeit van onse dier gecochte siele daer verlene
ons god syn genaede tŭe ame*n*

Willem Ia*n* soen wᵗ reynsbŭrch den 18 meij [1610.]

[A Letter from Dirk Pieters at Hoorn to Lubbert Gerritsz. at
Amsterdam, dated May 21, 1610, in which he excuses himself,
Abel Hendriksen, Gijsbert Dirks, and Jacob Adriaansz. from
attending the meeting on May 23 concerning a union with
the Remnant of John Smyth's Church.][1]

Anden Eersame Clas
Iansen brŭijn
om voort tee bestellen
Aen lŭbbert gerretzn
Tot
Amster dam[2]
Dr*ie* SS [stuivers] ...
die boed*e* sijn loon

Godts genade voer eenen vrintlijcken groete Amen
Eersame Heer hartelijcke lieŭe ende In godt beminde
broeder (vader) ende meede dienaer Inden here Lubbert
Gerretsen Also wij v 1 onder teijckenden brieff vanden
6 deses ontŭangen hebben ende den Selleŭen met andacht
well oeŭer (ende wederoeŭer gesien ende met Comer
[Commer] nae bedacht //. Soo hebben wij met onse
dienaren besproecken (ende onse mede die*naeren* / als
Aebell hendericksen Gijsbert Dircksen ende Iacop arien-
sen antboeden [)(?)] / met haer raet hoŭdende vinden wij t
voert beste voer onse gemoet (ende voer den heere) om
niet te coemen nae v 1 begeerten // bidde darom wilt het
ons ten besten hoŭden // t geschiet niet dat v 1 ons des

---

[1] MS. B. 1361 in the Mennonite Archives, Amsterdam. Apparently
not given in Dr B. Evans' "The Early English Baptists".

[2] This address is not a part of the text of the letter.

niet werdich en Sijt gensins Iae alwaert noch tien maell
meer dat weet die heere / dan om Sekere gewichtege oor-
sacke dien wij meenen datoe te hebben // Soŭeele noŭ
die Sacke belangt darom wij verschreŭen Sijn is onse
eenŭŭldige [?] raet ende beede dat ghij toch versichtich [?]
ende Sorrchŭŭldich [?] wilt handelen ende niet licht tot
eenen voort ganck en Consenteert om eenige perijckelen
die darouer ontstaen moegen / op dat wij niet ande eene
kant timmeren ende ande andere velmeer brecken // want
lieŭe broeder wij Sien well waner all enige gescheijden
volcken tesamen comen hoe Swarlick het valt den Selleŭen
in vrede tee behoŭden gelijck den tegenwoordigen stant
alte vell ons leert // nochtans weten wij dat die vrŭchten
der gerechticheijt wort in vreden geseijt bijden geenen
die den vrede hoŭden / darom lieŭe beminde broeder laet
ons het geene hoŭden dat ons de heere verleent heeft / op
dat wij niet en verliesen dat wij gewrach[t] hebben maer
vollen loon vanden heere moegen ontŭangen / hier toe wil
ons die heere helpen ende bijstaen [?] nŭ ende in Eewicheijt
amen Sijt hier mede den here beŭoelen ende van harten
gegroet met des heren vrede / dateert hooren den 2i meij
Anno i6i0

Bij mij dirrick Pieterzn v l
mede dienar Inden heere

[The Draft of a Letter sent by the Waterlanders at Amsterdam to the congregation in Leeuwarden, dated July 16, 1610
(New Style), asking for an early answer as to their opinion of
the enclosed Confession of Faith in 38 articles, and also of the
value of the baptism of John Smyth's followers.][1]

Gunstige & in Godt beminde broederen & mededienaren
in den heere Ian Schellingwouv, ofte Hans Mathijs met
vwe medehelperen daer ontrent in den dienst des heren
v wenschen wij toe des Heeren vrede, & een genadige
voorlichtinge in Christo op alle vwe wegen, Amen

[1] MS. B. 1362 in the Mennonite Archives, Amsterdam. Professor
Dr Müller's translation of this document is printed in Dr B. Evans'
"The Early English Baptists", Vol. I., pp. 215–16. This document is so
poorly written as to be most difficult to decipher with exactness.

Het belieue v by dese*n* te wete*n* dat wy seer v*er*lange*n*
nae bescheyt & antwoorde opt'gene wy een tytlanck ge-
lede*n* aen v liede*n* v*er*socht e*n* begeert hebben, aengaende
de saken der Engelse*n*, die wy v.l. bekent gemaeckt
hebbe*n*, en syn v*er*wondert waerom de sake by v soe
weynich behertict schynt te worde*n*, daer*of* wij beschaemt
syn voor de liede*n*, naŭlych weten wat antwoorde*n*, dat
de sake dus v*oor*trecht. Is derhalŭe*n* onse versoeck &
eernstich begere*n* aen v liede*n*, wilt de sake niet langer
v*oor*trecke*n*, maer ons cortelyck en binnen veertijen dage*n*
tyts nae dato deses antwoorde toeschicken door v comste
selffs in p*er*sone, ist mogelyck dat wy soe vele by v gelde*n*
moge*n* ofte soe niet, schriftelyck, op dese twe stŭcke*n*:
Eerstelyck wat ghij in de bekentenis, die wy v toegesonde*n*
hebbe*n* nae v begere*n* omdat ghij met vwe gemeente*n*
proeŭe*n* wolt metten woorde Godts te bestraffe*n* e*n* weder
te v*er*betere*n* hebt; te*n* andere*n* wat wt cracht van t
woort Godts van haere*n* doope te hoŭde*n* is. nae v ge-
voele*n*. En van dit laeste stŭck hadden wij insonderheijt
opt spoedechste geerne antwoorde; & goedt onderwijs.
Het welche soe ghij ons omtrent de tyt voorgenoemt niet
toe en schickt, soe sŭllen wy daer voor houden dat ghij t ons
beŭeelt en geheel in hande*n* stelt, om te doen en te
late*n* naedat wy t hier met onse gemeente best vinde*n*
sullen na de wysh*eijt* die wij hebbe*n* en dat ghy v daer in
gerŭst sult[?] hoŭde*n*, e*n* na der tyt te vrede*n* syn, dus
wilt v beneerstige*n* [= haasten], is onse bede..., soo ghij
ons met Gront van Godts woort ter eener oft-ter anderer
zyde*n* te waerschoŭwe[n ?] hebben [= hebt] e*n* ten beste*n*
te onderwyse*n* hebt, dat ons sŭlckx ylich [= spoedig] als
geseyt is toegesonde*n* werde, op dat wy te eer hoe beter
ter sake moeten doen gelyck wy schuldich syn. beneŭe*n*
ditte niet meer dan hertelycke groete ae*n* v onse*n* lieue*n*
br*oede*re*n*, & mededienare*n* in den eŭangelio des here*n*
daer in Frieslant, Iesus met syn geest blyŭe ewelyck by
v, Ame*n*

In Amsterdam dese*n* 16*en* Iŭly A*nn*o 1610. stilo noŭo.
by ons

[A Letter, dated July 18, 1610, from the Waterlanders in Leeuwarden (Friesland), stating their disapproval of the proposed union with the Remnant of John Smyth's congregation, whose baptism they term something unheard of, " een noeijtt gehoerde sake ".][1]

Myn harte is zeer well aen den regenten In ysraell
    de daer vriwillich *zyn* Onder den volke: Sed ne quid Nimis

Naer lieffelike groetenisse en*de* goeden genegentheit Onsers harten zeer *Lieŭe* en*de* wellbeminde *Broederen* en*de* mede di*enae*ren aen den Rike gods Lŭbbert Gerrijtzen samptt vwe mede di*enae*ren wij Ondergescreuen mogen v[.] L[.] n*iet* onthouden onse *verwondernise oŭer v ijŭerich en*de* driftich schriŭen aen ons gedaen int welke ghij heden vordertt onsen antwoirdtt bennen—14—dagen oft namaels ons gerŭst te dragen oŭer de aleantije ofte *verhandelinge van vereniginge metten engelschen aldaer by v gehoŭden en*de* voirgenomen *etc* wij syn L[.] mannen oŭer d sake zeer bedacht, waero*m* v L adŭijs van ons vvt vrieslantt soe driftich en*de* ijuerich vordertt en*de* versochtt hoe well hett een geheel nyewe en*de* noeijtt gehoerde sake is. de well behoerlyck maer datt alle *Gemeenten* In Prŭijsen als mede doer duijtslant en*de* all omme geseten bekent waer gelyck v Lieŭe [?] *Broederen* noch well bekendtt sall sy*n* watt woorden en*de* beloften geschiett syn by ons In voerige *ver*handelde saken n*iet* meer nyewes sonder *vra*gaen den [?] raadt van allen t hoŭden, watt opsichtt dese haestige t zamenlopinge ofte *ver*eniginge deses volcx mett haer absŭrden werck [?] standtt en*de* dienst by verscheiden *Gemeenten* als particŭliere personen oŭer all maken sall, Condtt ghij self L: Mannen aff meten is n*iet* nodich int breedste te extenderen, dan Cortelick voir [voor] ons dochte hett well raaetzaem Onder correctie In dese sake noch watt te vieren soe yŭerich en*de* vierich n*iet* te wesen doen wenden vele meer allen mogeliken vlytt arbeit en*de* nersticheit aen om de Rŭyne schaden *ver*darff en*de* onderganck der *Gemeenten* oŭer den waterlandeschen vredemakinge

---

[1] MS. B. 1363 in the Mennonite Archives, Amsterdam. Professor Dr Müller's translation of this document is given in Dr B. Evans' "The Early English Baptists", Vol. I., pp. 216–18.

oft vereniginge datt datt [*sic*] erst ouer een side mochte gebracht
worden dien brandtt gelesschett d *gemeen*ten gevredicht en*de*
wedero*m* In rŭste en*de* stillicheit gebrocht [gebracht] soŭde
ons een hartelike vruechde en*de* blijdtschap des harten sy*n*,
*ver*laett toch so licht de oŭde vrienden n*iet* met *ver*kiesen der
Nyewen de soelen velichtt [?] noch well soe goett n*iet* syn,
d *ver*meerderinge des rycx en*de* *ver*beteringe der kercken Cristi
is ons van harten lieff kendtt godtt d here, maer mett *ver*-
stroyinge der vrienden is n*iet* te wenschen, dese schade doett
ons int Harte wee, v onmatigen ijuer heeft datt mede gewrochtt,
wij willen datt daer bij affcorten oft wij well dien angaende
vele meer hadden t zeggen Watt aengaett t *ver*soeck om onsen
aduijs en*de* Proeŭe de ghij begeert oŭer de geconcipieerde –38.
gelooffs articŭlen is t *ver*geefs, d wile d selfde In gedrŭckte
boeken voir alle ma*n* aen den dach sy*n* gebracht mogen wij nŭ
mett v een algemey*n*[e ?] ordell va*n* all ma*n* daer van *ver*wachten
*ver*staen daerom Impartinent int besunder va*n* ons te vorderen
(den tydt sall leren d co*m*moditeit is bij velen noch n*iet* anders
geweest obiter [?] eens gesien en*de* oŭerlesen verwacht den tydt
men heeft hier oick mede watt anders te doene, Ten laetsten
datt v L voir all en*de* ten principale onsen aduijs en*de* In sien
oŭer haren doop vordertt, *ver*wondert ons seer aen gesien ghij
lieden v Insie*n* en*de* goedtbedŭncken oŭer dat stuck n*iet* en
*ver*toontt hett welke v behoerdtt hadde, datt dan gesien hebbende mochten wij t zelŭe proeŭen en*de* het onse daer by
stellen en*de* also t beste mett melkanderen *ver*kiesen, doch
Cortelick soe vele daer op voier een antwoirdtt onder Correctie
wij en kennen noch weten van sŭlken gebruijck ordinantie ofte
doen vth [wt] met der h. schriftŭren n*iet*, syn d*aer*om bloede
en*de* onvrymoedich vele daer van t zeggen t is een noeijtt
gehoerde sake willen d*aer*om dat In syn waer de laten en*de*
ons aen den woorde godes hoŭden daer wij op bescheiden zy*n*
en*de* n*iet* op menschen werck ofte doen, hier medde houden wij
voir desen Instancie v schriŭen en*de* *ver*soeck genoechsaem
beantwoordtt en*de* wiltt voirtan vwe dienst en*de* amptes plicht
In desen en*de* allen anderen bevorderen (In dien onsen ant-
woordtt v L n*iet* genoech en*de* vull kan doen mett *ver*willinge
en*de* ontbiedinge der saken gelegentheit oŭer all en*de* alomme

In allen Plaetzen voiren verhaeltt, houdtt goeden raadtt ende
beneffens oick d wachte ouer d kudde des heren Laett ons dese
Iegenwoirdige schaden eerst soeken toe boeten eermen watt
nyewes verneemtt datt bidden ende vermanen wij v ende blyfft
hier mede alle t zamen den ewigen ende allmogenden godtt
ende syn genaden rike woordtt In ewige ende genadige be-
waringe beuolen ende hartelick t samen van ons vwe onwerdige
Broederen ende mede dienaeren gegroett vaertt well den .18. Iuly.
1610

	Dijrck Doedesz	
Mͬ Douwe Sijbrants	1610	7
bij mij Hans mathijsz	18	houtt
Ick woorde haest moede in		mate
desen wtbecommeringe		

[A Memorandum made by Claes Claeszoon Anslo at
Amsterdam on Jan. 17, 1611/2 stating the wish of Lubbert
Gerritsz., expressed on his death-bed, that a union between the
Waterlanders and the Remnant of John Smyth's Congregation
might be speedily effected.][1]

Copije

Den 17ᵉ Ianuarij alsoe Lubbert gerretsz seer cranck te   1612
bedde lach heeft hij die dienaers alle / ende oock hans de [? New
Rijs / Ian munter / nittert obbesz / cornelis albertsz / ende Style]
mijn Claes claesz / (behaluen mathijs lutso [?] die absent
was) genraecht [?] Koefoot selffs sijn hertelijcke begeren
was soe hij scijde ende wel dudelijcke hem verklaerden oft
oock onser aller begeren was / dat Reijner wybrans [?]
inden vollen dienst mocht beuesticht werden / dewijl hij
een tijt lanck die gemeente int woort goods bedient
hadde / seggende dat hij daer wel in gerust was / dewijll
hij het woort goods het meeste wesende getrou in beuonden
was / dat hem het wiste [?] te weten die sacramenten wel
oock te betrowen waren / waer op wij alle Iae antwoorden /
ende dewijll het op senen [?] na met die gehele gemeijnte

---

[1] MS. B. 1366 in the Mennonite Archives, Amsterdam. Apparently
not given in Dr B. Evans' "The Early English Baptists."

met stillswygen vredelick bestempt was vraechden Lubbert
gerretsz doen oock Reynier wybrans / oft hij door goods
ghenaeden bereijt was den swaren dienst aen te nemen /
welcke onder die selūe genaeden oock Iae antwoorden /
doen heeft Lubbert gerretsz hem de handt opt hooft
geleijt / hem wenschende veele goede toewenschingen van
godt ende hem alsoe beūesticht ende hem nergent aen
verbonden als aen den woorden goods / seggende oock dat
hij groote blyschap hadde gehadt dat met alle die mannen
int [?] lestleeden alle Concepten neder geleijt waren ende
dat men alleen nae den woorde goods alles sall handelen
heeft vorder oock ernstelick begeert dat men die saecke
doch niet Int vergen soude stellen vande engelsche / maer
metten eersten voltrecken soe het mogelick ware dan seijde
Inden doop van M.r smidt [John Smyth] wat bedencken
hadde / alsoe hij daer geen scriftūer [?] toe en hadde / maer
nu well [wilde] gerūst alle die andere engelschen / sonder
weder te dopen op tenemen / vorder begerde hij oock aen
nittert obbes / dat hij die verkiesinghe voor desen geschiet /
wilde doch behertigen ende hem gelaten stellen ende door
goods ghenaeden sijn beste doen / het welck nittert obbes
oock onder die selue ghenaeden aen nam / ende wert door
Lubbert gerretsz oock alsoe begeert dat matheus [?] Iansz
oock doen soūde die welcke daer niet present was maer die
dienaers belooffden dat oock te vorderen ende hebben
Reynier wybrans alle met eenen kūsse ontffangen ende
alsoe in vreden vriendelyck gescheijden ende Lubbert
gerretsz met eenen cūsse des heeren ghenaden beūolen
ende goeden nacht gewenscht—ende hadde Lubbert
gerretsz oock te vooren hans de Rijs gebeeden alsoe
Reyner wybrans een Ionck man was dat hij hem doch in
alles met Raet ende daet wilde te hulpe komen / ende met
hem alle dingen ouerwegen ende handelen als sij tesaemen
hadden gedaen / het sij mondelingh ofte aen mallcanderen
te scrijūen nae gelegentheijt der saecken / verklaerden
lubbert gerretsz oock ende begeerden / datmen int ver-
handelen der sacramenten in alles soūden handelen tot die
meeste stichtinghe der gemeenten / seggende op somyge

plaetse*n* stellen bij ee*n* taffell daer omtrent 20 teffens aen
gaen sitte*n* / op andere plaetse*n* anders men soude daer in
handele*n* / wat met die meeste vreede mochtte geschiede*n* /
dat hij t wel aen ee*n* taffell inde Rijp[1] hadde toe gedient
en*de* oock op adere plaetse*n* etc

Claes claesz ansloo

Dit hebbe ick strach de*n* selŭe*n* dach voor een memorije
gescreŭe*n* soe haest als ick t hŭijs qŭam

[An early English Anabaptist Petition, probably written in
1614 (by Thomas Helwys ?).][2]

> To the right Hon*o*rable assemblie of the Commons-
> house of Parliament. /

> A most humble supplication of divers poore prisoners,
> and many others the king*es* ma*i*esties loyall subiect*es*
> ready to testifie it by y*e* oath of allegeance in all
> sinceritie, whose G r e v i a n c e s are lamentable, onely for
> cause of conscience. /

Most humbly sheweing.. That whereas in y*e* Parlia*ment* holden in
the 7th yere of the king*es* ma*i*esties Raigne that now is, it was
enacted that all persons whatsoever aboue the age of 18. yeres,
not comeing to Church &c. should take the oath of allegeance;
and for the refusall thereof, should be committed to prison
without baile &c. By w*h*ich Statute the Popish Recuzant*es*
vpon takeing the oath, are daily delivered from imprisonement*es* :
and divers of vs also are set at libertie when wee fall vnder the
hand*es* of y*e* Reverend Iudges & Iustices, But when wee fall
vnder the hand*es* of the B i s h o p s wee can have no benifitt by
the said oath, for they say it belongeth onely to P o p i s h
recuzant*es*, & not to others; but kept have wee bene by them
many yeres in lingering imprisonement*es*, devided from wives,
children, servant*es* & calling*es*, not for any other cause but
onely for conscience toward*es* God, to the vtter vndoeing of vs,
o*u*r wives & children. /

[1] De Rijp is a village in North Holland.
[2] MS. in the Library of the House of Lords, London, calendared under
the date, 1613.

Our most humble Supplication therefore to this
high & Honorable assemblie is, that in commiseration of
the distressed estate of vs our poore wives & children
it may be enacted in expresse wordes that other
the kinges maiesties faithfull subiectes, as well as Popish
Recuzantes may be freed from imprisonementes vpon
taking the said oath. /

And wee shall still (as wee do day & night) pray that the God
of heaven may be in your Honorable assemblie, for by him do
Princes decree Iustice. /

By his maiesties faithfull subiectes

most falsely called

reiected by the

Anabaptistes.

comittee

[An undated Latin Confession of Faith by Richard Overton,
probably written in 1615.][1]

Credo corde & confiteor ore

[? 1.] Vnum tantum esse Deum, vnum Christum, vnum
        Spiritum Sanctum, vnam Ecclesiam, vnam veritatem,
        vnam fidem, vnam veram Religionem.

2   In Dietate [sic] sunt tres personæ realiter distinctæ, Vater,
        Filius & Spiritus S. coeternales, coequales & coessen-
        tiales; omnes & singuli eorum vnus et idem Deus, non
        diuisæ sed distinctæ realiter inter se proprietatibus suis,
        viz. creatione, Redemptione & sanctificatione.

3.   Deus Pater est illius Esse à se non ab alio; Filius est
        idem illud Esse, non à se, sed a patre; Spiritus S. est
        idem illud Esse, sed non à se, sed a Patre & Filio: Ita
        Esse seu essentia diuina horum trium eadem est, et
        numero vna.

4.   Hæc Trinitas in vnitate coli et venerari debet in spiritu
        et veritate, et qui Deum sic veneratur fruetur vita

[1] MS. B. 1353 in the Mennonite Archives, Amsterdam. Professor
Dr Müller's translation of this document is given in Dr B. Evans'
"The Early English Baptists", Vol. I., pp. 254–56.

æterna, et modus Dei sic venerandi perfectè exprimitur per ipsum Deum in Veteri et Nouo testamento per manus prophetarum et Apostolorum, et qui vllo alio modo colit Deum, quàm illo his duobus testamentis expresso, fuerit ejectus è fauore & præsentia Dei cum Dæmonibus et suis Angelis in mortem æternam.

5. Quinto, credo et confiteor, quod Dominus norster [*sic*] Iesus Christus ab Apostolis prædicatus, fuit ipse Messias ab æterno promissus, de quo Prophetæ vaticinabantur & scribebant.

6 Sexto, credo omnia in Lege & Evangelio scripta & contenta esse vera, diuina & ab omnibus sic æstimanda & retinenda.

6 7°. Christum vnigenitum Dei filium esse Sacerdotem prophetam & regem secundem [*sic*] ordinem Melchesideci in æternum. Et ecclesia sua à nullo alio neque Cælo, terra & Inferis, sed ab ipso gubernari debet

Munus ejus propheticum est .1. reuelare voluntatem Patris; .2. instituere [?] ministerium; 3. intus docere seu efficacem esse per ministerium.

Munus Sacerdotale est, 1. docere nos, et aliter quidem, quàm alij sacerdotes, hoc est non tantum auribus per verbum, sed etiam in cordibus per S. S. .2. Offerre se victimam propitiatoriam pro omnibus & singulis totius mundi peccatis .3. orare & intercedere pro nobis perpetuò apud patrem. Ita vt ejus victima satis et sufficiens est pro omnibusque & [*sic*] singulis rationalibus in toto rerum vniverso degentibus, ad eorum redemptionem & salutem, si ijs propria fide adhibeatur & ad finem perseueratur.

Munus Regium constat in ejus resurrectione è mortuis et ascentione in cælum ad dextram patris vincens & sub pedibus ejus eijciens Orcum, mortem, peccatum & finalem condemnationem; omni potentia in cælo & terra spiritualiter gubernans suam Ecclesiam, adornans eam donis spiritualibus, ac tandem eam liberans ab omnibus malis; et planè debellatos in æternas pœnas detrudens.

vera & visibilis ejus Ecclesia est quidam numerus populi,

è mundo per verbum dei seperati, & per Baptismum
fidei et rescipiscentiæ collecti & constituti.

Concescit Christus hujus Ecclesiæ plenam potentiam &
autoritatem inter se juncto eorum beneplacito et vnanimo
mente eligere personas ad gerendum officia in hac
Ecclesia.   Et hæc et nulla alia sunt amplectanda viz:
pastorum Doctorum, presbyte[ro]rum, Diaconorum &
subministratorum; qui per verbum Dei ab om[n]i parte
qualificantur & approbantur.

Officia omnia Antichristiana cujuscunque fuerint generis
in hanc Ecclesia[m] non sunt admittenda sed funditus
exterpanda:

omnes humanæ traditiones & opiniones sunt odio cordis
prosequenda et fugienda; et si vnquam a quibusdam
sint assumpta, non sunt fouenda sed statim deponenda:
~: sed priusquam progrediar aut ad finem perveniar
ne sit quæso vobis molestum nosse me Anglicum esse
nuper Anglicanæ Ecclesiæ; sed convictus verbo Dei &
spiritu sanct[o] omnes ejus errores depono & in æternum
renuntio, et toto animo & mente cupio per baptismum
in veram Ecclesiam intrare.

porro credo duo tantum esse Sacramenta in Ecclesia
Christi administranda & amplectanda, videlicet, Baptismi
& Cæni Dominici: et hæc Sacramenta pænitentibus &
fidem exhibentibus administranda & communicanda ita
vt vterque eorum Infantibus omnibus et infidelibus omnibus sunt deneganda / quippe talibus non pertinent.

postremò, pænitet me plurimum peccati, et tristitiâ et
mærore confiteor me peccatorem maximum esse et
hucvsque in peccatis summis et quotidianis vixisse, sed
eorum remissionem expecto et quæro per Iesum Christum
æternum Dei filium, et post mortem in vitam æternam
intrare; In illius nomine itaque totis viribus Corporis et
animæ exopto et desidero in veram Ecclesia[m] per
Baptismum intrare et perseuerare

Quid restat ergo quin Baptizar. /

Richardus Overton

A Copie rightly related of an Anabaptists Letter, written to his sometimes accounted Christian Bretheren, shewing the cause of his separation *from the Church of England, indited by a principall Elder, in and of that Separation*[1].

BEloued Friends, the ancient loue that I haue had towards you, prouoketh me to testifie, that I haue not forgotten you, but am desirous still to shew my vnfained loue vnto you in any thing I may. I make no question but you haue heard diuers false reports of mee, although among the same some truths, and that you may be truely informed of my estate, I thought good to write a few words vnto you, hoping you will not speak euill of that you know not, nor condemne a man vnheard.

The thing wherein I differ from the Church of England, is, they say at their washing or baptizing in their Infantcy, They are mēbers, children of God, and inheritours of the kingdome of heauen. This I dare not beleeue; for the scriptures of God declare, that neither flesh, nor washing the flesh can saue. Flesh and blood cannot enter into the kingdome of God: for that is flesh, is flesh, and wee cannot enter into the kingdome of God, except wee be borne againe: They that haue prerogatiue to bee the sons of God, must bee borne of God, euen beleeue in his name: and the washing off the filth of the flesh, is not the Baptisme that saueth, but a good conscience maketh requests to God. If any bee in Christ, hee is a new creature. The consequence of this is, that Infants are not to bee baptized, nor can bee Christians; but such onely as confesse their Faith, as these Scriptures teach.

There is neither command, example, or iust consequence for

[1] From I. P.'s "Anabaptismes Mysterie of Iniquity Unmasked." etc., London, 1623, pp. 1–11. This letter, it will be remembered, was written by one who became an Anabaptist for a time, but returned into the Church of England before this book was printed. The letter is signed "H. N.", though Benjamin Stinton read it "H. H." Thomas Crosby printed it as Stinton read it, and followed Stinton in ascribing its authorship to Thomas Helwys, although the initials "H. H." are not those of Helwys. This letter as printed by Crosby has been used to show that Helwys lived until after the date May 10, 1622, a most false conclusion. See Vol. I., pp. 256–57.

Infants Baptisme, but for the baptizing of Beleeuers: There is
besides of the Church of God to be considered what it is: It
will plainely appeare, that Infants cannot bee of it; they that
know the language from whēce the word Church is taken, can
witnesse that it signifieth a people called out; and so the
Church of Christ is a company called out of their former estate
wherein they were by nature, out of *Babylon*, wherein they
haue been in spirituall bondage to the power of Antichrist, and
from hauing fellowship in spirituall worship with vnbeleeuers
and vngodly men, from all whosoeuer commeth out, they are fit
timber for his spirituall building, which is a habitation of God
by the spirit, and the houshold of faith: Those thus come out
of nature, Egyptian bondage, and the fellowship of the children
of Beliall, being newe Creatures; and so holy Brethren are
made Gods house or Church, through being knit together by the
Spirit of God, and baptized into his body, which is the Church.
This being vndeniable, the Church of Christ, Infants cannot
bee of it, for they cannot bee called out as aforesaid: knowne
wicked men cannot bᴐ of it, because they are not called out;
nor Antichrists spirituall bondage cannot bee of it, because that
is a habitation of Deuils, and all Gods people must goe out of
that. What can be iustly obiected against this? are not all
the sonnes of God by faith? If any be in Christ, or a Christian,
must hee not bee a new Creature? I pray you doe not take vp
the vsuall obiection which the Antichristians haue learned of
the Iewes: What tellest thou vs of being made Christians
onely by faith in the Sonne, and so being made free, wee are
the children of *Abraham*, and of Beleeuers. Wee are vnder
the promise, I will bee the God of thee and thy seed: thus are
we and our children made free, when as they neither doe nor
can beleeue in the Sonne. This is a Iewish Antichristian fable,
for *Abraham* had two sonnes, which were types of the two
Seedes, to the which two Couenauntes are made, the one borne
after the flesh, tiping out the fleshly Israelites, which were the
Inhabitants of materiall Ierusalem, where was the material
Temple, and the performance of those carnall Rites which
endured vnto the time of Reformation.

    The other by Faith, typing out the children of the faith of

Abraham, which are the Inhabitants of the spirituall Ierusalem, the new Testament in which is the spirituall Temple, the Church of the liuing God, and the performance of all those spirituall Ordinances which Christ Iesus as Prophet and King thereof, hath appoynted, which remaines, and cannot be shaken or altered.

Now if the olde Couenant bee abolished, and all the appertainings thereof, as it is, as being similitudes of heauenly things, euen the Couenant written in the booke, the people, the Tabernacle, or Temple, and all the ministring Vessels, and a better Couenant established, vpon better promises, and better Temple and ministring vessels come instead thereof, procured and purchased by the blood of Iesus Christ, who is the new and liuing way. Let vs draw neere with a true heart in assurance of Faith, sprinkled in our hearts from an euill conscience, & baptized in our bodies with pure water. Let vs keepe this profession of hope without wauering, and haue no confidence in the flesh, to reap Iustification or Christianitie thereby; but let vs cast it away as dung and drosse: For if euer any might plead priuiledge of being the child of the faithful, the Apostle *Paul* might, as hee saith, read the place, but it was nothing till hee had the Righteousnesse of God through Faith. Then was he baptized into Christ Iesus for the remission of his sinnes. This Couenant, that we as children of *Abraham,* challenge is the couenant of life and saluation by Iesus Christ, made to all the children of *Abraham,* as it is made to *Abraham* himselfe, to them that beleeue in him that raised vp Iesus our Lord from the dead; and also *Acts* 13. 26. 32 39. the children of the flesh are not they, Rom. 9. 8. they must bee put out, and must not bee heyres with the faithfull: If they that are of the Lawe bee heires, Faith is made void, and the promise is made of none effect: therefore it is by Faith, that it might come by grace, and the promise might bee sure to all the seed that are of the faith of *Abraham,* who is the Father of all the faithfull. They are his children, the promise of saluation is not made with both *Abrahams* seeds, but with his one seed, they that are of the Faith of *Abraham.* These things may bee strange to those that are strangers from the life of God, through

the ignorance that is in them, because of the hardnesse of their
hearts God hath written them as the great things of his Lawe,
but they are counted of many as a strange thing, but Wisdome
is iustified of all her children, & they that set their hearts to
seeke wisdome, as siluer, and search for her as for treasure, they
shal see the righteousnesse of those things as the light, and the
euidence of them as the noone day.   They that bee wise, will
trie these things by the true touch-stone of the holy Scriptures,
and leaue off reioycing in men, to hang their Faith & Profession
on them, the which I cease not to supplicate God, day and
night on the behalfe of you all, To whose gracious direction I
commit you, with a remembrance of my hartie loue to euery
one, desiring but this fauour, that for requital I may receiue
your louing answere.

London. 10. *Maij* 1622.

> *Yours to be commanded alvvayes*
> *in any Christian Seruice.*
>
> H. N.

I haue sent to my Friends a testimonie of my loue: one booke
to Master *Strowd*, one to Goodman *Ball*, one to Mistris
Fountaine, one to *Roger Seely*, one to *Samuel Quash*, and one
to your selfe.

*I beseech you reade, consider, and the Lord giue you vnder-
standing in all things.*

[A letter from the "teachers and Ministers of the dutch and
english Churches" in Amsterdam, dated May, 1624, to the
Congregation of Elias Tookey, which had been excommunicated
by John Murton and the then existing Five English Anabaptist
Congregations.][1]

> Vermeerderinge in godlijcke wysheijt, ende
> kennisse der goddelycke waerheyt, wenschen wy

---

[1] MS. B. 1367 in the Mennonite Archives, Amsterdam. This transcript is made from the contemporary copy of the original MS. The
original is becoming difficult to read. Professor Dr Müller's translation
of this document is given in Dr B. Evans' "The Early English Baptists",
Vol. II., pp. 32–7.

van gansher herten, onse gelieŭede vrinden, die
den voorsmaeck hebben der hemelscher dingen,
en*de* 16. int getal syn, mits [?] allen den geenen,
die ontrent haer syn, ende om de waerheijt
ijŭeren, van godt den vader en*de* Iesŭ Christo
onsen heere ende algemeynen salichmaker. Amen.

Seer behertichde vrinden, wij hebben onlancx v, l, schrijŭen
vanden 29. Maert stilo antiqŭo ontfangen, en*de* met
vreŭchden gelesen. Godt danckende vande genade, die hy
onver*dient*, door syn lyeffde ende vriendelyckheyt, oŭer v
lieden ryckelyck wtgestort heeft, daer in dat hij, in dese
ver*duijsterde [?] werelt, de eŭangelische waerh*eyt*, in v laet
schijnen, ŭwe oogen des gemoedts ver*licht, en*de* tot prys
synder heerlycker genaden, en vorderinge ŭwer sielen
salicheijt, met erkentenis syns wils v lieden aengedaen
heeft. Wij bidden by [*sic*] lieŭen Godt, dat hij dat aengevangen werck, door den dienst Christi, wil segenen, ende den
opganck der sonnen, die inden morgenstont doorbreeckt,
en*de* opgaet tot den vollen dach toe, in v lieden herten wil
gelyck maken, en*de* v allen daer by genade ende hemelsche
cracht geŭen, op dat ghij door een affgestorŭen heijlich
leuen, vwe ver*lichtinge onder dit ver*keert geslacht, dat
syn wandelinge heeft inde dŭijsterheijt der sonden, moocht
wtdrŭcken, ende bekent maken, tot godes eere, vorderinge
ŭwer salicheijt, en*de* veeler ver*lichtinge en*de* beteringe.
Amen.

Wij syn beweecht geworden aen v allen te antwoorden,
en*de* te bewijsen onse hertlycke goede genegentheijt, en*de*
Christlycke affectie tot ŭwarts; als oock die vreŭchde, die
wij geschept hebben indien aenvangk van ŭwe ver*lichtinge.
V lieder christlycke groete is ons aengenaem geweest. ende
oft het getal der geenre [geene], die de heere belieft heeft
met kennisse der waerheijt te begnadigen, noch cleen is, soe
hebben wij ons hertlyck ver*blydt, vertroŭwende dat godt
het aengevangen licht syner waerheyt by veelen sal laten
door breecken, gelyck de geboorte Christi naden vleesche
eerst weynige werdt bekent gemaeckt, maer daer nae wijdt

is wtgebreydt, also syn wy in goeder hoop en dat de
geboorte en*de* kennisse Christi naden geest, die in v
aengevangen is, oock wij der sal doorbreecken, tot veeler
behoŭdinge en*de* salicheyt.

Wij hebben met ve*r*langen ve*r*wacht op v lieder schrijŭen,
gelyck wij ve*r*staen dat ghy oock ve*r*langht hebt om
eenich schryŭen van ons te becomen. De oorsaken van v
lieder ve*r*treck gedenckt ghij, wij nemen [?] die in lyeffden
op. De onse syn geweest om dat wij, nae v l, afscheydt
van ons, geen schriftelyck bescheijt van v, l, en hebben
gecregen, hoe onse schriften en*de* mondtlycke redenen, die
wy met ŭwe boden gehadt hebben, by den ŭwen geacht
waeren, dit wilt ons oock int goede affnemen.

Wt v l. schrijuen ve*r*staen wij dat ghij van Ian Morton
met den synen geexcommŭniceert, ofte wt haere ve*r*-
gaderinge geworpen syt. De voornaemste oorsaecke soŭde
syn v lieder gevoelen vande ve*r*draechsaemheijt der
swacken, ofte cleen ve*r*standig*en* in schriftŭerlycke ve*r*-
standen, die nochtans conscientieŭs syn in alles dat sy
waerlyck weeten, en stil en vreedtsaen [*sic*] inde gemeinte
syn. etc   Dus is leedt geweest sŭlcx te hooren, en t'heeft
ons van herten misvallen. Wij wenschen die v lieden
ve*r*worpen hebben meerder wijsheijt; dat ghij lieden
ve*r*dŭldelyck draecht alle de iniŭrien, die v om gemelder
saken oŭervallen, die niet weynich ve*r*weest en syn, en*de*
noch niet op en hoŭden, en*de* v ve*r*laet op de oprechtiche*ijt*
ŭwer herten, de goedtheyt ŭwer saken, en*de* de beloften
godts, daer aen doet ghij soe Christenen betaemt, t'is ons
lyeff geweest te hooren, wij ve*r*manen, bidden, en smeecken
v, blyeft op dien padt, ve*r*gelt geen qŭaedt met qŭaedt,
lastert noch iniŭrieert niet weder, maer hoŭdt v inde
voetpaden Christi, en*de* volcht het lydtsaem exempel der
heyligen, en*de* laet ŭwe vrindelyckheyt, gedŭlt, en*de*
lydtsaenheijt [*sic*] eenen yderen kenlyck worden, acht het
geringe met Paŭlo van eenen menschelycken dage geoor-
deelt te wesen 1. cor: 4. hebt medelijd*en* met sŭlcker
lieden onve*r*stant, en*de* draecht v in sŭlcke zee-stormen
nade woorden Paŭli .1. cor: 6. als Dienaers godts met

grote verdŭldicheyt, met drŭck, met noodt, met anxt. etc.
ende laet ŭwe gebeden voor de gene, die v leedt doen, tot
godt opclimmen, nae d'exempel Christi, gedenckt dat ghij
mede onverstandich geweest zijt, ende mogelyck ymandt
te ontydt veroordelt hebt, dit doende sŭldij v bewijsen
Christi bryeff te syn, met den vinger des leŭendigen Godts,
inde tafelen ŭwes [? ŭwer] herten geschreŭen, ende ŭwe
wysheyt, lydtsaemheyt, ende verdŭldicheyt sal den onver-
standigen tot een licht, en beter gesicht dienen.

Dat ghy lieden veel middelen gebrŭijckt hebt om inde
eenicheyt met de gene, die v lieden wtgeworpen hebben,
te blyŭen, verblydt ons; want t'is Christelyck nae vrede
ende eenicheijt te staen, oft te iagen. De heylige geest
vermaent daer toe, wij beclagen dat ghij in desen te
vergeeffs gearbeijt hebt, ende dat ghij nŭ hopeloos zyt in
sŭlcke lofflycke saecke yet vrŭchtbaers wt te rechten, hebt
geen beroŭv van allen ŭwen arbeyt in deser saken; want
t'sal in v t'aller tijt veroorsaken een goede conscientie, die
boŭen alle schatten gaet; maer inde gene, die v verdruckt
en versmaedt hebben, droeffheijt en roŭwe, wanneer sy tot
beter kennisse sŭllen gecomen syn, t'welck wy wenschen
dat haest geschiede, eer den dach bij haer ondergae.

Ghy lieden wildet geerne v saken ten gerechte stellen voor
de Dŭijtsche ende engelsche Gemeente alhier, onpartijdich
wilden wy oock geerne v saken verhoren, ende affhandelen,
op dat de geschillen nedergeleijt [?], ende vrede mocht gevonden werden. Maer hoe sal dat connen geschieden also
lange als v partijen haer daertoe niet verstaen en willen?
t'moet [?] godt opgedragen, en den tijt beŭolen sijn.

Soe Ian Morton, oft ijmant vanden synen hyer tot ons
oŭercomt met vreedtlijeŭender herten, ende geseggelycken
gemoede, t'sal ons lijeff syn, ende oft godt gaŭe dat sy by
ons op soe een wyse verschenen, soe mocht wat goedts door
haer comste veroorsaeckt worden: Soo het oock op een
ander wijse geschiede, soe en hebt geen gedachten dat sy
lieden hier in onse gemeenten eenige beroerte sŭllen
aenrechten. onse broederschap is door ervarentheijt, ende
het aenmercken vande menigerleije twisten, die de

twistige volcken ronts om ons gehadt hebben, en*de* noch
dagelycx hebben, door het der*ü*en van dese vreed-voedende
leere der v*er*drachsaemh*eijt*, geleert geworden, hoe lyefflyck,
costelyck, en goedt het is, dat broeders eendrachtich
t'samen woonen, psalm 133. also dat wij door yemants
comste geen v*er*storinge onder den onsen en bevresen.

Oft wel de sendtbrijeff, die wij *ü*we boden medega*ü*en, en
v lieden, gelyck ghij claecht, ontho*ü*den wort, maer van
twee onser leeraren, namentlyck van Hans de ries en
Reynier Wybrants*en* onderteeckent is, soe affirmeren wij
by desen dat den inho*ü*de is het gemeen v*er*stant, en*de* die
leere onder alle onse gemeenten, insonderh*eijt* t'st*ü*ck
vande v*er*draechsaemheijt, en*de* wort by ons allen geho*ü*den
als eenen sodanig*en* artickel, die wij met vre*ü*chden
omhelsen, also de sel*ü*e is een vande bysonderste oorsaken
vande vrede en*de* eenicheyt, oft t'samen-ho*ü*dinge onser
gemeenten. Soe Ian Morton, ofte ymant vanden synen
anders seijt, dat moeten wij lyden, en*de* Christelyck
v*er*dragen. Maer tot ons comende salt inde ondersoeckinge,
gelyck als wij geschre*ü*en hebben, en*de* hijer in noch
schrij*ü*en, be*ü*onden worden, en*de* niet anders. daerom en
hebben wij geen vreese voor syne, ofte eens anders comste,
als oft wij so*ü*den sorgen, dat ymant onder onse gemeen-
schap, door s*ü*lck*en* middel, so*ü*de vande vreedtlije*ü*entheijt
affgeleijt worden

Nochtans en sal v l, niet v*er*staen dat wij de v*er*draechsaemheijt onbepaelt drij*ü*en, als oft wij alle onverstanden
hoe groot, oft hoedanich die wes*en* mochten, onder ons
plaetse so*ü*den g*ü*nnen, ô neen. Maer wij bepalen die
met de heylige schrift*ü*re, en proe*ü*ense met alle wijsheijt.

Wij v*er*staen dat v. l. een genoegen hebt aen de oorsaken
by ons gesteet, waerom wij aen ons*e* Magistraten naer v. l.
begeren niet ges*ü*ppliceert en hebben, dat laten wij ons
welgevallen.

Gelyck ons dan mede behaecht t'gene v l vande eerste
sche*ü*ringe hebt geschre*ü*en, te weten, dat ghij siet dat de
affgesche*ü*rde sch*ü*lt hebben, om dat sy haer aen een
waere Gemeente niet gege*ü*en en hebben, maer onordentlyck

een van selŭen opgerecht, en secten gemaeckt, oock dat sy de censŭre Christi misbrŭijckt hebben. etc. Also v. l. door godts genade soe veele verlicht syt, dat ghij de gemelde gebreecken siet en kent soe bidden ende vermanen wy v, dat ghij neerstich toesiet, v kennisse wysselyck beleeft, ende sulcker lieden onwyse drijŭinge tot geener tyt niet gelyck en wort. Wy hebben haer lieden int begin der scheŭringe genoechsaem gewaerschoŭt, ende sulcke onge-ordineertheijt affgeraden, ende tot lydtsaemheyt ende ver-draechsaemheyt vermaent, maer onse redenen en waren by haer niet ontfanghbaer, tot onsen leedtwesen.

Geerne hebben wij in v schrijŭen gelesen, dat ghij niet en syt van dat gevoelen als noodtwendich achtende alle eerste dach inde weecke broodt te breecken, maer laten sŭlcx in der gemeenten vrijheijt, alst gelegen zij, gelyck ghij lieden oock selŭe oeffent.

Wt de woorden, gelyck ghij oock scluc oeffent, verstaen wij dat ghij affgesonderde het broot des heeren onder malcanderen breeckt, ofte het Sacrament des .h. aŭontmaels met den anderen hoŭdt. Soe wij dit recht verstaen, soe connen wij niet saen oft ghij doet soe doende t'selŭe dat ghij in andere berispt, te weten, dat ghij lieden, eer ghij v aen een waere gemeente hebt gegeŭen, ende door de selue in Christlycke ordeninge gestelt syt, een nieŭwe gemeente oprecht, en valt also int oordeel ŭwer partijen. Ende oft wij v. l niet te gebieden en hebben, soe vermanen en raden wij v allen, in sŭlcke kercklycke saken stil te hoŭden, tot breeder onderhandelinge, op dat alles onder v lieden or-dentlyck geschiede, ende een schriftŭerlyck aensien hebbe. Voor den aenvangk ŭwer scheŭringe was v lieder gevoelen dat een particŭlier broeder, sonder der gemeenten beroe-pinge, mocht de Sacramenten wtdeijlen, als mede dat het niet geoorloft was, in tyde der vervolginge in een ander landt te vlŭchten, ende aldaer te wonen, wij soŭden geerne verstaen, oft hijer in bij v lieden veranderinge is, oft dat ghij noch staet inde selŭe meyninge.

Doen ŭwe boden hier waren, ende wy mondtlyck met haer spraken, verclaerden wij haer dat den strijdt artickel vande

15—2

hercomst des vleeschs Christi by ons gehoŭden werde verdragelyck inden genen, die Christi menscheijt niet en versaekten, maer hem beleden warachtich mensche te wesen; maer soe ymant dat soe verre wilde trecken, als oft wij oock verdragelyck hielden Christi godtheijt te versaken, oft te lochenen dat Christŭs waere godt zij, die soŭde ons niet wel, maer qŭalijcken verstaen hebben. Daerom sal v. l. belieŭen ons te ontdecken, hoe wij de woorden in v schrijŭen verstaen sŭllen, te weten, dese : wij en binden niemant te verstaen ofte vatten van Christo, als wy van hem verstaen als sommige oft andere doen, maer verdragen malcanderen etc. geerne wilden wy weeten oft dit alleen geseijt sy vande hercomst des vleeschs Christi, oft dat daer onder oock begrepen wort d'artickel vander godtheyt Christi. ende dat ghij lieden oock verdragelyck hoŭdt, en onder v verdraecht, de gene de godtheijt Christi versaecken, oft Christŭm niet en bekennen warachtich godt te syn inden vader, en met den vader, ende den .h. geest. v. l. sal belieŭen hier van ons toe te schrijŭen ŭwe rechte meyninge ende insien.

Int stŭck vanden eedt, ende het ampt der oŭerheijt schrijeff v. l. dat sommige met ons syn, ende andere niet. v. l. sal ons belieŭen te berechten, oft de gene, die met ons in beijde artickelen niet en stemmen, wt lyeffden tot der gemeenten vrede ende stichtinge, haer wel wilden ont-hoŭden om haer gevoelen te beleŭen, oft dat wanneer sy gevordert werden, insonderheyt tot het gebrŭijck der wapenen, haer verstant soŭden beleŭen willen. wy achtent noodtwendich hier van te hebben waere wetenschap en kennisse.

Dat de andere artickelen in onse confessie gemelt, by v allen voor Christelyck worden gehoŭden, ende daer door bekent ontfangen te hebben veel geestlycke verlichtinge, daer oŭer dancken wij den lieŭen godt, die den oorspronck ende aenvanger is alles goedes, ende van wijen alle goede, volmaeckte gaŭen affvloijen. wij bidden hem dat hij, tot syner eeren ende ŭwer aller heijl, v wil genade cracht, en gaŭen geŭen tot volcomen toeneminge, ende opwassinge

inde aengevangen kennisse der waerheijt, hoŭdt oock
gelyckmoedich aen in een heijlich leŭen, met smeecken en
bidden tot den alderhoochste*n*, gedenckt dat hij getroŭv is,
die syn beloften in v ver*v*ŭllen, iae en*de* amen maken sal.

Met vreŭchden en blydtschappen hebben wij ve*r*staen
ŭwer aller heijlich voornemen om in onse broederschap
aengenomen te worden, en*de* sichtelyck te ve*r*eenigen met
onse gemeenten. wij syn daertoe oock wilvaerdich, en*de*
des voornemens om t'selŭe met godes hŭlpe in goeder
ordeninge te volstrecke*n*, nae dat wij ŭwe antwoorde op
desen sŭllen ontfangen, en*de* ve*r*staen hebben dat wij
sodanige gelyckheijt hebben inde kennisse der waerheijt,
daer wt wij ve*r*troŭwen mogen vreedtsaem, als Christenen
toecomt, met malcanderen te mogen leŭen.

Van vwe opponenten en hebben wij geen schrijŭen noch
clachten, tot v lieder nadeel ontfangen. Soo ons nae
desen yet behandicht wort, soe sŭlle*n* wij ons, als on-
partydige toecomt, daer in hoŭden en vinden laten.

Wij ve*r*staen dat de gelden, die wij ŭwe boden behandicht
hebben, wel syn bestelt, gelyck wij ŭwe boden sonder
eenich achterdencken toebetroŭt hebben.

Aldŭs geantwoort hebbende op v. l. aengenaem schrijŭen
slŭijten wij desen, en sŭllen ŭwe bescheijden weder antwoorde met ve*r*langen ve*r*wachten. de genade onses heeren
Iesŭ Christi zy oŭer v allen, Amen.

In Amstelredam desen [blank space] May A*n*no 1624. onder-
teeckent met consent en*de* welgevallen der leraren en*de*
Dienaren der dŭijtsche*r* en*de* engelscher Gemeenten Iesŭ
Christi aldaer, by ons

[A Letter from Elias Tookey and his Congregation at
London to the Dutch and English united (Waterland) Church
at Amsterdam, dated June 3, 1624, in answer to the preceding
communication, and expressing the hope that they may be
received into the membership of that Church, etc.][1]

[1] MS. B. 1368 in the Mennonite Archives, Amsterdam. Professor
Dr Müller's translation of this document is given in Dr B. Evans' "The
Early English Baptists", Vol. II., pp. 21–4.

Seer diere vrienden tot ons, weetet, dat wy ontvangen hebben vwe graue ende gratieus antwoord : het welke onsen alder sielen groote vreuchde veroorsaect, want ghy hebt onser herten bequaemlich toe ghesproken daerin : hat [het] selue dat Godt doet, deur het licht des leuens Christum nae den gheest ende op het ontvancke van vwen brief (daer wesende een trouwe bode ghereet) wy versamelde terstont beyde te lesen ende ouerleggen wat besceyt [?] aen v. l. te seynden : deur wiens snelle afsceydt, wy sijn veroorsaect gheworden alle vwen wijse schriften ouer te scricken : maer het gheen alleen, het welke v. l. van onse begeert, dat wy onsen ghevoelen daer van scrijuen soude.

1. Eerstelich wy mercken, dat ghy ons acht ghefaljeert te hebben, int brecking des broodts ofte het ontvancke des nacht-maels onder malcanderen sedert onsen w^{t}werpinghe : etc ~ tot den welke, wy antwoorden, nae dien dat daer gheen waere voor-gaende ghemeenten waren, by wien wy ons by ghevoeght mochte hebben onder een volle order te comen wy hebben dus ghesinte gheweest, dat in sulke saecken, een gheemeente mochte die Sacramenten ghebruicken : maer wy willen noch onthouden (ghelijck ghy ons radet) tot dat wy hooren van v wederom : hopende die scriften beter gheopent te hebben tot ons by v. l. in desen stucke

2. Wy staen noc ghesint, dat een particuliere broeder mocht die Sacramenten bedienen wanneer die ghemeente hem daer toe roept, al is hy niet int officie van den pastoorscap : met desen proviso dat die ghemeente gheen officiers en hebt, maer heeft sy, dan houden wy dat een particuliere broeder gheensins doen macht : maer in desen wy sullen willich weesen te leeren / waerin wy faljeeren.

3. Wy houden het niet ongheorloft, int tydt der vervolginge te vluchten in een ander landt daer te woonen, ende sommighe onder ons hebben noyet so ghehouden.

4. Wy verstaen dat die heylige ende vreedsame leeringe der verdraeginge niet misbruickt en wort, hoe well sommige die

still sijn, in die ghemeente blijuen: die als noch niet well en weeten, wat van Christi godheyt te begrijpen: so sy [?] salichheyt alleen deur hem houden, ende in het gheen, waer toe sy ghecomen sijn, oprecht blijuen: deur welke vruchten der oprechticheyt wy verstaen, dat Christi Godheyt, hem selue in haer toont: welke ons versekert, dat sy Gods eygene sijn, hoe well sy als noch in het vernunft ende cerebro [?], dien verholentheyt of mysterie niet becoomen connen: maer ist dat eenighe die gheemeen verstant des ghemeents herein [*sic*] opponeren, ofte in eenighe andere stucken daer een onrustich eende domineerende gheest, wy houden dat sodanige niet te verdragen worden: maer om haerder onrusticheyt, ende om dat sy soecken [?] ouer anderen te hersscen, vermijdt hooren te weesen.

Veerder [?] wy laeten v. l. weeten, dat daer gheen onder ons sijn die den Godheyt Christi versaken: maer daer sijn 2 of 3 onder ons die in haer seluen een weynech anders van ghevoelen, als wy int generael doen, nochtans all comt op een in het leste: als wy het verstaen. die generael vatten, dat sijn Godheyt bestaet in den oneyndelich klont alias massa ofte onbegrijpelich substantie der goddelich natuer alleen: die andere vatten, het gheen te wesen all dat w^{t}vluyt natuerlich (als die licht van den Sonne) w^t dien oneyndelich substantie, ende dat desen w^{t}vloet bestaet in veel particulieren: als een lichaem bestaet in veele lyden: euen so is Christus 1 Cor: 12. 12 ver. ende het is goddeliche cracht, wijsheyt, ghenade, gherechticheyt etc ~ wien God w^{t}ghesonden heeft beyde die wereld te maken: ende den mensch ghevallen sijnde te versoenen: dese int corte is het gescill in het vernunft [?], aengaende die Godheyt Christi: ende sullen wy malkanderen ordeelen om desen ghevoeltingen: het sy veer maer in dien wy eenige sien van onser ghemeente Christum te cruiscigen of crucificeren, ofte die goddelich natuer waer van sy deelaehtich sijn, deur die bedroch der sonden: om desen oordeelen wy, om dat wy sakerlich weten dat die woort Gods sulken alrede gheordeelt heeft. in dese oock wy sijn ghewillich te hooren met alder snellheyt, wat God v. l. hierin kundich [?] ghemacht heeft: ende laeten het tot vwen discrete consideratie.

5. Een eedt, wort ons niet dickwills voorghestelt, ende sommige wy mogen weygeren, sonder veel scult ofte scaede: nochtans het weygeringe van sommige eedt in onsen land, willen brengen beyde scult ende scade: als of wy weigeren soude den eedt der trouwheyt aen onsen koninc: wy souden gheheeten wesen verraders, ende wilde sy het w^tterste extremiteyt ghebruicken: sy mochten tegen ons procederen als tegen verraders: waer deur wy vallen int' pericell haerder wett: ende oock die heylige waerheyt, welke wy belyden, soude wesen door boose mensken quaed gheacht, ende wy ghehouden als commerlich ofte onrustich persoonen in een stadt, om niet te doen, het gheen, dat wy versekert sijn, dat wy doen mogen sonder sonde in sodanich eenen saecke a[l?]s dese is: wy begeeren van v. l. te weeten welke v. l. ordeelt het slimste te wesen: te weten desen eedt te nemen ofte te weigeren: oock ofte het so vallen soude, doet sommige deur nood-dranck soude ghebracht werden te nemen, ofte het door vreede verdragen mochte werden: wederom in onse landt soude wy desen eedt weigeren, wy konde niet vrye borgers ghemackt worden binnen onse steden, noch op eenige tydt comen w^t onsen landt, het sy om traffique te doen om den cost te crijgen, of te vlieden van vervolginge om der conscientie wille: nochtans willen wy myden desen ende alle andere so veel onsen vermogen aengaet, nu, ende euwelich

6. Aengaende magistratie, ende waepenen of crijch-handell, wy willen in gheender manier aenveerden ofte ondernemen: sommige van conscientie, ende die reste om der vreede wille euwelich.

Aldus hebben wy int corde gheantwoort tot vwen begeerten, niet hebbende tydt te scrijuen yet breeder op desen tydt, ende ofte wy hadde, nochtans konde wy v. l. niet vorderen: want wy hopen dat ghy zijt in, ofte nae by den vullheyt der vreuchte [?], ofte stant der volkomentheyt, in dien manier, dat wy sien ende gheloouen: maer als noch veer te corte zijn: maer wy willen niet ophouden te bidden, dat die gheen die desen werke begont [?] heeft het sy in v. l. ofte in ons mochte het volbrengen tot den dach Iesu [?] Christi toe in onse beyde wy alle groeten v hertelich in den Heere: genade sy met allen   Amen.

Desgelijcks wy bidden v. l. in dien ghy ons in v. l. ghemeenscap ontvangen kont laet het v belieuen; te scrijuen sommighe woorden aen Ian [Iohn] Morton ende sijnen vrienden, streckende to[e?] vreede ende order: het sal oock vervordert worden so veel ons vermocht: ende sommighe die met hem houden, sijn well ghereet & will-veerdich om sulken vreede, als den stucke der verdraegsaemheyt ender order te omhelsen. Daer sijn twee (die aen sijnen kant waren) ghevallen op personael successie van den tydt der Apostelen: ende wilden gheerne weeten, ofte eenighe die nu staen waere gheconstitueerde ghemeenten konnen seggen, dat sy haeren afcomste hadde, van hand tot hand, van den tydt der Apostelen af. ende ist saeck, dat dese niet gheprobeert can werden: dan woude sy gheerne hooren van den opstandinghe of oprijsinghe der alder oudtste dat nu sy: ende op watt manier: ende of v. l. die gheene zijt: ofte van hun. sy sijn goede volke, ende begeeren God te behagen, ende te leuen in een waere order: daerom, laet hat [het] v belieuen, te doen wat v. l. kont om haer te vreede te stellen.

Iunij 3. 1624.	V. l. vrienden alleen, in, ende om die heylige
van London.	waerheyt, ende hemelsche Leeuen:
	Elias Tookey ende die andere.

[A Letter, dated Nov. 12, 1626, from the Five Early English Anabaptist Congregations at London, Lincoln, Sarum, Coventry, and Tiverton, to Hans de Ries, Reinier Wybrantsz., and their Congregations in Holland, expressing the wish that they might be united with them in one religious communion.][1]

Dilectis nostris amicis Hans de Reys et Reynero wybransono atque ecclesijs ex quibus sunt, simul ac cum omnibus alijs Ministris et ecclesijs in eadem via cum illis ambulantibus remanentibus in Hollandia, atque illis partibus: Ecclesiæ Iesu Christi, quæ in Anglia sunt, habitantes Londini, Lincolniæ, Sarum, Couentriæ, ac Tyuertoniæ,

---

[1] MS. B. 1372 in the Mennonite Archives, Amsterdam. Professor Dr Müller's translation of this letter is given in Dr B. Evans' "The Early English Baptists", Vol. II., pp. 26–30.

mittunt salutem ex córde optantes cunctas vobis multiplicari gratias a deo patre per Dominum Iesum Christum

Dilecti Amici, post salutationes ex corde optantes vestram assiduam prosperitatem ac salutem, eò quod Dominum Iesum Christum ac illius benedictam veritatem diligitis; cuius gratia, nos omnes eundem dominum Iesum, ac veritatem eius vobiscum diligentes, decet, omnibus modis conari vnanimes [*sic*] esse, cum omnibus quibuscunque, et in vna cumunione ac societate secum ambulare. ideo persuasi sumus nos in hoc deo gratos fore, nempe in tam bono laudabilique opere, vnde bonum domini populo redundet ad adiuvandum ac stabiliendum eos in veritate: porro cum antehac plurimùm vobiscum vnionem pacemque peractam fore a nobis et cupiuimus et quæsiuimus, quorum primi ac præcipui viri nunc mortui sunt ac cum domino requiescunt; nos igitur qui relinquimur, eodem desiderio affecti promovendi Dei gloriam, ac populi sui bonum, nunc denuo idem suscepimus [?], quamobrem hos duos nostros dilectos amicos ac fratres, homines a nobis approbatos ob illorum constantiam ac fidelitatem pro causa *chris*ti in patiendo constantèr, longam ac tediosam incarcerationem, ad vastationem et pene illorum ruinam qui vobis nostram mentem declarabunt, ad vos misimus: (si necesse sit) præter quod vobis in hoc scripto nostro patefecimus. /

Quod ad articulos vestræ fidei attinet, quos mundo excusos patefecistis [?], tanquam fidem vestrum omnium: (præcipue in fundamento) ante hac ad nos a vobis missos, nos sedulo legimus, et considerauimus [?], et cum alta et indissimulata laude Deo omnipotenti, sanctum nomen suum magnificamus eo quod differentiæ inter nos non sunt maiores: et quod principia Christi, tam purè a vobis agnoscuntur: attamen ad vos intellectum nostrum in quibusdam, in quibus aliquid invicem differre videamur, scripsimus: quibus tamen rectè intellectis vtrimque, nihil differre videatur. idcirco vos oramus, ad nos vestras mentes per hos legatos nostros conscriptas mittere, ac eatiam [?] hos nuncios nostros verbatim certiores reddere. /

1. De differentijs igitur nos dicimus tanqua*m* vos scripsistis, vnum agnoscente*m* Christum Deum ac hominem in vna persona, secundu*m* vestrum articulu*m* octauum, quamvis ignoret an substantia*m* a Maria sumpserat, an non; et nec opponit nec contendit aduersus fidem alioru*m*, in re illa hunc recipi, manere ac tolerari posse in societate fidelium sine reiectione seu conde*m*natione

2. De iureiurando nos nullam videmus discrepantia*m*, cum informati sumus ac partim noscimus vos legitimu*m* tenere, veretatem loqui coram Magistratu seu quocunq*ue*, et super iustam occasionem Dei reuerendum nomen ad testimonium sumere, veru*m* esse; secundu*m* scripturas has Ro: 1. 9. 2 Cor: 1. 2. 3. phill: 1. 8. et aliàs fas esse iurare non tenemus omnino secundum has scripturas, matt: 5. 34. Iam: 5. 12.

3: Oblata iusta occasione impedimenti, affirmamus cænam dominicam omitti posse donec tollantur impedimenta: aut aliter non audemus omittere quoque die sabbati quu*m* convenimus ad præstandu*m* cætera Dei publici Ministerij: cum exemplum [?] Ecclesiaru*m* Dei habemus approbantium nos hac in re hocq*ue* tam pretiosa*m* esse nostræ spiritualis consolationis, ac vnionis cu*m* christo, et mutuò, et coniunctionis invic[e]m partem: qua*m* vllam aliam Dei ministerij partem: aut aliter cum volumus, faciamus semel in .7. annis si velimus: et tunc cur non reliquæ partes publicæ religionis, quæ eiusmodi sunt cu*m* hoc, tam diu etiam deferantur. /

4. Ministrationem sanctoru*m* sacramentoru*m* inseperatim cu*m* ministerio verbi, coniunctam esse agnoscimus et cuiq*ue* membro corporis admin*i*strare sacramenta no*n* licere, hoc tame*n* affirmamus ministros esse, corporis qui non constituuntur per impositionem manuum in episcopatu*m*, qui prædicent, convertant ac baptizent, et ædificent ecclesiam, atq*ue* cæteras publicas actiones consentiente ecclesia præstent absentibus episcopis: solu*m* autem expedit cu*m* ecclesia episcopos habet [?], et cu*m* adfuerint, vt illi

ducerent omnes ecclesiæ publicas actiones, tanqua*m* ecclesiæ publici ministri ac serui. /

finaliter, pro ipso magistratu, Inprimis concepimus vos
non tantopere vestrum in hoc iudiciu*m* vrgere adeo, vt
neminem contrariæ mentis admittatis, at quosdam qui
vobiscu*m* non consentiunt, recipitis hac in re velut ac
nos vere instruimur, vos*que* quenda*m* magistratum con-
trouersias finientem, causas, lites*que* in posessionibus, ac
alijs rebus mundanis approbare iudicare si non sanguine*m*,
arma, bellaùe attigerit: adeo nostram, re vera differentiam non circa magistratum, sed circiter executionem
ipsius officij versari. scilicet an magistratus sit iure ex
ecclesia, vtens nulla parte suæ mundanæ authoritatis in
Christi spirituali regno, vel ecclesia; sed hoc potius an in
mundo illo gladio, quem Deus ei dabit [?] ad defenden̄du*m*
ius suorum subiectorum terrestriu*m*, contra om*n*es in-
vasiones, iniurias [?], ac eiusmodi malefactores puniat, qui
occidunt, &c. vtatur; hoc concipimus esse differentiam. /

In hac re vobis ne displiceat, nos libere pati vobis nostras
mentes significare, cu*m* nosipsos volentes instrui profitemur, vel a vobis, ceu a quovis in quocunq*ue* [?], quod
lucide nostris conscientijs apparebit per verbu*m* veritatis.
quod ad ipsu*m* magistratum attinet, nos vobiscum agnoscimus secundu*m* articulum. 37. Dominu*m* Iesu*m* *chr*istu*m*
in suo regno spirituali, vel ecclesia novi testamenti ipsum
magistratum nec aliqua*m* potestatis suæ partem consti-
tuisse: nec executionem illius illic intrare: quia regnum,
arma, ministri, et singula appertinentia eiusdem sunt
spiritualia et in hoc tanta*m* fiduciam habemus, vt vitas
nostras in testimoniu*m* dare parati sumus [?]. atq*ue* etiam
in hoc spirituali statu non respicere debemus personas,
nec multos [?] esse magistros: at in mundanis rebus sancti
debent respicere personas, vt cuncti inferiores, suos supe-
riores, vt liberi parentes &c: et multi simus magistri
immo om*n*es magistri in ecclesia, sint magistri in omnibus
rebus mundanis, suis credentibus seruis: et sic magistratus
regant [?] non in rebus ecclesiasticis, sed mundanis: namq*u*

est mundana ordinatio Dei ac bona; num potest aliquid
boni esse impedimento homini, ne sit discipulus *christi*.
vel christianus; an homines detineantur ab ecclesia, pro
agendo seu exequendo quod bonum sit; nequaquam possit;
nil nos impediat a deo nisi peccatum et malum idcirco
si magistratus nos impediat ab christianitate, est malum
ac peccatum: & tum debemus desiderare illius ruinam: et
nec supplicare, nec deum laudare pro ipso, tanquam pro
bona Dei ordinatione: at vero si nec peccatum, nec malum
at supplicandum, et pro eo gratias dandum [*sic*] est, tanquam
pro bona Dei ordinatione: velut ac est. tunc neminem
impediat ne sit christianus nam hominem futurum chris-
tianum, aliquid relinquere docebimus; quin peccatum;
Baptismus propter quem aduersus mundum contendimus,
est baptismus resipiscentiæ, ob peccatorum remissionem,
quem omnes qui suorum peccatorum pænitentiam agunt,
ac euang[e]lij doctrinæ credunt, habeant: num, pænitentiam illius, quod bona Dei ordinatio sit, docebimus; absit;
multum loqueremur, at cum vosipsi Authoritatem appro-
batis, de executione loquemur: in confesso est, ille qui
instituit hanc bonam dei ordinationem, posuit in manu
eiusdem gladium, vt vindex sit male agenti, ac remunerator
bene agenti. igitur tolle gladium, et tollas authoritatem:
nam quis sapiens cogitare possit cum magistratus decre-
uisset iustitiam, vt malefactores punirentur; quis illorum
decreta æstimaret, si non illis esset potestas compellendi
ad id quod rectum sit per gladium; nequaquam possit;
exempli gratia, si magistratus secundum mandatum Dei
potestatem non haberet sanguinem effundendi effundentis
sanguinem humanum, quid ipse homicida curaret pro
magistratu, seu quo pacto ab effundendo continuò sanguinem impediretur: et similliter pro armis, videmus
saluatorem approbrantem [*sic*] illa in cœtu discipulorum,
attamen illis non licere vti in defensione spiritualis regni
nec ipsius tanquam regis eiusdem, cuius causa Iudæi
quærebant illum occidere: adeo vt arma legitima sunt
inter discipulos suos, veluti ac cetera mundana: at in
regno suo non sunt vtenda [?] arma: cum arma militiæ sui

regni non sunt carnalia sed spiritualia, atque illius subditi,
solum vnum regem habent, qui spiritualis est, idcircò non
dominabuntur invicem tanquam principes gentium, eo
quod regnum eius non est simile regis mundanis. /

Multa alia ad hoc regnum pertinere dicuntur, vt spiritualis
thesaurus, ac sacculi, Lu: 12. 33. spiritualia ædificia, Ephe:
1. 20. spiritualis vestitus, 1 pet: 3. 3. spiritualis cibus
Ioh: 6. 27. ro. 14. 17. eo quod hæc omnia ac alia multa
dicuntur esse in regno *Domini* Christi, an non in mundo
habeamus ideo, ac vtamur illis, vt mundanis rebus, the-
sauris sacculis, ædificijs, indumentis, ac cibis; speramus
neminem hæc negaturum. /

Præterea qum [cum] vos vestra fruimini libertate, velut ac
scribitis, tenendo non licere armis vti, hoc nobis mirum
videtur: quoniam Magistratus qui testimonium habet sub-
ditorum fidelitatis, volentium suum regnum defendere, hac
in re istorum pax maiori pretio habebitur, quam illorum,
qui se suumque regnum perire, ac subditos obrui sinerent,
potius quam illum contra homicidas, fures ac terræ suæ
invasores defenderent: nos certi sumus sic foret nobiscum
in natione nostra, vtcunque sit cum vestris magistratibus,
et quod ad persecutionem tolerandam attinet, videmus pios
magistratus sæpissime passos fuisse magnam persecutionem,
a manibus inferiorum, ac superiorum Num: 14. 2. 10. &
16. 12. & 1 Sam: 18. 8. & Dan: 6. 1. & 3. 12. Ioh: 7. 50.
hæ sunt quædam rationes nostræ inter multa, pro nostro
iudicio, ac persuasione hac in re: atque hæ sunt omnes
differentiæ nostræ, quas nos concipiamus: reliqua vestro-
rum articulorum, nos libere tam corde quam ore, agnoscimus
atque vsque ad mortem Deo fauente agnoscemus. /

De quibus omnibus differentijs, nos precamur, vt vobis
placeat serio ponderare ac considerare, ac consideratis nos
certiores reddere, vtrum nos tolerare possitis, velut ac nos
vos tolerare possumus hisce in rebus: vt sic simus membra
simul vnius corporis cuius caput christus, atque ambulantes
in vna commvnione ac societate, simus vnanimes [*sic*], cohabi-
tantes in vnitate, ac veritate christi Iesu perinde ac fratres;

vt appareat cuius vere sumus discipuli, puta christi Iesu Domini no*st*ri ac vnici saluatoris, cui sit gloria in secula seculoru*m*, Amen.

Et sic Dilecti, ac plurimu*m* respecti amici, nos vos (venia nostra sumpta) ex corde gratiæ domini nostri Iesu christi commendamus, que*m* vos ducere atq*ue* conducere in omnem veritatem, atq*ue* etiam nos, et sic in illa inculpatos seruare vsq*ue* ad apparitione*m* gloriæ suæ, nos iteru*m* atq*ue* iteru*m* rogamus : Amen : /

Verbatim stylo nouo. 12.° Nouembris. 1626.
cu*m* methodo facillima transtuli ex anglico
in sermonem latinu*m*. /[1]

[A Letter of Cornelis Claesz. Anslo of Amsterdam to Hans de Ries announcing the arrival of the two representatives of the Five English Anabaptist Congregations, and dated November 13, 1626.][2]

Den [?]
Eersame discrete Hans
de Ries woonende op
de nieuwe sloot
Tot
Alckmaer[3]

port

In Amsterdam de*n* 13 November 1626 Waerde en in godt beminde Vade[r ?] in Chr*ist*o Hans de Ries sij vrede. Heden zyn bij ons geweest 2 Engelsche

---

[1] There is in the Mennonite Archives at Amsterdam a Dutch copy of this letter. The original was in English. The Dutch copy concludes with the following words: "Aldŭs getranslateert in Dŭijts wtte latynse copije die wtte engels, daer in het origineel geschreŭen was, oŭergeset was. den 18. Nouember A*n*no 1626."

[2] MS. B. 1373 in the Mennonite Archives, Amsterdam. This document like some others here published is wretchedly written and exceedingly difficult to decipher. Professor Dr Müller's translation of this letter is given in Dr B. Evans' "The Early English Baptists", Vol. II., pp. 24–5.

[3] This address is not a part of the text of the letter.

als gecommitteerde van 5 gemeenten in engelant met haar brengende seekeren brief aen v l, Reynier Wijbrants, en de andere dienaren onser gemeenten, de welcke door een onser engelsche broederen in latijn uit het engels is getranslatee[r]t, waeruit wij verstaan dat se onse confessien gelesen en met opmercken (soo sij schrijven) naegedacht hebbende wel zouden willen met ons vereenigen, also sij haar in alles daarmede vereenicht vinden uitgenomen in t' stick van eedt.

2. dat sij oock verstaan dat men het avontmaal alle sondagen behort [?] te celebreren ten sij dat het door rechtveerdich belet verhinde[r]t werde. 3. dat de broederen sonder oplegginge der handen of van den biscoppen daer toe bevesticht te zyn, vermogen en behooren in het afwesen der biscoppen te prediken en de sacramenten te bedienen. 4. het ampt der overicheyt verstaan sij dat van een christen mach bedient worden, doch niet als tot de kerke behoorende maar als een wereltlijck ampt: tot bewys van haare meninge brengen sij eenige redenen in, waar van de voornaamste is dat het ampt in hem selven goet is, en houden, dat het geene goet is den gebruicker des selfs niet kan houden noch stellen buiten de gemeente, noch beletten dat hy geen christen sij.

dit is in t' corte haare intentie, verstant en orsaack van haare komste, versoeckende dat wij met dese hare 2 gecommitteerde zouden spreken, ende haar schriftelicke antwoort laaten toekoomen. Wij hebben gesait dat wij vl advijs zouden versoecken alsoo de brief specialick aen vl hordt, over welcken versoecken wij vl advijs wat wij hier in doen zůllen, of het vl gelegen is hier te koomen, dan of wij haar tot ůwent zellen zenden. als mede of wij haar een schriftelijck antwoort op haren brief zůllen mede geven dan of wij die haar zůllen nae zenden, vl believe ons vl advijs met den aldereersten te laten weeten, wij hebben haar daar op uitgestelt, en ondertesschen onse engelschen belast dat sij haar onse laetste antwoort aen elias tokij zonden laaten leesen alsoo die van de sellifde materie handelt, t welck sij aengenomen hebben te doen, doch

deese hebben in t stick van den eedt en t ampt der
overicheyt noch eenen anderen grondtslach als elias tokij
ende de zijne.

dese zyn in engelant wel 150 persoonen starck sij zijn van
elias tokij afgeschaiden, en zyn van Ian mortons ofte
thomas elwijs volck, deese 2 die hier zijn schinen beqŭame
mannen te zijn, en redelick treffelick in het habijt[1], hebben
oock soo d'andere schrijven vele om den name christi geleden, en zyn langen tijt gevanckelick geweest.

Ick heb vl seker libel van de weeck gesonden hoope vl zŭlt
het ontfangen hebben.

....

Wij hebben aen den
grave noch 100 gl. ge-
ordoneert te betaalen.

vl Dienstwillige
Cornelis Claesz. Ansloo

....

[Questions asked by Hans de Ries, about November, 1626,
of the two Representatives of the Five English Anabaptist
Congregations, with their Answers.][2]

oft die 5 kercken die syn In haer schryft gedencken van
haer comste tot ons kennisse & wetenschap ghehadt
hebben

oft sy met eendracht van de selue geordent syn om tot
ons te comen, oft sy den brieff geconcipiert hebben. waer
by wy t zelue sullen weten also hy van haer niet onder-
teckent is [?]

---

[1] These words would seem to indicate that the early English Anabaptists wore a distinctive style of clothing as the Friends, or Quakers,
did later.

[2] MS. B. 1374 in the Mennonite Archives, Amsterdam. Professor
Dr Müller's translation of this document is given in Dr B. Evans' "The
Early English Baptists", Vol. II., pp. 30–32. The MS. is wretchedly
written throughout and can be deciphered only with the greatest difficulty,
as is the case with all the papers of Hans de Ries' that the present
writer has seen. The letters are often slurred, and such letters have been
printed in italics.

oft sy allen met malcanderen eendrachtich nae dinhout van
haer schrift van een gevellen syn, In sonderheyt datter
gheen onderschyt tusschen haer leeren & ons en is als In
de stucken die sy In haer schrift gedencken

dewyl wy hier eenighe van haer nacie hebben die van den
haren[?] gebannen syn waer voor sy nŭ de selue houden

oft sy de ghene die wt engelant hier weten commen woonen
souden banwerdich houden ende die hier woonen[?] souden[?]
houden[?] schuldich te wesen weder In engelant te comen

oft sy noch voor recht houden & dryuen & beleuen souden,
dat elck broeder sonder ordentlycke beroepinge & be-
lastinghe soude moghen de sacramenten bedienen & ock
de vrouwen als er geen mannen waren[?]

oft geen ander forme van waardy In haer lant gebruyckt
worde Int eetsweren als godt ende[?] syn getŭijgen

oft sy alle souden connen verdraghen dat eenighe ghe-
menten In engelant synde maer somwyelen des Iaers het
nachtmael hilden

oft eenich broeder In haer gemeenten wonende & het
alle sondach brootbreken niet voor godts ghebodt hilde
& derhaluen alle sondach met haer niet comŭnicerde[?]
by haer soude mogen geleden worden

oft door de belofte by getrouwicheyt den coninck ghedaen
souden haer verplicht houden den coninck met wapenen
voor te staen & haer seluen met wapenen totten bloede
toe te beschermen

nu wat wet sy houden een christen ouerheyt ghehouden is
de quade te straffen crych te vooren & met syn vyanden
te handelen.

oft ock een christen Int twisten[?] synes conincx & tegen-
staen synder vyanden[?] goederen[?] aentasten ontweldighen
& nemen mach ock de ontweldichde goederen als vry eyghen
goedt behouden en besitten mach

de 5 gemeenten hebben elck gheen leraer
en gheen leeraer hebben Wachten met den dienst tot datter
een comt ergo ist niet nut[?] wendich[?] alle sondach broot
te breken

sy lat*en* niemant toe te leer*en* oft niet bequae*m* gekent sy [?]
ma[ken?] onderscheyt tusse*n* ee*n* die leert & sacrament*en*
bed*i*ent & ee*n* die Ind*en* voll*en* dinst staet
2 [?] tweerley [?] gevoelen va*n* buyte*n* lant [?] te treck*en*
oft sy de engelsche soud*en* ontfang*en* is twyffelacht*ich* [?]
oft het nacht*mael* alle sondach te houd*en* verwerpelyck
by haer all*en* weten sy niet alle sondach broot te brec*ken*
hebb*en* sy gee*n* gebot noch wet maer [?] weten niet oft
soud*en* toelat*en* dat ee*n* [?] leeraer des sondags [?] soude
mog*en* sulcx [?] navolg*en* [?]

[A Letter of the early English Anabaptist Congregation at
Lincoln to the Congregation of Waterlanders at Amsterdam,
dated Sept. 5, 1630.][1]

So ist Beminde ende lief-hebbende Vriendt dat Ick v.l.
brief ontvanghen hebb (w^t handen van Ian Drew onsen
beminde vriendt) ghesonden aen ons ende die reste van
onse brocderen hier in dese natie ende vindande daer in
een ghetuighenisse van v.l. goede meyninghe neffens ons,
in onse Christelicke stant: wy connen niet nae laten onse
vriendelicke danckbaerheyt aen v te bewijsen voor deselue,
wenschende dat ghy ende wy mochten comen tot den
eenicheyt des heylighen gheest, ende tot dien bande des
vredes welke sy in der waerheyt Amen.
Weetet nochtans goede vriendt dat die haestighe hande-
linghe die ghy ons op leyt, wy connen niet bekennen, noch
die dinghen so gheringhe te wesen als ghy se schijnt te
achten: als voor Math: 18 nae de welke ghy niet en wilde
hebben dat wy elke ghescill des verstants ofte daedt soude
straffen: wy weten ende het is openbaer dat in ijegelicke
dinghe waer deur een broeder gherechtelich ghe-erghert
wort, boete wort gheeyscht welke gheweygert zijnde, die
onboetvaerdighe moet gheacht zijn als een heyden ende
publicaen: nae welke onsen salich-maker leert Math: 5 een

---

[1] MS. B. 1376 in the Mennonite Archives, Amsterdam. Professor
Dr Müller's translation of this letter is given in Dr B. Evans' "The Early
English Baptists", Vol. II., pp. 41–4.

yeder teghen wien een broeder yets heeft, met sijn broeder
versoent te wesen, yer hy eenighe gaue (op den Outaer)
offert voor den heere. ende op dat het niet te cleyn mach
schijnen in v.l. ooghen, besiet die woorden onsen salichmakers omtrent het beginsell des 18 Capittells, daer hy
·seyt het ware beter dat eenen molen steen aen sijn hals
ghehanghen worde, en in het diepste der Zee verdroncken,
dan dat hy eenen van desen cleynen vererghert die in my
ghelooven. etc.

Ende waer als ghy ons acht meer te wesen van den gheest
der Iongeren Christi dan van den gheest onsen salichmakers, indien ghy meynt dat gheest, doe sy vier van
den hemel wilde hebben om die samaritanen te verslinden
etc. wy moghen well segghen dat ghy qualoch dunckt:
want wy den en niet een ghedachte herberghen streckende tot lichamelichen verdruckinghe ofte leedwesen onses
naesten, ofte enighe van weghen religie, ofte in saecken
van conscientie, maer voor alle dinghen wy strijden met
alle menschen daer teghen. noch en sijn wy (hopen wy)
gheleyt met den gheest der ambitie ofte eergiericheyt te
strijden wie soude het grootste sijn maer wy ontvanghen
gheerne die menichderley leeringhe onses salichmakers in
het teghen deel: indien ghy het appliceren wilt tot dat
van onsen salichmakers dat die gheest is ghewillich ende
die vleych swacke: wy moeten bekennen dat het also met
ons gaet, nochtans derfen wy niet anders doen als hopen
dat den heere sijn belofte sal volbrenghen int aennemen
van onsen goede wille voor den daede, yae ende dat wy
ghevonden sullen worden eenichsins den gheest Christi te
hebben, anders behooren wy hem niet toe volgens dat
gheschreven staet Rom: 8. 9. Maer ghy seght dat Christus
droegh den ongheloof, (verachtinghe) ofte qualijcke nemen
onwetentheyt, & blinde ijever sijnder Iongheren, alleen
haer berispende etc. ende cont ghy ons rechvaerdelich
straffen, dat wy volgens dien regell niet en wandelen.
handelen wy andersins dan straffse-wijse met die ghene
die straffbaer of ergerlicke bevonden sijn, indien sy haer
bekeeren, ofte meynt ghy dat christus sijnder [?] Iongheren

souden [*sic*] hebben wille [willen] dooghen [gedoogen] indien
sy sijn straffe teghen ghestaen hadden ofte sijn onderwijsinghen ende vermaninghen gheweygerde," siet toe hoe ghy
sodanighen eenen ghedachte toe laet, tis waer om yets dat
wy lesen dat hy noyet handelde veerder met haer so is het
mede waer dat sy altoos ghewillich waren te ontvanghen
sijn berispinghen, ende van hem ghe informeert ende ghere-
formeert te worden. maer voor obstinate ende ongheregelde
persoonen die daer leest mach sien, dat hy overvloedich is
int leeren hoe men met haer moet handelen. Waer als
ghy procedeert te spreken van die abuisen ofte fauten in
die ghemeente tot Corinthum ende die kerken ghebout
deur den Apostellen (als of ghy niemant onboetvaerdich
wilde hebben in desen dinghen w^{t}ghedaen ofte ghebant:
wy bidden v in dese bedenckt so wy v hier in stemde toe,
wat ellende ende confusie soude het wesen te dooghen
die menschen te comen droncken, slaperich, ofte anders
ongoddelich tot den tafell des heeren, te vallen in twisten,
oneenicheden, te lochenen die verrijsenisse, te voeghen
recht vaerdich makinghe met het wett sonder Christo,
ende so van ghenade te vallen etc. voor alle ofte eenighe
waer van ghy seght dat men se behart te straffen, afraden,
ende also dooghen ofte draghen. In dien men dese dinghen
soude dooghen in plaets van eenen ghemeente der heylighen, die kerke soude groyen tot een ghesellschapp der
boose ende godloose persoonen tis waer dat wy niet en
lesen van eenighe persoon die w^t den ghemeente van
Corintho ghedaen was als den onkuische persoon: wy
lesen oock niet dat eenighe een sonde waer van den
ghemeente deur den Apostell was berispt dat het was
yemant van den ghemeente so eighen, ofte particulier,
dat also die gheheele ghemeente met hem handelen conde
daer voor, want alle die reste waren so vermenght, ende
so generalich besmett, dat sy mosten alle verbeteren ofte
alle ghestraft worden deur den Apostell, ende daerom
noemt hy sijn derde waerschouwinghe ofte vermaninghe
sijn 3 ghetuighenen seggende indien hy wederom quam
hy woude se niet sparen : het welke watt soude het anders

wesen als met haer voort te gaen tot den wᵗtersten straff
nae die cracht die hen Heere hem ghegeuen hadde tot opbouwinghe ende niet tot verdervinghe: als ghy mach sien
dat die ghemeente van Ephesus wort ghedreycht dat sy
ontkerkt ofte haer Candelaer soude versett worden, om
dat sy haer eersten hefde versaken hadde. maer te keeren
tot die ghemeente van Corinthen [?] die Apostle [*sic*] seyt
so yemant die hem een broeder laet noemen wort een
oncuische, gierighe etc: met sodanighen eene niet te
eeten, nu wy achten dat het hier ghemeynt wort van
gheestelicke eeten, ende niet van ghemeenen eeten want
dat soude te phariseesche wesen, so dat ghy sien meught
dat daer andere sonden sijn behaluen oncuisheyt waerₛom
dat men wᵗghebant mach sijn. dat meer is alle sonden
streckende tot lasteringhe, volgens den exempell der
Apostelen handelende met Hymeneus ende Alexander
behaluen den Apostell sijn begeerte dat sy afghesneden
ware die haer quelde, te weten die ghemeente der
Galateren, met valsche leeringhe, ende dat sy haer oordeel draghen soude wy sy waren, het welke wy hopen
dat ghy het met ons besluyten will deur excommunicatie,
ende niet lichamelicken doodte: wederom hoe souden die
ghene die daer twisten ende tweedrachten veroorsaeckte
ghescouwt worden, als deur banninghe ofte Excommunicatie: ende hoe connen wy scheyden die ghene die daer
leeren teghen die heylsame woorden onsen heere Iesu
Christi, als deur excommunicatie: siet ghy oock niet dat
die Heere dreight te vechten teghen die ghemeente
Pergami met het swaert sijnder monde om dat sy doochde
met haer die daer onderhielde die leeringhe Balaam͂ ende
waer als ghy vermelt dat die heere gaf Iesabell eenen tijdt
tot boete, wy hoopen dat ghy verstaet dat nae dat se
ghebant sijn, ofte wᵗ die ghemeente ghedaen dat haer
tijdt des boete niet gheheel afghesnijden wort: tis waer dat
alle dinghen soude ghescieden in der liefde, ende [?] in der
gheest der sachmoedicheyt, ende indien wy daerom connen
rechvaerdelich ghestraft worden het sy veer dat wy dat
niet en soude bekennen met beloften des verbeteringhe,

Gal: 5.
10, 12.

Rom.
16. 17.

maer nochtans niet nae latende die onghemanierde te
vermanen, want haer in haer onmanierlicheyt ofte mis-
bruicken te dulden soude gheen helfde maer haet wesen
levitici 19. & 17 verse [*sic*] noch en wort een Coninckrijck in hem selue ghedeylt, deur het straffen, castijdinghe
ofte afsnijdinghe der quaed-doendere maer veel eerder
die vrede ende ruste daer van behouden, tis waerachtich
beminde[?] dat ghelijck als Christus ons vergaue so
soude wy malcanderen, maer Christus vergaue niemant Act:
als die daer boete dede, ende tot hem keeren, ende daerom 3. 19, 20.
wat sijn wy dat wy meer doen soude: wy begeeren on-
gheveyns delich der allen versoeninghe, maer versoeninghe
moet wesen op bekentenisse des schults met belofte des
verbeteringhe, ende niet moetwillighe teghenstant ofte
onboetvaerdicheyt in sonde, ende all hoe well dat wy als
haestighe ende straffe menschen hebben ghehouden gheweest, nochtans dit weten wy voor seker dat als noch
noyet yemant van ons w^t der ghemeente ghedaen, eenighe
liefde tot God oft ijever tot religie bewijsde ten sy dat
deur boetvaerdicheyt hy wederom met ons vrede maeckte.
ende tot een besluit wy bekennen met v, dat het is een
bedroefde dingh ende seer beclaegdelich te sien die
gheestelicke steenen van des Heere bouwinghe, neder
gheworpen ende verstroyt, maer heijlaes hoe sal men
sulks connen helpen, niet deur haer in haerder boosheyt
te dooghen, want dat soude wesen des Heeren huise tot
eenen kuil der dieffen te maecken, ende grouwelich in
sijnder ooghen te brenghen in sijn heylichdom sodanighe
onbesnijden persoonen, ende gheen plaets ofte volk hem
gheestelicken offenhanden aenghenaem deur Ies: Chr: op
te offeren. ende dus met dancksegginghe voor v. l. liefde
biddende den Heere tot een vergeldinghe des selue v te
bewaren ende vermeerderen in waere liefde ende ijever
tot den heerlike Evangelie onses heeren ende salichmaker
Ies*u* Chr*isti* dat ghy deur hem mach ghenieten die ouer-
vloedighe gaven sijns h: gheest, tot vwer heylichmakinghe
in dese leven, ende verheerlichinghe in het toecomende
leven: die welke die geuer van alle goede gaven gheve

v ende ons ende alle die den Heere Iesum liefhebben.
Amen. ende dus met onse groetenisse saer vriendelich aen
v ende alle liefhebbers der waerheyt, wie [wy] bevelen v des
Heeren beschermínghe ende leydinghe wiens vrede segen-
inghen sy met v euwichlich: (bidden wy) Amen

Lincolne Septem: 5. 1630.

v ongheveynsde liefhebbers in die Heere, die broederen
daer woonachtich.

w^t ghecopieert Maij 31, ende Iunij primo 1631.
deur v. l. Dienstwillighen broeder:

Swithune Gryndall.

[A Letter written by James Toppe and Israel, his wife, of
the early English Anabaptist Congregation at Tiverton, to Hans
de Ries in answer to a letter of his dated Sept. 13, 1630.][1]

V.l. vriendelick acceptatie mijns brief, ende sorghvuldicheyt
om den selue te voldoen heef my op desen tijdt occasie ghegeuen tot v mijn danckbaerheyt te bewijsen, van weghen v.l.
goede regarde neffens my ende alle anderen hier, hiefhebbers
der waerheyt het welke is in Chr: Iesu onsen heere. dese daerom
connen ghetuighen, dat Ick ontvanghen heb v.l. vriendelicke
brief ghedateert Septem*ber* 13. 1630. waer in ghy begeert, als
ghy seyt, met ongheveynsder herte, die ijever godes ende sijnder
waerheyt, het welke wy desgelijx met ongheveynsder herten
ernstelich begeeren ende om strijden: maer dit moeten wy weten
dat onsen ijever moet wesen nae kennisse, ende aenghesteken
met het vijer van hemel, ofte anders soude het worden dwaese
ontsinnicheyt, meerder dan ijever: als wy meughen sien deur
droevich exempell aen het Ioodtsche volk, die daer hadden
volgens den ghetuighenisse des Apostells die ijever godes maer
niet nae kennis, deur het welke sy waren so onwetentlich
rasende dat sy die Messiah selue kruisde, die sy so lang ende

---

[1] MS. B. 1377 in the Mennonite Archives, Amsterdam. This letter is
undated but it was translated from English into Dutch on June 5, 1631.
Professor Dr Müller's English translation of this Dutch copy is given in
Dr B. Evans' "The Early English Baptists", Vol. II., pp. 44–51.

so seer waren verwachtende, ende hoopte dat hy Israel soude
verlossen Luc: 24. 21. ende daerom wy vrijelich met v bekennen
dat wy deur onwetentheyt dickwills meughen dolen jae doolen
int volbrenghen van het ghene dat wy behoren te doen van
weghen kennis, doende menich mael dinghen te haestelich ofte
all te traeghelich het ghene dat wy anders hadden behooren te
doen: nochtans die Heere in sijn woort ons klaerlich toont
sijnder wille, wat wy behooren te doen ende oock mochte doen
so die schult op ons selue niet en laghe: Niet te min hopen
wy dat God ons ghenadich sal worden ende onsen swackheyt
ende onvolcomentheyt, (noch het ghene dat wy des weghen
misdoen), niet toe rekenen wille, wy dagelix strijdende sulks
in ons seluc te verbeteren, ende van perfectie tot perfectie te
groeyen: maer indien wy onsen eighen willen soude soecken
te doen, ende ons te vreden stellen met den ghemeene custuyme
ende practijcke van anderen die wy beminnen etc. dan mochten
wy niet verwachten eenighe meerder openbaringhe van Godes
wille tot ons, noch eenighe ghenade van sijn handen. Nu tot
v antwoort op mijnen brief, waer in ghy seyt, die oorsaeck
waerom dat ghy lijdet ofte draeght een broeder nae vermaninghe, die daer hoorde een predicatie in England is dese
(als ghy seght) om dat ghy niet en derft, sijn verstant wesende
dat hy mocht hooren, ende deur het hooren ghesticht sijn van
een anders ghesint, leueren sodanighen eenen ouer tot Satan:
om dat den daet des hooren niet simpelich quaedt ofte vleeschelich sy, maer die leeringhe ofte persoon welke ghy seght
mach ghedisputable [sic] zijn (ofte twijfellachtich) etc. in welke
woorden van vwen, daer sijn 2 redenen: die eerste is seght ghy
dat sijn verstant was dat hy sulks doen mochte, ende sulks doende
ghebouwt zijn van een teghen ghesinte persoon: die tweede
(seght ghy) om dat die bloote daet van hooren is niet simpelich
quaedt ofte vleeschelich. Tot den eerste wy segghen, can die
bloote verstant van een broeder jae al ware het van den alder-
heylichste heyliche die hier oyet leefde zijn een goede regell,
voor sijn eighen ofte anderen directie in godes dienste, sonder
eenighe verseekaringhe w^t Godes woort, wy meynen vastelich,
dat ghy also niet en houdet, want dat ware te maken een
privaet verstant des sterffelicken mensche van ghelijcke waer-

die of valeur met den heilighe schrift, welke soude niet beter
worden als lasteringhe ofte blasphemie : wat boosheyt is daer
indien een mensch sijn privaet oordeel ware die regel, die men
niet toe laten ende excuseren soude deur een schijnsell ofte
andere van goedt, als die vwen te gaen hooren eenen valsche
propheet (want so oordeelt ghy van haer ofte anders waerom
noemt ghy se die teghenghesinte) om opghebouwt te worden.
wy hebben sommighe hier die het gheoorloft houden te gaen
hooren eenen valsche propheet, maer niet om eenighe loffe ofte
eer tot God te brenghen, noch goedt tot die menschen, tis
gheseyt dat sulks boosheyt ware te gaen om eenighe sodanighe
eyndt : maer die vwen houden het gheoorloft te gaen hooren
tot opbouwinghe : can een founteyne seyt St Iacobus w^{t}werpen
soete water ende bitter mede, niet meer (meughen wy vrie-
moedelich segghen [)] can een valsche propheet stichten ofte
opbouwen Christi ghemeente ofte eenighe lidtmaet daer van.
want als die waere propheten Christi, stichten ende opbouwen
het ghemeente Christi, desgelijcks doen die valsche propheten
het kerke Antichristi ofte sijn rijckdom stichten ofte opbouwen :
sy connen niet te samen ghevoeght zijn in des Heeren werke
tot opbouwinghe sijnder ghemeente niet meer jae veel min dan
die heydenen Esra 4. conde ghevoeght worden met die Iooden
int opbouwinghe van die materiael tempell, alleen Godes volk
die Iooden mosten opbouwen dien materiael tempell doen,
desghelijx nu, allen des Heeren propheten ofte volk die van
hem ghesonden sijn hebbende haer beroepinghe van haer
Meester Chr: Ies: bouwen op sijn gheestelicke tempell nu :
simon Magus noch gheen ander valsche propheet wie hy sy,
heeft eenighe deel ofte part in dese werke : wy sijn vermaent
deur St Iude ons op te bouwen in onse heylighe ghelooue :
maer indien wy by die teghen ghesinte soude gaen om opbouwinghe wy mochten draghen des Heeren straffe tot die
Iooden, daer hy seyt dat sy versaken hadden den founteyn des
levendich water ende haer putten ghemaeckt die gheen water
conde houden, den gheheele loop der schrifte is teghen alle
sodanighe Balaamitische trinckende : so die religie die ghy
belijdet waerachtich sy, dan die religie die den teghen ghesinte
belijdet moet immers valsche zijn dese reden will v leeren.

Nu tot den tweede, dat die daedt des hooren niet simpelich quaedt sy, ofte vleyschelich etc. wy segghen indien ghy meynt die actie van hooren een valsche propheet, ofte propheten predikende ofte biddende w^t cracht van sijnder gheestelicke beroepinghe, (ghelijck het scijnt dat ghy doet) want anders wy achten dat ghy niet lochenen will, maer dat men sondighen mach int hooren, so well als int sien ofte spreken etc. dan segghen wy dat alle sodanighe hooren quaedt sy ende vleysch-elich, niet wesende van het gheest Godes, noch bevestight deur sijn woort, alse dese plaetsen der schrifture proberen sullen: Ier: 23. 16. daer die Heere radet sijn volke segghende hoort niet die woorden der propheten die daer propheteren ende leeren v Idellheyt etc. ende Hos: 4: 15. comt niet tot Gilgal, noch [?] gaet niet tot Beth-haven: in den eene sijn sy verboden te hooren met den w^{t}wendighen oore, ende in den anderen niet so veel als te comen tot den plaets der valscher God-dienst om haer te hooren ofte besien: ende die stemme van hemel Math: 17. 5. seyt dese is mijn beminde in wien Ick een wellbehaghen heb, hoort hem: ende Ioh: 10 mijn scapen hooren mijn stemme, maer eenen vreemdelinch willen sy niet hooren: ende van die ghene die Chr: w^{t}stierde, hy seydt die v hoort, hoort my, maer van die teghenghesinte seyt hy nergens so: Daerom wy besluiten, indien Godes volke verboden wort te hooren die predicatien, ghebet ofte ghebieden der valsche pro-pheten als dese schrifturen ende veele meer willen betuighen: dan segghen wy dat het int gheheel ongheoorloft sy die schapen Christi te hooren der vreemdelinghen stemme, vernamentlich tot die tijdt, plaets, ende vergaderinghe der ghenen die daer vergadert sijn in die name Christi: maer ghy seght dat hy het doet w^t gheloove in hem selue, oh sluit v ooghen niet toe, wy bidden v, wat ghelooue can hy hebben, wanneer dat gheen woordt des gheloofs sy daer voor in het gheheel boecke Godes te weten voor sodanighe een oeffeninghe: want die H. gheest seyt dat ghelooue compt van hooren, & hooren van het woordt godes: nu hy heeft gheen woort Godes om dese sijn gheloof ende daerom heeft hy gheen gheloove daer in: ende het ghene dat niet van gheloove sy is sonde: ende dat niet alleen, of hy niet en blijfde in het oeffeninghe van desen quaedt, want so

ghy selue acht het, anders waerom afradet ghy hem van sulks,"
wilt ghy een broeder afraden om yet anders als sonde, het welke
hooren eens ghedaen hebbende, het wort hem sonde, ghelijck
als wy probeert hebben: ende indien hy gheen boete en doet,
vermaent zijnde den 1/2, & 3 mael nae die ordentelich regell
van onsen Meester Chr: Ies: die eenighe wett-gever sijnder
ghemeente laet hem v wesen als een heyden etc. maer indien
hy boete doet vergheeft hem, anders niet: dese is het wett
Chr*ist*i het welke wie niet gheoorsamen willen, sijn niet waerdich
die name der Christenen, want niemant is een Christen als die
sijnder wetten ende gheboden subject sy ende onderdanich.
want als niemant can ghenoemt sijn des koninck ondersate, die
sijn rechvaerdighe [*sic*] wetten niet ghehoorsamen will: so oock
in Chr: gheestelicke coninckrijck daer sijn wetten ghanschelich
gherechtich sijn, die welke wij [? hij] niet en ghehoorsamet can
niet Christo toebehooren, ende so hy hem niet toe behoort, dan
can hy het gheest Christi niet hebben, ende hebbende niet het
gheest Chr: tis sonder questie dat hy ofte sy selue ende haer
leeringhen syn quaed ende vleeschelich, beyde propheten ende
volke wie sy sijn die andere ofte teghen ghesint sijn die
waerachtich professie Christi: maer ghy acht het bequaem
hem te draghen deur lang-moedicheyt etc. jae den Heere te
bidden voor sijn verlichtinghe etc. als in v.l. duitsche broederen
brief: wy stemmen dat toe met v.l. dat wy met sodanighen
eene moeten handelen. als met eenen broeder, ende hem niet
achten als een vyandt die gheheele tijdt dat hy onder vermaninghe sy, maer dit wilden wy van v.l. bidden in v.l. naeste
schrijvens te toonen hoe lang men eenen broeder draghen sal
in sijn sonde, het sy altoos ofte tot dat hy vriendelich vermaent
heeft gheweest den 1, 2, & 3, mael, ofte tot wat respijt des
tijdts. van weghen God ghevende die menschen tijdt tot boete
als hy dede Iesabell: tis waer die Heere gheeft som wijlen
die menschen eenen langhe tijdt des boets, sommighe 60 ofte
80 jaeren, jae den gheheele tijdt haerder leven: maer hy heeft
sijn ghemeente ghepaelt met die 3 vermaninghe, ende so hy
dan gheen boete en doet laet hem dy worden als een heyden
etc. ende nochtans is hy deur dese niet berooft van alle middelen des boets, maer dese is het leste remedie die die kerk

ouer hem te ghebruicken heeft tot boetvaerdicheyt, als alle
vermaninghen hem niet dienen will : do dat ghy sien meught
dat Chr: sijn ghemeente eenen tijdt ghestelt heeft, welke die
ghemeente niet verby can gaen : desghelijcks woude Ick v
bidden te toonen waer die Apostelen ghedooghen hebben lang
(als ghy seght) grooter sonden Ick can sulks niet ghedencken
dat Ick het oyet ghelesen heb dat die Apostelen ofte eenighe
van die eerste kerk ghedooghen hebben eenighe broeder bouen
die ghesette tijdt van onsen salichmaker a[l]s te voren gheseyt
is.   Ende waer als ghy seyt in v.l. brief dat die schrifture die
Ick allegeerde van die ghemeente tot Ephesus. Apoca: 2. 2. my
niet en diende, Ick moet hersegghen dat het my dient, want
hoe cont ghy het daer toe binden te weten van quaede leeraeren,
wanneer die woorden sijn generael, ende dat ghy contse niet
draghen die daer boose sijn, ende particulier ende hebtse ondersocht die daer segghen dat sy Apostelen sijn, ende en zijnse
niet etc. welke leste woorden ghy neemt, ende beduitse te
wesen die boose te vooren ghenoemt : hoe well dat sy te samen
ghevoeght sijn met een woordt van byvoeghsell die haer te
samen voeght : so dat alle quade worden ghemeynt int generael
ende by name die ghene die daer seyden dat sy Apostelen
waren, & waren niet. te volghen den regell van Godes woort,
is die beste & behoudenste wech te wandelen tot reformatie
beyde van minder ende meerder sonden, tot den welke, ist dat
wy opsien, wy sullen sekerlich niet qualoch doen : hoe well in
menschelich pollicie wy mochten nemen andere weghen, maer
pollicie die daer menschelich sy moet gheen plaets hebben in
Chr: kerke. so wy ghewillich sijn reformatie te soecken, dan
moeten wy het doen nae sijnder woort, dan sullen wy seker
gaen, in den reformatie des minder quaedts des meerder te
voorcoomen : als mede den ghemeente Christi in der liefde te
bouwen : ende hoe meughen wy onsen broeder meerder liefde
toonen, als hem w^t sijn sonde te plucken ofte trecken, ende
vernamentlich door sodanighe middelen als Chr: selue voorghestelt heeft. so een vleeschelick vriendt soude int ghebreck
leggen, so dat sommighe lidt most afghesnijden worden, ofte andersins het woude het gheheele lichaem bederven, soude men hem
niet veel grooter liefde bewijsen, om het gheheelich aftesnijden;

dan deur teerheyt [teederheid] beteen te laten tot perijkell des
gantsche lichaem etc. ende van sodanighe nature is die sonde
so men het heen laet gaen, ende dat men het toelaet in die
ghemeente, het will versueren den gheheele deegh treckende
van boven die gramschapp Godes ouer den gheheel ghemeente,
als ghy sien meught in die ghemeente tot Corinthum, om dat
sy toelieten den onkuische persoon onder haer boven het gheene
dat betaemde 1 Cor: 5. die so het schijnt, oeffende het selue
leeringhe der draeghsaemheyt als ghy doet, ende waren daer
ouer scherpelich van den Apostell berispt ofte beschuldicht.

Van weghen die vnie ofte eenicheyt (ghy seghl) het faljeert
aen onsen cant, om dat sommighe onder ons houden ende
oeffenen het materiael sweert, het welke (ghy seghl) noch Chr:
noch sijnder Apostelen oijet oeffenende: het welke hoe ghy
het versaken cont weten wy niet, nae-dien dat die schrifture
bewijst dat effen onder die Iongheren Christi die hem altoos
verghelschapte, daer waren swaerden, als wanneer onsen
salichmaker een weynich voor sijn lijdinghe ofte apprehensie
in die tuine, doe hy sijn Iongheren onderwijsinghen ende
directien gave wat sy doen soude nae sijn afscheyt: segghende
doe Ick v wᵗstierde sonder buydell sonder tessche ofte schoenen
hebt ghy oock yet ghebreck gehadt etc. maer nu wie een
buydell heeft etc. ende die niet en heeft die vercoope sijn
rocke ende coope eenen sweert, ende sommighe onder haer
seyden Heere siet hier sijn twee sweerden: ende Petrus had
een sweert doe hy het misbruickende snijde af Malchus oore.
tot dat hy het misbruickte, was hy noyet berispt om dat hy
het hadt: ende sonder twijfell sommighe wettelich ghebruick
had hy daer van te voren, ende dan oock, als mede nae-maels
ofte anders waerom waren sy gheboden sweerdten te hebben,
jae haer rocken te vercoopen, ende sweerdten te coopen, so dat
in sommighe saeck ofte in eenighe dinghen sonder twijfell sy
mochte se ghebruijcken. wederom doe die soldaten tot Ian
quamen met het ander volke sy vraeghden hem wat sy doen
soude hy seyde haer dat sy niemant gheweld soude doen etc;
daer hy leerde [?] haer hoe dat sy haer draghen soude in haer
plaets als christenen, ende nochtans behouden haer beroep als
soldaten.

Indien ghy noch seggen soude dat noch Christus noch sijn
Apostelen oyet ghebruickde die materiael sweert: dan bidden
wy in v.l. naeste schrijvens te toonen nae v.l. verstant wat sy
deden met haer sweerden te vooren vermelt, so sy se op
gheenderley wijse ghebruicken mochte, dan bekennen wy met
v.l. volgens die schriftuer plaetsen by v.l. ghe⸱allegeert met
veel meer daer toe streckende in v.l. brief, die sulks beve-
stighen: dat die materiael sweert het gheestelicke rijckdom
Christi niet toe-behoort: desghelijcks oock noch buidell noch
tessche noch schoenen etc noch verscheyde [sic] andere dinghen
van diergelijcken aert, nochtans mach men se als wy sijn vleesh
ofte menschen van deser werelt wettelich ghebruicken tot
maintenantie ofte onderhoudinghe van onsen natuerlich leven,
welke wy ghehouden sijn te behouden ofte te beschermen, eve
ofte effen als onse salichmaker doe hy w^t dese werelt scheyden
soude, nu seyt hy die daer een buydell heeft, laet hem het
nemen etc onder het welke daer was een materiael sweert:
nochtans sien wy dat sy het niet en mochte ghebruicken int
bescherminghe van haer christelicke professie of van haer
Meester Christo: wanneer hy Petrum strafte, seggende steecht
v sweert in sijn schee etc. noch en houden wy het wettelich
te ghebruicken tot defensie van ons als wy sijn belijders des
evangelie, voor het welke wy moeten, hebben, ende noch lijden
vervolginghe: noch om te verwerven eenighe aerdsche croon,
ofte wereltsche digniteyt die wy nae haecken: maer volgens
onsen schuldighe plicht tot onsen Coninck & landschapp in
alle civijle dinghen ende wettelich, ende als wy aerdsche onder-
danen sijn van sijn aerdsche rijck tot defensie van sijn persoon,
digniteyt ende rijck wy ghebruicken die materiael sweert: op
sodanighe wijse houden wy het gheoorloft te ghebruicken:
nochtans segghen wy ende oordeelen dat indien wy noyet
occasie sullen hebben te ghebruicken dat sulks beste ware:
noch en oordeelen wy v.l. noch eenighe andere die sulks wey-
gheren eenichsins te ghebruicken: maer wij sijn versekert (als
wy meynen) so wy het in sommighe saken ghebruickte, dat wy
niet sondighen soude. Maer ghy heden oordeelt ons gheheel
onweerdich eenighe vnie ofte ghemeensaemheyt in Chr: kerke.
van weghen dese onsen verstant ende ghebruick: hoe well dat

ghy lieden siet dat wy bevestiginghe hebben daer om w^t Godes
woort : ende willen niet toe laten dat wy met v.l. ghemeen-
schapp soude hebben tot dat wy boete doen van weghen het
ampt der ouerheyt, ende het ghebruicke des w^tterlicken
sweerts. het ampt der ouerheyt leert den heylighe gheest is
die goede ordinantie Godes ende woude ghy hebben ons ofte
eenighe die gheworden sullen een lidtmaet der ghemeente
Christi, boete te doen van het ghene dat goedt sy, ofte hem
anders niet toe te laten, het sy verre, niet maer sonde can
yemant onbequaem maken een Christen te worden, van het
welke hy moet boete doen, hoe cleyn het sy, want so het sonde
sy so is het des wetts ouertredinghe, ende een yeder trans-
gressie oft ouertredinghe daer van sal een rechtvaerdighe
vergeldinghe des loons ontvanghen, te weten het toorne ende
vloecke Godes, sonder boetvaerdicheyt. maer te gaen hooren
een valsche propheet so het niet en worde der broederen
erghenisse, ofte vervolginghe te mijden etc. welke niet te min
is openbaerlich quaedt, als te voren ghetoont heeft gheweest :
voor dese acht ghy hem niet weerdich in den ban te doen, hoe
well hy gheen boete bewijst om dat hy sulks doet maer acht
het leuen [?] bequaem, hem te draghen ofte haer (hoe well dat
sy boose sijn) die daer boose zijn, om welker oorsaeck wy oordeelen dat die schult op v leyt, ende dat het aen v Cante
mankeert ofte ghebreckt dat daer gheen eenicheyt en sy
onder ofte tuschen ons : want hadden wy gheweten dat ghy
lieden sondanighe verstant hadde ghehadt doe wy eenicheyt
met v.l. sochte wy souden eerstelich v.l. reformatie, voor
eenicheyt ghesocht hebben. daerom wy bidden v.l. van ghene
dat hier gheschreven staet te considereren, als mede van het
ghene dat onse vrienden ende beminde broederen van Lincolne
gheschreuen hebben tot antwoort van v.l. brief tot haer ende
so te stieren ons ouer v.l. verstant van weghen dese saecken
dat so ghelijck als wy alle een dingh meynen ende om strijden
te weten oprechticheyt in die professie des Evangeliums, wy
mochten te samen alle eens ghesint worden, als die ghene die
daer sijn van den huisghesin des gheloofs, ghegrondt ende
ghebouwt op die fundament der Apostelen & propheten Chr:
Iesus wesende die vernaemsten hoeck-staen : ende also in hem

opgroopen tot het euwighe leven. van weghen eenen Eedt het was (mijns heugens) tot dese ghebracht doe wy lesten met v waren, dat daer gheen onderscheyt was in onse houdinghe, alleen wy noemden dat eenen Eedt, ende ghy lieden niet : want ghy l. desgelijcks willen ghetuighen die waerheyt van een saeck voor den ouerricheyt nemende die Eer-waerdighe naem Godes tot ghetuighenisse, ende dese houden wy gheoorloft te doen wanneer wy daer toe gheroepen sullen worden & niet anders. Ende dus met ongheveynsde groetenisse aen v, ende v.l. huisvrouw ende die reste van onse beminde vrienden met v woonachtich by namen Alexander Hodgkin Ian Drew met haer wijven & die reste als ghenaemt, niet verghetende die 4 Oudtsten aen wien Ick bidd v maeckt kondich den inhoudt deser brief, als mede van dat ander gheschreuen van ons lieve vrienden te Lincolne. die Heere leyt v altoos in die waerheyt Amen.

Van Tyverton gheschreuen.   v.l. lieve & ghetrouwe vrienden

in die Heere altoos :

Ouerghesett w^t d'Engelsche spraeck   Iacobus Toppe : & Israel,

Iunij 5. 1631.   sijn huisvrouw.

per v.l. D.[ienaer ?] Broeder Swithune Gryndall.

———

[A Letter from Leonard Busher to Abram Derikson, dated Delft, Dec. 8, 1642, giving certain facts concerning Busher's old Age.][1]

Den [?]

. Eersamen vroomen

Abram Derikson in

de gecroonde Reed

tot

Amsterdam[2]

poort

In Delph de 8 december 1642.

[1] MS. B. 1378 in the Mennonite Archives, Amsterdam.
[2] This address is not a part of the text of the letter.

Ongunstige (Ik wou dat Ik (met waerheit) mogen seggen gunstige broeder in Christo, Abram Derikson, Salut: Ik heb diverse[1] brieven aen ul.[ieden]gesonden, maer geen Antwort become*n*; Ik heb ooc van tho: Cŭyp niet gehoort, sedert September doe hy wt England quam: Sin heb ic hem een brief geso*n*den, de 18 November, maer geen Antwort; Ik begeere dat ul. hem dat seggen, om dat ic mogen weete*n* hoe het met hem is: Hem ul. sal believe*n* my antwort te geve*n*, op my brieve*n* aen u & ul. confraters gesonde*n*, Ik ben een oŭt swack man, diep in de 71 yaren, end ligge*n* onder myn Pack ongeholpen, bedenct so het ubelieven, of hierin u & ul. Confraters, Gods geboden houden, die gebiet u nasten lief te hebben als u selven, end hem te helpen, so als onder sijn Pack, hy mogen niet blive*n* ligge*n*: vl. kent my staet wel, beyde nade geloof & na de weerlt, nochta*n*s in beyde, laet ul. my onder myn Pack liggen ongeholpen, overleg het wel, of God daerom niet vertoornt is? gyl*ieden* verstaen dat ic onder doolingen ook liggen, nochtans help u my niet wt, welc Godde meer mishaegt, om dat Ik dicwills aen ul. help versocht hebbe; haet my niet om dat ic ul. alle lief hebbe, end u niet flattere: gelijc de Schriftge-leerde*n* & Phariseen christum & sijn discipule*n* gehaet hebben: ul. mogen vremt dincken, dat ic u alle broeders

1. Ioh. 5. 1. 2.

noemen, gy sijntet, of gy moet niet[2] geloove*n* dat Iesus de Messias is, na dien ul. sulx gelooven, & Ic geloovet ook, so moet wy broeders in christo sijn, of ul. moet bewysen, dat ic daerin ongeloovich ben, welc ul. niet doenlic is: dan na dien wy alle sulx gelooven, en dat de Apo: seyt, die sulx geloove*n*, is wt God gebooren, so hebben wy een Hemels vader, dan moet het noot sakelik volgen, dat alle syne soonen, broederen met malcander sijn, doch onse broeder christus de outste is, nŭ na dien dit waer is, so ic begeere dat ul. alle, my in beyde, liefde bewijsen; gelijc

---

[1] Evidently an English word.

[2] My transcript reads "niet", but from the sense it is evident that it should either be omitted, or another "niet" inserted after "Iesus" and before "de Messias".

christus & syn Apostelen vermanen : hopende een troosteling Antwort cortelix te onfangen, Ic bevel ul. alle met my selven, de Salich genade des Heeren Iesu de[1] Messias, vl. d.w [?] : & desolate broeder in christo, Mark Leonard Busher .. in de blaw Clawe tusken de Pieterstraet, end Browery van der de [?] verkerde weerlt.

[1] Surely the writer of such Dutch was not a Dutchman, as Dr Whitley has contended !

XVII

DOCUMENTS CHIEFLY RELATING TO THE EARLY BROWNIST (BARROWIST) AND INDEPENDENT CONGREGATIONS ON THE CONTINENT

[A Letter of "G(eorge) Abbot, Archbishop of) Can*terbury*", probably written to Sir William Boswell, and dated "From Croydon Sept: 4: 1622."][1]

My verie good Lord.....

You are therefore to knowe, that his ma*ies*tie beinge much troubled and greived at the hearte, to heare eu*er*ie daie of soe manie defecc*io*ns from our Religion, both to Poperie and Anabaptisme, or other points of Sepa*r*ac*io*n, in some parts of this kingdome, and Consideringe w*i*th much Admirac*io*n, what might [be] the Cause thereof, especiallie in the Raigne of such a kinge, who doeth soe Constantlie professe him selfe an open adu*er*sarie to the superstition of the one and madnesse of the other, his princelie wisedome Could falle vpon noe one greater proba[bi]litie then the lightnesse affectednesse, and vnprofitablenesse of that kinde of preachinge, w*hi*ch hath beene of late yeeres two much taken vpp in Courte, vniu*er*sitie, Cittie, and Countrey :/
......

[An interesting Letter written by John Cotton to the "Lord Bishop of Lincolne, Lord keeper of the great Seale", dated "Boston [England]. Ian*uary* 31. 1624."][2]

[1] Add. MS. 6394 (Boswell Papers, Vol. I.), fol. 29–30, in the British Museum.

[2] Add. MS. 6394 (Boswell Papers, Vol. I.), fol. 35–36.

My honourable & very good Lord,

As your Lordship hath dealt honourably, & Christianly with me: so might I iustly be esteemed impiously vngratefull, if I should deale otherwise, then ingenuously, & honestly with your Lordship. When my cause first came before your Lordship, your Lordship wisely and truely discerned, y^t my forbearaunce of ye Ceremonyes was not from wilfull Refusall of Conformity, but from some doubt in my Iudgement (wch I confesse is very shallow) & from some scruple in Conscience, wch is indeede as weake. And therefore vpon mine humble, & instaunt Petition, your Lordship was pleased in much goodnesse, to graunt me time to consider further of these things for my better satisfaction. Your Lordships gentlenesse hath not since bred in me any obstinacy in mine owne Opinion: much lesse emboldened me to depart the further from ye receyved Iudgement & practise of ye Church in any point. The point of kneelinge in Receyvinge ye holy Communion, was noe lesse doubtfull to me (if not more) in ye dayes of your Lordships Prædecessour, then it is now. His Lordship knoweth, that in Westminster by his Commaundement, I propounded my doubts about it before himselfe, & the Reverend & learned Bishop of Sarisbury. y^t now is. Vnto whom I did so freely open my selfe, out of deepe desire to helpe my selfe by their deeper Iudgements, y^t my Lord discerninge my simplicity, became (as I conceyved it) ye more favourable & willinge not onely to beare with me, but also to give some way to my Restitution, & in the windinge vp to leave me in such Estate, as your Lordship found me. I humbly beseech your Lordship thinke not I have so abused your Lordships Patience, as to harden my selfe by your Lordships Lenity. Noe, I assure your Lordship, out of an vnfeigned Desire, to improove your Lordships Gentlenesse to mine owne Peace, & the Churches satisfaction, I have thus farre gayned (what by Conference, what by study, what by seekinge vnto God) as of late to see the Weakenesse [?] of some of those groundes against Kneelinge, wch before seemed too stronge for me to dissolve. The Experience of ye faylinge of my Iudgement in some of these thinges, maketh me the more to suspect it in other

Arguments & grounds of like nature. Besides I shall never forgett, what your Lordship gravely & wisely once said vnto me, The Ceremonyes I doubted of, „were noe where expresly „forbidden in Scripture: the Arguments brought against y^m „were but by Consequence deducted from Scripture: deduction „of Consequences was a worke of ye Iudgement: other mens „Iudgements (so many, so learned, so godly) why should I not „conceyve, did as infallibly deduce iust Consequences, to allowe „these thinges, as mine owne, to doubt of y^m. Alas, alas, (my deere Lord) I see by often Experience, the shallownesse of mine owne Iudgement, especially in comparison of many Centuryes of Godly-Learned, who doubt not of the Lawfull liberty of these Ceremonyes, especially of this Gesture. Their Consent herein doth further strongly persuade me, to suspect the motions of mine owne minde, when I see my selfe in any thinge to dissent from ye receyved Iudgement of so many Reverend Fathers, & Brethren in ye Church, whom I doe not onely highly reverence, but admire. I see, it is commonly a Palsey-distemper in any member of ye Body, when it is carryed by a Motion different from ye rule of ye rest of ye members. And I iustly suspect y^t Spirit, in my selfe, or in another, y^t breatheth a motion different from ye rest of ye members of ye body of Christ, ye Church of God.

Thus may your Lordship well perceyve, how little, your Lordships forbearaunce of me hath hitherto stiffened me in any private Conceyte. And though it hath bene suggested to your Lordship (as I heare) y^t it hath emboldened our Parish to Incomformity, & induced divers others to come from other Parishes, to Communicate with vs in ye like Liberty: Yet surely your Lordship hath done honourably & Christianly, & well beseeminge the æquity of your High & Honourable Court [?], Not to give Credit to such a Suggestion, till your Lordship hath Enquired, & heard our Answer. The trueth is, the Ceremonyes of ye Ringe in Marryage, & standinge at ye Creede, are vsually performed by my selfe: & all ye other Ceremonyes of Surplice, Crosse in Baptisme, Kneelinge at ye Communion are frequently vsed by my fellow-Minister in our Church, & without disturbance of ye People. The People on

Sabbaths, & sundry other Festivall dayes, doe very diligently, & throug[h]ly frequent y° Publique Prayers of y° Church, appointed by Authority in y° Booke of Common Prayer: neyther doe I thinke, y^t any of y^m ordinarily (vnlesse it be vpon iust occasion of other buisinesse) absenteth himselfe. It is true indeede, y^t in Receyvinge the Communion, sundry of y^m doe not kneele: but (as I conceyve it, & as they Expresse themselves) It is not out of scruple of Conscience, but from y° store & multitude of Communicants, wch often doe so thronge one another in this great Congregation, that they can hardly stand, (much lesse kneele) one by another. Such as doe forbeare kneelinge out of any doubt in Conscience, I know not, how very few, they be: I am sure, in comparison of y° rest, they be nullius numeri. That divers others come from other Parishes for y° Purpose, to Receyve without Kneelinge, is vtterly vnknowen to me, & (I am persuaded) vtterly vntrue. All y° neighbour Parishes, Ministers & People rounde about vs, are wholly Conformable. Once indeede (as I heard) one of y° Inhabitants of our neighbour Parish, comminge to visit his wife (who then nourced a Gentlemans child in our Towne) did here Communicate with vs. And whether for his not kneelinge, or for some further Cause, I know not, but (as I heard) y° Court beinge Informed of Him, did proceede severely against Him, But otherwise, the man (as I have since bene certefyed) hath alwayes vsed to receyve Kneelinge, both before, & since. Yet his Case beinge further bruited abroade, then well knowen, might easily breede such a Suspicion, & afterwards a Report, wch in time might come to your Lordships Eares, y^t divers did come from other Parishes to vs, for this purpose, To Receyve Incomformably. But your Lordship is wise, easily discernninge [?] betweene Report & Evidences.

Let me now therefore humbly intreate your Lordship, in y° bowells of Christ Iesus, since your Lordships Lenity hath hitherto neyther hardened me to any selfe-conceyted Obstinacy, nor wrought any Præiudice, eyther to your Lordship, or to y° Church of God: Your Lordship will therefore be pleased To allowe me yet further time, for better Consideration of such doubts, as yet remayne behinde That if vpon further search,

I can finde them too weake to deteyne me, as I have done
yᵉ former I may then satisfy your Lordships Desire, & Expectation: If Otherwise, yet I trust your Lordship shall ever
finde me (by yᵉ helpe of God) a peaceable, & (to my best
endeavour, accordinge to my weake abilityes) a serviceable
member of yᵉ Church of God. I dare not præsume, with more
wordes to Presse your Lordship, whom yᵉ store & weight of
so many important Affayres, presse continually. The Lord of
Heaven & Earth give me still to finde favour in your Lordships
Eyes: And even He prosper your Lordship with Longe life, &
Happynesse, & Favour with God, & man. So humbly cravinge
Pardon for my great boldnesse, I desire leave to rest

> Your Lordships exceedingly much bounden Oratour /

Boston. Ianuary 31. 1624. /   Iohn Cotton. /

[A Petition of English and Scottish ministers in the Netherlands to King Charles I of England against six articles
   exhibited by Sir D.(udley) Carleton. Dated " Att Rotterdam the 4.ᵗʰ of Iune 1628."][1]

Articles exhibited & delivered unto the Synod
of the English & Scottish Ministers in the
Netherlands, in the name of his Majestie of Great
Brittanie, by the right hono:ᵇˡᵉ the L. Carleton
Baron of Imbercourt, Ambassadour extraord:ⁱᵉ to the States
Generall of the united provinces, May 19. 1628. /

1   It is his Majesties pleasure, that the said Ministers meddle
     not with the making or composing, much lesse yᵉ pub-
     lishing of any new Liturgie or sett forme of prayer for
     their congregations.

2.   That they by no meanes do exercise the power of Ordina-
     tion, but that they leave both English & Scottish to
     receive holy orders only from their owne mother-Churches
     established in these two kingdomes: And that they
     accept of no other into any pastorall charge, but those
     only who have beene so ordained.

     [1] Add. MS. 6394 (Boswell Papers, Vol. I.), fol. 41–44.

A very plain and well grounded

TREATISE

CONCERNING

BAPTISME·

Wherein it is very cleerly shown, *and out of
good grounds demonstrated that* Baptisme *was instituted and
ordained by the Lord Christ*, *for those that believe and repent*,
and was so taught and used by his Apostles, *and observed and
followed by the Primitive Church.*

As also how that in processe of time the Baptisme
of Children in stead of true Baptisme was brought in
and received, and by divers Councels, Popes, and
Emperours commanded to be observed.

Marke 16. 26.
*He that shall believe and be Baptised shall be saved,
But he that will not believe shall be damned.*

Printed in the yeare of our Lord and Saviour
JESUS CHRIST.

TITLE-PAGE OF THE SECOND IMPRESSION. (*Facsimile.*) Probable date
1648. See Vol. I., pp. 263–4 and Appendix B, p. 370.

3   That they bring in no novelties in any rites or Ceremonies
    which either concerne the actuall admission of Lawfull
    Ministers unto their pastorall charge, or which may be
    used in any other sacred act whatsoever.

4. That they assume no power to themselves to meddle with
    any point of doctrine : but that in doctrinall points they
    keepe themselves to what hath beene established by the
    English & Dutch Churches.

5. His Majestie is well content that they should still keepe
    that power, wch K. James his Royall Father intended
    to them ; viz: To suppresse those who tooke vpon them
    the function of preachers, without lawfull vocation or
    admission to ye Ministery.   And 2.^{ly} to examine, re-
    straine & punish the ill manners of such as give scandall
    by their vitious lives.   And moreover, his Majestie doth
    recommend unto them, to make diligent inquisition
    after those who write books or pamphletts any way
    derogatory to ye Church or state of England; & as
    much as in them lieth to suppresse them.

6. In case any doubt or difficulty arise concerning ye true
    meaning or execution of these particulars; that they
    then repaire to his Majesties Ambassadour or Agent for
    ye time being, who will ever have, or be able to procure
    such directions from his Majesty whereby so godly a
    worke, may be duely & rightly advanced.

                            Signed
                            D. Carleton.

May it please your Sacred Majestie graciously to receive
& consider this humble declaration of us your Majesties
most loyall & duetifull subjects (the English & Scotch
Ministers) now living under the power of a forraine
state, touching these articles exhibited unto us in your
Majesties name, as your Royall pleasure, by the right
honorable the Lord Carleton, Baron of Imber Court,
your Majesties Ambassadour extraordinary to ye States
generall of ye united provinces ye 19th of May 1628. /
First in generall, we humbly beseech your Royall Majestie

to consider how unjustly, without any occasion by us
ministred to these Churches of England & Scotland,
a needles trouble hath beene raised unto us. First in
the time of K. James of happy memory; & now againe
in your Majesties time upon some sinister suggestions
only, as though our proceedings in our Synodall assemblies should be derogatory to the Churches of the
said kingdomes; whereas that solemne protestation
made by us to the contrary att our first embracing
& undertaking that authority given us by the most
Illustrious Lords the States Generall by the procurement of his Majesties Ambassadour doth sufficiently
cleare us of that imputation: the contents of wch protestation here following, we humbly present to your
Majestie.

The said Ministers for the removing of all jealousy of innovation,
separation, faction or schisme, did all jointly & severally
protest, That as they did entertaine the liberty & benefitt
of the said order & governement to be practised and
administred only according to the French Churches, &
as is contained in the grant from the most Illustrious
Lords the States, without any purpose or intention to
do any thing in any other forme to the least offense of
the Churches in these provinces; or any way to impaire
any particular lawfull priviledge wch hitherto hath beene
enjoyed by any of the English Churches in these provinces, being in nature & quality neither offensive or
contrary to the order of the Dutch or French Churches
among whom they reside, nor any way repugnant to the
power & grant aforesaid. So likewise did they protest
their entertainement of the said forme & order to be
(notwithstanding the bond of our uniforme obedience to
the power & grant aforesaid during our abode in these
parts) free in their soules & consciences from any dis-
respect, censure, prejudice, or condemnation of the
Churches in his Majesties dominions; reserving unto
them all due reverence as to the true Churches of
Christ, equally precious in the sight of God (through

the same most precious faith) with our selves resolving
still to hold communion with them, notwithstanding
any difference of externall order; & evermore to pray
for, & procure their happines & wellfare with our owne.
......

And 1. concerning the making or publishing of any new
Liturgie. We are sorry, that our best intentions are
so misconstrued, it never havinge entred into our minds,
to frame or publish any new Liturgie: or to oppose or
condemne the Liturgies of any other Churches: but only
to enlarge that allready extant (: [*sic*] wch by authority
& command of the States we are enjoyned to observe :)
by adding thereunto from other Liturgies; & among
the rest from the Liturgie of England, so much as
without offense or scandall in these Churches might be
practised: wch foresaid Liturgie hath beene in continuall
use in all Churches here, from the time of Q. Elizabeth
of famous memory, whilst the Earle of Leicester did
governe in these provinces; & agreed upon & practised
in the Churches of the Brill & Vlissinghe, then absolutly
depending upon ye authority of the Kings of England,
& maintained by them. Such was the care of your
Ma*jesti*es royall pr*e*decessor*s* to have all things among
their subjects here residing to be done in conformity
to the Churches of these lands, thereby to prevent all
offense, & to maintaine the peace & unitie of the
Church: wch course we trust assuredly, your Ma*jesti*e
intends we should follow; not purposing we should putt
in practise any Liturgy never as yett authorized in
these parts; or that we should leave every man to his
owne liberty to use what Liturgie he pleaseth; seing
thereby as great, if not greater confusion & disorder
should raigne amongst us after order established, as
was before the erection of our Synode.

Touching the practise of Ordination forbidden us in the
2.^d Article: We humbly beseech your Ma*jesti*e to weigh
the nature of ordina*ti*on, being an essentiall point of y^e
function of our Ministery, for the well ordering ye house

of God, over wch we are sett, as well as the preaching of the gospell & administration of the Sacraments; so that with good conscience we cannot omitt it, nor leave it wholly to others without being guilty of neglect of the office laid upon us by Christ. And we are persuaded, that your Majestie considering this, will never prohibitt us the exercise of any thing, the power whereof is conferd upon us by him, there being (as we hope) no just cause in our persons or carriadge to ye contrary.

2. Ordination is of such a nature, that the exercise thereof being taken from us, the practise of all other points of Ecclesiasticall discipline over others of the Ministery are taken away with it; Seing none can displace that have no power to place; nor take away authority, where they cannot give it. The Ordainors may maintaine the ordained by them against all others; it being the order of all Churches, that Ministers in their Ministery be subject to their Ordainors. This point is also confirmed by the Popes owne law............

3. If we should leave this practise wholly to these Churches, & thereby leave to them all the rest of the points of Ecclesiasticall governement we consequently give way to a forraine Ecclesiasticall power over ye Churches within ye dominions of this State; & so should not only prove ourselves most unthankfull persons, but also wrong the state, in transferring the liberty & power graunted us by them to strangers; so enthralling them to a forraine authority./

4. Your Majestie may consider what infamy & disgrace by this course shall be brought upon us your Majesties subjects, as the only men in these Churches, who are unworthy to enjoy the freedome, wch other strangers (& namely the French) do peaceably possesse. We beseech your Majestie graciously to respect the credit of your owne loyall subjects, that they be not herein made inferior in estimation to other strangers, & so exposed to the prophane derision & contempt of all men.

5. We beseech your Majestie to ponder what a dangerous

president this were to have the practise of any affaires
Ecclesiasticall to depend upon a forrain power, without
the limits of the kingdome or state, where it is exercised.
What confusion should fall amongst States & Princes,
if once this practise should take place ? For why may not
a forrain civill power, order the affaires of another state,
if a forraine Ecclesiasticall power shall once have place
to order the Ecclesiasticall affaires of another State?
Was not this a speciall reason wch moved your Majesties
Father of happy memory to take such paines in writing
that famous Apologie pro juramento fidelitatis against
such usurped power by the Pope? We beseech your
Majestie to consider, if any state under heaven, except
papisticall, would willingly suffer such a practise, so
dangerous, to creepe in, & take place in their dominions:
considering, that even in this point of ordaining of
Ministers, the Popes owne law doth not permitt a
Bishop to ordaine any without the limits of his owne
Bishoprick, much lesse in a forrain state, as hereby doth
manifestly appeare......

6. We beseech your Majestie to conceive, that if we
should continue a Synodall body without practise of
ordination ; we should be such an Ecclesiasticall body,
as is not to be found in any reformed Church in the
world. And therefore we leave it unto your Majesties
wise judgement, if the leaving this practise wholly to
the Churches of England and Scotland, should not
worke in all abroad a greater distaste of the Churches
of England & Scotland, & Episcopall governement in
them (: if once it begin to extend its authority to
forraine nations without the compasse of your Majesties
dominions :) for suppressing in their owne brethren
abroad, the ordinary practise of all other reformed
Churches? May not all Churches thinke; yea do
they not allready conceive hereby that if they could,
they would both condemne & overthrow all their
governement? Whereas otherwise, they might have
all other Churches to hold peace & communion with

them, if they should not incroach so strangely upon them, & their practise in our persons.

....

[Information concerning the English Congregations in the Netherlands between 1621 and 1633.][1]

Concerning the Classis.

> That in the yeare 1621. M^r forbes obtaining a Commission for the English Classis Mr Paget, & Mr Potts refused to be members of it: And being pressed to come in they made their case knowne to the Amsterdam Dutch classis of which they were. & gave their reasons. which were so approved That the Classis made an Act, That they thought it best the English should have no classis, & that Mr Paget & Mr Potts should not be drawn from the Dutch classis they were in. This Act with the reason are [*sic*] vpon register. & recorded.
> That Mr Paget &^{c} [?] being yet farther pressed by the Engl classis; The busines was presented to the North Holland synod: where the former Act of the Amsterdam classis was confirmed; this is likewise to be seene vpon record. /
> Mr Forbes notwithstanding this once with Mr Scott the Vtrecht minister, & another time with Mr Batchelour came to Amsterdam privately to the Burgomasters to desire them to constraine Mr Pagett & Mr Potts to be of their classis...
> That the two maine reasons why the English Classis is condemned are these (as they may be seene vpon record) 1. Because the Ministers of England which come over hither are of severall & inconsistent opinions differing from one another & from all reformed churches. as expressely that some are Brownists. some Brownistically affected in particular opinions. as .1. in allowing private men to preach. 2. In denijng [?] formes of praier. 3 In admitting Brownists to their Congregations not

[1] Add. MS. 6394 (Boswell Papers, Vol. I.), fol. 146, recto and verso.

renouncing their Brownisme. Some are Iacobites who require a New Covenant for members of a church to make before they can be Communicants, 2. Condemne the Decisive & Iudging power of all Classes & Synods; & that they have only a power of Counsailing & advising, because every particular Congregation is a church; and that a Compleat church, and that it is Immediately given vnto every congregation *from* Christ to be a single & vncompounded policy: (These are the very words of Mr Iacob, & Parker, & Baines,) And now the Dutch Classis & Synods conclude that such opinions as these do cleane overthrow the nature of their goverment; and y^t amongst such diversity of opinions no true Classis can be...

2. Because of the Complaint of the french & wallons in those countries..because they have a Classis graunted vnto them: It were bet*ter* (they say by experience) that they had no classis but were (as Mr Paget is) mixed into the Dutch Classes. for by reason of the distan[ce ?] of their dwelling they cannot have Monthly or quarterly Meetings, as Classes have, but only annuall as Synods: and that then there[?] is such trouble in their gathering togeth*er* some dwelling in one province & some in anoth*er* at such great distance that they never all...& by reason of their few meetings the[re ?] grow vp many Enormities in *pa*rticular congregations vnpunished:...

That now in this pr*e*sent yeare 1633. M^r forbes & his Classists obtaining a new commissi[on] for their classis *from* the Councell of State, Mr Paget hath pr*e*sented the busines againe to his Classis at Amsterdam the 4th of Aprill: being the first Monday in the month. And they have promised their vttmost endeavour to hinder it...

....

Concerning Mr Peters ordina*c*ion

1. There was a *New Covenant made* w*i*th [?] certaine pr*e*cise & strict obliga*c*ions to wh*i*ch they should bind themselves. and he would be chosen by none but them

that would put there [?] hands to that paper. This saith
Mr Paget was a kind of Excommunicac*i*on to above two
p*ar*ts of the congregac*i*on in former times. & hath caused
the difficulty of adminis[t]*er*ing the sacrament because he
will give it to none but them whose names are at his New
Covenant. Those New Covenanted must choose & Call
him. so before these a sermon was made by M^r forbes.
2. There was χειροτονεια. first by all the men, but said
M^r forbes, I see w*hat* the men do: but w*hat* do the
weomen do. Therevpon they fell a χειροτονising too &
Lift vp their Hands.
3. There was χειροθεσία. The Imposing of all the hands
of the p*re*sent Ministers except Mr Daye who was not
desired (*Mr Grim of weasell was present* and confirmes
all this) and Mr Forbes held them above halfe an hower
laijng [laying] his burthen vpon him in these words &
manner, as if he had never beene made minister. /

One Thomas Cranford: who doth vsually eate at Stephen
ofwoods: is putting out the Bibles. they are printing in a
house by the South Church. and one Stasmore a Brownist.
who is discontented about the busines if it be well carried
will easily tell all; & bring you to the place, Stephen
ofwood is certainly the man wh*i*ch procures the printing
of all the blew bookes...

[A Letter of Alexander Browne to Sir William Boswell,
dated "Rotterdam the first of Nouem*ber*", 1633.][1]

Sence my laste beinge wth you I haue littell or noe newss to
Informe you of only Mr Peter reported to sum of his peopell
that he was to preach his farewell sermond at delft the last
sunday: and to leaue it A dessolaite plaice wheer their [?] was
wepinge Amongest his femall [female] saintes to heir of the
sad stories he related vnto them heir at Rotterdam before he
departed: for nowe insteed of preacheinge wee should haue A
littell seruice..read with many other skandolous wordes he

---

[1] Add. MS. 6394 (Boswell Papers, Vol. i.), fol. 153 recto.

eussed [used] vpon the Common prayer:...his prefaice to the fresh supplie is printed and I am promissed one of them but I shall noe sonner [sooner] receaue it but I will send it forwarde to your Honnor. I haue heir sent you Mr Peters Couenant w^ch [?] he maide and vnless wee will all subscribe to this his Couenant wee shall not be admitted to the lords Table neither ould members nor newe: so that it semes to me our Church formerly was noe Church: but what authoritie he haith to doe these thinges: I knowe not: for he him sellf saith the C[h]urch of Eingland doth Tije [*sic*] the Concienc of men to do this and that, and he for his parte in this his Couenant Tieth both Concienc: and purss...

[A Letter of Henry Elsynge's to Sir William Boswell, dated Amsterdam Iune the 6:^th 1633 ".][1]

There are very pretty differences now *in motion betweene the Brownists heere* [in Amsterdam], *they haue diuided their Brotherhoods, some goe along with Iohn D'ecluse, some with Mr Kan* [Canne], *the two heads of that diuided Bodye,* of which indeede there are none willing to bee feete, or any other enferior members, they would all bee heads: *Iohn D'ecluse has deliuered vp to Sathan Mr Kan, & his Sectaries, & Mr Kan will shortly bee ready, to doe him & his, the like courtesie.* Stephen Offwod my Host was once one of the Brotherhood, but tis long since hee fell from it: but his wife & children continuing still among them, hee has written a booke which hee directs to them, in which hee layes the Brownists very open, & layes downe motiues & reasons to his wife & children, why they should forsake (as hee termes them) their abominac[i]ons: but that hee maye shew himselfe *auerse to the Church of England & the discipline therein* setled & approued of, hee *has a Tract* wherein hee shewes that the *English of these Churches heere,* had very good reason to leaue the Church of England, *bringes in a short Narratiue of the Troubles of Franckfort, when the English first endeauored in the beginning of Queene Maryes tyme, to erect a Church there,* & vpon that occasion, brings in likewise the...opinion of Mr Calvin,

[1] Add. MS. 6394 (Boswell Papers, Vol. i.), fol. 142.

Bullinger & others of our Booke of Common Prayer: but that I feare your occasions, would not dispence with soe vnworthy an Interruption, I had *sent you the Booke.* There is heere alsoe an English Bible now printed, according to the Exemplary of that Bible, which was printed in the Queenes tyme (Anno 1599[)], & (as they saye) *since by King Iames prohibited* to bee any more printed: & that it may passe the better in London & with the more *securitie, it beares the same date with the other, & is soe punctually the same with it, that it is I thinke impossible to distinguish them.....*

[Part of a letter probably written by Stephen Goffe, of the date 1633.][1]

......

It is to be observed that of those Engl: Minister[s] [in the Netherlands] which vse not the English forme [of Liturgy]
1. Some vse the Dutch translated. as M[r] Paine. but yet that mended much left out, and some things added, as may appeare by M[r] Paines booke. /
2. Some vse none at all as M[r] Forbes. but every time they administer the Sacraments a new. they [?] doe [?] not stand to one of their owne. /
3. Some vse another English forme putt out at Midleborough. 1586. This M[r] Goodyer saith he vseth at Leyden. and M[r] Peters saied to me that was the forme he found in his consistory. But whether he vse it or no I cannot tell, I beleive he goes the Forbesian way.
4. Some vse our English forme in the sacraments but mangle them Leaving out and putting in whole sentences......

M[r] Pagetts 20 Proposicions to M[r] [Thomas] Hooker
with his answere thereto :∼/[2]

Quest: 1 Whither it be lawfull for any to resort vnto the Publique Meetings of the Brownists, and to Com-

---

[1] Add. MS. 6394 (Boswell Papers, Vol. I.), fol. 168.

[2] Add. MS. 6394 (Boswell Papers, Vol. I.), fol. 67–72. Only a small portion of the contents of this document is here given.

municate with them in the WORD of GOD.//
Negatur

Answ: To seperate from the faithfull Assemblies, and
Churches in England, as noe Churches is an error
in Iudgment, and sinne in practize, held and
mayntained by the Brownists, & therefore to
Comunicate with them, either in this their opinion
or practize, is sinnefull & vtterly vnlawfull, but for
a Christian both their opinion, & practize, to heare
occasionally amongst them, & so to Comunicate
with them in that part of Gods worde (which I
conceauc to be the meaning of the first Quære) is
not so farre, as I yet see simply vnlawfull, but may
prove occasionally offensiue, if either by goeing, wee
should encourage them to goe on, in their Course of
seperation, or els by our vnwise expressions, might
serue to weaken ours, to like of it our selves, and so
to drawe them to a farther approbation of that way,
then was before meet, wherevpon it followes, if wee
giue these occasions of offence, wee sinne if wee do
not abstaine [?], but if these occasions of offence may
be remoued, by our Constant renouncing of their
Course of the one side, and by our free and open
profession of our intents, on the other side. That
wee goe only to heare some sauorie point opened,
and to benefitt by the guifts of some able Minister,
that may come amongst them, if I say the giving
of any Iust offence by these, or any other meanes,
may be avoided, I conceive then it is not a sinne to
heare them occasionally, and that some men may
prevent such occasions, it is to mee, it is to me [*sic*]
a very disputable question not hauing euer studied
this point before. /

Quærs 2 Whether those Members of the Church [of England]
which somtymes heare them, & stifly maintaine
a Libertie therein are to be tollerated or rather
censured. // censured

18—2

Respo:　For the practise of members according to the former
　　　　Caution & interpretation, being taken vp & mayn-
　　　　tayned though stiffly, which Argumente, because it
　　　　is but questionable and disputable before they be
　　　　fully convicted of their sinne, they ought to be
　　　　tollerated rather than censured: And this modera-
　　　　cion in things which are disputable, and not
　　　　absolutely necessary to salvation......

Qu: 3　Whether such of the Brownists as haue not re-
　　　　nounced their Seperation from the Church of
　　　　England, Nor yett allow Comunion with the
　　　　Publique estate thereof may lawfully be receiued
　　　　for members of our Church // Negatur.

Resp:　The not renouncing seperacion from the faithfull
　　　　assemblies in England and the not allowance of
　　　　Comunion with the Publique state of the Church of
　　　　England This meer opinion can in no wise make
　　　　a man vnfitt to be receaved a member of this
　　　　Congregation, vnlesse wee will say that such a man
　　　　(being in his iudgment & life otherwise altogether
　　　　vnblameable) in Judicious Charitie is not a visible
　　　　Christian, which is a more ridged Censure then
　　　　the wisest of the seperation would giue waie vnto,
　　　　in a proportionable kinde, and I suppose a pious
　　　　hart dare affirme,......

English Preachers in the Netherlands [in 1633][1].

Of yᵉ Regiments.

e Lord Vere. Mʳ Goffe.
c [?] Gen: Morgan. Mʳ Batchelour.
e Col. Paginham. Mʳ. Day.
e Col. Herbert. Mʳ Sclaer.

Of yᵉ Merchants.

c Mʳ Forbes. and his
c Assistant Mʳ Hooker.

[1] Add. MS. 6394 (Boswell Papers, Vol. i.), fol. 175. In the original
the list of names is given in three columns.

[Of yᵉ] Garrisons.

Vtrecht. Mʳ Fortree.
Gorichom. Mʳ Batchelour. idem.
Tergoo. Mʳ Day. idem.
e Gittredenberge. Mʳ Firsby.
Busch. Mʳ Gribbins.
c Husden. Mʳ Widdowes.
c Bergen. Mʳ Paine.
Dort. a Dutchman w*hi*ch
    speakes English.
c Nimmegen Mʳ Sibbald. Scotchm.
Wesell. a Dutchman w*hi*ch
    speakes English.
Tiel. Mʳ Sclaer. idem.
Doesborough. Mʳ Parsons.

[Of yᵉ] Towns.

Amsterdam. Mʳ Iohn Pagett.
c Rotterdam. Mʳ Peters.
Flushing. Mʳ Roe.
Middleborough. Mʳ Drake[1].
Leyden. Mʳ Goodyer.
Hage. Mʳ Balmeford.

The towne Ministers haue meanes allowed them by the States.
of the Garrisons none haue any Meanes from the States but
only Vtrecht. 500ᵍ: per ann*um* and Bergen. 200ᵍ: per ann*um*
the rest are payd by the Captaines, w*hi*ch is about 2. gulders
a weeke, as long as they bee in the Garrisons, So that when
they are in the field they haue nothing but only of those
Companies w*hi*ch are left at home.
Of all those there belong to yᵉ English Classis Mʳ Forbes.
Mʳ Peters. Mʳ Balmeford. Mʳ Batchelour. Mʳ Paine. Mʳ Widdowes.
Mʳ Sibbald. this last came within this yeare (and though they
haue had noe classicall meeting) yet must be named here
because hee was placed by the authority of yᵉ classis at
Nimmegen, and doth reckon himselfe of that classis.

[1] Could this by any chance have been Thomas Drakes who has already
been mentioned elsewhere ?

Those y^t refuse to be of ye English Classis, some are of
the Dutch, and some are of none. Mr Pagett. Mr Fortree,
Mr Gribbins are of ye Dutch. (what Mr Roe and Mr Drake doe
is not knowne, but they refuse to be of ye English classis.)
Mr Goodyer desired to bee of ye Leyden classis, but they will
not admitt him, And ye reason giuen is because they doe
obserue by a longe and sharpe controuersy which hath been
betwixt him & his parishioners hee is of a rigider Discipline,
then ye Dutch Discipline is.

Mr Gribbins was commended by ye Lord Vere to ye Busch,
being a Palatinate man that wanted meanes, & hauing studied
well in England, ye officers report nothing but well of him. /

Mr Fortree was chosen by ye officers, and is well approued of
by them, for a quiet man.

Mr Paine was called from Schonehouen by ye Englishe classis
to Bergen op Zone. after y^t by their Authority, they had
depriued one Mr Clarke the Scotch regiment Preacher to y^e
Earle of Bucklough.

Mr Parsons is the regiment preacher to Coll: Belford, (it is
likely hee is of noe Classis at all) Mr Sibbald : to Coll: Broge.

[A letter of Stephen Goffe's to Sir William Boswell, dated
"Leyden. Feb. *28* stil. no." (1634/3 ?)][1]

Worthy Sir.

I hope you have receaued a lettre from Amsterdam
on Sunday wch did acquaint you with the comming of m^r
Damport [Davenport] vnto you, & the cause of it. And by
this time m^r Damport appearing to you hath shewed the truth
of it. Since that m^r Pagett hath given me another relacion
wch with his most humble service he desired me to make
knowne vnto your selfe : vnto whom he desires to approve him
selfe, and give account of his actions. After that in many
discourses with m^r Damport He had found his difference from
him in the poynt of Baptisme, wch is not only a matter of

[1] Add. MS. 6394 (Boswell Papers, Vol. I.), fol. 192 recto and verso.

judgement but practice both ministers joyning in baptizing
every child according to the Dutch custome ((1) one reading
the forme, & explicacion of it. and the other sprinkling the
water with those words In the name &c.) He told him that it
was necessary for him to admitt all the infants wch were
brought, as he & the Dutch alwaies vse to do, or els they could
not be fitt colleges in that pastorall charge. Herevpon Damport
& his frends made the first cry, complained to the Dutch
ministers, obtained of two of them, to come vnto m^r Pagett, to
reprehend him for his difficulty in admitting so reverend[?]
a College &c. Those two (.. one Roulandus. & Goldorpius)
comming to m^r Pagett & hearing[?] the case were presently
made of his mind, & concluded that a more sollemne meeting
should be had, & Damport perswaded to a better sense, or els
no admission. Wherefore shortly after 5 of the Dutch ministers
came vnto m^r Pagetts house, and there expected m^r Damport
who could not be brought to come vnto them, notwithstanding
that they proceeded to their consultacion, wrought in Lattine
the condicions they would require of Damport & Pagett, &
subscribed them with their 5 names, These condicions were on
Pagetts part That if the Parent or frends of the infant did
signifie vnto him before hand that they would have a child
baptised, That then m^r Pagett should send them to Damport,
to be examined, as he desired. On Damports part That if the
Parent or frends being desired to go to him should not go. or
comming should be so ignorant as not to be able to give account
of their faith, or if they should suddainely bring the child into
the church without forewarning that he should not venture to
refuse to baptize it. Damport having this paper of condicions
brought to him gave such an answere, as m^r Pagett vnderstood
he meant to rest satisfied in them. Wherevpon he preached
before m^r Pagett & they were to proceed to his Calling. After
sermon m^r Pagett desired him to speake plainely whether he
would rest in those condicions, & resolve to performe them.
His answer was, That in the Consistory one of the Elders
should expresse his mind; but m^r Pagett pressing him to
expresse his owne mind him selfe, He seemed to take the
Condicions vpon wch they in the Consistory concluded on him

for their pastor, made an Instrument of his Election, w[c]h yet m^r Pagett would have to include in it The Condicions about baptisme. wch was done. Now their worke was to obtaine the consent of the magistrates, & the Classis. The magistrates for a good while were hard to be entreated, alleadging his offending our king, his deserting of his former charge, His preaching since he came hither &c but at last were overcome by the importunity of the merchants that pressed for him. The Classis made no difficulty supposing the acceptance of those Condicions. So that now nothing was remaining but Damports receaving their call. wch when He saw with the Condicions about baptisme mencioned in it, he desired to be excused, that he could not with a good conscience performe them. So all that busines was vndone againe. And thus it now stands. Since that his clients have beene very malicious against m^r Pagett, most grievously reviling him, & exasperating both him & those frends wch he hath against a 2^d election wch is thought willbe very hardly obtained, the Dutch ministers being offended at this precise Iesuitissme æquivocating him selfe in to their election. Yesterday was their Classis day, in wch their purpose was (as m^r Pagett told me) to speake of Damports dealing. And that He might avoyde the discoursing with them or any of them he would absent him selfe. either this is the cause of his jorney, or it is believed so, because yet no Dutch minister could come to speake with Damport since his comming though they have sought it many times, severally & alltogether, as when he was chosen the whole Classis desired his company to dinner, but non est inventus. nor ever since could be. wherin we are litle beholding to him, for they sticke not to say His Latine tong is the cause of it. /

......

Leyden. Feb. *28* stil. no. [1634/3 ?]

Tewsday. morn. /

Your humblest Servant

Stephen Goffe. /

[A letter of Stephen Goffe's to Sir William Boswell, dated "Leyden March .9 " (1634/3 ?).][1]

Worthy Sir.

Since the receiving of your–March–6. from Brill. for which I give you many thankes, M[r] Paget hath sent his kinsman to me, to relate what was done in the Classis last weeke. The ordinary busines being dispatched in their mondayes meeting they resolved of purpose to come together the next day to heare m[r] Damports [Davenports] matter. On one side m[r] Paget declared that after the consent of the magistrates by order from the classis he with the Elders had offered m[r] Damport his Call in writing. but that He refused it his conscience not suffering him to vndertake those condicions w[ch] yet were thought necessary by 5 of themselves, and were in appearance accepted by him selfe. On the other side were two of the Elders of the Church deputed & instructed by m[r] Damport; who indeed confessed the refusall, & the tendernes of his conscience, but in the name of the *most* & *cheifest* of the congregation desired the Classis that they might have him established amongst them, not Pastor but Assistant in preaching. alleadging the excellency of his guifts, & his *discreet* & *peaceable* carriage. / Vpon the notice of his refusall some of the Dutch ministers who (by the merchants m[r] Damports frends) were brought to be sticklers for him professed themselves much wronged, that m[r] Damport had putt them vpon the displeasure of the magistrates. for that the magistrates did alledge, as his deserting England, so his differing from the Belgicke constitutions w[ch] they had answered vnto them, & warranted vpon their creditts that he would be a fitt and conformable man. But now in his plaine flying off, & that for such easy condicions, he did lay them open to shame to the magistrates, who were difficulte before, but now would be possessed; that many other differences were hidd in his brest besids those. / To that matter of being lecturer or assistant in preaching only, that was a

---

[1] Add. MS. 6394 (Boswell Papers, Vol. i.), fol. 194 recto—195 recto. This letter I take to be dated according to New Style, as was often the case in the Netherlands at this period.

species of creatures wch was not in their church, besids that
therein they should exceedingly wrong m^r Pag*et* whose age
required a College in all the burthens of the church, wch were
as many & more heavy in the businesses of the Consistory for
government, and in administering the sacraments, then [?] in
the pulpitt for preaching.　And that vnlesse he were legittimate
Pastor he could have no place in the consistory. &c.　In fine
There conclusion was that 3 Dutch ministers should be deputed
to go vnto him in the name of the Classis to expresse the just
cause they have to be offended at his refusall, they having
through so many objections made his way for him.　And to
take his reasons why he will not accept of those condicions
concerning baptisme.　And that next classis those 3 must
report w*hat* his reasons be that so they may sett a finall conclusion to this matter........................
Leyden. March .9. /. [1634/3 (?)]

Your most humble &
thankfull Servant
Stephen Goffe. /

[A Letter of John Davenport's to "Sir William Boswell
Knight", dated "Amsterda*m* March 18. 1634(/3 ?)".][1]

Honorable Sir,

　　　　When I first Came into these parts, my purpose
was to stay he[re] but 3 or 4 moneths, and, that time being
expired, to returne for England my nati[ue] Countrey, had not
the sinister & slanderous informac*i*on, whereof I complained
in [my?] last, exasperated the ArchB^p. of Cant:[erbury] to
reproachfull inuectiues, and bitter mena[ces?] against me in
the High Com*m*ission, whereby my returne is made much more
difficult, and hazardous then I could suspect. when, in that
letter, I sayd, I am willing to excercise [*sic*] those gifts which
God hath giuen me &c I vsed that expression not in affectation,
but as fittest to represent my present state, and to intimate
that I am not engaged by any relation of office for Continuance
here. which, being added to what I then wrote, and the

---

[1] Add. MS. 6394 (Boswell Papers, Vol. i.), fol. 196.

vnseasonablenes of two or three moneths (after my arriuall) for trauayle, and that I was but once at the Hague, in transitů, before the last time, when I trauayled thither purposely to present my selfe and seruice to your Ho:[nour], will make a full apollogy for my seeming neglect in that particular. The particulars, wherein I haue changed, are no other then the same, for which many worthy ministers, and lights eminent for godlines & learning haue suffered the loss of theyre ministry and liberty; some whereof are now in perfect peace, and rest, others are dispersed in seuerall countreyes, and some yet liue in England as priuate persons, who were and are loyall and faythfull subiects to theyre soueraigne, and haue witnessed against hæresyes, and schysme and against all sectaryes, as Familists, Anabaptists & Brownists, against all which I also witnes, in this place, wherevnto I had not come, if I could haue bene secure of a safe and quiett abode in my deare natiue country.

If that way of questioning should pass vpon all men, which your wisdom iudgeth meete in this case...I thinck, they that iudge me will be found, in some particulars, to haue spoken against the gouernment of England. All that I spake was concerning the gesture of sitting, vsed in this countrey, in receiuing the Sacrament of yᵉ Lords Supper, which I approued, and præferred before Kneeling, grounding what I sayd vpon Luke 22. 27 to 31,...nor did I euer heare that any man tooke offence thereat, but this informer who was discontented the weeke before at a sermon wherein some Arminian errours were touched vpon by me, which quickened him to watch for some aduantage, wherevpon he might ground an accusation.

Whereas it pleased you to question vpon oath whether I haue not bene Cause, or Conscious of any English bookes, or treaties printed or published in these parts since my Coming ouer, or now in press, wherein the present orders and gouernment of Engl: in church affayres are traduced and vndermined? my answer (but without oath till I shall be lawfully called there-vnto) is negatiue. Dᵣ Ames his last booke & intitled a fresh suit against Ceremonies is the onely booke, that I know of, which hath bene published since my coming into these parts, that booke with y⁰ præface was printed before I came from England, yea before the authors death, who was buried before my arrivall here, nor haue I dispersed any of them in England, or in these countryes. my profession of to [*sic*] being still his Maiesties Loyall & faythfull subiect is in simplicity and trueth, neyther shall they disproue it, who traduce me, and if they proceed according to those beginnings, I shall be constrained to declare myne innocencie in an Apollogy printed to the vew [view] of the world, and therein to communicate the grounds, where-vpon my iudgment and practise was altered, and the reason of my departure thence hither; with such obseruations as I haue made in both places. But it is not my purpose so to doe, vnles the continuance of iniurious aspersions make it necessary, in which case the law of God and of nature bindeth men to such a Vindicacion of theyre innocency as the Case requireth. oh that the good hand of God would bring it to pass that those vgly vizzards of disloyalty and schisme being pulled off, the persons that are besmeared and deformed with these obloquies might be represented to his Maiestie in theyre owne shape and colours, viz. in the tendernes of theyre conscience, in the peaceablenes of theyre disposition, & in the simplicity of theyre intentions for the good of church and Commonns. vnder his Royall Gouernment for the continuance of whole life [*sic*], and raigne in peace and prosperity I doe and shall (as I am bound) daily prostrate my selfe with my poore prayers before the throne of grace......

[A Letter of Stephen Goffe's to Sir William Boswell concerning the difficulties between John Davenport and John Paget, of the year 1634/3.][1]

Sir:

The newes of Amsterdam that is the difference concerning Baptisme wᶜʰ is betwixt mʳ Pagett & mʳ Damport & the difficultie of his proceeding there Stephen ofwood who hath beene with you hath better related than I can, that heard it only at large at Delph [?], whether mʳ Damport him selfe was

---

[1] Add. MS. 6394 (Boswell Papers, Vol. i.), fol. 179 recto.

comming to consult with m^r Forbs. The Crowne of Chri*stian* martyrdome [?] could not be found because m^r Voot [?] was not in towne. Mr Widdowes [?] was there newly returned fro*m* Leyden, where he desired me if I would do him no good to do him no harme, it seemes (not that he feares obstacles (as he saith) but for expedition) he hath some good book a printing wch I must inquire after. It is no vnvsuall thing to suspend men fro*m* the sacrament. for as I was served here so was one m^r Brooks a gentleman of very good worth & more than ordinary desert & goodne*s* putt by at Rotterdam. m^r Petter*s* to avoyd the blame of it made great love vnto him, but so ordered it that his Elders refused him without alledging any reason at all that I can heare. This business is of that consequence that many honest gentlemen of my Lo*rds* company at Delph take it very ill. for that they went of purpose some of them—(one Captaine Robberts by name) to Rotterdam having not opportunity at Delph; to have reccavcd but hearing this of m^r Brooks desisted in their suite. & complaine of the difficulty of the way to Heaven here more then in England or the Gospell. I came so late. home last weeke, that I have nothing to say fro*m* Leyden......
Leyden $\frac{22}{13}$./[?][163$\frac{4}{5}$]

Your most humble thankfull

Servant

Stephen Goffe.

[A letter of Griffin Higgs' to Sir William Boswell, dated "April .9. S.[tilo] Vet. i634....at the Hage."][1]

......M^r. Damport [Davenport] is still a Non-Conformist to the Dutch Church as well, as to the English; in many points: [?] one is the not-baptizing of Infants, vnles he approve the [?] parents faith, and life: wherevpon the Dutch ministers have silenced him, and (without Conformitie to their orders before the first of may) they doe peremptorily reject him...it is manifest, that the Dutch ministers doe mislike our Non-Conformists, and would more Easilie entertaine Conformable men of Learning, and good life, and moderation. For they doe

---

[1] Add. MS. 6394 (Boswell Papers, Vol. i.), fol. 200–1.

now professe at Amsterdam, that they will not continue the
stipend to any English minister, who comes against the King
of Englands pleasure......

[A letter of John Paget's to Sir William Boswell, dated
"Amsterdam, March 13 1636 Stilo nov."][1]

Honourable S[r],

According to *your* desire I have sent vnto you this book
of the forme of of [*sic*] com*m*on prayers & administration of
sacram*entes* printed at Midlebu*rg* this being the fourth edition.
Some parts of it are translated out of the Dutch formulier; in
some things it varies, Though I never accurately compared
them together, yet I think vpon the view of some places, it
had bene better if there had bene lesse variation.   I can well
misse it for twise so long a time as you mention; yet seing I
have no more but this copy, neither know where they are to be
got, I would willingly at *your* leasure receave it againe, when
you have done with it.   The God of heaven be wi*t*h *you* &
cover *you* wi*t*h the shadow of his winges:......

Amsterda*m*, March 13   Y*our* Honours to be Com*m*anded
1636 Stilo nov.

......   I*o*hn Paget:

A true Relation of the first Erection
of an English Church in Vtrecht,
with the proceedings synce. / .[2]

Before the yeare i622 there was noe settled Congregation, but
only Regiment Preachers whoe duringe the tyme that the
soldiers were in Garrison preached vnto them, but they goeinge
into the feild the English Cittizens and inhabitants were
destitute of preachinge and other diuine administrations. / .
Vpon which occasion some of the most eminent of the Cittizens

---

[1] Add. MS. 6394 (Bosvell Papers, Vol. I.), fol. 228 recto.
[2] Add. MS. 6394 (Boswell Papers, Vol. I.), fol. 270–75.   This account
appears to have been written about 1637 or a little later.

of the English nation, propounded among them, to erect a
settled Congregation, because they were of a good number,
w*h*ich they could not doe without permission of the Lords
the staites of the Province, and Magistraites of the Citty of
Vtrecht, the Chiefe difficultie beinge then for to finde meanes
for the maintenance of the Minister. / .

Wherevpon they made a Muster of the families, & inhabitants,
and found them to be aboute i20 in number, whoe framed a
petition, which they all signed with their owne hands, and sent
one Ralph Wase, and Ephraim Buttler into the Haghe [Hague]
vnto S*ir* Dudley Carelton [*sic*], then Lord Ambassadour of his
Ma*je*stie of great Britaine, entreatinge his letters of recommend*ations* [?] to the Lords to the staites of this Province that
they would be pleased to grant them some Meanes for the
Minister, and permitt them to erect a Congregation &c, which
the said Lord Ambassador vpon their request did, w*h*ich petiti*on*
of the Cittizens, and Letter of the Lord Ambassador are yet to
be seene in the staites Chamber dated 20th [?] Aprill 1622. / .

The said Cittizens of the English Nation in Vtrecht petitioned
the staites of the Province and Magistraites of the Citty of
Vtrecht, for a grant of a Church to meet in, and for a stipend
towards the Maintenance of their Minister. / .

The states consented and allowed i50 gulders [?] yeerly towards
the Preachers maintenance and the Citty allowed as much, and
the Church of st[.] Katherine was designed them for their
meetinge in, [?] com*m*on with the soldiers of the Brittish
Nation w*h*ich was done the 8th of May i622 as we finde it
recorded by M*r* Thomas Scott his owne hand, the first Minister
of this settled Congregati*on*: / .

The said Thomas Scott hath likewise recorded that then the
Captaines ioyned with the Cittizens, and desirous to haue an
English Preacher sent expresse messengers to m*r* Thomas Scott
then Preacher of the English Garrison at Gorchum, to call him
to this place, and they promised (to witt the Cittizens) to make
a certaine stipend of 600 guldens by the yeare, and to allow
him a house, And that besides he should haue the benefitt of
the Garrison, w*ch* was 2g by the short month of euery syngle
Companie and rateably of the rest. / .

The Consent of the states of this Province dated the 14 May, and of the Citty dated the 13th May 1622 is with a proviso, that they (to witt the Congregation) shall not goe to the callinge of a minister then with dew Correspondence, and xamination [?] of the Minister, & wch purpose they of the Citty gaue Commission vnto the Schepon [Schepen] Wttenwell [?], and vander Lynghen of the Citty Counsell.

The aforenamed mr Scott beinge called he was inducted by mr John Forbes Preacher to the Marchants adventurers at delft, whoe then preached, mr Barkeley preacher at Rotterdam, mr Andrew Hunter preacher to the Scottish Regiment and mr Gualter Whitestone preacher to the Regiment of Viscount Liste./. Also their were present the Committyes of the States and Magistrates, besides diuers english Officers of the Garrison then at Vtrecht with all dew solemnitie on the 20th May 1622./

The Cittizens of the English and Scottish Nation resident at Vtrecht made amongst them a muster of them that were able for to furnish the 300g, wch they had promised, to make the 600g, and euery one of the Contributors names, and their promised Contribution set downe in a list, and performed it accordingly as diuers of them that are yet aliue and then were Contributors can testifie./.

This Contribution continued but one Yeare, and because there were many to whom this Contribution fell heauy the Congregation resolued againe to entreate the aforenamed Lord Embassador to writte in their behalfe for increase of meanes, wch he did accordingly and vsed divers reasons, that they were Cittizens, & ought not to be treated otherwise then the other Cittizens, and alsoe as the French Nation, and other more reasons, as by the said letter in the states Chamber of this Province is yet to be seene./.

Hauinge obtained this letter, mr Thomas Scott writes with his owne hand in the records of the Church, that the 12th of June in place of change of Church officers the Elders were continued, because the Ministers stipend beinge not yet fully settled it was thought fitt to employ them still in the businesse whoe were best acquainted with it. And alsoe because the Church beinge Newly gathered the Deacons were best acquainted with such members as had need of assistance, and wth the estate of thosse who should assist and Contribute. Then they put vp a request vnto the states and another to the Magistrates of the Citty for increase of meanes towards the Maintenance of the Minister, that soe the Cittizens of the English Nation might be eased. The states granted an increase of 100g yearly and the Magistrates the like some*m*e, so that the Minister fro*m* the states and Magistrates received yearly 500g, and fro*m* the Cittizens 100g and this was paid quarterly by equall portions. /.

In June 1625 the Preacher Elders and Deacons of the English Congregation petitioned to the states and Magistrates of the Citty that because the Church of st Katherine was somewhat toe farr out of the way that they might haue againe the vse of st Peters Church; And procured to that end the Letters of recom*m*endation of Henry Earle of Oxford, and Generall Cicill, wch was granted vnto them, and tooke now possession therof 24th July 1625. /.

The 8th of June 1626 m^r Thomas Scott was killed goeinge to the Church by one John Lambert soldier of Viscount Wimbletons Comp*anie*. /.

The Consistorie of the English Congregation fearinge that their church might fall to the ground beinge but newly raised, writ the 19th of June Letters in the name of the Congregation to one m^r Jeremie Elbrough then at Montford, Lamentinge their heavy Losse, entreated his presence to accompanie the dead corps, and to conferre with him further in acceptinge the place of m^r Scott.

The said m^r Elbrough came, yet could not accept the call vntill he was freed fro*m* Colonel Levistone to whose regiment he was lately taken to be minister, wch leaue he shortly after obtained. /.

The 20th June the Synod of the English and Scotch Nation was kept at Vtrecht, and the Elders put vp a petition to the said Synod that the said Elbrough might be admitted for their Pastor wch was granted, wherevpon the Synod with the Elders put vp requests to the Lords the states and Magistrates of the Citty that they would be pleased to afford m^r Elbrough the same allowance to be continewed to him as was before granted to m^r Scott; wch requests were granted, and the same Meanes continued. /.

Then the Elders and Deacons acquainted their Pastor m^r Elbrough how many of the Cittizens were not able to pay the som*m*e that was formerly agreed on generally to make vp to make vp [*sic*] the yeerly 200g vid:t 100g to the Preacher, the other to the Reader: Wherevpon m^r Elbrough discharged them of his stipend, and left it free to some of abilitie to giue, wch were before bound by couenant to pay. /.

Mr Jeremy Elbrough hauinge received Letters testimoniall out of England as he was inioyned by the Synod, was confirmed in his pastorall charge of the English Church at Vtrecht, by m^r John Forbes Preacher to the English marchants at Delft, on Thursday the iith Janu*ary* 1627: there were present m^r Samuell Batchelor Preacher to the Regiment of Sr Charles Morgan Knight and Colonel; m^r Flaman [?] one of the Dutch Preachers of the Citty; alsoe John Innis [?] Wenwall [?] one of the Magistrates of the Citty, with the Captaines English of the Garrison, and the Burgers of the Citty. /.

The 29th August 1627 vpon the request of the Minister, Elders and Deacons of the Church, the states and Magistrates of the Citty allowed eich an augmentation of 50g by the yeare: soe that now the states and Magistrates eich of them haue giuen and doe giue still 300g. yearly. /.

Note that all this While the English Church at Vtrecht was gouerned by it selfe, and many disputes and questions thereofe arisinge troubled as well the states as Magistrates and the Classis, they tooke notice therof, and resolued to make them a member of the Classis, yet did they continue by themselues as long as m^r Elbrough was here. /.

In the yeare 1629 m^r Elbrough was called to be Minister at Hambrough to the English Marchants theere, and in his place succeeded Doctor Alexander Leighton a scotchman and at his beinge taken on there was observed the Order of the Classis; as alsoe he tooke session with them and the English was admitted as a Member of the Classis. /.

..................................¹

---

[1] I have given here only about half of the contents of this manuscript.

[A Letter of Robert Crane's to his Cousin, Sir Robert Crane, Knight and Baronet at Chilton, Suffolk, dated "Vtrecht ye 16[..?] 1640", concerning the English Church at Arnheim.][1]

S^r

Since I came into these Countryes I haue bin in a perpetuall Motion, still rooleinge from Citye to Citye, so as yet I could not gather any thinge worth your notice, nor truly is there almost any discourse but of the lamented state of England. I meete here with many sects, but few Religions, and see more super-stion [superstition] in theire houses then in theire Temples, 'tis vsuall to prophane the Churches without contradiction, whilst the very ground of their Chambers is held as holy; either wee must walke bare-foote, or else noe admission into theire Paradise, and if accidentally wee enter into a Garden, we find euery Tree bareth forbidden fruite; In Gelderland at the Citie of Arnham [?] [Arnheim] I receiued greate fauors from diuers worthy gentlemen of our Nation who haue theire seated themselfs, especially from these Sr William Constable, Sr Mathew Boynton, Sr Richard Saltingston of Yorkshire, as also from Mr Laurence who within few yeares liued neere Berrye [Bury St Edmunds?], They haue two Preachers, and this the dis-cipline of theire Church; Vpon euery Sonday a Communion, a prayer before sermon & after, the like in the afternoone [?], The Communion Table stands in the lower end of the Church (which hath no Chancell) Altar-wise, where the Cheifest sit & take notes, not a gentlewoman that thinkes her hand to faire to vse her pen & Inke, The Sermon, Prayer and psalme being ended, the greatest companie present theire offeringes, which amounte to aboute two or 3 hundred pounds a yeare Sterlinge. the Ministers content themselfs with a hundred pounds a man p*er* Annum the Remainder is reserued for pious vses;......

Vtrecht ye 16
[..?] 1640

Your most humble & most obe-dient Cosen & Seruant
Robert Crane

[1] Tanner MS. 65 (fol. 24), in the Bodleian Library, Oxford.

XVIII

SELECTED DOCUMENTS FROM THE GOULD MANUSCRIPT[1]
ILLUSTRATIVE OF THE HISTORY OF SEPARATIST AND
INDEPENDENT CONGREGATIONS IN ENGLAND BEFORE
1642

A REPOSITORY of Divers Historical Matters relating to
the English Antipedobaptists. Collected from Original Papers
or Faithfull Extracts. [By Benjamin Stinton.]

ANNO 1712.

I began to make this Collection in Ian: 1710--11.

Page I.

Numb: 1.

[So-called Jessey Records or Memoranda.]

The Records of An Antient Congregation of Dissenters
from wch many of ye Independant & Baptist Churches in
London took their first rise: ex MSS of M^r. H. Iessey, w^ch
I rec^d. of M^r. Richard Adams.

Of M^r. Iacob the Cheif beginner of this Church his Works
& proceeds about this Way.

Henry Iacob a Preacher, an eminent man for Learning, haveing
wth others, often & many ways, sought for Reformation, &
shewed the Necessity thereof in regard of the Church of
England's so farr remoteness from ye Apostolical Churches in

---

[1] At Regent's Park College, London. I do not italicize letters which
were manifestly first underlined by the Rev. George Gould of Norwich.

his 4 Assertion dedicated to King Iames, & he made an offer 1604.
of Disputation therein

A Humble Supplication to his Majesty (viz) King Iames for 1609.
permission to enjoy ye Government of Christ in lieu of humane
Institutions, & abolishing that of the Antichristian Prelacy, as
more opposite to Monarchy & to his Royal Prerogative : And
haveing set forth

An Attestation of ye most famious & approved Authors 1610.
witnessing wth one Mouth y^t each Church of Christ should be
so independent as it should have ye full Power of all ye Church
affairs entire within it selfe : And Published

The Divine Beginning & Institution of a Visible Church, 1612.
proveing ye Same by many Arguments, opening Matth: xviii. 15
wth a declaration & fuller evidence of Some things therein :
And haveing published

An Exposition of ye Second Cõmandement, shewing that 1610.
therein now is required a right vissible Church State & Govern- 1610
ment independent

He hav ing had much conference about these things here ;
after y^t in ye low Countries he had converse & discoursed much
wth Mr Jn.º Robinson late Pastor to ye Church in Leyden & wth
others about them : & returning to England In London he held
many several meetings wth the most famious Men for Godliness
and Learning (viz) Mr Throgmorton, Mr Travers, Mr Wing[1],
Mr Rich Mansell, M^r Jn.º Dodd [(]to whom Dr Bladwell was
brought y^t by his opposition ye Truth might ye More appeare)
these wth others haveing seriously weighed all things & Circumstances Mr Jacob & Some others sought ye Lord about
them in fasting & Prayer togeather : at last it was concluded
by ye Most of them, that it ware a very warrantable & com-
mendable way to set upon that Course here as well as in
Holland or elsewhere, whatsoever Troubles should ensue.
H. Jacob was willing to adventure himselfe for this Kingdom
of Christs sake, ye rest encouraged him.

---

[1] I think this may have been John Wing, who in 1632 was " Pastor to
the English Congregation at Vlishing in Zeeland", and who published
in that year a book entitled, " The Crowne Conjugall, or the Spouse
Royal,...", 8º.

The Church Anno 1616 was gathered

Hereupon ye said Henry Jacob wth Sabine Staismore [Staresmore], Rich Browne, David Prior, Andrew Almey, Wm Throughton, Jn° Allen, Mr Gibs, Edwd Farre, Hen Goodall, & divers others well informed Saints haveing appointed a Day to Seek ye Face of ye Lord in fasting & Prayer, wherein that perticular of their Union togeather as a Church was mainly comended to ye Lord: in ye ending of ye Day they ware United, Thus, Those who minded this present Union & so joyning togeather joyned both hands each wth other Brother and stood in a Ringwise: their intent being declared, H. Jacob and each of the Rest made some confession or Profession of their Faith & Repentance, some ware longer some ware briefer, Then they Covenanted togeather to walk in all Gods Ways as he had revealed or should make known to them

Thus was the begining of that Church of which proceed, they within a few Days gave notice to the Brethen here of the Antient Church.

After this Hen Jacob was Chosen & Ordained Pastor to that Church, & many Saints ware joyned to them.

The same Year ye Said Hen Jacob wth ye advice & consent 1616 of the Church, & of some of those Reverend Preachers beforesaid published to ye World

A Confession & Protestation in the Name of certain Christians, therein showing wherein they consent in Doctrine wth ye Church of England, & wherein they ware bound to dissent, with their evidences from ye Holy Scriptures for their dissent in about 28 perticulars viz

1. Christs offices.
2. Scriptures all Suffic.
3. Churches Distinction.
4. Visibile Church.
5. Synods & Counsels.
6. Cathol. Church Politick.
7. Provinciall Church.
8. Parish Chu. Bondage.
9. L. Arch: Bp^s. L. Bp^s.

10. Makeing Ministers.
11. what Comũnion wth them.
12. Pluralists. No[n]residents
13. Discipline Censures
14. Pastors Number & Power
15. Mixt Multitude.
16. Humane Traditions.
17. Traditions Apostolick.
18. Of Prophecy.
19. Reading Homilies.
20. Christs descent to Hell.
21. Of Prayer.
22. Holy Days so called.
23. Marriage, Burying, Churching, &c.
24. Ministers being Magistrates.
25. Lords Days Offerings.
26. Tiths Church Dues
27. Magistrates Power
28. Necessity on us to obey Christ rather than Man herein.[1]

With a Petition to ye King in ye Conclusion for Tolleration to such Christians.

At ye Same time also he published a Collection of Sundery Reasons. 20 & 4 Conclusions proveing how necessary it is for all Christians to Walk in all ye Ways & Ordinances of God in purity, in a right Church way. part of them were made by Mr Wring [? Wing] the Preacher.

About eight Years H. Jacob was Pastor of ye Said Church & when upon his importunity to go to Virginia, to wch he had been engaged before by their consent, he was remitted from his said office, & dismissed ye Congregation to go thither, wherein after [blank space] Years he ended his Dayes. In the time of his Service much trouble attended that State & People, within & without.

1624

After his Departure hence ye Congregation remained a Year

[1] In the Gould Manuscript these twenty-eight "particulars" are arranged in two columns of fourteen each.

or two edifying one another in yᵉ best manner they could according to their Gifts received from above, And then at length Iohn Lathorp sometimes a Preacher in Kent, joyned to yᵉ Said Congregation; And was afterwards chosen and Ordained a Pastor to them, a Man of tender heart and a humble and meek Spirit serveing the Lord in the ministry about 9 Years to their great Comfort.

1632. the 2ᵈ Month (called Aprill) yᵉ 29ᵗʰ Day being yᵉ Lords Day, the Church was seized upon by Tomlinson, yᵉ Bps Pursevant, they ware mett in yᵉ House of Hump: Bornet [Barnet], Brewers Clark in Black: Fryers, he being no member or hearing abroad, At wᵒʰ time 18 were not coṁitted but scaped or ware not then present. 1632

About 42 ware all taken & their names given vp. Some ware not coṁitted, as Mʳˢ Bernet, Mʳ Lathorp, W. Parker, Mʳˢ Allen &c Several ware coṁitted to the Bps Prison called then the New Prison in [blank space] Crow a merchants house again) & thence Some to yᵉ Clink, some to yᵉ Gat house, & some that thought to have escaped he joyned to them, being in Prison togeather viz

John Lathorp	Widd Ferne
Sam House	Broʳ Arnold
John Woddin	Marke Lucar
Mʳ Granger	Mʳ Jones
Mʳ Barbone	[blank space]
Mr. Sargent	Sam Hon [How ?]
Sister House	Mʳ Wilson
John Milburn	Mʳ Crafton [Grafton]
Henry Parker	H. Dod, deceased, a Prisoner
Mʳ Jacob	Mʳ Lemar.[1]

1632   Elizab. Milburn, about 26 coṁited yᵉ 12ᵗʰ of yᵉ 2ⁿᵈ Month (called May 12ᵗʰ) being yᵒ Lords Day. Just a fortnight after was yᵉ Antient Church so seized upon & two of them coṁitted to be fellow Prisoners with these. The Lord thus tryed &

---

[1] In the Gould Manuscript these names are written in four columns, and the word "Prisoner" in the entry relating to "H. Dod" is there placed in the margin.

experienced them & their Friends & foes ye Space of some two Years, some only under Baill, some in Hold: in wch time ye Lord Wonderfully magnified his Name & refreshed their Spirits abundantly, for

1. In that time ye Lord opened their mouths so to speak at ye High Comission & Pauls & in private even ye weake Women as their Subtill & malicious Adversarys ware not able to resist but ware asshamed.

2. In this Space ye Lord gave them So great faviour in ye Eyes of their Keepers y^t they suffered any friends to come to them and they edifyed & comforted one another on ye Lords Days breaking bread &c.

3. By their Holy & Gratious carriage in their Sufferings, he so convinced others y^t they obtained much more faviour in the Eyes of all Such generally as feared God then formerly, so that many ware very kind & helpfull to them, contributing to their Necessities, some weekly sending Meat &c, to them.

4. Their Keepers found [them] so sure in their promises that they had freedom to go home, or about their Trades, or buisness whensoever they desired, & set their time, & say they would then returne it was enough without the charges of one to attend them.

5. In this very time of their restraint ye Word was so farr from bound, & ye Saints so farr from being scared from the Ways of God that even then many ware in Prison added to ye Church, viz

Jo. Ravenscroft	Willm ⎰
Widd Harvey	Thos ⎱ Harris
Mary Atkin	Jane
Thos Wilson	Widd. White.
Sarah.........	Ailce ⎱
Hump: Bernard [Barnet or	Eliz ⎰ Wincop.[1]
Bernet]	Rebec
G. Wiffield	

6. Not one of those that ware taken did recant or turne back from the truth, through fear or through flatterry or cunning Slights but all ware ye more strenghtened [*sic*] thereby.

[1] In the Gould MS. these names are arranged in four columns.

7.   When in y⁰ time of their Sufferings, Mʳ [John] Davenport had so preached that some brought the Notes of his Sermon to these, as if it ware to condem their practice, & would have them answer them if they could: they sent a letter to him desireing he would Send them his own Notes to avoid Mistakes hoping that either he might inform them or they him in some things discover to him wᵗʰ[wᵗ] was made known to them, He loveingly performed it, they having perused his Notes, wrote back to him a large answer; after his receipt thereof he never did coῆunicate with them any more, but went away when y⁰ Sacrament day came, and afterward preached, publickly & privately for y⁰ truth, & soon afterward went to Holland, where he sufferd somewhat for y⁰ truths sake, & then went to New England where he now preacheth the same Truth that these do here, 'though there without such Persecution.

8.   The Answers of Mͬꜱ Jones & Some others in yᵗ time of their Sufferings are not Yet Extent for y⁰ Comfort and Encouragement of others against taking that Oath ex officio against false Accusers. Their Petitions to his Maj.ᵗʸ

Sarah Jones her Grievances given in & read openly at y⁰ Coῆission Court.

Her Cronicle of Gods remarkable Judgments & dealings that Year &c   wonderfull are the Lords works its meet he should have all y⁰ Praise.

After y⁰ Space of about 2 Years of the Sufferings & Patience of these Saints they ware all released upon Bail (some remaining so to this day as Mʳ Jones &c, though never called on) only to Mʳ Lathorp & Mʳ Grafton they refused to shew such faviour, they ware to remain in Prison without release.

At last there being no hopes yᵗ Mʳ Lathorp should do them further Service in y⁰ Church, he having many motives to go to new England if it might be granted After the Death of his Wife he earnestly desiring y⁰ Church would release him of yᵗ office wᶜʰ (to his grief) he could no way performe, & that he might have their consent to goe to new England, after serious consideration had about it it was freely granted to him Then Petition being made that he might have Liberty to **1634** depart out of y⁰ Land he was released from Prison 1634, about y⁸ 4ᵗʰ Month called Iune, & about 30 of the members, who desired leave & permission from y⁸ Congregation to go along with him, had it granted to them, namely, Mʳ Io: Lathorp, Sam. House, Iohn Wodwin, Goodwife Woodwin, Elder & Younger, Widd: Norton, & afterwards Rob.ᵗ Linel & his Wife, Mʳ & Mˢ Laberton, Mˢ Haṁond, Mˢ Swinerton

1620   joyned those wᵗʰ Mʳ Iacob, these inhabiting in Coulchester (though an old Church of y⁸ Separation was there) viz Ioshua Warren, Henry Ianuary, St Puckle a.............. Manasses Kenton, Lemuel Tuke &c who afterwards by Concent became a Church. Tuke left them & is a Preacher at Dry.

1630   Mˢ Dupper had been of this Congregation he wᵗʰ Tho: 1630 Dyer yᵗ was one of them & Daniel Chidley y⁸ Elder.............. ....these joyned togeather to be a Church, Mʳ Boy joyned himself to them & Mʳ Stanmore [Staismore?] Benj: Wilkins, Hugh Vesse, Iohn Flower, Bro: Morton, & his Wife, Iohn Ierrow.

1633.   There haveing been much discussing these denying Truth 1633 of y⁸ Parish Churches, & y⁸ Church being now become so large yᵗ it might be prejudicial, these following desired dismission that they might become an Entire Church, & further y⁸ Coṁunion of those Churches in Order amongst themselves, wᶜʰ at last was granted to them & performed Sepᵗ 12. 1633 viz

Henry Parker & Wife

Widd: Fearne	Marke Luker	......Hatmaker
Mˢ Wilson	Mary Milburn	Thoˢ Allen.
	Io: Milburn	
	Arnold	

To These Ioyned Rich: Blunt, Tho: Hubert, Rich: Tredwell & his Wife Kath:, Iohn Trimber, Wᵐ Iennings & Sam Eaton Mary 1633 Greenway——Mʳ Eaton with Some others receiving a further Baptism.

    Others joyned to them,

1638. These also being of y⁸ same Iudgment wᵗʰ Sam. Eaton & desireing to depart & not to be censured our interest in them was remitted wᵗʰ Prayer made in their behalfe Iune 8ᵗʰ 1638. They haveing first forsaken Us & Ioyned wᵗʰ Mʳ Spilsbury, viz.

Mr Peti. Fener	Wm Batty
Hen. Pen	Mrs Allen (died 1639)
Tho. Wilson	Mrs Norwood

Other Persecutions besides the Persecutions befores[d]

The Good Lord Iesus gave, (Satan still envying ye Prosperity of Zion, stirred up against this Church) several Tryalls afterwards wherein still ye Lord gave occation of Triumphing in him; It's good to record & bring to remembrance our Straights & ye Lords Enlargements, Experience works Hope & Hope maketh not asshamed because ye Love of God is shed abroad in our hearts.   to instance in

Iohn Trash was taken by Rag at Mr Digbeys & not Yelding **1636** to Rags general warrant was had to ye L. Mayor........& was comitted to ye Poultrey Counter for ten days & then was released upon Bail, wanted his health & was shortly after translated.

11th Month (vulgarly Ianuary) ye 21 day at Queenhith (where Mr Glover, Mr Eaton, Mr Eldred & others ware wth us) **1637** after Exercise was done, by means M^r........the overthwart Neighbour, Officers & others came, at last both ye Sheriffs, & then Veasy ye Pursevant who took ye names; The Lord gave such Wisdom, in their Carriage y^t some of their opposers afterwards did much favour them & bail'd them. The next Day Veasy the Pursevant got Money of some of them, & so they ware dismissed, 4 ware comitted to ye Poultrey Counter viz

R. Smith Mrs Iacob S. Dry

3 Month 8th Day At M^{rs} DeLamars Veasy wth others came **1638** upon them in Barnaby Street by Male all taken 4 bound to answer at High Comission. viz Br. Russell & Cradock

11th Month at Lambeth Mrs Lovel & Mrs Chitwood by Doctor **1639** Featly were sent to Kings Bench & by Doct^r Lauds direction bound to ye Assizes

2 Month Vulgo Aprill 21. At Tower Hill at Mrs Wilsons **1640** where some ware seeking ye Lord wth fasting for ye Parliament (like to be dissolved unless they would grant Subsidies for

Warrs against ye Scotish) by Procurement of Male ye Arch Prelates Pursevant, S^r W^m. Balford Leivetenant of ye Tower sent theither H Jesse (who he found praying for ye King as he told his Mag^ty) Mrs Iones, Mr Brown wth others about 20.

Then S^r W^m asked his Magesties Pleasure concerning them who would have them Released but Dr Laud ye Arch Bishop being Presant desired the men might be bound to ye Sessions wch was perform & no Enditement being there against them at their appearance they ware freed.

Also 6 Month 21. at our Brother Goldings by ye Constables 1641 means, Alderman Somes came who took ye Names of Mrs Puckle & Iohn Stoneard, ye Constables carried them with Mr Golding, Mr Shambrook & some others to ye Mayor who bound them to ye Sessions, from whence their Accusers being called then to take ye Protestation wth their Parishoners none appearing against them they ware freed.

Also 6 Month 22^d day at the L Nowels house ye same 1641 L Mayor Sr Iohn Wright came Violently on them, beat, thrust, pinched & kicked such men or Women as fled not his handling, among others Mrs Berry who miscarryed & dyed the same week & her Child.   He comitted to ye Counter H. Iessey, Mr Nowel, Mr Ghofton [Grafton], & that night bound them to answer at ye House of Comons where they appearing he let it fall.

Covenant Renewed.

Whilst Mr Lathorp was an Elder here some being greived 1630 against one that had his Child then Baptized in ye Common Assemblies, & desireing & urging a Renouncing of them, as Comunion wth them, Mr Can also then walking   Saints where he left Mr How (he going wth Some to Holland) He desiring that ye Church wth Mr Lathorp would renew their Covenant in Such a Way, & then he with Others would have Comunion wth them: Mr Dupper would have them therein to Detest & Protest against ye Parish Churches, Some ware Unwilling in their Covenanting either to be tyed either to protest against ye truth of them, or to affirm it of them, not knowing w^t in time to come God might further manifest to them thereabout Yet for peace Sake all Yelded to renew their Covenant in these Words

To Walke togeather in all ye Ways of God So farr as he hath made known to Us, or shall make known to us, & to forsake all false Ways, & to this the several Members Sub-scribed their hands

After this followed several Sheets containing ye Names of ye Members of ye said Congregation & ye time of their admission[1]

Numb: 2

[So-called Kiffin Manuscript.]

An Old MSS, giveing some Acco^tt of those Baptists who first formed themselves into distinct Congregations, or Churches in London. found among certain Paper given me by Mr Adams.

1633. Sundry of ye Church whereof Mr Iacob & Mr Iohn Lathorp had been Pastors, being dissatisfyed wth ye Churches owning of 1633 English Parishes to be true Churches, desired dismission & Ioyned togeather among themselves, as Mr Henry Parker, Mr Tho. Shepard Mr Sam^ll Eaton, Marke Luker, & others wth whom Ioyned Mr Wm Kiffen.

1638. Mr Tho: Wilson, Mr Pen, & H. Pen, & 3 more being 1638 convinced that Baptism was not for Infants, but professed 1638 Beleivers joyned wth M^r Io: Spilsbury ye Churches favour being desired therein

1640 3^d Mo: The Church became two by mutuall consent just 1640 half being wth Mr P. Barebone, & ye other halfe with Mr H. Iessey Mr Richard Blunt wth him being convinced of Baptism y^t also it ought to be by diping ye Body into ye Water, resembling Burial & riseing again. 2 Col: 2. 12. Rom: 6. 4. had sober conferance

---

[1] It is a great pity that Stinton did not think it worth while to transcribe this extended list of the members of the church.

about in ye Church, & then wth some of the forenamed who also ware so convinced: And after Prayer & conferance about their so enjoying it, none haveing then so so [*sic*] practised in England[1] to professed Believers, & hearing that some in ye Nether Lands had so practised they agreed & sent over Mr Rich. Blunt (who understood Dutch) wth Letters of Com̃endation, who was kindly accepted there, & returned wth Letters from them Io: Batte a Teacher there, & from that Church to such as sent him.

They proceed on therein, viz, Those Persons y^t ware persuaded   1641 Baptism should be by dipping[2] ye Body had mett in two Companies, & did intend so to meet after this, all these agreed to proceed alike togeather.   And then Manifesting (not by any formal Words a Covenant) wch word was scrupled by some of them, but by mutual desires & agreement each Testified.:

Those two Companyes did set apart one to Baptize the rest; So it was solemnly performed by them.

Mr Blunt Baptized Mr Blacklock y^t was a Teacher amongst them, & Mr Blunt being Baptized, he & Mr Blacklock Baptized ye rest of their friends that ware so minded, & many being added to them they increased much

The Names of all 11 Mo. Ianu: begin

Richard Blunt	Sam. Blacklock	Tho Shephard)
Greg. Fishburn	Doro: Fishburn	his Wife)
Iohn Cadwell	Eliz. Cadwell	Mary Millisson
Sam. Eames	Tho. Munden	
Tho. Kilcop	William Willieby	
Robert Locker	Mary Lock[*er* ?]	

---

[1] That is perhaps more accurately in London.

[2] In Vol. I., p. 334, I speak of this mode of baptism by "dipping" as having received about 1641 the nickname of "ducking over head and ears". This expression, however, seems to have been of much earlier origin, for in Stephen Denison's "The Doctrine of both the Sacraments", London, 1621, p. 23, occur the following unexpected words :—"*Be Baptized*, the word translated baptizing doth most properly signifie dipping ouer head and eares,..." He also says, p. 11, that "by report" there were "not a few Anabaptists" about London in 1621, but gives no suggestion that they then practised immersion.

Iohn Braunson	Iohn Bull
Rich. Ellis	Mary Langride
Wᵐ Creak	Mary Haman
Robᵗ Carr	Sarah Williams
Martin Mainprise	Ioane ⎫ Dunckle Ann ⎭
Hen: Woolmare¹	Eliz. Woolmore
Robᵗ King	Sarah Norman
Tho. Waters	Isabel Woolmore
Henry Creak	Iudeth Manning
Mark Lukar	Mabel Lukar
Henry Darker	Abigal Bowden
Eliz Iessop	Mary Creak
	Susanah King

41 in all

* 11ᵗʰ month understood as appears above, & this was Ianuʸ 9ᵗʰ.

11* Ianuary 9 added

Iohn Cattope	George Denham
Nicholas Martin	Tho: Daomunt
Ailie² Stanford	Rich Colgrave
Nath Matthon³	Eliz Hutchinson
Mary Burch	Iohn Croson
	Sybilla Lees
	Iohn Woolmoore

thus **53 in all**

Those that ware so minded had comunion togeather were 1644 become Seven Churches in London.

Mʳ Green wᵗʰ Capᵗ Spencer had begun a Congregation in 1639 Crutched Fryers, to whom Paul Hobson joyned who was now wᵗʰ many of that Church one of yᵉ Seven

These being much spoken against as unsound in Doctrine as if they ware Armenians, & also against Magistrates &c they joyned togeather in a Confession of their Faith in fifty two 1644

Se yᵉ Notes at yᵉ End of yᵉ Confession. Articles wᶜʰ gave great satisfaction to many that had been prejudiced.

---

¹ [? Woolmore].　　　² [? Ailce, i.e., Alice].　　　³ [? Matthew].

Thus Subscribed in yᵉ names of 7 Churches in London :

Wᵐ Kiffin
Tho: Patience
Geo: Tipping
Iohn Spilsbury
Tho: Shepard
Tho: Munden

Tho: Gun
Io: Mabbet
Iohn Web
Tho: Kilcop

Paul Hobson
Tho: Goore
Io: Phelps
Edward Heath

[Part of] Numb: 23. [which is]

An Account of A Church that usually met in Southwark near Sᵗ Mary Overys Church, consisting partly of Pædobaptists, & partly of Antipædobaptists, from their first Constitution in yᵉ Reign of K. Iames I, to their Dissolution in 1705.

taken out of their Church Book, &c.

[Supposed to have been written by old Mʳ (Iohn ?) Webb.]

This Church I find was constituted in Gospell Order about yᵉ Year 1621. The first Pastor thereof was one Mʳ Hubbard, a learned Man of Episcopal Ordination, who having left the Church of England, took his Ministry from this Church, & with them went into Ireland, & there died. They returned again to England, and chose Mʳ Iohn Canne, (famous for filling up a Bible with Marginal Notes to this day much valued) to be their Pastor, who attended that service for some time, and then with some of the Members left the Church, and went to Amsterdam, and there continued with the English Church many years, and tho' he came into England afterwards, yet he returned to Amsterdam, and there died. During which time they continued without a Pastor, and then chose Mʳ Sam: How, who served in the ministration about 17 years and died in peace very much lamented. In his time they were persecuted beyond measure by the Clergy and Bishops Courts, and he dying under the Sentence of Excommunication, They with a Constables guard secured the parish ground at Shoreditch to prevent his being buried there so that he was buried at Anis a Cleer, and several of his Members according to their desire was buried there likewise. He wrote that little Book so often printed, called Hows Sufficiency of the Spirits teachings, and was very famous for his vindication of the Doctrines of Separation, and both he and his People were much harrassed for it by their Enemies, and were forced to meet together in fields and woods to avoid them.

They afterwards chose one Mʳ Stephen More to be their Pastor. He was a Deacon of their Church excellently gifted for the work of the ministry, a man of good reputation and possessed of an Estate. In his time their Case was altered for the better, and they who used to be avoided, and who were hardly reckoned among men, but look'd on as a kind of Wild Creatures, and greatly persecuted, met with some respite of peace. Indeed once on a Lords day when they were met together, they were taken, and by Sʳ Iohn Ludhall [Lenthall] committed to the Clink Prison and some of them had before the house of Lords as aforementioned. But after that I find little interruption given them.

A Brief Account of this Church of Christ, from the be- gining: Togeather wᵗʰ yᵉ Progressions down to this present Year. 1699.

According to yᵉ best Account from Ancient Members therein, & such Notices as in Old Books we find: That about yᵉ Year 1621 was this Church constituted in Gospel Order, & carried on by one Mʳ Hubbert; who in that time of Trouble then all did pass to Ireland, where he for some time continued with them & dyed. He was a Man brought up in Learning, & was formerly an ordained Man of the Church of England, but renounc'd it, & took his Ministry from that Church. This one thing is remarkable of him, That on his Death-bed he said, He thought there was Some Spell in his first Ordination, Seing that tho he knew yᵗ Some of yᵉ Members had as good gifts as himselfe & more Grace Yet could not get over this, but think of himselfe aboue them & thought this did arise from yᵉ Impressions in his mind made at that Ordination. This Church returned into England, & kept close their Coṁunion here about London, where one Mʳ Tho: Hancock, a member of this Church, preaching to them as a Brother for some Months. After wch ye Church called Mr Iohn Can, (who was since famous for filling up a Bible wth Marginal Notes, to this day much Vallued) whom ye Church called & Chose their Pastor, who attended that Service for Some Time, & then wth Some of ye Members left ye Church, & went to Amsterdam, & there continued wth ye English Church many Years; And tho he came into England after yet returned & there dyed. All wch time ye Church planted by Mr Hubbard, wth Such other as Ioyned wth them continued serving the Lord wth Singleness of heart, & in process of time had ye Oportunity of enjoying as a Member Sam: How.

At wch time, they Solemly renewed & confirmed their Antient League & Covenant one wth another, & then did freely Elect, Choose, & Ordain ye Said Sam.[1] How to be their Pastor, who faithfully & painfully served in this Ministration about the Space of Seven Years, till, according to ye will of God, he fell asleep [& died in Peace] in a troublesome Day, being much lamented.

Before I go further take these remarks on this Sam! How who lived about 1634 or 35, wch was a time of great trouble by the Bpp^s Courts in King Charles ye 1st time, in many Vexatious Conditions by Pursevants &c, & Excomunications: & This Servant of Christ dyed under this Punishment, & therefore they would not let him have y^t wch they call Christian Burial, but wth a Constables gaurd secured ye Parish ground at Shoreditch against them, who very quietly was buried at Anis, a Cleer, where several Members desired & when dead was buried by him. This is y^t How so much talked of in latter Years who wrote ye little Book so often printed, called Hows Sufficiency of ye Spirits Teaching &c. And as farr as I can find by them y^t were of ye Church at y^t time (for I know many of them) he was famous for ye Vindication of ye Doctrines of Seperation, & were for it much harrassed up & down in Fields & Woods; but God was wth them, & they cheerfully passed along.

After these things, some considerable time after, finding ye want of a Pastor, & desireing ye Groth of ye Church, & their

Edification, they chose out among themselves, & pitched upon Stephen More, a gifted Brother, & a Deacon to ye Church, & did freely Elect, Choose & Ordain him unto that Office about ye Year 1641.   He was a Cityzen of Good Worth, & possessed of Some Estate, & lived in good Reputation, yet did he willingly comply wth all ye Providences of God in all their Afflictions & Sufferings to Serve our Lord Iesus, & purchased to himselfe a good degree & great boldness in his Work, &c.[1]

....

....

[1] Since this material was prepared for the press, Dr Whitley has published the entire document with some useful annotations ("Transactions of the Baptist Historical Society" for May, 1910).

XIX

THE NAMES, TRADES, AND POOR ESTATE OF ALL THE
SEPARATISTS LIVING IN GREAT YARMOUTH ABOUT
JULY 17, 1630

The names of all such Seperatistes or Brownistes as are resident
within the Towne of great Yarmouth ["Julij. 17. 1630"][1]

1 William Vring now in Norwich Castle and comitted to the
  Goale in Yarmouth by W:m Buttolphe & Henry Da[..]
2 his wife. /
3 Raphaell Bishoppe
4 Andrew Purkis
5 et vxor
6 William Birchall now in Yarmouth Goale. /
7 Thomas Caine in the same Goale. /
8 et vxor

9 Samuell Butler   19 Alice Witherell
10 Edmond Cannon   20 Margarett Neave
11 et vxor   21 Effa Wiseman
12 Marie Ladd widdow   22 Alice Smith
13 Ioane Balles   23 Dyonis Springall
14 Iane Blogg   24 Valentine Porte
15 Iane Bridgwell   25 vxor Boberti Baffam
16 Ellen Tilles   26 vxor Thomæ Parker
17 Anne Trindle   27 Ruth Burton
18 Widdow March   28 Ellen Smith

  Marie Ennis and Adam Goodwins of Castor tw[o]
  miles distant from Yarmouth who sometimes fre-
  qu[ent?] them. /

  [1] S. P., Dom., Charles I., Vol. 171 (9).

A true relation of the estates and Condicons [*sic*] of theise people. /

William Vring a poore Mariner now in prison lives on the baskett. /

Raphaell Bishopp a Shoomaker not worth 5.[*libras*]

- Andrew Purkis sometime a brewer not worth 20.[*libras*]

William Birchall a poore dyer being now in prison liv[es ?] on the baskett. /

Thomas Caine [?] now in prison lives on the basquett. /

Samuell Butler in shew the Ablest of them all a grocer far[r ?] indebted and one that dealeth altogether vpon Creditt his estate vncerten but valued at 100[*libras*] at the most. /

Edmond Cannon a Compasse maker not worth x.[*libras*]

Marie Ladd a poore widdow not able to satisfie her husband[*es* ?] debt*es*

Ioane Balls the wife of Richard Balles Blockmaker a poore man. /

Iane Blogg the wife of Edward Blogg Sailor poore.

Ellen Tilles the wife of Iohn Tilles a poore man

Effa Wiseman the wife of Robert wiseman Tailor

Iane Bridgwell poore, Widdow march poore, Anne Trindle poore, Alice witherell poore, Margarett Neve poore Alice Smith poore Dyones Springell poore, Valentine Port a poore labourer, Ruth Burton, poore;

vxor Roberti Baffam sailor poore; Ellen Smith poore

vxor Thomæ Parker a poore Ioyner. /

XX

REPORTS RELATING TO THE APPEARANCE OF CERTAIN
SEPARATISTS BEFORE THE COURT OF HIGH COM-
MISSION BETWEEN APRIL 19 AND JUNE 21, 1632

[Under the date April 19, 1632.][1]

Keepers of Conventicles would not pay their Fees to be *Fees by Con-*
discharged after their answere, it was said therefore, they have *venticlers.*
not made their answere, & they were committed for not answering,
although they had, but had not paied their Fees.
....

In the Court of high Commission
3 Maij. 1632.

_____

This day were brought to yᵉ Court out of prison divers persons *Conventiclers.*
(and some of them appeared by bond) which were taken on
Sunday last at a Conventicle mett at yᵉ house of [————]
Barnett a brewers Clarke dwellinge in yᵉ precint of Black
Fryars. By ,name Iohn Latroppe their Minister Humphrey
Bernard [Barnett], Henry Dod, Samuell Eaton [————] Granger
Sara Iones, Sara Iacob, Pennina Howse, Sara Barbon, Susan
Wilson : and divers other [*sic*] there were which appeared not
this day.   Mʳ. Latropp yᵉ Minister did not appeare at yᵉ first,
but kept himself out of yᵉ way a while, therefore the man of

[1] From Rawl. MS. A. 128, in the Bodleian Library.   As has been said
in Vol. ɪ., p. 322, note, these reports were published in full by S. R. Gardiner
in his " Reports of Cases in the Courts of Star Chamber and High Commission ", Camden Society, 1886, but the portions required ought also for
convenience to be found here.

the howse wherein they were taken was first called: who was asked when he was at his parish Church? He answered that he was then at his parish Church when they were in his house, and that he vseth to goe to church, but his wife will not, then said the ArchBishop of York, will yo^u suffer that in your wife? Then said the Kinges Advocate these persons were assembled on Sunday last at this mans house in black Fryars & there vnlawfullie held a Conventicle, for which there are Articles exhibited in this Court against them, I pray that they may be put to answere vppon their oathes to the Articles, & that they sett forth what exercises they vsed, & what were the wordes spoken by them. And as for yo^u m^r. Dod (quoth ye Advocate) yo^u might well haue forborne seing yo^u haue been warned heertofore, & passed by vpon promise of amendment: good m^r Advocate, spare that, saith Dod: He was asked whether he vseth to come to his parish Church: He saith he hath come to his parish Church as often as he could & vseth to come thither, but he endeavoureth to heare the most powerfull Ministery. and therefore said ye Bishop of London yo^u heare m^r Latroppe, what ordination hath he? He is a Minister saith m^r Dod. did yo^u not heare him preach & pray? [?] saith ye Bishop. nay yo^u your self & the rest take vpon yo^u to preach & to be Ministers, Noe saith m^r Dod, London, yes, yo^u doe, and yo^u were heard preach & pray. Dod, I shalbe readie in this particuler to confesse my fault, if I am convinced to be in any. Then two of them were put to their oath, but they desired to be excused for this tyme, & that they might have some time to consider & be informed of the oath.

Then said the ArchBishop of Canterbury, yo^u shew your selves most vnthankfull to God, to ye King & to ye Church of England that when ([?] God be praysed) through his Maiesties care & ours yo^u have preaching in every Church, & men haue liberty to ioyne in prayer & participate of ye Sacramentes, & haue Catechizinges & all to enlighten yo^u, & which may serue yo^u in the way of Salvation; yo^u in an vnthankfull manner cast of [sic] all this yoake, & in private vnlawfullie assemble your selues togeather, making rentes & divisions in the Church: If anie thing be amisse, let it be knowen, if any thing be not

agreeable to the word of God, we shalbe as readie to redresse it
as yo[u], but whereas it is nothing but your owne imaginations,
& yo[u] are vnlearned men that seeke to make vp a religion of
your owne heades! I doubt noe perswasion will serue the
turne. We must take this course. yo[u] are called heere. let
them stand vpon their bondes, and let vs see what they will
answere, it may be they will answere what may please vs.
London. It is tyme to take notice of these, nay this is not the
4th parte of them about this Cittie, yo[u] see these came of sett
purpose they mett not by chance; they are desperatlie hereticall:
they are all of different places, one of Essex, S[t] Austins, S[t] Martins
le grand, Buttolphs Algate, Thisleworth, S[t] Saviours: let these
be imprisonned. Let me make a motion, There be Fower of
the ablest men of them, let these 4 answere & be proceeded
against, & the while if the rest come in, they shalbe received,
but if they will not, I know noe reason why 4 or 5 should [not?]
answere for all.

....

[Under the date May 3, 1632.]

Then came in m[r] Latropp, who is asked what authority he   Latroppe.
had to preach, & keepe this Conventicle? and saith the Bishop
of London, how manie woemen sate crosse legged vpon y[e] bedd,
whilest yo[u] sate on one side & preached & prayed most de-
voutlie? Latroppe, I keepe noe such evill companie, they were
not such woemen. London, are yo[u] a Minister? ArchBishop
of Canterbury, are yo[u] a Minister? Bishop of S[t] Davides, were
not yo[u] Doctor King the Bishop of Londons Sizer in Oxford?
I take it yo[u] were; and yo[u] shew your thankfullnes by this.
He answered that he was a Minister, London. how, & by whom,
qualified? where are your Orders? Latropp. I am a Minister
of the gospell of Christ, and y[e] Lord hath qualifyed me. Will
yo[u] lay your hand on the booke, & take your oath, saith y[e]
Court? He refuseth the oath.

....

Samuell Eaton and two women & a maid appeared, who were   Samuell
demaunded why they were assembled in that Conventicle when   Eaton
others were at church? Eaton. we were not assembled in contempt of the Magistrate. London. Noe? it was in contempt

of yᵉ church of England. Eaton. it was in conscience to God
(may it please this honor*a*ble Court) and we were kept from
Church, for we were confyned in yᵉ house together by those
that besett yᵉ house, els divers would haue gone to Church and
manie came in after the sermons were done. London. these
were first discovered at Lambeth & then at other places & now
taken heere, they haue in their meeting*es* bookes printed against
yᵉ Church of England. ArchBishop of Canterbury. Where were
yoᵘ in the morninge before yoᵘ came hither to this house ? We
were in our owne families. Canterbury. what did yoᵘ ? we read
yᵉ Scriptures and catechized our families (saieth Eaton): and
maie it please this this [*sic*] honor*a*ble Court to heare vs speake
the truth, we will shew yoᵘ what was donne, and (free vs of yᵉ
contempt of Authority) wee did nothing but what yoᵘ will allow
vs to doe. London. who can free yoᵘ ? these are dangerous ꞵen,
they are a scattered companie sowen in all the Citty) [*sic*], and
about Sᵗ Michaell of yᵉ Querne, Sᵗ Austins, Ould Iury, Redriffe,
& other remoter places. Hould them yᵉ booke Eaton. I dare
not sweare, nor take this oath, though I will not refuse it, I will
consider of it. S*i*r Henry Martin, Heare, heare, yoᵘ shall sweare
buṭ to answere what yoᵘ know, and so far as yoᵘ are bound by
law : yoᵘ shall haue time to consider of it, and haue it read over
& over till yoᵘ can say it w*i*thout booke if yoᵘ will, when yoᵘ
haue first taken yo*u*r oath that yoᵘ will make a true answere.
Eaton. I dare not, I know not what I shall swe*a*re to. Kinge*s*
Advocate. It is to giue a true answere to articles put into yᵉ
Court against yoᵘ, or that shalbe put in touching this conventicle of yo*u*rs, and divers yo*u*r hereticall tenent*es* and what
wordes, and exercises yoᵘ vsed, and things of this nature.
Eaton I dare not.

Sara Iones.   Arch Bishop of Canterbury. What say yoᵘ woman ? S. Iones.
I dare not worship God in vaine, but saith the Bishop of London,
will yoᵘ not sweare and take an oath when yoᵘ are called to it
by the Magistrate ? S. Iones. yes, I will answere vpon my
oath to end a controversy before a lawfull Magistrate. Earle
of Dorsett. what doest thou thinke woman of these grave
Fathers of the church, that these heere be not lawfull Magistrates ? I would doe any thing that is according to Gods word.

ArchB*ish*op of Yorke. would yo^u ? then yo^u must take yo*ur* oath now yo^u are required by yo*ur* governo*urs*. yo^u must sweare in truth, in iudgement in righteousnes. S. Iones. yes, and they that walke in righteousnes shall haue peace. but I dare not forsweare my selfe.

Canterbury. Come what say yo^u ? Pen. I dare not sweare this *Pennina* oath till I am better informed of it, for w*h*ich I desire tyme: *Howes / a maide.* Sir Henry Martin. Must yo^u not be readie to giue an answere of yo*ur* faith ? Pen. yes, I will giue an answere of my Faith if I be demaunded, but not willinglie forsweare my selfe. / .

King*es* Advocate. what will yo^u take yo*ur* oath good woman? *Sara Bar-* S. Barbone. I dare not sweare, I doe not vnderstand it. I will *bone.* tell the truth w*i*thout swearing. ArchB*ish*op of Canterb*ur*y. Take them away. Soe they were all com*m*itted to ye New prison. And it was appointed, that at ye next Court, being a fortnight after this, because of Ascention day they should be brought againe to the Consistorie at Paules, because of trouble & danger in bringinge soe manie prison*ers* as there were over the water to Lambeth. /

In the Court of high Commission at
ye Consistory in Paules 8 May 1632.
———

This day all those that were taken in ye Black-Fryars were *Con-* brought to ye Court vnder ye Custodie of ye Keeper of the New *venticlers.* prison. The King*es* Advocate shewed that they were taken at a private Conventicle and prayed that they may take their oathes to answere ye articles w*h*ich arc putt in against them. First Sara Iones was asked, of what parish she was ? She said *Sara Iones.* she dwelleth at Lambeth. London. Doe yo^u come to ye church ? S. Iones. None accuseth me to ye contrary. London. where were yo^u vpon Sunday was sennight ? S. Iones. when I haue done evill & my accuser come, I will answere. King*es* Advocate. I doe accuse yo^u, take yo*ur* oath & yo^u shall knowe yo*ur* accu-sac*i*on. S. Iones. I am afraid to take Gods [?] name in vaine, I knowe noe other worship then God hath appointed. London. This yo^u are Com*m*aunded to doe of God who saieth yo^u must obey your Superio*urs*. S. Iones. That wh*i*ch is of God is according to Gods [?] word and ye Lord will not hold him guilt-lesse y^t taketh his name in vaine.

Sara Iacob.
Marke Lucar.

S. Iacob was called to ye booke but she refused alsoe; [?] Then was called Marke Lucar : who was asked of what parish he was & when he was at Church ? M. Lucar. I am yet to chuse of what parish to be. [?] and I doe not remember ye day of ye moneth when I was at Church. London. He doth not remember I dare say ye day of ye moneth nor ye moneth of the yeare when he was at Church, but he dwelleth in St Austins parish : offer him ye booke. M. Lucar. If I may knowe a law & ground for takeing this oath, I will take it, but I desire to know my articles before I take my oath. ArchBishop of Yorke, whether doe yo^u knowe or noe that ye King hath power to take an account of *your* proceeding*es* ? London. att their perrills. aske [?] the next.

Iohn Ireland.

Iohn Ireland was asked where & when he was at Church. He saith at Mary Maudlins Church in Surrey, And that he was at morninge Church *within* this halfe yeare. but being asked ye booke. refused to sweare.

Toby Talbot.

Then were called 4 others. Toby Talbot. Will*ia*m Pickering. Mabell Milbourne. Will*ia*m Attwood, & were put to their oathes. and first Talbot saieth in his excuse that he knoweth not ye articles what they are, and before he would take his oath he would know his accuser. S*i*r Henry Martin. The Law is, that those y^t are taken in these Conventicles & remaine obstinate, that they shalbe made to abiure ye Kingdome, and if they returne, or obey not, it is felony therefore freind*es* take heed to *your* selves, and know y^t yo^u have more favour then yee

Will*ia*m Pickering.

deserve. Pickering. I trust I haue done nothing against ye law, and for this oath, I doe not know what belongs to it. and he refuseth to take it. Attwood saith, he doth not know what

Will*ia*m Attwood.
Mabell Milborne.

ye Booke is. M. Milbourne being asked whether she would take her oath, she said that she would not.

London. speake to Dod. Latroppe. & ye man of ye house. Henry Dod yo^u are ye obstinate & perverse ringleaders of these folkes : you had a faire admonition ye last Court day. and yo^u haue this day assigned yo^u to answere vpon *your* oath.

Henry Dod.

Dod. I hope we are not soe impious. we stand for ye truth : for takeing yᵉ oath I craue your patience, I am not resolved vpon it. Brewers Clarke. I was at yᵉ Church, but for takeing yᵉ oath I desire to be resolved[1]. London. Mʳ Latroppe. Hath the Lord qualifyed yoᵘ, what authority, what Orders haue yoᵘ! the Lord hath qualifyed you, is that a sufficient answere? yoᵘ must giue a better answere before yoᵘ & I part. Latropp. I doe not know that I haue done any thing which might cause me iustly to be brought before yᵉ iudgment seat of man: and for this oath I doe not know the nature of it. Kinges Advocate. the manner of yᵉ oath is, that yoᵘ shall answere to that yoᵘ are accused of, for Schisme. York. & London. if he will not take his oath, away with him. Latropp I desire that other passage may be remembred, I dare not take this oath. wherefore the Court ordered, that they should be kept in straight custodie especiallie Latropp. for yᵉ Bishop of London said he had more to answere then he knew of.

Barnet.

Iohn Latropp.

Samuell Eaton being demaunded whether he would take the oath. He answered, I doe not refuse it, though I doe not take it: it is not out of obstinacie, but as I shall answere it at yᵉ last day I am not satisfyed whether I may take it.

Samuel Eaton.

Samuell Howe (saith yᵉ Kings Advocate) yoᵘ are required by your oath to answere to yᵉ articles. Howe. I have served the King both by sea & by land[2], and I had been at sea if this restraint had not been made vpon me: my conversacion I thank God none can taxe. Register. will yoᵘ take your oath? How. I am a yong man, & doe not know what this oath is: Kinges Advocate. The King desires your service in obeying his lawes.

Samuel How.

Then P. Howes was called, and required to take her oath. but she refused. London. Will yoᵘ trust mʳ Latropp & beleive him rather then yᵉ Church of England. Pennina. I referre my self to the word of God, whether I maie take this oath or noe. Then were called Ioane Ferne & Elizabeth Denne: who refused to sweare till they were informed, and one of them said she

Pennina Howes.

Ioane Ferne.

Elizabeth. Denne.

---

[1] This answer would seem to suggest that Humphrey Barnett, though not a strict separatist, was after all probably a member of the congregation at this time. This view is contrary to a statement made in Vol. I., page 321.

[2] How this statement agrees with the well-known fact that Samuel How, the separatist, was a cobbler, has not yet been made very clear.

could not read a letter in yᵉ booke: the King*es* Advocate saith their oath was yᵗ they should answere trulie as farre as they knew to the Articles.

Elizabeth Sargeant saith she must not sweare, but when she is before a Magistrate. Why now saith the B*isho*p of London. yoᵘ are called before yᵉ Magistrate, are yoᵘ not? Iohn Egge, will yoᵘ take y*our* oath? He refuseth. Henry Parker will yoᵘ take y*our* oath to answere yᵉ articles? H. P. I doe not deny the oath though I dare not take it, till I shall know what I shall sweare. Iohn woodwyne, He being tendered yᵉ booke, said, I desire to know what I shall sweare to, & what is the end of [t]his oath before he will sweare. Iohn Melborne. I am not well perswaded of this oath, yet I will not deny it. Eliz*abeth* Melborne. I doe not know any such thing as a Conventicle. we did meete to pray & talke of yᵉ word of God, wh*i*ch is according to the law of the land. York. God wilbe served publiquely not in y*our* private house. Thomas Arundell of Sᵗ Olaves parish refuseth to take the oath for the present, till he knew yᵉ Articles that he might informe himself. Will*ia*m Granger of Sᵗ Margarett*es* in Westm*inste*r. He being called, the Bishop of London spake vnto him saying, Granger, yoᵘ looke like a man of fashion will yoᵘ take y*our* oath to answere to yᵉ articles according to y*our* knowledg, and as farre as yoᵘ are bound by law? Granger, I desire to have some tyme to consider of it. London. I would not have any of the standers by thinke that yoᵘ or any of these have not had tyme to consider of this, yoᵘ rent & teare the Church & will not submitt y*our* self to yᵉ tryall of law. yoᵘ must know, the Iustice of this Court is lymited, & yoᵘ may be driven to abiure the Realme for y*our* offence. Then Robert Reignold*es* of Thistleworth was tendered the oath. He desired to speak 2 or 3 wordes: If I have done any thing against the Law, lett me be accused by the Course of the law: if I thought this oath might be taken with a good Conscience, I would take it; and I doe for the present desire yoᵘ, though yoᵘ doe not pitty me yet to pitty my poore wife & smale Children. York. Pitty y*our* wife & Children y*our* self, and lay y*our* obstinacy to y*our* conscience. /

(margin notes)
Eliz*abeth* Sargeant.
Iohn Egge.
Henry Parker.
Iohn woodwyne.
Iohn Melborne.
Eliz*abeth* Melborne.
Thomas Arundell.
Will*ia*m Granger.
Robert Reignold*es*.

Abigail Delamar a Frenchmans wife, was brought from the Abigal Delamar. New prison to y⁰ Court, & required to take y⁰ oath. She demanded whether it were the oath of Alleageance; the King*es* Advo*cate* said, it was to answere the truth to y⁰ Articles in Court against her as farre as she knew & was bound by law. She said. I neither dare nor will take this oath till I am informed of it, that I may with a good conscience. London. Her husband is y⁰ Queenes servant, & a stiffe Romane Catholique, and she a deepe Familist & Brownist, & one of the Conventiclers taken at BlackFryars, the last weeke ther was a generall fast held in y⁰ prison, that they might be delivered out of prison, I gaue order that all that came to them that day should be stayed, This woman came,......Canterbury. I see yoᵘ are an obstinate woman, as all the rest of *your* Companie are. Ab Delamar. yoᵘ *per*secute vs *with*out a cause yoᵘ haue sent 26 of vs to y⁰ prison, but since we were imprisoned what course haue yoᵘ taken to informe vs? Which of yoᵘ haue sent anie man to vs or taken any paines to informe vs? London. There was a day sett for them to answere at y⁰ Consistorye in Paules: but they haue y⁰ last Sunday peti*cio*ned his Ma*ies*tie, shewing that it is not out of obstinacie, but they decline y⁰ Ecclesiasticall Iurisdic*c*on [*sic*] altogether. Woman, take *your* oath. Ab. Delamar. Noe this oath is condempned by y⁰ law of the land, & I refuse it as an accursed oath, & appeale to y⁰ Kinge. I heard that y⁰ Saboth day after this Court she deliv[er]ed a peti*cio*n to the King in the name of all the rest, shewing that they refused not this oath obstinately, but yᵗ they were afraid, it was against y⁰ Subiect*es* iust libertie, to be compelled to take this oath and shewed that they would willinglie be tryed by his Ma*ies*ties lawes, or by his Ma*ies*tie or any of his Lord*es* & Nobles.

Amy Holland did not appeare because of sicknes, as it was Holland. given in answere for her

....

Grafton an vpholster [*sic*] one of y⁰ BlackFryers Companie Grafton. is ordered to giue bond for his apparance [*sic*] at y⁰ next Court.

Sara Barbone being bound to appeare is escaped, & hideth Barbon. her selfe, her bond to be certefyed in y⁰ Exchequer.

Wilson.

Phillis Wilson, being one of them that were taken at B*lack*-Fryers was tendered ye oath, but she refused saying, she durst not sweare vnadvisedly.   King*es* Advocate.   It is before ye Magistrate by authority of an act of parliament.

Escape of some of ye Con- venticle^rs out of prison.

London. 7. or 8. of those that were best able to beare it are let out of prison, & therefore for my p*art* I will consent that it be ordered that noe more be sent to ye new prison, till these be brought againe.   The keep*er* prayed their lor*dsh*ipps pardon, & promised to endeavour to finde them againe: London: Let these women therefore for ye honour of ye Court be sent to other prisons, & the rest to be removed some to one prison & some to an other.

....

[Under the date June 14, 1632.]

....

Con- venticlers.

Rawlins, Harvy, Arthur Goslin, Howland, Robert Bye, Iohn Smith, & others were taken at a Conventicle in a wood neare Newington in Surrey vpon the Saboth day last. and being now brought to the Court they were required to take their oathes to answere ye Articles put in against them.   Two of them answeare they will not sweare at this time: and as they were goinge out, Harvy put on his hatt, w*hich* was presentlie taken offe and he was complayned on, & being called back to answere it, he saith, he was shiftinge [?] away, & putt on his hatt. Another saith that a lawfull Magistrate had examined them alreadie, and therefore he will not sweare to be heere examined. London. yo*ur* examinations taken before S*ir* [————] he sent to me. there is nothing in it but that yo^u mett togeather to conferre vpon ye word of God as farre as yo^u vnderstood the same, & to pray, w*hich* yo^u might answere heere: but yo^u tell this Court that it is not a lawfull power & authority: And of the same minde are those that were taken att BlackFryers: for they petic*i*oned ye King to be tryed by his Iudges, by his Lord*es*, declyning the Ecclesiasticall Iurisdicc*i*on: this they tendred ye last Sunday: This yo*ur* obstinacie will cause yo^u to be proceeded against at the common law, & be made abiure the

Kingdome, & if yo^u returne to be hanged. King*es* Advocate speaketh to another of them. yo^u are required to take yo*ur* oath to answere the Articles put in against yo^u. Prisoner. I cannot sweare, because I know them not in certeinty. London. Let these (may it please yo*ur* grace) be sent two and two to other prisons, & none to the new prison, because the keep*er* hath lett some of ye principall of ye other Companie to escape. Andrew Sherle will not lay his hand vpon the booke. Robert Bye com*m*inge into the Court, the Bishop of London spake kindly to him saying, come, thou lookest like a good fellow that will take thy oath. Bye. I am Christ*es* freeman; I owe obedience to God & ye King, and those that are lawfullie sent by him, but to noe others: Att w*hi*ch there being some laughter he said, I am in deed & good earnest, I dare not take this oath: An oath is for the ending of a controversie, but this is made to be but the beginninge of ye controversie. ArchBishop of Canterbury; yo^u doe shew yo*ur* selves the most vngratefull to God & to his Ma*ies*tie the King & to vs the Fathers of the Church: if yo^u haue anie knowledg of God, it hath come through & by vs or some of our predecessors: We haue taken care vnder God to give milke to ye babes & yongling*es* and strong meate for the men of vnderstanding, yo^u haue ye word of God to feed yo^u, the Sacrament*es* to strengthen yo^u, and we support yo^u by prayer, for all this what despight do yo^u returne vs: yo^u call vs abhominable men, to be hated of all that we carry the Marke of the beast, that we are his members: We doe beare this patiently, not because we haue noe law to right vs, but because of yo*ur* obstinacie: But for yo*ur* dishonouring of God & disobeyinge ye King, it is not to be indured: when yo^u haue readinge, preaching, singinge teaching, yo^u are yo*ur* owne Ministers, the blinde lead ye blinde, whereas his Ma*ies*tie is God*es* vicegerent in ye Church, the Church is nothing with yo^u, & his Ministers not to be regarded, and yo^u runne into wood*es*, as if yo^u lived in p*er*secution, such an one yo^u make the King, to whome wee are soe much bound for his great care for ye truth to be preserved amonge vs and yo^u would haue men beleiue, that he is a Tyrant, this besides yo*ur* wickednes, vnthankfulnes, & vngraciousnes toward*es* vs the Fathers of the

Church. Therefore let these men be put 2. and 2. in severall prisons.

Iohn Cooke, Iames, Margery Cleaver, Iohn Iapworth, Anne [————] One was a yong girle, these were all taken in another Conventicle, but where I cannott directly say, I heard about Christes Church in London: These alsoe all denyed to take the oath, and were all sent to severall prisons, two, and two. /

[Under the date June 21, 1632.]

....

Against
Ralfe
Grafton
one of
the Con-
venticlers.
Ralfe Grafton an Vpholster dwellinge in Cornehill, London, was required to take his oath to answere y⁰ Articles. He was said to be a principall ringleader of those Conventicle's that mett at BlackFryers. Kinges Advocate this is a rich man dwelling within the Citty, my Motion is, that your Grace & the Court would sett a Fine vpon this man if he shall refuse to answere, that other [sic] may be warned for contemning of y⁰ Court. London. Mᵣ Advocate I thanke yoᵘ for this Motion. Kinges Advocate, I require yoᵘ, & the Court requireth yoᵘ to take your oath to answere to matters of your owne fact as farre as yoᵘ know, & are bound by law. Grafton. An oath is a matter of an high nature, & must not be taken rashlie, I dare not therefore take this oath. We have done nothinge against y⁰ law: it was noe Conventicle, there was nothinge spoaken against y⁰ King, nor against the State, I dare not take y⁰ oath and I am noe Ringleader of any to evill. Canterbury. Yoᵘ mett without law, yoᵘ had no authority. Pœna ad paucos, metus ad omnes. Wherefore, the Court for his Contempt in refusing y⁰ oath sett a Fine of two hundred pound vpon him, & committed him to prison. Grafton. I have bayle heere readie if yoᵘ please to take it, I doe tender it to yoᵘ. London. Canterbury. Noe away with him to prison: if he come not in by the day of mittigation, let the Fine stand.

XXI

NOTICE OF A SEPARATIST CONVENTICLE TAKEN AT A HOUSE IN "REDERIFFE" IN DECEMBER, 1638

Surrey *to wit.*

The Examinacion of Edward Hurst late of Cambridge Tayler taken the 23 of December. 1638.[1]

bailed

He saith that he came to london on thursdaye laste. and lodged at the bull in Bishopsgate streete and this daye he enquiringe for a freind of his, was tould that he might finde him att a howse in Rederiffe, which made him goe thither, where he founde aboute, 20. or 30. persons men & woemen. beinge all strangers vnto him & knewe not the names of either of them, where they did all pray togeather and dispute & exhorte one an other, and there Contynued aboute 2. howers togeather vntill the Constables & officers of Rederiffe came in tooke some of them awaye. this Examinate denyeth that he did exhorte or dispute with them or any of them Edward [?] hurst [?]

bayled.

Phillippa Cowlake. St Giles Cripplegate parishe
Frances Greene the wife of Phillipp Greene

bayled

of the same. Clothworker.

Iohn Dyer of Barmondsey Lastmaker he saith that they were all Readinge a Chapter & expoundinge of it

[1] S. P., Dom., Charles I., Vol. 404 (118).

bayled— Beniamyn Pratt of oldstreete weauer.

word taken— Martha Elliott of S^t. Gyles Cripplegate.
Thom*as* Tyle
bayled. John Ellis of St Pulkers Cordwainder

Nicholas Rothwell and Peter Blake Churchwardens of Rederiffe togeather w*i*th John
Stoakes & John Lingwood Constables goeinge
aboute in tyme of devine service to see good
orders kepte did finde the said p*er*sons & diuers
others that ran & Convayed themselues awaye
gathered togeather in a howse where on [one]
hayward dwells, he beinge at sea And his wife
w*i*th her frends in the Countrye, but howe
they came into the howse the said officers
knowe not.

nicolas Rothwell ⎫ Church
peter blake   ⎬ wardens

John Lingwood ⎫ Constables
John stokes   ⎬

Thomas Laish
John Lewis

XXII

DOCUMENTS RELATING TO THE PRISON LIFE AND DEATH OF THE SEPARATIST, SAMUEL EATON

[A Petition concerning him which was probably sent to Archbishop Laud in 1638.]¹

To the most Reverend Father in God William Lord [Laud] Arch⸱Bᴾᴾ of Canterbury his Grace Primate and
Metrapolitan of all England.

Humbly   The most humble Peticion of Frauncis Tucker
Sheweth.   Bachelour of Divinity and Prisoner in Newgate
            for Debt.

That whereas there is one Samuell Eaton Prisoner in Newgate committed by your Grace for a Scismaticall and dangerous Fellowe. That the said Eaton hath held diverse Conventicles in the said Gaole some whereof hath bin to the number of 70 persons, or more and that hee was permitted by the said keeper openly, and publiquely to preach vnto them, and that the said Eaton hath oftentimes affirmed in his said Sermons, that Baptisme² was the Doctrine of Devills, and its Originall was an Institucion from the Devill and oftentimes hee would rayle against your Grace, affirminge that all Bᴾᴾˢ were Heretickes Blasphemers, and Antechristians, That the said keeper haueinge notice hereof by the peticioner whoe desired him to bee meanes that these greate resorts and Conventicles

---

¹ S. P., Dom., Car. I., Vol. 406 (No. 64), in the Public Record Office, London.

² [? in the Church of England.]

might bee prevented and that hee would reproue the said Eaton for the same, and remoue him to some other place of the Prison. That herevpon the said keeper in a disdainfull manner replyed that the peticioner should meddle with what hee had to doe and if hee did dislike the said Eaton and his Conventicles hee would remoue the peticioner into some worser place of the Prison, That at this time there was a Conventicle of 60 persons or more that the said keeper comminge into the Roome where this Conventicle was, and the said Eaton preachinge vnto them and maynteninge dangerous Opinions, havinge viewed the said Assembly hee said there was a very faire, and goodly Company and stayinge there some season departed without any distaste thereat, to the greate encouragement of the said Eaton, and the said persons to frequent the said place &c That the said keeper had a strict Charge from the highe Commission to haue a speciall Care of the said Eaton &c, that since this the said keeper hath severall times permitted him to goe abroad to preach to Conventicles appointed by him the said Eaton. That dayly there doth resorte to the said Eaton much people to heare him preach....[that just before the death of the petitioner's wife, after she had been removed from the chamber she had occupied in the prison] the said Chamber was by the keeper assigned over to the said Eaton, it beeinge the most convenient place in the prison for keepinge his Conventicles—.

......

....

[An Account of his Burial, evidently written on " Aug: 31: 1639."][1]

Mᵣ Alsop, I wrote to you the other weeke, how yᵗ I had beene with Eaton [i.e., Samuel Eaton]. This is further to let you understand yᵗ upon sunday, being Aug. 25. I was accidentally at his buriall, for being to visit one in Bethelem comming

[1] S. P., Dom., Car. I., Vol. 427 (107), in the Public Record Office, London.

home, I met Brownists & Anabaptists (I thinke) at least
200 with Eatons corpes, so I went backe with y^m to see how
they would bury ye dead, & I observed how they answered such
as met y^m, demanding who y^t was to be buried, they said it
was one of ye Bishop's prisoners, but when they came to y^e
grave, it being made ready for y^m in ye new Church yard neere
Bethelem; they like so many Bedlams cast ye corpes in; &
with y^r feet, in stead of spades cast & thrust in ye mould till y^e
grave was allmost full: then they paid ye grave maker for his
paines, who told y^m y^t he must fetch a minister, but, they said,
he might spare his labour.

I could wish y^t you would certify my Lord of this, also y^t
I had beene at ye gate house...

XXIII

A BROADSIDE WHICH MENTIONS THE EXCOMMUNICATION
OF SAMUEL HOW, AND THE PLACE AND DATE OF HIS
BURIAL IN 1640.

The Coblers threed is cut.

OR,

The Coblers Monument : wherein, to the everlasting memory of the folly
of *Samuel How,* his doctrines are detected, and his life and death
described : together with an Epitaph written on him at the
Last, with an exhortation to the ignorant to avoid
such phantastick spirits ; he being buried
in the high-way neer *Dame Annes*
a Clear (a place so called,
neer Shores-ditch, on
tuesday, Sept. 29.
1640.[1]

T is an ancient and worthy custome to
weep for the deceased; but How? not
for this *Samuel How,* who being a Cobler,
took upon him beyond his Last, the
mending of soules, and in a Sermon
preached to above an hundred persons in
the Nags-head Taverne neere Coleman-
street, delivered many absurd Doctrines
& Vses, against humane Learning : and afterward published
and entitled his Sermon, *The sufficiencie of the Spirits teaching
without humane Learning, for the light and information of the*

---

[1] This definite information serves to correct a misstatement as to the
date of Samuel How's death made in Vol. i., p. 201. On account of the
exigencies of space the heading of the broadside, as here reproduced, has
been differently arranged from that of the original, which consists of only
six lines in all.

ignorant: wherein he published his owne folly, it being a knowne truth, that Learning is no essentiall immediate cause of grace, but an instrumentall cause, whereby the knowledge of the Scriptures are gained; and humane learning doth prepare the soule, and enlarge it to receive divine mysteries, and by judgement assisted by Gods Spirit, to finde out hidden truth, and to defend fundamentall Principles. How durst then this lump of ignorance assume so much boldnesse, with reasons drawne *ab absurdo*, from absurdity, to detract from learning, or with his blacke Thumb wax so impudent to touch, much lesse to handle humane Science or Learning; who will thus requite him with an old saying:

Scientia non habet inimicum nisi ignorantem.

The ignorant will onely be
To humane Learning an enemie.

But his folly hath been formerly enough derided: For as sober obedient knowledge is rewarded, so foolish ungrounded opinions are disregarded: they are like *Solomons* thornes, crackling under the pot; & it is likely these flames of the Coblers zeal proceeded from pottles of wine, it being preached (as above said) in the Nags-head Taverne, neere Coleman-street: a fit place for such a preachment, tending to the disgrace of all humane learning; which scorning to answer a foole according to his folly, it seems that this selfe-conceited Cobler, *Samuel How*, being stricken with shame, and afterward with sicknesse, sneaked out of this world and died; and being formerly excommunicated out of the Church, he was buried in the high-way, after his threed of life was cut. And therefore let the Reader take this as a monument of his folly; whereupon in conclusion may be engraven this Epitaph.

An Epitaph on *Samuel How* a Cobler, the unlearned enemy of humane Learning.

THis *vnlearned Cobler, by the Spirits discerning,*
Was a great enemy to humane Learning.
How could that be? Why How *that in a stall,*
Could sing Queen Dido, *or the Ladies fall,*

Would in a Taverne needs set up his stage,
And against humane Learning shew his rage.
Doctrines and Vses from his Text he drew,
That was us'd to draw threeds through an old Shew:
And with sharp argument he seemed to prick,
As with an Aule, all learning to the quick.
And having wrought himselfe so out of breath,
The Coblers thred of life was cut by Death.
And in the high way buried under ground,
Studies how he all learning may confound.
He needs no Monument, nor Epitaph,
For at his folly every one doth laugh,
To think how he did go beyond his Last,
The Coblers end is shame for folly past.
Then let no ignorant above his reach,
Speake against learning, or attempt to preach.
Lest having spet and spoke, they doe come off,
Like this unlearned Cobler with a scoff.
Who having done his worke, by death is paid
His wages, and in the high-way is laid.
Where he no foolish Arguments can hold:
For How, *his zeale, and corps in ground are cold.*
He that was humane Learnings great Kil-kow,
Lies in the high-way, you need not ask How ?[1]

Printed for *Richard Harper* at the Bible and Harp
in Smithfield. 1640.[2]

---

[1] In the original this epitaph is printed in two columns.
In the original the imprint consists of only one line.

INDEX

NOTE. The numerous names of streets, lanes, and parishes of London which occur in the early pages of Volume II. have not been included in the Index.

𝕮𝖆𝖒𝖇𝖗𝖎𝖉𝖌𝖊:

PRINTED BY JOHN CLAY, M.A.

AT THE UNIVERSITY PRESS

Printed in the United States
4225

9 781579 788957